WINES OF THE LANGUEDOC

THE INFINITE IDEAS
CLASSIC WINE LIBRARY

Editorial board: Sarah Jane Evans MW and Richard Mayson

There is something uniquely satisfying about a good wine book, preferably read with a glass of the said wine in hand. **The Infinite Ideas Classic Wine Library** is a series of wine books written by authors who are both knowledgeable and passionate about their subject. Each title in **The Infinite Ideas Classic Wine Library** covers a wine region, country or type and together the books are designed to form a comprehensive guide to the world of wine as well as an enjoyable read, appealing to wine professionals, wine lovers, tourists, armchair travellers and wine trade students alike.

Port and the Douro, Richard Mayson
Cognac: The story of the world's greatest brandy, Nicholas Faith
Sherry, Julian Jeffs
Madeira: The islands and their wines, Richard Mayson
The wines of Austria, Stephen Brook
Biodynamic wine, Monty Waldin
The story of champagne, Nicholas Faith
The wines of Faugères, Rosemary George MW
Côte d'Or: The wines and winemakers of the heart of Burgundy,
    Raymond Blake
The wines of Canada, Rod Phillips
Rosé: Understanding the pink wine revolution, Elizabeth Gabay MW
Amarone and the fine wines of Verona, Michael Garner
The wines of Greece, Konstantinos Lazarakis MW
Wines of the Languedoc, Rosemary George MW
The wines of northern Spain, Sarah Jane Evans MW

WINES OF THE LANGUEDOC

ROSEMARY GEORGE MW

with photographs by Gary MacDonald

infiniteideas

Rosemary George MW was lured into the wine trade by a glass of the Wine Society's champagne at a job interview and subsequently became one of the first women to become a Master of Wine, back in 1979. She has been a freelance wine writer since 1981 and is the author of twelve books, including *French Country Wine*, which first took her to the south of France. Back in the mid-1980s she realized that this was a region of enormous potential and consequently went on to write *The Wines of the South of France* (2001). This was the beginning of her enthusiasm for the Languedoc, which she has followed up most recently with *The wines of Faugères*. President of the Circle of Wine Writers, she writes a blog on the region (www.tastelanguedoc.blogspot.com) and contributes to various magazines such as *Decanter* and *Sommelier India*.

The right of Rosemary George to be identified as the author of this book has been asserted in accordance with the Copyright, Designs and Patents Act 1988.

First published in 2018 by
Infinite Ideas Limited
www.infideas.com

A CIP catalogue record for this book is available from the British Library
ISBN 978–1–908984–86–9

All web addresses were checked and correct at time of going to press.

All photographs © Gary Michael MacDonald

Maps © Editions Benoit France pour CIVL

Printed in Britain

CONTENTS

INTRODUCTION: SETTING THE SCENE

The first thing to do is to set the parameters. What is the Languedoc? So often it is lumped with Roussillon in the one breath of Languedoc-Roussillon, but in fact the two areas are separate and very different. Roussillon is Catalan; the Languedoc is French. Their history and traditions are not the same. Their original languages are different. Roussillon speaks Catalan; the Languedoc, Occitan. However, France has recently been amalgamating some of its regions, so that Occitanie, which you might think is the equivalent of the Languedoc, has been extended to become Languedoc-Midi-Pyrénées, with the regional capital shifting from Montpellier to Toulouse. However, for the purposes of this book, the Languedoc extends from the appellations of Malepère, Cabardès and Limoux, to the west of Carcassonne, as far as the vineyards of Sommières and Pays des Cévennes, east of Montpellier.

In the west, the boundary is very clear cut. After the last vineyards of Cabardès, the scenery gives way to the pastoral fields of the Lauragais, with sunflowers and wheat. No vines grow there. In the south, the departmental boundary of the Pyrénées-Oriéntales and the Aude separates Roussillon from the Languedoc and the vineyards of Corbières. The Terrasses du Larzac and the Pic St Loup are the most northern vineyards, with climate and geology placing a limit on the vineyards. Above them are the *causses* of the Larzac, sheep grazing country for Roquefort cheese. It is in the east that things become more blurred, and administrative geography comes into play. Although to my mind, Costières de Nimes is *languedocien*, French wine administration

1

places it within the Rhône Valley. Likewise, the newest appellation of the area, Duché d'Uzès, opted to join the Rhône, even though it is more *languedocien* in approach, and the parallel IGP, Pays de Cévennes, is considered to be part of the Languedoc. Consequently, I have written about the Pays des Cévennes, but only mention the Duché d'Uzès in passing and Costières de Nimes not at all.

I have been visiting the Languedoc regularly for over 30 years, researching previous books, *French Country Wines* and then *The Wines of the South of France, from Banyuls to Bellet*. My visits became much more frequent after we bought a *maison sécondaire* outside the historic town of Pézenas. You could say that it was the many visits to the area for the second book that enabled us to ascertain exactly which part of the south of France appealed the most. Faugères is our nearest appellation, so that seemed the natural choice for my next book (published in 2016), and now this one is the logical corollary.

Why write about the Languedoc now? Quite simply, and without exaggeration, it is the most exciting wine region of the whole of France. The pace of change in the past few years has been breathtaking, and for that reason I have chosen to concentrate on the Languedoc of the twenty-first century and on the new wine growers who are behind those changes. In a nutshell, the region has become, in the words of one grower, more confident, while another suggested wiser and more grown up. It is not only that work in the vineyard and cellar has improved dramatically but also that the atmosphere has changed, with a buoyancy and optimism apparent. While there are still problems, and indeed dull wines, there is now an underlying realization that the Languedoc has so much to offer. The lure of the Languedoc for outsiders, and newcomers to wine, is very strong. Many of the new producers say that it was more welcoming than other regions they explored. The newcomers have brought ideas from elsewhere and that all adds to a vibrant melting pot of dynamic attitudes, with an extraordinary enthusiasm and energy amongst the wine growers. I have lost count of the times somebody said: '*C'est ma passion*'. Life may be hard, with vineyards affected by frost, hail or drought, but they simply could not imagine doing anything else, and they are all making the very best wine they can. They enjoy the liberty that the Languedoc offers; if you make an appellation, you must conform to its regulations, but if you make an IGP, the rules are much more flexible, and if you make Vin de France, the restrictions are minimal. For this reason, the Languedoc is a hotbed of experimentation, with a wonderful choice of grape varieties. The appellations retain the established varieties but the producers of IGP and Vin de France may experiment virtually to their heart's content; some indeed make all three.

While I have been visiting the Languedoc regularly for the past thirty years this book is essentially the fruit of cellar visits between July 2016 and October 2017. I have enjoyed every moment, well almost every moment. It has taken me off the beaten track of the Languedoc, with so much to discover. I love the scenery. The hills of the Corbières are wild and rugged, dominated by the Montagne d'Alaric and Mont Tauch. The Minervois has the backdrop of the Montagne Noire, which does indeed appear black in the distance. As you travel east, you encounter more distinctive skylines: the Caroux, or *la femme allongée*, dominates the vineyards of St Chinian; Faugères lies at the foot of the Espinouse; and Cabrières nestles underneath the dramatic Pic de Vissou. Driving south down the motorway, the A75, that runs through the centre of France, there is a moment when you come over the Pas de l'Escalette and it seems that the whole Languedoc opens up before you. You can almost see the sparkle of the blue Mediterranean on the horizon, with a pimple that is the Mont Sainte Clair, outside Sète. Driving out of Aniane one can follow the Hérault up through winding gorges to the village of St Jean de Buèges, past the Pont du Diable; or walk up in the vineyards above Montpeyroux where you have views of Mont Saint-Baudile, known as la Sentinelle du Larzac. Further east, the scenery is dominated by the two peaks of the Pic St Loup and the Montagne de l'Hortus, and to the east of Montpellier, the land becomes softer, with gentle undulating hills, and then you reach the Cévennes, with its national park, and more off the beaten track villages around Anduze, while down on the coast there are the lagoons, with their oyster beds, and the Mediterranean beyond.

The principal towns of the region, Narbonne, Béziers and Montpellier all have much to offer, as have the smaller, picturesque towns of Limoux, Lagrasse, Sommières and Pézenas. There are awe-inspiring old abbeys, like St Guilhem-le-Désert, Fontfroide and Valmagne, as well as countless little villages that merit a detour on a brief visit. Some only come to life on market day; in others, barely a dog stirs in the summer and the most demanding activity is a game of *boules* in the village square under the shade of the plane trees.

There has been much to discover. As a local wine merchant observed, new estates are popping up like mushrooms. The newest appellation of the Languedoc, the Terrasses du Larzac, has absorbed 25 new estates since 2011; Faugères had four new wine growers in 2014, and a further four since then. There are new arrivals at every vintage, and those are the people on whom I wanted to concentrate for this book, for they are the people who are creating the Languedoc of the twenty-first century. Of course, I could not ignore the long-established estates, or indeed some of the cooperatives, where they continue to perform well for their appellation, but my focus is on the new developments and the newcomers of the past 17 years, making for a very personal and possibly idiosyncratic selection. There are well over 2,500 wine estates in the Languedoc, so I apologise for all the omissions, of which there are many, but I hope that I have paved the way to new discoveries, the future stars of the Languedoc, in the 200 or so estates covered in this book. But first comes some history before a consideration of the developments of the twenty-first century.

1

THE HISTORY OF THE LANGUEDOC: FROM THE GREEKS TO THE TWENTY-FIRST CENTURY

The viticultural history of the south began with the Greeks, when they founded Massalia, now Marseilles, in the sixth century BC, and brought vines with them. A few years later they settled further along the coast around Agde. Excavations at Lattes, just outside Montpellier, have uncovered a vast quantity of grape pips from the fifth century BC, indicating with certainty the presence of vineyards in the Languedoc, before the arrival of the Romans, who founded a colony at Narbonne in 118BC. Viticulture flourished under the Romans, despite the temporary braking effect of Domitian's edict of AD92 ordering many existing vineyards to be pulled up, in an attempt to ensure that land suitable for the cultivation of wheat was retained for that purpose, but this lasted only until the repeal of the edict by the Emperor Probus in AD276. Viticulture has been a vital element of the agricultural activity and economy of the Languedoc ever since. The archaeological museum in Agde contains a magnificent collection of amphorae used for transporting wine.

During the Middle Ages, the increasingly powerful Catholic Church contributed considerably to the development of viticulture throughout the Languedoc. At one time, there were as many as fifty Benedictine abbeys in Languedoc-Roussillon, including St Guilhem-le-Désert and Lagrasse, as well as the magnificent Cistercian abbeys at Fontfroide and Valmagne, to mention just four that are still standing and well worth a visit. The production of wine was an essential part of monastic life, as it was needed not only for the Eucharist but also for hospitality. The monasteries were the four-star hotels of medieval travel. The monastic houses played an important role in continuing the viticultural traditions of the south throughout the Middle Ages, especially during the periods of social upheaval caused by the Albigensian Crusade and the Hundred Years War.

Once the Languedoc was assimilated into France, wine began to travel north, and there are records of Languedoc wine being enjoyed at the Valois court of Charles V towards the end of the fourteenth century. Nonetheless the Massif Central represented a substantial barrier throughout the Middle Ages and difficulties of transport would ensure that the wines of the south remained unknown.

Viticultural fortunes continued to fluctuate. The end of the Wars of Religion with the accession of Henri IV in 1589 offered a hope of prosperity. Vineyard plantings increased enormously in the seventeenth century as a result of the clearing of scrubland in the hills, while the coastal plains remained indispensable for the production of wheat. Taverns flourished, trade developed and the market opened up towards Italy and Catalonia with Agde and Béziers becoming important commercial centres.

Nevertheless, the region remained relatively isolated from the rest of the country with poor communications until the building of the Canal du Midi, which opened in 1681, under the impetus of Jean-Baptiste Colbert. It is also appropriately called the Canal des Deux Mers, for it links the Mediterranean with the Atlantic. To appreciate this colossal feat of engineering, it is well worth visiting Fonséranes, just outside Beziers, where there is a series of nine locks, one after the other, like a flight of steps, that changes the water level by 25 metres. Pierre-Paul Riquet, the engineer who masterminded the whole project at great personal cost, is commemorated with a statue in the Allées Paul Riquet, the broad promenade in the centre of Béziers. However, competition from the *bordelais* remained fierce and during the eighteenth century only 5 per cent of the wines and *eaux de vie* of the Languedoc were exported along the Canal du Midi. The port of Sète provided another opportunity for trade, but it was only accessible to merchants from northern Europe, notably the Dutch, through the straits of Gibraltar.

THE INDUSTRIAL REVOLUTION

It was not until the nineteenth century that the vineyards of the Languedoc experienced a period of real prosperity. With the Industrial Revolution came a new clientele, the factory workers and miners of the north, who wanted a cheap energy-inducing drink, namely wine. The Midi adapted itself to this demand and created an industrial vineyard for the production of thin, acidic wine that barely reached 7 or 8% abv and would be further watered down by its consumers. Today it would be considered quite undrinkable. However, it was the basis of the economic and agricultural success of the Midi. Many fine châteaux were built, with immense cellars that catered for enormous quantities of wine. A building such as the Château de Grézan in Faugères may look from the distance like a medieval castle, but it dates from the nineteenth century and is one of many designed by the *bordelais* architect Louis-Michel Garosse, who offered potential clients a catalogue of different buildings.

Considerable technical progress in wine making occurred during the nineteenth century. In a vineyard near Mauguio in the Hérault, Henri Bouschet created a new grape variety, Alicante Bouschet, by crossing Grenache Noir with a hybrid of Aramon and Teinturier du Cher, which had been developed by his father, Louis, a few years earlier. Alicante Bouschet was to become one of the most widely planted varieties of the Midi following the phylloxera crisis.

At the beginning of the nineteenth century, France had the largest vineyard in the world, with the Hérault one of the most productive departments, but many of the wines were for distillation. Marcel Lachiver in his history of French vineyards sees 1850 as the year that saw the end of the traditional vineyard all over France, for it was about to be transformed by cryptogrammic disease, notably oidium, as well as by consequences of the advent of the railways, and then phylloxera, which meant that the Languedoc would be replanted as a *vignoble de masse*, completely changing its traditional practices of cultivation and production.

The nineteenth century authorities wrote of the wines of the Languedoc with varying degrees of enthusiasm, sometimes singling out specific *crus*. Victor Rendu in 1862 classified the wines of the

Languedoc into three categories: the vines of the hills or the *garrigue*, which provided wines for export; the vines of the terraces, where the soil consisted of pebbles mixed with iron, which gave wines suitable for commerce; and then finally the vineyards of the plains, planted with Aramon and Terret Bourret, which produced wines for distillation.

In the 1860s Jules Guyot undertook a very detailed report on the vineyards of France for Napoleon III. He enthused about the quality of Mourvèdre, called Espar in the Midi, and regretted development of what he called the 'common' grape varieties. In the Hérault he found wines for distillation, ordinary wines and great wines, as well as fortified wines and brandy. He also mentioned that some eminent wine growers in the Hérault were experimenting with Pinots, Cabernet, Syrah, Cot, Sauvignon and Semillon, as well as Spirans, Espar, Carignan, Grenache, Morastel and Clairette, which gave some very superior wines and drinks that were much in demand. There were apparently as many as 150 different grape varieties grown in the south. Sadly, many of them were to disappear completely in the aftermath of phylloxera.

Yields increased enormously in this period. In 1848, the Hérault overtook the Gironde as the department with the largest area of vines. Between 1861 and 1867, the six years during which Guyot was preparing his report, production in the Hérault rose from 9 to 14 million hectolitres. The all-time record harvest was 1869, when the Hérault produced a breathtaking 15,236,000 hectolitres from 226,000 hectares of vines. The average yield per hectare works out at almost 68 hectolitres, which was enormous for the period. The year 1875 saw the record harvest for France, with 84 million hectolitres. Between 1878 and 1899 there was never a harvest larger than 50 million hectolitres and consumption was always greater. However, in 1900 production soared to 68 million, dropping again to 58 million hectolitres in 1901.

The development of the railways during the second half of the nineteenth century coincided with the period of industrialization and encouraged the growth of the Languedoc vineyards, providing an easy means of transport to the capital and the industrial north. The Paris–Lyon–Marseilles railway opened in 1856 and links were also provided with Sète, Montpellier, Béziers and Narbonne.

PHYLLOXERA

But there were problems too. In 1863 the phylloxera louse was found in the village of Pujaut in the Gard, in the vineyards of a wine grower who had imported some American vines. The louse began its steady munch westwards and northwards, although it did not reach the Aude until 1885. Growers hoped to escape its devastating effects but its progress was relentless.

In the later part of the nineteenth century enormous energy was devoted to finding a remedy. The louse was identified by Emile Planchon, a professor of chemistry at the University of Montpellier, who made the connection with the American vines that had been brought into France. The effects of phylloxera were dramatic, with plantings in the Hérault falling from 222,000 hectares in 1872 to less than 90,000 in 1881. The French government offered a reward of 300,000 francs to whoever discovered a remedy. The Hérault alone produced some 696 different suggestions, of which about half were tried out in an experimental vineyard near Montpellier. Suggested remedies included the flooding of the vineyards on the coastal plains, for the life cycle of the louse includes 40 days underground. The soil around the roots was injected with carbon bisulphite; occasionally you still see the piece of equipment used, carefully preserved as a museum piece. Gaston Bazille from Montpellier was the first to experiment with the grafting of European vines onto American rootstocks, but this procedure was not initially seen as the sought-after remedy and the reward was in fact never paid. Eventually however, it was realized that this was the only viable solution. By 1870, there were 450 hectares of grafted vines in the region.

Vines adapted more easily to grafting on the more fertile, less chalky soil of the coastal plains and as the vineyards of the Midi were replanted in the last years of the nineteenth century, there was a definite shift away from the hillsides, leading to the neglect of many quality vineyards, the *coteaux* and *terrasses* mentioned by the nineteenth-century authorities, that was to endure until almost the end of the twentieth century. When it was noticed that phylloxera did not survive in sandy soil, vineyards were developed on the coastal sand dunes notably under the impetus of the Compagnie des Salins du Midi.

In 1900 there were 200,000 hectares of vines in the Hérault, while between them the three departments of the Languedoc, the Aude, Hérault and Gard, produced 21,346,000 hectolitres from 384,560 hectares. The average yield of the particularly prolific vineyards of the Hérault was an extraordinary 66 hectolitres per hectare, when the national average was only a meagre 29 hectolitres per hectare. In 1899 these three departments, with 23 per cent of the country's vineyards, accounted for 44 per cent of the total French wine production. For most of the nineteenth century vines had been grown alongside wheat and olive trees, but by the turn of the century, the Midi had become a region of monoculture.

ALGERIA, FABRICATION AND OVERPRODUCTION

Meanwhile the vineyards of Algeria, then a French colony, were being developed, with a phenomenal increase in production from 338,000 hectolitres in 1878 to 22,762,000 ten years later. Wine growers from the Gard, Hérault and Aude, as well as from Spain and Italy, settled in Algeria and planted the grape varieties of the Midi, namely Grenache Noir, Cinsaut, Carignan, Aramon and Alicante Bouschet. The wines of Algeria soon became known as *vins de médicin*, for the rich full-bodied wines of Algeria had the necessary low acidity and deep colour to complement the pale thin wines of the Midi.

Sète, or Cette as English writers of the time called it, developed a flourishing trade in all kinds of spurious wines. Writing in 1877, Charles Tovey talks of Cette as a byword for adulteration: 'It is alleged that if you tell a Cette merchant at 9 a.m. that you wish to have 50 pipes of port, 50 butts of sherry and 50 hogsheads of claret, he will promise to deliver them at 4 p.m'. There is no doubt that with an ample choice of every type of grape juice, honest blending was the order of the day. Much of this wine was sent 'to the Brazils and all parts of America; some to India and Australia', but he did not think much was imported into England.

The process of fabrication was described in *L'Art de faire le vin avec les raisins secs*, by Joseph Audibert, which first appeared in 1880 and sold out of five editions, each of a thousand copies, in six months. Audibert explained how to make a wine from raisins soaked in eau de vie and hot water, recommending mixing this so-called wine with wine from the Languedoc, or the Var. It is impossible to know how much spurious wine was fabricated in this way. There were wines on the market that had never been near a grape, coming from glycerine, sulphuric acid and some colouring matter, while the most common process was simply to use sugar and raisins.

But underneath the apparent prosperity and the recovery from the phylloxera crisis, there were economic and social problems. The Languedoc had become such an important source of supply that a bad harvest in the region automatically meant a wine deficit for the whole of France, while an abundant crop resulted in a surplus on the market. With the large vintages at the turn of the twentieth century, the price of wine fell and in 1901 supply exceeded demand by about 10 million hectolitres. Prices collapsed. In the 1880s a hectolitre of Languedoc wine cost 30 francs and in 1900 10 francs, while the cost of production was 15 francs. Prices picked up temporarily with the smaller crops of 1902 and 1903, but then the crisis reappeared with the large crop of 66 million hectolitres in 1904, which sold at an average price of between 6 and 7 francs per hectolitre. Things came to a head in 1907.

The viticultural community blindly refused to see that the root of the crisis lay in overproduction, but insisted the fault lay with fraud of the type practised in Sète, and also with the incompetence of the French authorities. The inspiration for revolt came from a humble wine grower, Marcelin Albert, who was born in the village of Argeliers in the Aude, a few kilometres north of Narbonne, in 1851. He was a simple man, but possessed of a powerful command of words, who inspired others to follow him in what he hoped would be peaceful demonstrations. He began with a petition in his village. In 1905, 400 signatories refused to pay their taxes and asked for the resignation of the local council, under the cry of 'Vive le vin naturel. A bas les empoissoneurs!' The village council did resign. A commission given the task of investigating the crisis stated clearly in May 1907 that the viticultural crisis was not due to overproduction because the vineyard area was smaller than 30 years earlier. What they had failed to recognize was that the average yield was much higher. And the wines of Algeria were not seen as contentious, but accepted as French.

Meanwhile the tide of protest swelled, with the numbers growing at each demonstration, and 80,000 people attending a protest in Narbonne on 5 May 1907. The demonstrators demanded that wine be sold at a remunerative price and their banners cried 'Pas de revenue, pas d'impôts. Mort aux fraudeurs, le Midi veut vivre. Nous voulons du pain. Pas de politique.' The demonstrations finally culminated in 600,000 people collecting in Montpellier on 9 June, the day before the expiry of an ultimatum to the government that if it did not take the necessary steps to redress the wine market, a tax embargo would be declared. There was no action from the government and in the days that followed, some 618 town councils resigned, hanging black flags outside the town halls. The Chamber of Deputies voted for an increase in the tax on sugar from 25 to 45 francs, which was seen as a small gesture of appeasement, but meanwhile the Prime Minister, Georges Clemenceau, called in the troops, and things came to a head in Narbonne on 19 June, when the situation deteriorated, resulting in one death and several injuries.

Meanwhile Marcelin Albert, who had gone into hiding to avoid arrest, travelled to Paris and managed to surprise Clemenceau in his office. However, he was not equal to the politician's cunning and was duped; accepting a 100 franc note for his train fare home, he was accused by his fellow demonstrators of being bought. Back in Argeliers, he was ostracized and, from being seen as the saviour, he became a traitor in the eyes of his fellow wine growers.

The demonstrations of 1907 were not in vain. A law, passed on 29 June in an attempt to ease the situation, introduced some sensible measures, such as the déclaration de récolte, alongside the déclaration de stocks, which together determine the availability of wine for sale during the following 12 months. These two measures remain in force today, all over France. Action was also taken against fraud, imposing some control over the sugar producers and taxing sugar destined for the wine industry. The following month saw the creation of Répression des Fraudes, which still exists today, and the legal definition of wine, as coming, 'exclusively from the alcoholic fermentation of fresh grapes or from the juice of fresh grapes'. But the real problem, the overproduction of mediocre wine, remained and would stay with the Languedoc for most of the twentieth century, mainly lying dormant but erupting, sometimes violently, from time to time.

COOPERATIVE CELLARS

The creation of *caves coopératives* (cooperative cellars) was suggested as a possible solution to the problem of overproduction. The idea was not new; the very first village cooperative had been set up in the Ahr Valley in Germany in 1868 and others followed elsewhere. The concept appealed to the socialist unions who saw cooperatives as an opportunity to resist the large *négociants* and landowners. The first cooperative of the Languedoc was founded in the village of Mudaison in the Hérault in 1901 and was followed by that of Maraussan, which took the stirring name of les Vignerons Libres. By 1914 there were 27 village cooperatives in the Languedoc.

Initially the cooperatives were intended to help with sales, while each grower continued to make his or her own wine. Only gradually did they begin to produce wine as well, and share equipment and cellars. The First World War placed a brake on their development but in the 1920s and 1930s the movement really took off. Three hundred and forty cooperatives were founded in that period in Languedoc-Roussillon alone. At the same time, French consumption per capita increased from 103 litres in 1904 to 136 litres in 1926. Cooperatives continued to function as an important factor in the viticulture of the Languedoc throughout the twentieth century, and the best still play a vital role in their appellations and villages.

The 1930s were also difficult times, with the worldwide Great Depression and further overproduction caused by the two enormous vintages of 1934 and 1935. France and Algeria between them produced almost 200 million hectolitres of wine in those two years, when the average annual consumption in France was 70 million hectolitres and the export market was moribund after the loss of traditional markets following the First World War. These problems were not confined to the Midi and the French government had already attempted to resolve the situation with the Statute de la Viticulture in 1931. This contained four important principles: it limited yields, restricted new plantings, blocked stock at the property in order to regulate the market and introduced the obligatory distillation of part of the crop in order to reduce the excess. *Primes d'arrachage*, or subsidies for pulling up vines, were introduced and various hybrid varieties forbidden, although they often remained in the small family plots destined for personal consumption. The much lower crop of 1936 and the outbreak of the Second World War in 1939 relieved the situation to some extent. Meanwhile 1936 saw the creation of the very first appellations, including Muscat de Frontignan in the Languedoc, as well as Rivesaltes in Roussillon. Significantly the first Languedoc-Roussillon appellations were for *vin doux naturel*. The Languedoc had to wait until 1948 for its first table wine appellations, namely Fitou and Clairette du Languedoc.

CHANGES AFTER THE SECOND WORLD WAR

The Midi continued to be a vineyard of mass production and mass consumption but changes were necessary. For Marc Dubernet, one of the region's leading oenologists, 1956 was a turning point in that French consumption fell for the very first time. France was emerging from the austerity of the post-war years, with changes in social habits such that the French were beginning to drink less but better quality. Consequently, the demand for wines from the south began to fall. A very hard winter destroyed vineyards in the north, and olive trees in the south. The 1950s also saw the creation of the Common Market, with the signing of the Treaty of Rome in March 1957. The region was unprepared for change; the wine industry was out of date, with a market dominated by large landowners complacent in their monoculture, with unwieldy *négociants* and cooperatives. As will be seen in the following chapter, both *négociants* and cooperatives have changed, bringing a plethora of smaller wine estates.

In the 1950s, Algeria was still an important factor in the wine market, with the port of Sète owing its prosperity to trade with the colony. The low-alcohol wines produced from the high-yielding vines of the Midi desperately needed a boost of alcohol and flavour from the so-called *vin de médicin* to render them acceptable. The young *négociants* of that period learnt their trade, and above all their blending skills, in Algeria, in the same way that a young winemaker today might go to Australia or California for new horizons. When Algeria gained independence in 1962, many families obliged to leave the country migrated to the Languedoc, bringing with them their experience of winemaking in a warm climate. The Languedoc *vigneron* tended to be interested only in his vines, whereas the *pieds noirs*, the immigrants from north Africa, were very much concerned with their cellars. The number of large *négociants* without any vineyards of their own has declined significantly; *négociants* these days want to control the process from vineyard to bottle. In Narbonne between the two world wars there were as many as 100 *négociants*; today only one remains.

The creation in 1973 of *vins de pays*, now called *Indication Géographique Protégée*, or IGP for short, helped give the mass of *vins de table* some regional identity. The development of Vin de Pays d'Oc in 1987, with its emphasis on varietal wines, was ground-breaking, enabling the Midi to meet the New World on its own terms. The appellations continued to develop, based on the earlier *Vin Délimité de Qualité Supérieure*, with St Chinian and Faugères in 1982, followed by Minervois, Corbières and the Coteaux du Languedoc, which incorporated the original VDQS of the Languedoc as *terroirs* in 1985. Coteaux du Languedoc has subsequently been replaced by the all-embracing appellation of Languedoc, which covers Roussillon, as well as Minervois and Corbières.

The second half of the twentieth century also saw the creation of *groupements de producteurs*, such as Vignerons du Val d'Orbieu, which now trades as Vinadeis. The role was essentially a commercial one. Its members, both cooperatives and wine growers, make and mature their own wine, while the group is responsible for any blending and also bottling and sales. Although the winemaking is not the group's responsibility, it will none the less play an important role as adviser and consultant, instigating changes and improvement in vineyard and cellar. At one time, there were as many as 80 such groups in Languedoc-Roussillon, but many have now disappeared, as they are losing their market force alongside the new breed of *négociants* and the smaller dynamic wine growers of the twenty-first century.

In the mid-1980s, the European wine lake was the result of overproduction, not only in the Languedoc and Roussillon, but also in southern Italy, and a cause for concern. Distillation was the immediate solution but the problem has gradually disappeared as the vineyard area of the Languedoc, as well as Roussillon, has shrunk. In 2017 there were 224,00 hectares in Languedoc-Roussillon, compared with 292,00 in 1997, and 431,000 in 1968. At the same time yields have also decreased significantly. *Primes d'arrachage* have played their part, encouraging the pulling up of vineyards, particularly on the coastal areas, that never produced anything other than inferior *vin ordinaire*. And there has been a shift in location, with greater value placed on low-yielding hillsides in the hinterland, with the consolidation of vineyard areas like the Terrasses du Larzac and Pic St Loup.

The Midi is now financially viable in a way that was simply not envisaged in the mid-1980s. Where once the bulk of the income came from government and EU subsidies, viticulture is today very buoyant. The protesting *vignerons* of the twenty-first century are not concerned with excess production in their own region, but with the encroachment of foreign wines, notably from Spain and Italy, onto the domestic market, fuelled by a confusion of labelling so that the origin of these wines is often unclear. The next chapter addresses the successes and challenges of the twenty-first century.

2

THE LANGUEDOC IN THE TWENTY-FIRST CENTURY

The Languedoc is the wine region of France that has evolved the most during the past 20 years or so. Remembering my early visits to the Languedoc in the mid-1980s, the viticultural landscape was very different indeed. The region was only just beginning to shake off its notorious reputation as a producer of *le gros rouge*, of eye-watering quantities of *vin ordinaire*, with no distinguishing characteristics whatsoever, that merely fed the European wine lake. Now long-forgotten, it was a significant issue at the time. The early appellations for table wine, Faugères, St Chinian and Coteaux du Languedoc, were in the pipeline and production was dominated by the village cooperatives. How things have changed, almost beyond recognition, in every aspect of wine growing in the region. This chapter is an attempt to consider some of those changes.

The answers to my question – what has changed since 2000? – have been many and varied. However, I think Miren de Lorgeril, the dynamic president of the *cru* of Cabardès, who runs her husband's family property, Château de Pennautier, hit the nail on the head when she replied without a moment's hesitation: 'self-confidence'. The Languedoc now has confidence in its own ability to make great wine, which it completely lacked as little as 20 years ago. As Miren says, 'We are rediscovering that we have fantastic *terroir*; people now realize that. We do not have to follow the fashions of Bordeaux or Burgundy; we are the Languedoc. And we should be proud of it.' The Languedoc can make everything from very simple but hugely enjoyable wines to truly great wines, with a depth of personality and character.

Viticultural techniques and winemaking technology have evolved dramatically all over the world in recent years, and the Languedoc is no exception in benefiting from those advances. Miren went on to observe that what people look for in their winemaking and in their wines is freshness, and that quest for freshness has necessitated changes in vineyard and cellar. There has been a significant shift towards cooler hillside sites. The most notable example of this is the development of the new appellation of Terrasses du Larzac. When the appellation of Coteaux du Languedoc was created in 1985, many of the villages of the now well-established Terrasses du Larzac were not included because they were deemed too cool for grapes to ripen successfully. There has since been a complete shift in attitude. The coastal plains that once provided the viticultural wealth of the Languedoc are no longer significant in the quest for quality and the focus is on higher altitude vineyards. You can walk in hills above the village of Montpeyroux and see wonderful vineyards, les Cocalières, planted in what was only recently an expanse of *garrigue*.

In the cellar, the significant change has again been the quest for freshness, for digestibility and drinkability. Twenty years ago, most of the oenologists will tell you, and I certainly remember it, overextraction was the dominant factor, but of course we did not realize it then. The Languedoc had for so long produced feeble, anaemic wines that it needed to prove it was capable of something so much better, so wines with any quality aspiration were macerated on their skins for weeks and aged in new oak, and the result was far from elegant. But with time came experience and the realization that more is not necessarily better.

For Jean Natoli, of Mas des Quernes, one of the key consultant oenologists for the Terrasses du Larzac, the Languedoc has quite simply become more professional, after the excesses of the 1990s. There has been a learning curve, with more restrained winemaking and more thoughtful viticulture. He cited the example of Syrah. When it was first planted in the Languedoc, people did not really know how to grow it, and it took time to realize that it needed to be trained on high wires and that a single wire was not enough. There is now a greater respect for the soil and, indeed, any wine producer worth their salt will tell you that it all begins in the vineyard; that is the most important aspect of their work.

TECHNIQUES AND EQUIPMENT

With a greater understanding of the vineyard comes the development of '*sélection parcellaire*', or site selection. Many are the wine producers who make numerous small vinifications based on a grape variety and a particular plot, with distinguishing characteristics. The enormous vats of the past have been abandoned in favour of a diversity of blending options, a veritable artist's palette of choices. When a wine estate produces a range of several wines from the same appellation, the top wine will usually come from the best identified vineyard of the estate.

Progress has been made in the cellar. Grapes need to be sorted; pickers may do that in the vineyard, and even mechanical harvesters can sort grapes, but many people have the backup of a sorting table. Cement vats, once deemed old fashioned, and usually much too big for today's requirements, are once again viewed in a favourable light, but on a more modest scale. They are often preferred to stainless steel vats, for the simple reason that temperature changes are much slower and less dramatic than with stainless steel. People have a much better understanding of *élevage*, of the impact of new wood, and the advantages of larger barrels, *demi-muids* of 500 or 600 litres rather than small *bordelais barriques*. Older barrels are often preferred to new wood, and the market for second-hand barrels has shrunk, as people keep their barrels for much longer. The enormous *foudres* may be a thing of the past but smaller *foudres* increasingly have their place in the cellar, as do the tapered tronconic vats, in wood or cement. Some growers are experimenting with chestnut or acacia barrels, and at the lower end of the quality scale, the use of oak chips is now allowed for simpler wines. Another more recent technique is *vinification intégrale*, whereby the wine is not only aged but also fermented in a small barrel from which the top is first removed in order to fill it. The aim is more integrated oak and supple tannins. There is also interest in concrete eggs, in which the wine is constantly moving, effecting a natural *bâtonnage*. Amphorae too are a subject of interest, but above ground, rather than buried, as is the long tradition in Georgia. A company in nearby Castelnaudary produces amphorae for the adventurous Languedoc producer.

Much less sulphur dioxide is used, not only by those who favour more natural and minimal intervention wine making but also by anyone who is serious about their cellar hygiene. Natural yeast is another option, favoured by some but not by others. Jean Natoli, for one, remains unconvinced by natural yeast, observing that the 20 per cent of his clients who do not use cultured yeasts are the source of 95 per cent of the problems! As Jean-Louis Escudier of INRA, the Institut National de la Recherche Agronomique, asserted, these days a wine should not have faults. With the growth in technology, faults are much easier to avoid, and also easier to remedy. However, you must not confuse technology with industrial wines; technology opens doors and adapts to market demand. He concluded that '*la bonne innovation* will be the tradition of tomorrow'.

The tools available to winemakers today are extraordinary. I visited Marc Dubernet in his laboratory outside Narbonne. I could only describe it as amazingly complex, with technical advantages that are nothing short of breathtaking. Marc observed that back in the 1970s when he started working as an oenologist, one person could make 30–40 calculations per hour, with the help of the appropriate technical and analytical equipment. Today that figure stands at 1,600, and with calculations to the finest degree. I was left feeling that there was nothing that a machine would not be able to determine about a wine.

In 2017, Marc worked his fiftieth vintage, and consequently he has a very broad overview of the development of the Languedoc and its evolution over the past half century. 'Whereas previous generations were content with *vin de table*, the younger generation looks for authenticity and personality; it is the individual wine producers who will develop the image of the Languedoc. Technology is available for the wine producers to use; each vineyard owner can find his own path, and the oenologist accompanies him and helps him understand his *terroir*, so that he can obtain the best possible wines from it. We can't do it for him and if he does not understand, it won't work. Oenology represents the *savoir faire* of man.'

For Marc, the best wine will be made tomorrow. He commented on what he sees as the next stage in the development of the Languedoc. 'We will continue to maintain our technical knowledge, and communication is all important, allowing each estate to connect with the consumer. We will cease to have doubts, but be proud of what we do, and accompany it with research. The focus will be on the individual, and each wine producer must find his own path.' When Claude Gros, another oenologist, began

working 30 years ago, he would have described his role as a wine docu
solving faults, whereas these days an oenologist must ensure that the
wines are good and will find their market, with a commercial future.
Claude also observed that ideally an oenologist should have the practical
experience of their own vines, which he does in his association with
Château La Boède in La Clape and Clos des Truffiers.

CLIMATE CHANGE

A current issue is water, or rather the lack of it, compounded by climate
change, which, for every Languedoc wine grower, is indisputable. They
see its effects every year and, as I write, the Languedoc has experienced
one of the driest years ever, with no serious rainfall between the middle
of May and the middle of October 2017. In the past, you could rely
on two good storms, perfectly timed for the two public holidays of the
summer, 14 July and 15 August, but no longer. In fact, 2017 turned out
to be a very good year, with the production of some very good wine,
but in tiny quantities. However, had there been rain at the right time,
it would have been a great year, for rainfall not only affects quantity but
also quality. Too low a yield makes for vines that are out of balance, and
yields that are too low also have economic implications. Many wine
growers will have suffered financially in 2017 from drastically reduced
yields, for the simple reason that without any wine to sell, you do not
make a living.

Lack of rain raises the thorny issue of irrigation. In the past, French
appellation laws have always been firmly against irrigation but these
days the INAO allows irrigation, though each appellation decides
for itself and many of them still take a traditional view. But there are
signs that attitudes are beginning to change. At INRA, they are more
broad-minded, observing that irrigation has always been cast in a bad
light because it is seen to increase production, which is something that
the Languedoc now avoids for historical reasons. However, if it is well
managed, with finely tuned drip irrigation, it will improve both the
quality and the quantity of the wine. In contrast, irrigation by aspersion
is a waste of water; nor is it not good for the vines as it creates humidity
and causes disease. Today, probably about 15 per cent of the region's
vineyards are irrigated, mainly those on the plain, where water is

more easily accessible. That is the problem; in some areas, it is almost impossible to find water.

Some grape varieties are more sensitive to drought that others. Syrah cannot cope with drought, whereas Cinsaut behaves like a camel in the desert. Some work is being done on purifying waste water for irrigation, but that would be an expensive option. Jean-Louis Escudier at INRA also suggested that shading could be an option, helping to alleviate water stress. *Gobelet* (bush) vines naturally provide some shading, and those who leaf pluck take care not to expose ripening grapes to intense sun or consider the direction of the rows for planting to make for more shade. However, INRA suggests more strategic shading in the form of solar panels could not only provide shade but also energy. The panels are high, so that their position and angle can be adjusted and the extent of the shading altered. There is already one grower at Domaine de Nidolères, at Tresserre in Roussillon, who has erected panels over some of his vines, for the moment purely on an experimental basis.

The effects of climate change are also manifesting themselves with increasingly early harvest dates. On that front, 2017 probably broke all the records. Gavin Crisfield of La Traversée began picking his Cinsaut on 20 August in 2017, and admitted that he was too late. It is important to get the right date, and he missed it; you can lose the right moment in a day. Nowadays, with the trend to lighter, fresher wine, the picking date becomes a crucial decision, and Gavin finds Cinsaut increasingly difficult to make as a result of climate change. The producers of Muscat also broke all the records in 2017, with Domaine de la Rencontre in Mireval starting the harvest of their Muscat for sparkling wine as early as 27 July.

ALCOHOL LEVELS

Alongside ripe grapes stands the issue of alcohol levels. There is no doubt that alcohol levels are much higher than they were 20 years or so ago. Once people understood the concept of phenolic ripeness, whereby not only was the sugar at the appropriate level but also the fruit tasted ripe, they began picking grapes with fruit flavours in mind, and with that comes higher alcohol levels. It is difficult to know what to do about the higher alcohol levels. Jean-Louis Escudier observed wryly that

France cannot follow the Anglo-Saxon or New World solution to high alcohol and dilute the wine with water. You can lower the alcohol level if you increase the yield but that is not really an option either if water is in short supply. There are grape varieties that naturally produce less alcohol, such as Cinsaut. Yeasts were originally chosen for their ability to produce alcohol; in contrast, today they are selected for the opposite function, and form a subject of research. Jean-Louis Escudier began his career in 1983, and laughingly observed that back then he worked on *enrichissement*, on chaptalization, that is not allowed in the Midi; now at the end of his career he is considering the opposite problem, trying to find ways to render wines lighter and more balanced with less alcohol. Claude Gros commented that you must not confuse ripe with overripe grapes and you must avoid overripe and, above all, raisined grapes. Balance is the key, and often wines that are quite high in alcohol do not necessarily taste out of balance if there is sufficient fruit and flavour to support the alcohol.

Typicity is a crucial word in the discussion of the characteristics of a wine and its appellation. Hernan Ojeda, the director of INRA, observed that typicity changes with the climate, so the change in climate will doubtless bring about a change in the grape varieties of the region. In the 1970s and 1980s, people looked for varieties that would improve the quality of the existing varieties, such as Carignan, Cinsaut and Aramon, which led to the extensive planting of Syrah, Grenache Noir and Mourvèdre, not to mention the international varieties such as Cabernet Sauvignon, Merlot, Chardonnay and so on. Most of the Aramon was pulled up, and Carignan was relegated to a secondary position in the *cahier des charges* of each appellation, while Cinsaut was considered only suitable for rosé. It still is very suitable for rosé, but there is a growing recognition that it also makes some delicious red wines, which are more elegant than the fuller-bodied structured Syrah. Not for nothing is it sometimes called the Pinot Noir of the south. As will be seen throughout this book, Carignan is enjoying a happy revival in its fortunes, and not just Carignan Noir, but also Blanc, and maybe even Gris.

Late-ripening grape varieties that can withstand drought have a future in the Languedoc. In that context, the success and future of Syrah in some areas is questionable. Grown in conditions that are too hot and dry, the flavours can turn distinctly jammy, or *confit* as the French more elegantly say. Another disadvantage of Syrah is its much higher mortality rate than Carignan or Grenache Noir.

Other, older, grape varieties are being 'rescued' from oblivion. There are several plantings of Oeillade, which is recognized as a cousin of Cinsaut. Thierry Navarre in Roquebrun has Ribeyrenc Noir, as do François Henry in St Georges d'Orques, Patricia Domergue in the Minervois and Damien Coste of Domaine Belle Pierres. Patricia also has some forgotten white and gris varieties, such as Ribeyrenc, Terret, Picardin and Araignan. The INRA station at Domaine de Vassal at Marseillan is a repository of vine varieties, with the intention of preserving many of the 'ancestral varieties', as Jean-Louis Escudier described them. Altogether, there are more than 2,700 varieties of *Vitis vinifera*, with rootstocks and hybrids as well.

GRAPES FOR WHITE AND ROSÉ

One of the most dramatic developments is the exciting improvement in the white wines of the region. Historically the Languedoc always produced red wines, with very few areas known for their white wines. The vineyards of Picpoul de Pinet were once the source of the base wine for Noilly Prat and other vermouths and Jean Ségura at Château Rivière Haute in La Clape was very unusual in focusing on white wine in the 1980s. When they were created in 1982, the appellations of Faugères and St Chinian only allowed red and rosé; the white appellations were not added until 2005. Pic St Loup and Terrasses du Larzac are still only red, so that any white wines in those areas are either IGP or plain AOP Languedoc.

Modern vinification methods, essentially temperature control for fermentation, have had a fundamental impact on the flavours of the white wines of the region, as has the introduction of grape varieties like Marsanne, Roussanne and Vermentino. There has been a new appraisal of the more traditional varieties, notably Carignan Blanc, Bourboulenc, which forms the backbone of La Clape, Grenache Blanc and also Grenache Gris; in other words, grape varieties with good acidity that are better able to withstand the summer heat. Terret Blanc and Gris are also enjoying something of a revival, as later ripening grapes with refreshing acidity. Other varieties have come from elsewhere. Viognier is now very much an established part of the Languedoc portfolio for IGPs and in some appellations it may be permitted in a very small percentage, but often the flavours are deemed too powerful, dominating the palate. Chardonnay and Sauvignon remain very firmly within the IGPs, while other varieties are being evaluated. Laurent Miquel, who is unusual in focusing more on white than red wine, has planted Albariño in the hills above Lagrasse. There are pockets of Chenin Blanc around St Saturnin, and lone examples of Riesling, Gewürztraminer, Petit Manseng and even Petite Arvine. Muscat, originally grown for *vin doux*, now increasingly makes unfortified sweet wines, and also refreshing dry Muscat.

The focus of the Languedoc is on blends rather than single varieties, and the diversity of the blends is infinite. Take No. 7 from Domaine la Croix Belle, made from seven different varieties, Chardonnay, Viognier, Grenache Blanc, Sauvignon Blanc, Grenache Gris, Muscat à Petits Grains and Carignan Blanc. Las Clapas Blanc from Domaine du Pas de l'Escalette is a blend of Grenache Blanc and Carignan Blanc, with a little Terret Bourret, or Terret Gris, and Grenache Gris, and L'Etincelle from Cal Demoura comes from Chenin Blanc, Grenache Blanc, Roussanne, Viognier and Petit Manseng. These are just three examples, none of which existed 20 or possibly even 10 years ago. It is not only the cooler hillsides that are suitable for white but, as is seen in the appellations of La Clape and Picpoul de Pinet, also the maritime areas. As Béatrice Fillon of Clos du Serres observed, for white wine, there is a whole history to build, and it will take time, with new areas to discover and develop. Vincent Goumard, talking about white wine in relation to the purely red Terrasses du Larzac, observes that they are just embarking on white wine; they need to start at the beginning and work out which grape varieties are suitable. It is an enormous task, but it will happen.

Rosé is also growing in importance, despite the reputation of Côtes de Provence, which has set the fashion for paler than pale rosé. The Languedoc actually produces twice as much rosé as Provence, both appellation and IGP. Technical advances in the cellar, temperature control and protection against oxygen, have had an enormous impact and some more adventurous wine growers are experimenting successfully with oak *élevage*.

VINE DEVELOPMENT AND ORGANIC WINE PRODUCERS

INRA is working on developing vines that are more resistant to mildew and oidium, with new varieties based on *Vitis rotundifolia*, or Muscardine, a variety that is native to the south-eastern United States. This work will result in the creation of new varieties, with the development of crossings that are 99 per cent *Vitis vinifera*, but with just 1 per cent that makes them much more disease resistant. Domaine de la Colombette outside Béziers has also developed its own vines that are similar to those of INRA (see p. 328). Both are convinced that this is the way to limit the use of treatments in the vineyards. The October 2017 issue of the magazine *Sciences et Avenir* stated that while vineyards account for 3 per cent of the cultivated land in France, the wine industry is responsible for 13 per cent of pesticide usage, which is a pretty shocking statistic.

Another significant current problem in the Languedoc is that of a vine trunk disease, called esca, which attacks the wood of the vine. Currently there is no cure for it, as a previously accepted treatment was based on arsenic and, for obvious reasons, has now been prohibited. It is probably not an exaggeration to describe it as the phylloxera of the twenty-first century, affecting not just the Languedoc, but the whole of France; according to INRA, as much as 14 per cent of the vineyards of the country. Some grape varieties, such as Mourvèdre and Cinsaut, are more susceptible to it than to others, such as Grenache. Essentially it is a type of airborne mushroom, carried in the wind, that will also live in the soil. The vines are particularly vulnerable at pruning because the disease may also be spread by the secateurs. Another suggested risk factor is the type of grafting: the mechanical omega shaped graft, rather than the manual pointed *greffe anglaise*, makes the vines more susceptible to esca. Suffice it to say, that for the moment there is no obvious solution.

The Languedoc does have one significant climatic advantage over many other regions of France, namely the drying wind that usually blows hard after any rain, which means that oidium and mildew are much less prevalent than elsewhere. This makes organic viticulture much more viable and widespread than in most other parts of France. Claude Gros has noticed an explosion of organic viticulture in the past few years: in 2000 about 10–15 per cent of his clients were organic; today that figure has leaped to 80 per cent.

In fact, there are now over 1,300 registered organic growers, cultivating 22,000 hectares of vineyards, accounting for one-third of all the organic vineyards of France, and many more who may not be registered but none the less follow the criteria of organic viticulture. They may reserve the right to treat conventionally in the case of an emergency, or may feel that the money they have to spend on the membership of one of the several organizations that control organic viticulture, such as Demeter or Nature et Progrès, is simply not cost effective. If you are a small vine grower, with say just 6 hectares, it will cost you about €2,400 per year to register your vines, and to recoup that money you need to increase the cost of your wine by quite a high margin. Increasing your production is usually not an option.

Organic viticulture is really a return to what the growers did before the development of systemic treatments; it depends upon copper and sulphur. The first organic growers appeared in the 1980s. Jean-François Coutelou of Domaine Coutelou in Puimisson remembered that when his father planted his first vines in 1987, he was one of just seven organic growers in the Hérault, with just 40 hectares of organic vineyards in the department. However, copper, which is allowed with organic viticulture, is criticized as it is a hard metal and remains in the soil virtually for ever. Cyril Bourgne of Domaine la Madura in St Chinian is very eloquent on the subject, considering that some organic producers are too dogmatic in their approach. He prefers an organization that was created in 2007, Haute Valeur Environnementale, which concentrates on the diversity of the soil and the management of water, while reducing the number of treatments and respecting the carbon footprint. 'It is not because it is organic that it is good, and that it is not toxic'. He is not the only grower to suggest that some organic treatments are as toxic as conventional ones. The encouraging aspect is that a growing number of *vignerons* are increasingly aware of the need to care for the soil and focus on biodiversity.

BIODYNAMICS AND NATURAL WINE

The next step after organic viticulture is biodynamics, which follows the phases of the moon when programming vineyards treatments. The biodynamic calendar divides the year into days of fruit, flower, leaf and root. Some days are much better than others for particular treatments and some days, such as Good Friday, are best avoided. There are various biodynamic treatments. The cynics joke about cow horns full of manure that are buried in the vineyards, but I wonder if that is so different to giving my roses bone meal. Those who have converted recently to biodynamics are convinced that they have seen an improvement in their wines. For me, one palpable example is Domaine du Pas de l'Escalette in the Terrasses du Larzac: their red wines seemed so much fresher and more finely crafted than on a previous visit, which Julien Zernott unhesitatingly attributed to their conversion to biodynamic viticulture

From biodynamics, it is an easy step to the thorny subject of natural wine. There has been a growing trend in recent years, not just in the Languedoc but all over France, to question the use of additives in winemaking. The most obvious example is sulphur, which has been used since Roman times as an efficient antioxidant and antiseptic, but its critics argue that it can deform the flavour of a wine, making tannins harder and masking the fruit. Cultured yeast, as opposed to the natural yeast on the bloom of the grape, is another issue. In a nutshell, the natural winemaker aspires to make his wine as naturally as possible, without the use of any additives whatsoever. This entails absolutely impeccable hygiene in the cellar and very rigorous attention to detail in both vineyard and cellar. The concept is highly laudable. Wine comes from grapes. What more is needed? However, the sad fact is, that left to its own devices, after wine, grape juice turns to vinegar, which means the wine needs help to stop it doing so necessitating protection from the effects of oxygen.

One of my criticisms of natural wines is that they can have a tendency to taste very similar, masking regional variations. This hit me most strongly with a comparison of two *cuvées* of Corbières, from Domaine Ollieux Romanis; one was natural and the other conventional. In the conventional wine I recognized the characteristics of Corbières, the spicy fruit and the notes of the *garrigue*. In contrast, the natural wine was fresh and perfumed, and quite unlike any other Corbières I have tasted. It was Gregory White, a natural winemaker in Aspiran, who explained why. With the need to protect against oxygen, so many natural wines are fermented using a form of carbonic maceration, with grapes added to a vat of carbon dioxide and left to infuse. Carbonic maceration can mask other flavours and that is what so often happens. Gregory manages to make natural wines using a classic vinification, so that his wines have a greater diversity of flavour.

With natural wine comes orange wine, white wines that have enjoyed a long maceration on their skins. It was John Bojanowski at Clos du Gravillas in the Minervois who asked: 'Who decided white wine should be made without skins and red wine with skins?' He makes a very successful orange wine from Muscat. And there are other examples of orange wine scattered throughout the Languedoc, demonstrating the multifaceted diversity of the region.

One of the problems of natural wine is that there is no real charter or common understanding as to what constitutes natural wine. There is an Association des Vins Naturels, with about 60 members, including half a dozen from the Languedoc, but by no means all the natural winemakers are members, and there are currently discussions with the INAO for a *cahier des charges*, but as yet nothing concrete. It would be fair to suggest no cultured yeast and no sulphur are the essential tenets of natural wine, with the assumption that the vineyards are farmed organically or biodynamically. As a result of this lack of control, most natural wines tend to be labelled Vin de France, as they often fail to conform to the norms of the appellation.

APPELLATIONS OF THE LANGUEDOC

The appellations of the Languedoc are evolving, with the creation of a hierarchical form pyramid. The appellation Languedoc is the base, replacing the former appellation of Coteaux du Languedoc, covering almost all the appellation land of the region, including nearly all of the appellations covered in this book. The default for all the table wine

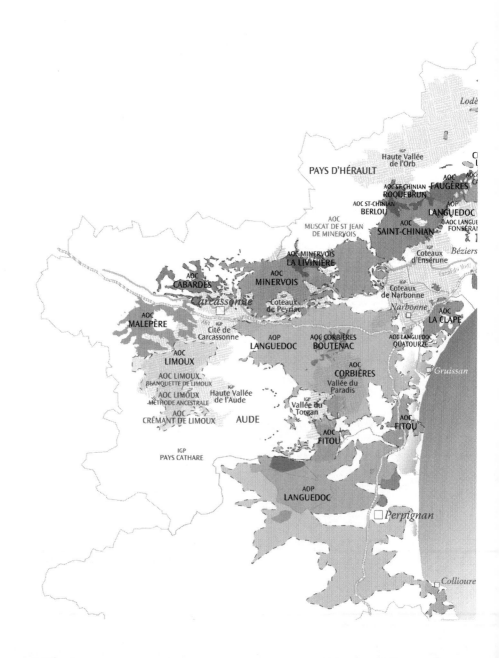

Lodè

IGP
Haute Vallée
de l'Orb

PAYS D'HÉRAULT

AOC ST-CHINIAN
ROQUEBRUN   FAUGÈRES

AOC ST-CHINIAN
BERLOU   AOP
LANGUEDOC

AOC
MUSCAT DE ST JEAN
DE MINERVOIS   AOC LANGUE
FONSERA

AOC
SAINT-CHINIAN

AOC MINERVOIS
LA LIVINIÈRE   *Béziers*

IGP
Coteaux
d'Ensérune

AOC
CABARDÈS

AOC
MINERVOIS   IGP
Coteaux
de Narbonne

Carcassonne   *Narbonne*   AOC
LA CLAPE

Coteaux
de Peyriac

AOC
MALEPÈRE   IGP
Cité de
Carcassonne

AOP
LANGUEDOC   AOC CORBIÈRES
BOUTENAC   AOC LANGUEDOC
QUATOURZE

AOC
LIMOUX   AOC
CORBIÈRES   *Gruissan*

AOC LIMOUX
BLANQUETTE DE LIMOUX   Vallée du
Paradis

AOC LIMOUX
MÉTHODE ANCESTRALE   Haute Vallée
de l'Aude   IGP
Vallée du
Torgan

AOC
CRÉMANT DE LIMOUX   AUDE   AOC
FITOU

IGP
PAYS CATHARE   AOC
FITOU

AOP
LANGUEDOC

□ *Perpignan*

□ *Collioure*

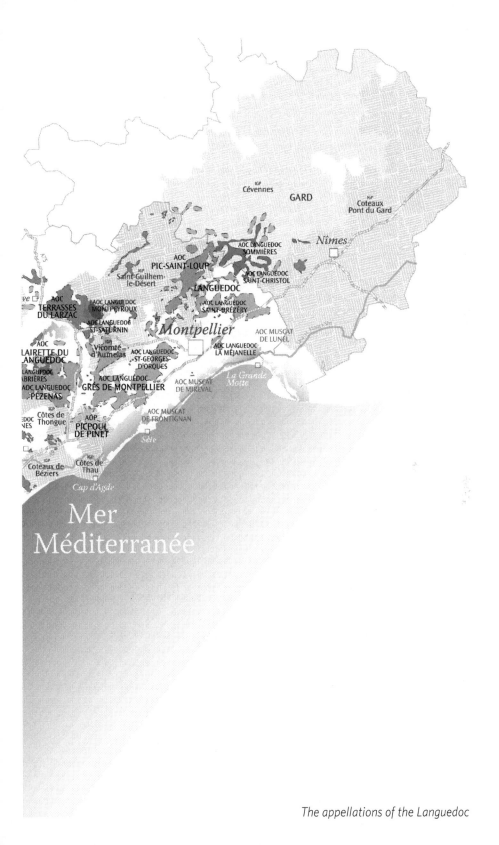

GARD

IGP
Cévennes

IGP
Coteaux
Pont du Gard

AOC LANGUEDOC
SOMMIÈRES

Nîmes

AOC
PIC-SAINT-LOUP

IGP
Saint-Guilhem-
le-Désert

AOC LANGUEDOC
SAINT-CHRISTOL

LANGUEDOC

AOC
TERRASSES
DU LARZAC

AOC LANGUEDOC
MONTPEYROUX

AOC LANGUEDOC
SAINT-DRÉZÉRY

AOC LANGUEDOC
ST-SATURNIN

Montpellier

AOC MUSCAT
DE LUNEL

AOC
CLAIRETTE DU
LANGUEDOC

IGP
Vicomté
d'Aumelas

AOC LANGUEDOC
ST-GEORGES-
D'ORQUES

AOC LANGUEDOC
LA MÉJANELLE

LANGUEDOC
CABRIÈRES

AOC LANGUEDOC
PÉZENAS

AOC LANGUEDOC

GRÈS DE MONTPELLIER

AOC MUSCAT
DE MIREVAL

*La Grande
Motte*

DOC
NES

IGP
Côtes de
Thongue

AOP
PICPOUL
DE PINET

AOC MUSCAT
DE FRONTIGNAN

Sète

IGP
Coteaux de
Béziers

IGP
Côtes de
Thau

Cap d'Agde

Mer
Méditerranée

The appellations of the Languedoc

appellations, with the one exception of Malepère, is Languedoc. You also find the occasional wine producer whose land is appellation Languedoc, but nothing more specific. To confuse the issue, the default position for most of Roussillon is also Languedoc. There is at least one grower based in the Languedoc who buys grapes in Roussillon and makes a wine that he labels Languedoc. Next in the hierarchy come the broader appellations, such as Corbières, Minervois, Terrasses du Larzac and so on, and within those fairly large appellations, some smaller *crus* have been recognized, such as Boutenac in Corbières and La Livinière in the Minervois.

The old appellation of Coteaux du Languedoc included various *terroirs*, the former VDQS of the region. Here, local pride and politics come into play, as most of these small areas would like to retain their individuality by becoming what is called an *appellation communale*, so that Languedoc-Montpeyroux would become plain Montpeyroux. French appellations have a very strong sense of place and the hapless consumer is expected to know that Montpeyroux is in the Languedoc, without it saying so on the label. So far, the new appellations that have grown out of the Coteaux du Languedoc are La Clape, Picpoul de Pinet and Pic St Loup. Terrasses du Larzac is a new appellation, a recognition of the quality of the high hills in the hinterland of the region. Areas like Pézenas and Grés de Montpellier are aspiring appellations in their own right, and St Georges d'Orques, for example, would be a *cru* of Grés de Montpellier, and Montpeyroux a *cru* of the Terrasses du Larzac, at the top of the pyramid. The situation continues to evolve and the goalposts shift, with the evolution of the appellations seen as work in progress. It took Burgundy several centuries to establish its system of *village*, *premier cru* and *grand cru*; the Languedoc is merely at the beginning of that journey. Another more cynical observation is that the hierarchy is a quarrel of *clochers*, of parish politics, a jostling for position rather than a real strategy.

For Vincent Goumard of Domaine Cal Demoura, the real subject today is the identification of the *terroirs*, which is why he has called one of his wines Terres de Jonquières, as he wants the wine to reflect the *terroir* of his village, with a contribution from each of his vineyards. When he began making wine in 2004, you needed to know the individual estate rather than the appellation; you bought wine by grower rather than appellation, but now the appellations have progressed, achieving a good quality level, with a growing number of estates working well. Vincent observed that if Languedoc-Roussillon were an independent country, it would be sixth or seventh in world production of wine, after Spain, Italy, the rest of France, as well as China, the USA and possibly Argentina or Chile. He feels that the success relates to the collective effort focusing on the improvement in the appellations, combined with a very good price–quality ratio, what the French elegantly call *rapport qualité–prix*. The best wines of the Languedoc are still affordable, which is no longer the case with Bordeaux or Burgundy. However, Laurent Miquel was keen to point out that the Languedoc is not an area for cheap wine. Labour costs are much higher in France than in South America or South Africa, and the hillside vineyards are more labour intensive than those of the plains.

The 1990s saw what Jean-Claude Mas described as the glorious years of *vins de cépage*, with the south of France competing successfully with the New World on its own terms with varietal wines. Vin de Pays d'Oc, created in 1987, with just 24 grape varieties, was the vehicle, and grape varieties from other parts of France were introduced to the Languedoc, with the development of a plethora of wines based on a single varietal, Merlot, Cabernet Sauvignon, Chardonnay, Sauvignon Blanc and so on, as well as grape varieties more traditional to the Languedoc. Over the years, the varieties permitted for what is now Pays d'Oc have extended to 58, with Albariño the most recent addition to the list. In contrast, the identity of the appellations of the Languedoc depends firmly upon blends, which may vary from appellation to appellation and from grower to grower. If you do not wish to make either an appellation or an IGP, there is the option of Vin de France, which has replaced anonymous *vin de table* with something more precise, in that information about the vintage and the grape variety is allowed on the label. In the hands of a talented wine producer, Vin de France can prove an original and rewarding choice.

The commercial face of the Languedoc has also changed dramatically. Time was when virtually every village had a cooperative. The first cooperatives helped with sales, usually *en vrac* to a *négociant*, and then they began to produce wine, sharing equipment and cellar facilities. Today the cooperatives, with certain exceptions, are a waning force. Some are vital to their appellation, and work well for it, such as Cabrières, the two

Picpoul cooperatives, Montpeyroux and Castelmaure et d'Embrès in the Corbières, to cite just a handful. The cooperative in Faugères does its appellation a gross disservice in selling its cheapest wine as Faugères, and at half the price of the average Faugères. The cooperative of St Georges d'Orques is no better. The cooperatives were let down by the *viticulteur* who worked badly, reducing quality to the level of the lowest common denominator. In contrast, the forward-thinking cooperatives have instituted systems of remuneration that concentrate on the quality of the grapes and they have been able to make the shift into the modern commercial world.

Many others have been unable to make that transition, and consequently they have closed, and joined forces with neighbouring cooperatives. In the villages close to my home village of Roujan, the Roujan cooperative now works with neighbouring Neffiès and Abeilhan; Pouzolles and Alignan du Vent also work together, while Gabian and Magalas have ceased to function. In 1980, there were 550 cooperatives, responsible for 70 per cent of production; in 2017 there were 220, still accounting for 70 per cent of production, but with a much smaller area of vines, and significantly lower yields. As Marc Dubernet observed, the cooperative system is dying because they produce industrial wine without any personality, and that is not what the consumer wants. The image of the Languedoc is now carried by the individual winemakers.

INDEPENDENT PRODUCERS

The generation change has been positive. The children of growers have not merely followed in their parents' footsteps; they are likely to have studied, and to quite a high level. Many are those who have not only learnt from their parents but also have a degree in oenology, and they will have travelled, working elsewhere in France, or indeed much further afield, learning from that experience, in many cases what not to do, and finding out what they can adapt to their own circumstances. These days the independent producers have become so much more important, with new estates being created at an astonishing rate. As will be seen, the people behind them may come from the region, and may be the children of cooperative members who want to make their own wine, or they may come from other parts of France, having worked in wine elsewhere, or wine may represent a complete change of career. The same applies to the numerous foreigners who have settled in the area. The lure of the Languedoc is very strong. One of the key reasons for this is the relative affordability of the land compared with other parts of France. The Languedoc is seen as a land where everything is possible. The climate makes for relatively easy viticulture compared with some of the northern parts of the country. The appellations may lay down production rules, but it is very easy to elect to make an IGP or a Vin de France if you wish to experiment and try something unusual. There is a feeling that there is everything to discover and nothing stands still.

One of the key problems of the Languedoc today is marketing. How do the plethora of small wine producers sell their wine? Many are those who are talented winemakers but inept in the commercial field. Competition is fierce. I can think of people who make sound and reliable wine, and who sell successfully because they have marketing skills; then there are others whose wines deserve to succeed but who simply do not manage to crack the commercial nut. I have lost count of the times somebody has lamented to me that the British market is so difficult.

The role of the *négociant* has changed too, with an increasing emphasis on the ownership of vineyards. A company like Jeanjean will produce an extensive range of wines, accounting for its bread and butter, but its quality focus is above all on its wine estates. The same goes for the likes of Domaines Paul Mas and Gérard Bertrand. Even the somewhat anonymous Grands Chais de France, one of the biggest but fairly silent players in the region, is buying vineyards: first Domaine des Belles Eaux from AXA and now Domaine du Plan de l'Homme in St Jean-de-Fos, with vineyards in Terrasses du Larzac.

Someone like Jean-Claude Mas wants to control the whole process from vine to bottle either by owning his own vineyards or by contracts with other growers, so that he can develop his individual style of wine, which is in complete contrast to the cooperative system. Jean-Claude observed that once the Languedoc was a land of *viticulteurs* who produced grapes but since about 2000, many of the *viticulteurs* have turned *vigneron*, with essentially four or five different professions: growing grapes, making wine, marketing and selling their wine, and also simply running their estates, with all the resultant bureaucracy, financial issues and paperwork. A *négociant* activity will always have its place, with some much larger than others, such as the Vignerons du

Val d'Orbieu, now called Vinadeis, which began life as a *groupement de producteurs*. Some smaller producers also have a *négociant* activity to supplement their wine offer, but essentially it is the name of the domaine that provides the identity and signature for the wine.

Languedoc has had a reputation for cheap wine, but that is gradually changing. When Aimé Guibert at Mas de Daumas Gassac set the bar in the 1980s, asking a price that was more in line with Bordeaux or Burgundy than a humble Vin de Pays de l'Hérault, he gave others the confidence to follow his example. When we are prepared to pay a sensible price for a wine, which means that it should be neither too expensive, nor too cheap, we are giving its producers the possibility of investing some money in better cellar facilities or new vineyards. More recently Gérard Bertrand talked of a *prise de conscience* about price. You must not be afraid of selling at a higher price, as he is with his new *cuvée* Clos d'Ora, from Minervois La Livinière, which currently averages about £150 on Wine Searcher (www.winesearcher.com), making it the most expensive of all Languedoc wines. However, an immense amount of care and attention to detail has been lavished on producing this micro-*cuvée* and there are customers for it. At the other end of the scale, there remains the economic challenge to sell the wine at an appropriate price and there are still stories of people selling below cost price in order to make room in the cellar for the next harvest.

BUILDING THE BRAND

Communication remains a problem. There is virtually no communication about the appellation Languedoc, which is the region's most extensive, and fastest growing in volume, thanks to a demand for rosé. For the moment, Corbières is still the largest, but it is not very homogenous, with considerable variations of *terroir* and climate. Half the region produces IGP, and mainly Pays d'Oc, but the two organizations of the CIVL, the Comité des Vins du Languedoc, and the Pays d'Oc do not work together. The Languedoc remains very individual. As Laurent Miquel put it: 'Everyone is a pioneer. It's like herding cats and dogs. The challenge is to obtain more recognition.'

Others are less optimistic. Xavier Brajou of Terrasse d'Elise thought that too many people were doing the same thing, bringing about a standardization of the appellations. Maybe there are simply too many estates, with not enough room for everyone. Consider that the Terrasses du Larzac alone has absorbed 25 new wine producers in the past six years. There is a limited number of wines that an importer or wine merchant can deal with from the same area. The pessimists raise doubts as to whether there is a market for so many wines that are in some ways relatively similar. They each need to find their individuality, and yet it is the energy of the newcomers that has helped bring the Languedoc into the limelight.

There is also the tricky question of money and land values. People obviously want a return on their land but according to Xavier Braujou of Terrasse d'Elise, very few of the newcomers are 'real farmers, real *paysans, les vrais gens de la terre,*' and they have increased the land values, which can pose a problem for the local people and can also have an impact on inheritance taxes. In Terrasses du Larzac, for instance, half of the growers do not come from a family of growers. They may be investors; they may be doing it for pleasure, and not necessarily need to be profitable; or they may choose to sell their wine at what some consider an excessive price. Then, as Damien Coste from Domaine Belles Pierres put it, the journalists are seduced, and fail to realize that these people have a completely different perspective from the original *viticulteurs.* The micro-*vignerons* accentuate the competition and the impact of their micro-*cuvées* makes for an imbalance, so that the people who were there at the beginning are completely overlooked. Virgile Joly in St Saturnin would suggest that there are two sorts of *vignerons*, the small producers who may only have a couple of hectares, and do everything themselves, or the investors who do not need to make a living but take pleasure in creating something, and then there are those for whom their vineyards are their livelihood and need to be made profitable. As he put it so eloquently, the two realities are not the same but the market does not see the difference – and journalists should be aware of this and take the size of an estate into consideration.

Along with importance of communication, there is a growing awareness of the value of oenotourism. Most of the appellations now have some kind of annual fête that encourages tourists to visit the area. The Grand St Jean in Faugères in the middle of July is always a lively occasion, as is the Caveaux Ouverts in Montpeyroux in the spring. There are also *ballades vigneronnes*, combining an opportunity to walk and taste in the format of a meal. You walk a kilometre and reach your aperitif stop, with an appropriate *amuse-bouche*, and some wines to taste and enjoy with it, and then walk to the next course, with more wines to taste. Each grower who wishes to participate mans a barrel and shows a wine of their choice. The Pic St Loup walk, with its proximity to Montpellier, is particularly popular but I have also enjoyed walks in Terrasses du Larzac and around La Clape.

Few are the wineries that have a restaurant, but they do exist and their number is growing. La Table Cave du Château at Château Pennautier was a pioneer. There is also Côté Mas, run by Domaines Paul Mas outside Pézenas, and Folia at Château Flaugergues in the suburbs of Montpellier, and a restaurant about to open at the Prieuré de St Jean-de-Bébian outside Pézenas. Many are the wine estates that organize concerts and other events to attract visitors during the summer months.

When asked about changes, Catherine Roque of Mas d'Alezon in Faugères suggested that, 'We have finished our adolescence, and have become *sage*, or grown up.' She is optimistic: 'We are evolving in the right direction; we have magnificent vineyard land.' Jean-Claude Zabalia, who has been involved with the region for a number of years, considers the Languedoc to be *en pleine évolution*: it is developing its own culture of wine and not blindly following Burgundy and Bordeaux. 'The Languedoc is for those who like a risk; we are at the beginning of our modern history, though it all began with the Greeks 2000 years ago. The Languedoc stands for diversity, yet it does need to be known for something with which it can achieve a world-class standard. It has taken a giant step, but it is still finding its way.'

The chapters that follow cover the various appellations and show how each wine producer is finding their way in the twenty-first century.

3

MALEPÈRE

Malepère is the most non-*languedocien* of all the appellations of the Languedoc, for the simple reason that the appellation does not demand any of the usual five red varieties of the other Languedoc appellations. France divides broadly into three large viticultural regions and Malepère is where two of them meet, for it lies on the frontier between the Languedoc and Aquitaine. What the French call *le partage des eaux*, the watershed between the Atlantic and the Mediterranean, is at Castelnaudary, some 40 kilometres to the west.

The Massif de la Malepère is just south-west of the city of Carcassonne and north-west of the small town of Limoux. It covers some 30 square kilometres, rising to 440 metres, and is an ancient geological formation, even older than the Pyrenees, forming a promontory between the Mediterranean and the plain of Aquitaine. The vineyards are on its lower slopes, at about 250 metres, with pastures on the higher land. The lower slopes are peppered with little villages, such as the Cathar village Montréal with its imposing church, neighbour to Foujean, which was Catholic. Alaigne is a *circulade* village, built to resist invasion during the Middle Ages.

The vineyards of Malepère have been a melting pot of grape varieties, allowing those of the Languedoc to mix with those of Bordeaux. Although the appellation of Malepère is situated in the Aude and belongs geographically to the Languedoc, climatically it is in a transitional zone with more affinity to the Atlantic climate of south western France. Unlike the other appellations of the Languedoc, the wine growers of Malepère cannot produce an appellation Languedoc if they choose not to produce their own particular appellation. Aptly, the slogan of the appellation is 'L'Autre Languedoc'. Conditions are quite different. There are fewer hours of sunshine than on the coastal plain and usually no lack of summer rain, so that the vines do not have to withstand periods of drought. They are more likely to be affected by spring frosts, as indeed they were in 2017. The natural vegetation reflects the climatic mix. There are the holm oaks and Alep pines of the Mediterranean, the *chêne pubescente* of the sub-Mediterranean and the common or pedunculate oak of the Atlantic and, finally, the beech of the mountains. The various oaks give an indication as to which grape varieties grow best on which part of the Massif. As for the soil, it is very mixed. Malepère translates literally as bad stone, stone that was not good for building and therefore good for agricultural land. As well as stony sandstone terraces of glacial origin, there are slopes of clay and limestone. The north and south faces of the massif contain more gravel, as a result of the river Aude changing its course at some time.

Work at a local research station, Domaine Cazes, in the 1960s resulted in the introduction of Bordeaux grape varieties, so that the appellation of Malepère now includes Merlot, which must account for 50 per cent of the blend, with Cabernet Franc, Cabernet Sauvignon, and Cot or Malbec. As for the southern varieties, there is Grenache Noir and its near relation Lledoner Pelut, as well as Cinsaut, which is only used for rosé. Syrah has been removed from the decree to differentiate Malepère from neighbouring Cabardès. It would be possible to make Malepère without any Midi grape varieties at all but it is impossible not to include any *bordelais* varieties. Malepère is only ever red or rosé; any white wine is Pays d'Oc or Côtes de Prouilhe. A more recent proposal for a white appellation was refused by the INAO, with the suggestion that the wine growers of the appellation first needed to optimize the production of their red and rosé wines. Any thoughts of white wine were distinctly premature.

The appellation covers 39 villages, with the greatest concentration of vineyards on the southern side of the Massif de la Malepère. This is still a region dominated by cooperatives and, needless to say, there are estates in the area making serious wine that has nothing to do with the appellation. However, Gérard Bertrand's recent purchase of Domaine de la Soujeole should have a beneficial effect on the reputation of Malepère because, as Guillaume Mallafosse from Château Belvèze observed, '*il est moteur*'.

Producers

Domaine Rose et Paul

Arzens 11290
www.rose-paul.fr

This estate outside the village of Arzens is named after Gilles Foussat's grandparents. Paul was taken prisoner at Dunkirk in 1940 and it was Rose who ran the estate during the Second World War. Gilles's father joined the cooperative and was also part of the experimental estate of Domaine de Cazes. Gilles took over in 1992 with another professional and did not extract his vines from the cooperative until 2009. He began with 13 hectares and now works with 70. He tells a story of his battle with bureaucracy to get water connected to his cellar on the eve of the harvest. The threat to deliver a trailer of grapes to the door of the relevant office had the desired effect!

We enthused about Chardonnay, which could, with Grenache Gris, be the backbone for the potential white appellation. Currently it is IGP Côtes de Prouilhe, named after a nearby monastery, with three different *cuvées*, from young vines, a Sélection with some *élevage* on lees, and a *cuvée* Vieilles Vignes, fermented in wood, which was rich and buttery.

The rosé is based on Cabernet Franc, a minimum of 50 per cent – Merlot is not obligatory in the rosé. The balance consists of Grenache Noir, Malbec and Cabernet Sauvignon, with fresh elegant flavours. The simplest red Malepère is a blend of 55 per cent Merlot, with 30 per cent Cabernet Franc, some Cabernet Sauvignon and Malbec and just 10 per cent Grenache Noir. The wine was nicely rounded with fresh fruit after a ten months' *élevage* in vat. All five varieties are fermented together: 'We fought to have all five varieties in the appellation,' asserted Gilles. He enthused about the complexity of Malepère, with its two different *terroirs*, some clay and limestone at a higher altitude and some sandy limestone on warmer, south facing slopes, with a more Mediterranean climate. Grenache Noir here is quite different from anywhere else. Rondel, after the vineyard, consists of Merlot planted in 1965, Grenache Noir planted in 1968 and Cabernet Franc from 1976, given seven months in wood after blending, with some ripe structured fruit.

Gilles is currently president of the growers' syndicat and you sense that he is intensely committed to his appellation and optimistic about its future, enjoying its originality. The quality has improved with a strict *cahier des charges*. In 2007, when he became president, 90 per cent of the appellation was sold *en vrac* and when he took a bet that he could reverse that figure, everybody laughed, but that is what has happened. The volume of Malepère has reduced, but the quality has risen, and most of the wine is now sold in bottle. Our tasting finished with a 2013 Rondel, showing some elegant cedary notes of development.

Domaine La Louvière

11300 Malviès

www.domaine-la-louviere.com

Domaine La Louvière outside the village of Malviès belongs to the Grohe family, who bought their first vineyards in Malepère about 25 years ago. They now have 50 hectares, of which 35 are Malepère, and built a state of the art cellar in 2007. Their wine is made for them by the talented Australian winemaker, Jem Harris, who originally came to the Languedoc as a part-owner of Domaine les Fusionnels in Faugères. He is left pretty much to his own devices; the family's tap business is going well and wine is a hobby for them, but none the less they do expect results.

Jem compared Malepère with Faugères. Climate is obviously the biggest difference, and the soil is much richer, making for higher yields – the yield for Malepère is 50 hectolitres per hectare but the cooperatives produce excessively, as much as 200 hectolitres per hectare, but obviously not for Malepère itself. Jem makes a range of Pays d'Oc, including Chardonnay and some satisfyingly stony Sauvignon Blanc. La Muse is a blend of Viognier, Chardonnay and Chenin; la Souveraine is an oak-aged Chardonnay; le Coquin a pure Merlot with supple tannins. As for Malepère, there is a rosé from Cabernet Franc, Syrah and Merlot. La Mainesse is a blend of 60 per cent Merlot, 30 per cent Cabernet Franc and 10 per cent Malbec. Jem observed that Cabernet Franc has a superior performance to Cabernet Sauvignon, ripening better, and that Malbec is not widely planted. He is still learning about it. He is working on reducing the tannins, making for riper, more supple wines. La Séductrice, from poorer, drier soil, includes an oak-aged component and is given a longer maceration, while L'Empereur comes from the oldest and best plots on the plateau, and is fermented in 400-litre barrels before spending 12 to 18 months in wood. It is ripe and concentrated but not heavy, with well integrated oak, making a serious age-worthy glass of wine.

Domaine Gayda
Brugairolles 11300
www.domainegayda.com

This estate, with an international reputation, does not make Malepère, but a range of intriguingly original IGPs. Although the estate dates back to 1749, the current history began in 2000 when Anthony Record bought the property as a holiday house. However, as an energetic entrepreneur he was not going to neglect his land, and so the wine estate is the result of an association of four people, Anthony himself, Tim Ford who had run a large business exporting roses grown in Kenya and Zimbabwe until he was expelled by Mugabe; Mark Kent, a South African winemaker who runs Boekenhoutskloof in Franschhoek, and Vincent Chansault, the winemaker. All four have some link with the Cape.

Vincent arrived in the Languedoc in 2003, after working for a number of years in South Africa, and examined the soil and the climate, totally disregarding the fact that the land was appellation Malepère. For Malepère he should have opted for Merlot but instead he planted Cabernet Franc. He also chose Chenin Blanc, Sauvignon Blanc and Syrah. The concept of oenotourism is particularly strong in South Africa, and that is something that they wanted to develop, with a wine school, Vinécole, and also a rather elegant restaurant.

In addition to the vineyards at Gayda, they have bought 10 hectares in the Agly valley, in Roussillon, and have vineyards in Minervois La Livinière, with a cellar, which means that they can sell the wine as Minervois La Livinière, under the name La Villa Mon Rêve, after the little house in the middle of the vines.

Vincent exudes enthusiasm and you sense that he is very competent and focused. He recognizes the differences between his experiences in the Cape and in the Languedoc, observing that if he were starting again, he would plant smaller plots, not the long rows to which he was accustomed in South Africa. Domaine Gayda has been farmed organically since the beginning and now they are considering biodynamics. The cellar is well equipped, with numerous small stainless steel vats, for different vineyard sizes. They are experimenting with eggs, for Grenache Gris and Chenin Blanc, *foudres* for *élevage*, and also *demi-muids*, which are good for Grenache Noir, while Syrah does better in *barriques*. Vincent observed that tradition is an experiment that worked, and that they are creating their own history.

As for the wines, they are all Pays d'Oc. Flying Solo is their biggest brand, for which the white is Grenache Blanc and Viognier, while the red is based on Grenache Noir and Syrah with supple fruit, and the rosé is a blend of Grenache Noir and Cinsaut. The name recalls early aviation, with a tree on the estate a way marker for pilots like Antoine de St Exupéry flying from Toulouse to Barcelona. A Viognier Pays d'Oc comes from three different *terroirs*, the schist of Roussillon, limestone from the Minervois and Gayda and granite from Roussillon. Each is vinified separately in vat and then gradually blended and the result is a lightly peachy wine.

Figure Libre Freestyle, Pays d'Oc is a blend of Grenache Blanc, Marsanne, Roussanne, Macabeo and Chenin Blanc grown on granite, with Grenache Blanc accounting for over half the blend. Each grape variety is vinified separately, and spends nine months in wood, with blending just before bottling. There is good acidity, a saline quality and some minerality, as well as white blossom and a hint of oak. Figure Libre Chenin Blanc, Pays d'Oc occasionally has some noble rot, and is kept in an egg for several months. The flavours are honeyed with good acidity.

The red Figure Libre Freestyle is a blend of 45 per cent Syrah, 10 per cent Mourvèdre, 25 per cent Grenache Noir and 20 per cent Carignan from 20- to 80-year-old vines, while Figure Libre is pure Cabernet Franc, with lovely fresh fruit and supple tannins. Chemin de Moscou takes its name from their address, which was also the name of the air corridor for the aéro-poste after it left Toulouse in the early days of the flying postal service. The wine is a blend of Syrah, Grenache Noir and Cinsaut, given a total of 24 months' *élevage*, making for an intense flavour, with supple tannins and black fruit. Finally, Villa Mon Rêve, Minervois La Livinière, is a pure Syrah, with fresh *garrigue* fruit.

Le Mas de Mon Père

Arzens 11290

lemasdemonpere@yahoo.fr

Frédéric Palacio works from a back street in the village of Arzens, with 5 hectares planted with eight different varieties, namely Merlot, Cabernet Sauvignon, Cabernet Franc, Malbec, Grenache, Cinsaut, Carignan and some Chasan, but not in Arzens. He has come back to his *pays natal*. His grandfather made table wine and his father was a cooperative member. Frédéric made his first wine here in 2005. He is ardently organic asserting that you cannot talk about *terroir* if you add artificial chemicals to your soil. Above all he wants *vins de terroir*. He notes that working organically makes you more observant about your vines and the mechanization of vineyard work for the cooperative destroys the natural *terroir*. 'It is all a question of balance. Of course, it is fundamental to have good fruit.' His work is the accumulation of lots of small details and, as he says, ' I do the best I can'. He reckons that it took him ten years to understand his *terroir*; he keeps every plot separately and makes four wines. You have to know your *cuverie*; he compares his vats to saucepans and knows how they will behave, admitting that he is not a cook but he does enjoy good food. 'With the fermentation, you are creating heat and the more the vat heats up, which depends on its size, the more you extract.' He might destem or not; it depends on the quality of the juice. 'You must be aware of the *effet millésime*, the characteristics of that particular harvest.' He will destalk if there is less juice as otherwise there is too much tannin. The shape of the vat can have an effect too. He has a tronconic vat and would also like to try an amphora, but not an egg.

Of Frédéric's four wines, just one is a Malepère. We began with two Vins de France; they were rejected as IGPs. The first was intriguingly called Tu m'intéresses, which he said is a blend of everything left over from the other three, with some fresh fruit. The second Vin de France, C'est comme ça, used to be a pure Carignan but now includes Malbec and Merlot. It had youthful fruit with more tannin and body. A Malepère, Comme je suis, comes from 50 per cent Merlot, 20 per cent each of Cabernet Franc and Sauvignon and 10 per cent Malbec, with firm youthful fruit and structure, and freshness on the finish. A Pays d'Oc, Cause toujours, is a blend of two-thirds Grenache Noir to one-third Cinsaut, with some dry cherry fruit and tannins. I left with an impression of a very committed wine grower, taking his own path, and a feeling that the Malepère is quietly forging its own way in the Languedoc after celebrating the tenth anniversary of its appellation in 2017.

4

CABARDÈS

Cabardès is the appellation where you find both the grape varieties of the south west and those of the Mediterranean in the same wine. The name Cabardès originates from the local Lords of Cabaret, who defended the nearby Château de Lastours against Simon de Montfort during the Cathar crusade of the thirteenth century.

The vineyards of Cabardès cover 18 villages, of which Aragon and Moussoulens are the most important, around the small town of Conques-sur-Orbiel to the north west of the city of Carcassonne. They are separated from the Minervois by the river Orbiel. The climate is warmer than that of Bordeaux, and also hotter and drier than nearby Limoux and Malepère, but cooler and wetter than the rest of the Languedoc, making a diversity of grape varieties possible. On the western edge of Cabardès the vineyards give way to fields of wheat and to the north there are the first foothills of the Massif Central, the Montagne Noire. The vineyards are on the sunnier slopes of these hills, rising in terraces at an altitude of 120–150 metres until you reach the *garrigue* where no vines will grow. In the spring, you can see the snow-capped hills of the Montagne Noire in the distance. It is a windy region, for both the Marin and Cers can blow hard, although the Montagne Noire, the last outpost of the Massif Central, protects the area from the northerly winds. Nights at the end of summer, when the grapes are ripening, are cool, with a diurnal difference of as much as 15°C, which makes for freshness in the wine. The soil is mainly clay and limestone, with large chunks of limestone reflecting heat and light and retaining warmth.

Cabardès became an appellation in 1999. It is pink or red, but never white. Any white wine is an IGP or AOP Languedoc. The appellation regulations are unique in requiring a minimum of 40 per cent of each of the two families of grape varieties, *bordelais* and Mediterranean, so that it is impossible to make a pure *bordelais* or a pure Mediterranean blend, or indeed a varietal wine. The choice of the Bordeaux varieties, also described as oceanic, is Merlot, Cabernet Sauvignon, Cabernet Franc, Malbec and, curiously, Fer Servadou, which is more commonly found in the Aveyron, and indeed rarely in Cabardès. The Mediterranean varieties are Syrah and Grenache; Carignan and Cinsaut have virtually disappeared from the region. Freshness is the dominant theme; that is what all the wine growers emphasize above all.

Producers

Château de Pennautier, Pennautier

Pennautier 11610

www.chateaudepennautier.com

Château de Pennautier is the largest property of Cabardès and indisputably the flagship of the appellation. It belongs to the de Lorgeril family. The very first time I visited Cabardès, back in the 1980s, I met Françoise de Lorgeril. The place left me with the impression of a sleeping beauty. The elegant château was built in the 1620s by Bernard de Pennautier and two wings were added at the end of the seventeenth century, designed by Louis Le Vau, the architect of Versailles, while André Le Nôtre landscaped the gardens. Some renovation and restoration was needed, and the same could also have been said for the cellar. These days it is the next generation, Nicolas de Lorgeril with his energetic wife Miren, who run the estate, and Miren is also the president of the growers' syndicat, while Bernard Durand has been the winemaker since 2012. The family has other properties in the Languedoc: Château de Ciffre for St Chinian and Faugères; Domaine de la Borie Blanche in the Minervois; as well as Mas des Montagnes in Roussillon. The château has been beautifully restored with an elegant Louis XV salon and Aubusson tapestries from the 1780s.

Miren is very focused on the development of the estate and on the appellation, with a keen appreciation of the *patrimoine* and the importance of wine tourism. She was one of the first to open a winery restaurant in the Languedoc and today it is well worth a journey. Miren laughingly recalled that when they opened it, in 2002, 'everyone said I was mad!'

They have a tasting room with a view, looking down on the modernized cellars with bright orange vats. They make two Cabardès Rosé. The first is a blend of Merlot, Syrah, Grenache and Cinsaut, with some fresh raspberry fruit, while Cuvée Terroirs d'Altitude, coming mainly from Grenache Noir, with smaller quantities of Syrah, Cinsaut, Merlot and Malbec, is rounded and riper, with more body. There are three red Cabardès. The simplest, emphasizing the fruit, is predominantly Cabernet and Merlot, but that depends upon the year. Terroirs d'Altitude is more oceanic, with more Merlot than Cabernet Sauvignon and with some cedary notes; the blend varies according the conditions of the vintage, but generally the grapes for this *cuvée* come from the higher vineyards. Our tasting finished with a comparison of 2012 and 2013 L'Esprit de Pennautier, which represents a selection of the best wine of the year, with an emphasis on the oceanic varieties. Then to show just how well Cabardès can age we compared 2003, 2001 and finally 2000, which simply did not taste 16 years old in the summer of 2016.

Domaine de Cazaban

Villegailhenc 1160
www.domainedecazaban.com

Clément Mengus, who set up Domaine de Cazaban in 2007, comes from a wine-producing family in Alsace. Chance led him to Cabardès. His wife, Claire, is a primary school teacher and was posted to Carcassonne, so he looked for vineyard land and found Cazaban on a limestone plateau outside Conques-sur-Orbiel. He now has 10 hectares, mainly around his cellar, but also on the northern edge of the appellation, at Limousis, where the soil is schist. He often finds fossils in his vineyards, for the sea was there some 40–50 million years ago. Clément learnt his winemaking in Burgundy and has also worked in Australia. Since 2015, the business has been registered as biodynamic with Demeter.

Clément makes an exemplary range of wines. Coup de Foudre Blanc, Pays d'Oc, is a blend of Grenache Gris, Marsanne, Roussanne and Vermentino, which he planted to make a first vintage in 2011. For the 2016 vintage he has also included Grenache Gris and Grenache Blanc from his new vineyards on the schist at an altitude of 450 metres. All the different varieties are fermented together and vinified in a large Alsace *foudre*, and the wine is left in *foudre* on its lees until bottling in early spring. The 2015 vintage had notes of honey and white blossom with refreshing acidity. Clément asserted that he looks for finesse and not structure, and the wine changes each year, with the addition of another grape variety.

His first red, Jours de Vignes, IGP Côtes de Lastours comes from Grenache Noir, Syrah and Carignan and has a warm southern note about it, with some supple tannins. As Clément observed, it is very *gourmand*, which is what he intended. His first Cabardès, Demoiselle Claire, comes from 60 per cent Syrah with 40 per cent Merlot, with some fresh, elegant fruit and supple tannins. Part of the Syrah is aged in wood. Next came Petites Rangées, a blend of 50 per cent Syrah, with 25 per cent each of Merlot and Cabernet Franc, grown on warmer limestone, and aged in both smaller and larger wood: 227-litre, 500-litre and 20-hectolitre barrels. Youthful, cedary notes were balanced by some ripe spice. Domaine de Cazaban is a blend of 60 per cent Merlot and 40 per cent Syrah, grown on schist and limestone, and aged in relatively new wood for nine months. It is a selection of the best plots, a wonderful crescendo of flavour, richer and riper, but firmer, with potential. Finally, we tasted Le Coup des C, with the three Cs, Claire, Cazaban and Cabardès, which was made for the first time in 2010. If Clément has some particularly good barrels in the domaine wine, he gives them as much 30 months of *élevage*. The 2013 had some wonderful complexity, with spice and elegance, with Clément insisting that he is looking for complexity and not power.

Domaine de Cabrol

Aragon 11600

www.domainedecabrol.fr

Claude Carayol took over his father's property in 1988 and bottled his first wine in 1990. I first visited this estate at the end of the last century, when Claude was making some of the best Cabardès as he still does today, even though little has changed in his somewhat ramshackle cellar, full of old *foudres*. He has however, invested in his vineyard and now has 21 hectares. There is an image in Claude's cellar from a house in nearby Conques-sur-Orbiel of two faces, and that is Cabardès, looking both to the east and to the west. Consequently, Claude makes two *cuvées*, Vent de l'Ouest with 60 per cent Cabernet Sauvignon and 40 per cent Syrah, with cassis and cedary fruit, and Vent de l'Est, from Syrah with some Cabernet Franc, and sometimes some Grenache Noir, with the fresh peppery fruit of the Syrah. They are appealing examples of the diversity of Cabardès. Cuvée Quinze, Vin de France, is the white wine of the estate, an intriguing blend of Grenache Blanc, Viognier, Gros Manseng, Chenin Blanc and Semillon, one-third of which is fermented in wood and the rest in vat. The wine has herbal notes, with fresh acidity and a hint of dry honey and layers of nuances. It is one of those wines that keeps you guessing.

Domaine Guilhem Barré

Ventenac-Cabardès11610
guilhem.barre@gmail.com

Guilhem Barré is a genial man, with a bushy beard and a ponytail, and a broad, welcoming smile. After studying psychology, he turned wine producer, taking over 8 hectares in 2008 and building a simple cellar, an elegant shed, in 2011. His father comes from the Hérault and his mother from the Gers and when his wife found a job in the area, they realized that they liked the Aude. Guilhem particularly appreciates the freshness of Cabardès. There is always what he called *une belle tension*. He makes his wines as naturally as possible, with no filtering, natural yeast, and as little sulphur as possible. He has some barrels and has bought an amphora. Tasting in the cellar, Guilhem exudes enthusiasm. He loves the Languedoc: 'you can enjoy yourself and have fun'; he wouldn't work in Bordeaux. He makes a variety of different wines, two Vins de France and three Cabardès from Merlot, Syrah and Cabernet Sauvignon. He would like some Cabernet Franc, and he would also like to plant some Cinsaut and Grenache Noir, and is planning on Chenin and Viognier for white wine.

The two Vins de France are La Peyrière, a pure Merlot, with some ripe plummy fruit, characteristic of the variety, and Fantasie Singulière from Cabernet and Merlot, with some intense cassis. For Cabardès, there is La Dentelle, a blend of 60 per cent Syrah with 40 per cent Merlot, aged in vat, to make for some rich cassis fruit with an appealing balance of acidity as well as tannin; in other words, richness combined with freshness. Sous le Bois is Merlot with some Syrah, with ripe cassis and youthful tannins. Natural Mystic is Merlot and Syrah, kept in barrel so that the oak fills out the palate, with some good fruit and supple tannins. I enjoyed Guilhem's enthusiasm and he deserves to succeed.

For a final taste of Cabardès, we popped into La Cave des Oliviers, a small wine shop and a treasure trove of bottles in the village of Montolieu, run by an Englishman, Adrian Mould, who did much to promote Cabardès during the early days of the appellation. The shop is well worth a detour and Adrian usually has a bottle or two open for tasting. On this occasion, it was Château Jouclary, Cuvée Tradition, a very accessible spicy wine with supple fruit, and a good taste on which to leave Cabardès.

5

LIMOUX

Limoux is a cheerful, bustling town. An arcaded square provides the focal point, and the Café du Commerce is the local meeting place. Inside it is the epitome of the traditional French brasserie; sit outside long enough and you will see *tout* Limoux go by. There are the occasional market stalls, with fresh produce, and one of the better wine shops of the Languedoc is tucked into a corner of the square. In the late winter the town comes alive with carnival festivities, with masked pirouettes in the square. Crossed by the Pont Neuf, the river Aude flows through the town and provides extensive riverside views. The outskirts of the town proclaim its vinous activity with gaudy signs advertising Blanquette and Crémant and offering cellar visits and tastings

Altogether there are five different appellations, as well as an IGP Haute Vallée de l'Aude. First came Blanquette de Limoux, created in 1938 and based on Mauzac. The *méthode ancestrale*, a pure Mauzac, also dates from 1938 and involves a slightly different procedure from the traditional champagne method used for both Blanquette and Crémant. Crémant de Limoux is a more recent creation, recognized in 1990, and includes higher proportions of Chardonnay, Chenin Blanc and, from 2003, Pinot Noir. The first appellation for Limoux Blanc dates from 1959, with Mauzac. Chardonnay arrived in the 1970s and the current appellation for the still whites of Limoux was created in 1993, and is the only appellation in the whole of France that demands a compulsory *élevage* in oak, until the beginning of May following the vintage. Limoux Rouge, recognized in 2003, is based on Merlot but also allows Malbec, Syrah, Grenache, Cabernet Franc and Cabernet Sauvignon, though, illogically, no Pinot Noir. It appears that politics came into play here and consequently all the delicious Pinot Noir produced in the area is IGP Haute Vallée de l'Aude.

This is a wild, undulating area, with the valleys defined by the Aude and its various tributaries. The Pyrenees are not far away and play their part in the climate, making Limoux one of the coolest and wettest areas of the Languedoc. However, the variety of microclimates and aspect has led to the definition of four different zones, Autan, Océanique, Mediterranéen and Haute Vallée. Autan is the area around Limoux itself, with vineyards at an altitude of 250 metres, protected by hills on both the east and the west, making for a warmer climate and early ripening grapes. The Haute Vallée is the highest and coolest part of the appellation, with vineyards in the Aude valley, including villages such as Antugnac and Couiza. The Mediterranéen area lies to the east with a warmer climate tempered by some maritime influences from the sea, while the Océanique zone to the east has a higher humidity than the others. Altogether the appellation covers 41 villages, of which the most significant are Roquetaillade, Antugnac and Cépie.

Limoux proudly claims to be the oldest sparkling wine of France, with an even longer history than that of champagne. The monks of the Benedictine abbey of Saint Hilaire take credit for the discovery of the vinification process. Their twelfth-century abbey, a Romanesque church with peaceful Gothic cloisters, still stands in the sleepy village of St Hilaire. Authorities have set the date of the discovery of sparkling wine as early as 1531, which predates Dom Pérignon in Champagne by more than a century, for he was the cellar master of the abbey of Hautvillers from 1668 until his death in 1715. The monks realized that their wine began to ferment again in the spring after the winter cold, and managed to contain the carbon dioxide. Blanquette de Limoux was made in this way for several centuries until the champagne method was adopted but the tradition still lingers on in the small production of *méthode ancestrale*.

The production of Limoux is dominated by two cooperatives, Sieur d'Arques and Anne de Joyeuse, which account for about 70–80 per cent of the appellation. Some of the big players of the Languedoc have moved in to the region. Gérard Bertrand has bought Domaine de l'Aigle; Jean-Claude Mas began his activities with the purchase of Domaine Astruc and has subsequently acquired Domaine de Martinolles following the untimely death of Jean-Marc Vergnes; and most recently Jean-Louis Denois has sold Metairie d'Alon to Badet Clément, which is run by the Burgundian winemakers Catherine and Laurent Delaunay. Their first wines promise well. Another Burgundian house, Albert Bichot, made its first Limoux, from Chardonnay and Pinot Noir, from purchased grapes, in 2017. Salazar is owned by the *négociants* Bonfils. However, the small, independent producers are growing in number, for both still and sparkling wine. Some make both; others concentrate on one or the other, and may use a *prestateur* for the riddling and disgorgement of their wine, as the necessary machinery is simply too expensive.

What follows are brief introductions to some of the wine producers I have enjoyed visiting, most of whom made their first wine in this century.

Producers

Domaine Jo Riu
Pieusse 11300
www.domaine-joriu.com

This small estate is run by the elegant Caroline Giraud, with the help of her *régisseur* Arnaud, who is a trained oenologist. The story is a familiar one. Caroline's great-grandparents were cooperative members and her grandfather, Jo Riu, was happy to sell varietal wines *en vrac*. Then, ten years ago, Caroline, having studied commerce and worked as an events organizer, responded to her grandfather's request to take over his vineyards. She was able to take advantage of *primes d'arrachage* to change the composition of the vineyards, beginning gradually, first making IGPs. She then developed still red and white Limoux and now makes Crémant but as yet no Blanquette de Limoux. She has 35 hectares in production from which she produces now an extensive range of wines. You sense that she and Arnaud are open to experimentation.

The Crémant comprises 70 per cent Chardonnay with 20 per cent Chenin Blanc and 10 per cent Pinot Noir, with 12–16 months on the lees, while l'Inattendu has been fermented in oak, which gives more depth and weight. A Limoux Cuvée Capucine is an oak-aged Chardonnay to which she occasionally adds some Chenin for extra freshness. For her still wine, she is quite innovative, with some Petit Manseng, Vermentino, Viognier and Sauvignon Blanc as well as the more obvious Chardonnay in her vineyards. She is aspiring to make a *moelleux* Petit Manseng. Fortunately the wild boars tend to leave these grapes alone, and she likes the acidity that is characteristic of the variety. As for red wines, she has Merlot and Syrah and a little Cabernet Sauvignon, and favours less rather than more oak, observing that you do not need oak for Limoux Rouge, unlike for Limoux Blanc. Our visit finished with a look at her great-grandmother's charming Italian garden, albeit in the rain.

Domaine Cathare

St Hilaire 11250
www.cathare.tm.fr

Franck Schisano is bright, intelligent and focused. He makes only still wine, with as many as ten different wines from the same number of plots, mainly around the villages of Festes and St André. He really wants to concentrate on the coolest and highest part of the appellation, with vineyards in Festes at 400 metres, facing due north, and he also has 2 hectares at nearby Bouriège. For Limoux Blanc he has Chardonnay, Chenin Blanc and Mauzac, as well as Sauvignon for an IGP, and he would like to plant Riesling. This is a possibility now that Alsace has relaxed its grip on that particular variety. For red wine he has Merlot, Malbec, Cabernet Franc and Pinot Noir.

We sat and tasted at Franck's dining table and he talked passionately about his perception of Limoux. He works by plot and by grape variety, firmly believing that *terroir* influences the taste of his wine more than the grape variety. He sees high altitude as the principal quality of Limoux; the more extreme the *terroir*, the more unexpected the taste and the better the wine. For him, Limoux is a triptych of climates, the Mediterranean and the Atlantic, for the *partage des eaux* is close by, combined with a climate of mountains, which makes for a range of temperatures. He has almost picked the late-ripening Cabernet Franc in the frost and the temperature may rise to 25°C on an October afternoon. There are also differences in the soil, with Festes being based on *calcaires lacustres*, lacustrine limestone, while Bouriège is on a plateau, a former sea, with *calcaire marnes*, calcareous clay/marl, and fossils, 'not unlike Chablis'. Altitude makes a difference because 1°C is lost for every 120 metres, which helps to maintain acidity in the grapes. Anticipating rising temperatures in the future, Franck can envisage vines growing at 800 metres.

All Franck's vineyards are cultivated organically. He is convinced it adds to the taste, giving more acidity to the wine as the vines have deeper roots and explore the subsoil. He focuses on hand-picked grapes in small boxes and made his first wine in 2009. And how did he come to make wine? He comes from Toulon and played rugby with Gérard Bertrand, who encouraged him to change directions after he gave up rugby. And why Limoux? His wife, who comes from Toulouse, teaches in the village school of St Hilaire.

His range of wines is wonderfully eclectic and original, and mostly with names that recall the Cathar era. A pure Limoux Chardonnay Melhorier has a lovely salinity, while Consolament is a pure Mauzac – he is one of a handful of wine growers to make such a wine – that is fresh and sappy with good acidity. Caretas is a pure Chenin Blanc, and not a Limoux Blanc, for the simple reason that it is not aged in oak, of which rigid appellation regulation Franck is critical. This is pure and very austere, with dry honey and firm acidity. Inquisition is a Sauvignon, Haute Vallée de l'Aude and very stony and mineral, with no oak and excellent concentration. Château de Festes includes some Mauzac with the Chenin, with some oak ageing making for a firm stony palate. Evangelia is a Cabernet Franc, aged in old wood, with some fresh red fruit and silky tannins, and 2014 les Parfaits is a blend of Merlot, Cabernet Franc and a little Malbec. A pure Merlot is in the pipeline, while Hérésie is a pure Malbec, aged in wood and made for the first time in 2012. It is firm and stony, and in subsequent vintages the oak component has been reduced to merely 20 per cent. As for Pinot Noir, that is work in progress.

Domaine Mouscaillo

Roquetaillade 11300
www.mouscaillo.com

I always enjoy seeing Marie-Claire and Pierre Fort because the enthusiasm they have for their work is so infectious, while at the same time they proffer astute observations about Limoux. The biggest development since my last visit was the introduction of a sparkling wine. They ignored bubbles when they first arrived in Limoux from the Loire Valley in 2004. Pierre had deemed Crémant and Blanquette too industrial and they did not want to do the same as everyone else. But then they did some experiments and the result is a delicious Crémant, a blend of Chardonnay and Pinot Noir with creamy fruit and acidity. Pierre currently keeps all the wine in *demi-muids* for seven or eight months, though he is considering reducing the percentage of oak ageing to just half of the *cuvée*, but increasing it to ten months. There is no *dosage* and the time on the lees is currently 18 months and may well be extended. I thought the wine delicious, with some nutty, bready notes, and packed with character and flavour.

Next we were treated to a vertical tasting of Limoux Blanc, beginning with a vat sample of 2016 and finishing with Pierre and Marie-Claire's very first vintage of 2004. The wine spends 12 months in barrel. Pierre's vineyards enjoy the influence of both the Pyrenees and the Mediterranean and have a lot of clay so the vines do not suffer from any stress. The longer the grapes take to ripen, with more time between *véraison* and harvest, the better it is. Pierre observed that if yields are low, ripening is faster, so low yields are not necessarily a good thing if the vines are out of balance.

I particularly enjoyed the 2013 Limoux Blanc, the result of a small harvest and a cool year, with the grapes ripening slowly so that the vintage finished in October. The wine underwent a malolactic fermentation and the taste in the spring of 2017 was lightly leesy, with some nutty notes of maturity, and quite delicious. Pierre is adamant that Limoux Blanc has great ageing potential and based on this very generous tasting, I could not possibly disagree with him.

He also makes Pinot Noir Haute Vallée de l'Aude, cheerfully observing that he likes Pinot Noir but simply does not understand it; it is always a surprise. The flavours are fresh, with dry raspberry notes. Pierre and Marie-Claire are happy in the knowledge that their children are keen to follow in their footsteps and indeed, since that last visit, Pierre has officially retired and their son, Thomas, is now working on the estate.

Domaine Monsieur S

Bouriège 11300
www.monsieur-s-limoux.com

Étienne Fort is an engaging young man, with a mop of curly hair and a winning smile. Wine runs in his genes, for his father has 35 hectares of vines in the cooperative and as a boy he worked in the family vineyards.

His first vintage was as recent as 2011. His uncle is Pierre Fort of Domaine Mouscaillo, who encouraged him to become a wine producer, as did Gilles Azam, another producer nearby. He works from an old *bâtisse* at Bouriège, just outside Roquetaillade. It is nicely tumbledown and picturesque, with a large cellar that was originally used for bulk wine. S is for San Salvadou, the *lieu dit* of his vineyards, of which he has 15 hectares, all cultivated organically. Talking to Étienne, you sense that he is a thoughtful and sensitive winemaker. We wandered round the cellar tasting vat samples, which were quite austere, with firm acidity, and that is what he wants, keeping his wines on their lees until bottling.

Our tasting from bottle began with Blanquette de Limoux, a pure Mauzac that spends 12 months on the lees, to keep fruit and freshness. The vines are 35 years old. Apparently, there were few very old vines in the area. The wine had some characterful, creamy herbal fruit and a nice depth of flavour. Étienne observed that you must not extract too much with Mauzac, otherwise it is bitter. Crémant Monsieur S en rose was fermented in old *demi-muids*, with about 18 months on *lattes* – ideally, he is aiming for 24 months – and he aspires to producing a rosé that is pure Pinot Noir, but the INAO refuses to countenance such an idea. He was planning no oak and a longer maceration for the 2016 vintage. The 2015 vintage that I tasted had some satisfying depth. The white Crémant is a pure Chardonnay, fermented in 600-litre barrels and the taste is nutty and characterful. As well as sparkling wine, he makes a delicious Vin de France Syrah, with some fresh peppery flavours. He is also considering a variation of the *méthode ancestrale*, blocking the fermentation and then adding more yeast in a *prise de mousse*. None of his wines have any extra *dosage* because he does not like sugar and wants to keep the flavours fresh and pure. This is an estate that will go far given Étienne's questioning attitude and aptitude for pushing the boundaries.

Domaine les Hautes Terres

Roquetaillade 11300
www.domaineleshautesterres.com

Gilles Azam in the village of Roquetaillade explained how he left the village in 1984 to work elsewhere. He returned in 2000 and now lives in the house where he was born and uses the cellar that was once his grandfather's. Roquetaillade means *roche taillée*, or cut rock, and one of the six original quarries in the village still operates. Gilles took us to a very windy viewpoint just outside Roquetaillade from where you could see some of his vineyards. He has Chardonnay on a north-facing slope, which is slow to ripen, and on another, warmer slope there is Chenin, Malbec and Cabernet Franc, with a ten-day difference of ripening between the two slopes, the south-facing slope making for much richer wines. Altogether Gilles has 9 hectares in ten plots, with altitude ranging from 350 to 590 metres, and with a similar diversity of soil.

A Chardonnay Cuvée Louis, with 20 per cent Chenin, was quite rich and leesy. The Chenin gives some minerality and dry honey as well as very good acidity. Cuvée Joséphine is a Crémant de Limoux Brut Nature without any *dosage* and a blend of 60 per cent Chardonnay, 30 per cent Chenin and 10 per cent Mauzac, with about six months' *élevage* in wood and 18 months on the lees. Gilles was the first in Limoux to experiment with oak ageing, inspired by the champagne producer André Salosses. Old wood makes for a natural oxidation and provides fullness in the mouth; he thinks that ageing in vat can be too severe and that sugar masks any defects. Gilles favours minimum intervention in his winemaking, maybe a little sulphur at bottling by nothing more, observing that his cellar is much more hygienic than his house!

Limoux Cuvée Maxime is 80 per cent Malbec with 10 per cent each of Merlot and Cabernet Franc, with *élevage* in vat – Gilles is giving up on *barriques* for his red wine, which really should be predominantly Merlot to conform to the requirements of the appellation. The wine has a lovely freshness with fruit and tannin, and certainly does not need any supporting oak. Gilles talked about the characteristics of Limoux and how they would like an appellation for Roquetaillade. There are six producers in the village, which is not enough, so they are opening up the area to include other villages with similar characteristics, such as Antugnac, Bouriège, La Serpent and Montazels. Gilles also believes fervently that Limoux deserves a stronger image; the other Crémants of France, he says, 'have exploded but not Limoux. People don't fight for it; there is a lack of energy.' You sense that Gilles is doing his best to counter that.

GAEC Taudou

Loupia 11300
www.domaineloupia.com

Jean-Pascal Taudou has a small cellar in the *circulade* village of Loupia. He mainly makes sparkling wine from 15 hectares of his mother's vineyards, in seven separate plots, while the other 15 hectares, in the cooperative of Anne de Joyeuse, are used for still IGP. His grandfather grew grapes in the 1950s and his father began bottling some wine in the 1980s, mainly *méthode ancestrale* and then Blanquette de Limoux, and then they developed some Crémant de Limoux. Jean-Pascal studied at Montpellier but apart from a *stage* at the cooperative and another in the Minervois, he has never worked anywhere else, as he was eager to set up his own estate. He explained that Loupia is the most western of the Limoux villages so it has an Océanique climate; the nearby villages of Alaigne and Douzac are already Malepère. The prevailing winds are the cers from Toulouse and the marin from Narbonne, and it is cooler and wetter than the other parts of Limoux. Jean-Pascal follows Terra Vitis and is considering converting to organic viticulture; he limits the use of weedkiller and uses an *intercep* to weed between the rows.

Jean-Pascal particularly likes the fruitiness of Limoux, giving his wines quite a long ageing *sur lattes*, and they tend to have a richer *dosage* than some. His Blanquette is 90 per cent Mauzac, with three years on the lees, with some herbal fruit; for Crémant, the blend is 65 per cent Chardonnay with 15 per cent Pinot Noir and 20 per cent Chenin Blanc, the same proportions for both the white and the rosé, using the pinker juice for the rosé. He is also considering a pure Mauzac, without any *dosage*, asserting that there is renewed appreciation of the originality of Mauzac. A 2010 Crémant de Limoux with longer ageing on the lees was richer with more weight.

As for still wine, Obarra is an Haute Vallée de l'Aude, as it is an unoaked Chardonnay, with some ripe, rounded fruit, while Limoux Relève is aged in 500-litre barrels. The appellation regulations do not stipulate the size of barrel, just the length of ageing. Most originally, Jean-Pascal makes a *méthode ancestrale* as it used to be made; these days the process can be much more controlled but he prefers the traditional method. He uses pure Mauzac, picking it towards the end of September so that it is fermenting in October when the cellars are cooler, making for a slower fermentation. He decides when to stop the fermentation, which he does by chilling, and filters the wine gently before bottling in late winter, checking that there is enough yeast for the fermentation to start again when the temperature warms up. The wine is disgorged in the normal way so that there is no deposit, and there is a natural sugar content of 100 grams per litre. The pressure is lower, 3.5–4 kilogrammes as opposed to 5 for Crémant, and the alcohol level is 7% as opposed to 12–12.5% abv. The taste was honeyed and herbal, ripe Mauzac with good acidity. And when would you drink it? With dessert or as an aperitif with some foîe gras, suggested Jean-Pascal.

Domaine la Coume-Lumet
Cépie 11300
www.la-coume-lumet.com

We tracked down Luc Abadie up a dirt track high outside the village of Cépie. For the moment, he is economizing on signs and we thought we had embarked on a mystery tour until we finally reached a small cellar and a house dated 1788. Luc worked for Airbus in Toulouse before turning to this second career, encouraged by his brother-in-law, Mathieu Dubernet, son of the oenologist, Marc Dubernet. And why choose Limoux, apart from its relative proximity to his home in Toulouse? Luc enthused about the wonderful *terroir* and the fact that Mauzac is not very well known. He has 18 hectares of vines as well as a lot of woodland, at an altitude of 200–300 metres. There are wonderful views across the valley. He took over his vines in time to prune them for the 2013 vintage and made his first wine that year.

His range of wines has evolved to include Maset Haute Vallée de l'Aude as his entry level; La Coume for Limoux, with oak ageing, and a Crémant de Limoux from 70 per cent Chardonnay, 20 per cent Chenin Blanc and 10 per cent Mauzac, which is given 18 months on the lees. It was nicely creamy and rounded, with a fresh finish. Luc is quietly enthusiastic and committed to his new life, seeing it as a voyage of discovery. When I asked about the name of the estate, he explained that there are so many *lieu-dits*, including *coume*, that you need to distinguish it and *lumet* in Occitan means *la petite lumière*, the small light, with a reference to a poem by Rimbaud, conjuring up the image of plots of vines in rays of sunlight.

J. Laurens

La Digne d'Amont 11300

www.jlaurens.fr

Jacques Clavel arrived in Limoux in 2001 after a career in IT, having bought the company of J. Laurens from a *champenois*. Consequently, he makes no still wine at all, observing that he did not wish to dilute things. His 30 hectares of wines are at La Digne d'Amont. The range is classic. Le Moulin is Blanquette de Limoux, 90 per cent Mauzac with 10 per cent Chardonnay; the Crémant de Limoux, les Graimenous, is the core of the range, a blend of 60 per cent Chardonnay with 30 per cent Chenin Blanc and 5 per cent each of Mauzac and Pinot Noir, with 12 months on the lees and some rounded fruit; while the Crémant Rosé is 60 per cent Chardonnay with 25 per cent Chenin Blanc and 15 per cent Pinot Noir with some delicate raspberry fruit. His Le Clos de Demoiselles is a selection of 60 per cent Chardonnay with 25 per cent Chenin Blanc and 15 per cent Pinot Noir with longer ageing on lees and more depth of flavour.

There were two new wines since my previous visit. La Matte, after the *lieu-dit*, is a Crémant, a blend of Chardonnay, Chenin Blanc and Mauzac, but no Pinot Noir, with a minimum of 24 months on the lees, and no *dosage*, so the flavour benefits from the longer ageing, making for a rich palate balanced by good acidity. Jacques has also developed a *méthode ancestrale*, although less artisanal than that of Jean-Pascal Taudou, to take away the element of uncertainty in the method. Jacques explained how he uses tiny sachets, *billes*, filled with yeast, which dissolve once they come in to contact with liquid. He stops the fermentation by chilling when the alcohol level is around 4.5% abv and clarifies and filters the wine to remove any remaining yeast. He then adds more *billes* and the fermentation starts again with the yeast feeding off the remaining natural sugar, and the wine is disgorged in the usual way. For Jacques, it is a dessert wine, or to be enjoyed instead of a cup of tea with a piece of cake.

Jacques is a perceptive observer of Limoux and recognizes there are problems, particularly from the lower prices imposed by those with a pressing need to sell simply in order to maintain their turnover. 'We are at a bend in the road. There is no real solidarity amongst the disparate producers. The future lies with the small growers who are working to create their own reputation.' Fortunately there are young people taking over from their parents, but sadly not Jacques' own children.

Château Rives-Blanques

Cépie 11300

www.rives-blanques.com

Caryl and Jan Panman are an Irish–Dutch couple who came to Limoux in 2001 after successful careers in other fields, in different parts of the world. It was then time for a change and they settled outside Limoux, buying their vineyards from Eric Vialade, who has stayed on as their winemaker. The arrangement has continued to work well over the years and now their son Jan-Albie, otherwise known as Jan Junior, has joined the team. They have some spectacular vineyards in the hills outside the village of Cépie, with James Kingslake at Domaine la Bégude as their neighbour. He concentrates on IGP rather than Limoux.

I always enjoy tasting with Jan and Caryl and visit them regularly. The view of the Pyrenees from their tasting room on a clear day is spectacular, and their estate is named after the mountain that usually dominates that view. Caryl and Jan's wines have evolved over the years. Initially they made only Blanquette but not Crémant, although now that has been added to the range. They give the two wines equal attention, considering them equally important, and consequently there is no price difference between the two. With other producers, Blanquette tends to be cheaper, even though it is the most characteristic and original wine of Limoux. The Blanquette at Rives-Blanques, 90 per cent Mauzac with 10 per cent Chenin Blanc, is lightly herbal, while the Crémant, with 80 per cent Chardonnay and 10 per cent each of Chenin and Mauzac, has spent at least 18 months on lees and is lightly creamy. A rosé comes from roughly two-thirds Chardonnay with one-third Chenin Blanc and just 5 per cent Pinot Noir. The Pinot Noir makes for a pretty colour and adds an element of fruit and structure.

They take their still wines as seriously as their sparkling wines. Cuvée Occitanie is a pure Mauzac, picked three weeks later than for the sparkling wine. Caryl describes it as a real Cinderella, as it is not really appreciated, and they are only one of about three or four producers to make a pure Mauzac. I am so glad they do. Limoux Chenin Blanc, Dédicace, with the wine dedicated each year to a different person who has helped them, is a lovely example of Chenin, and shows how well it suits the Languedoc, with some dry honey and good balancing acidity. The 2004 vintage was drinking deliciously when it was 12 years old, demonstrating just how well the white wines of Limoux can age. Limoux Odyssée is a pure Chardonnay, rich and buttery and again with some ageing potential, while Limoux Trilogie is a blend of all three varieties, with the blend varying from year to year. It always has some wonderful nuances of flavour with length and depth.

Jan and Caryl Panman, Château Rives-Blanques

Things never stand still at Rives-Blanques. The last time I saw Jan and Caryl, they had made an unoaked Chenin, named appropriately Aude à la Joie, or Ode to Joy, and Jan Junior had produced a couple of barrels of Chardonnay, made in the Burgundy style, with a malolactic fermentation and from slightly riper grapes. As Jan Senior observed, in Burgundy they have 10,000 vines per hectare as opposed to 4,500–5,000 in Limoux, producing the same yield of 40 hectolitres per hectare, and in Burgundy they pick at a lower potential alcohol and add sugar and want a malolactic fermentation, whereas in Limoux there is no sugar and usually no malo. The final *bonne bouche* of a tasting is usually Lagremas d'Aur, a Vendange d'Hiver and Vin de France, made from late harvested Chenin Blanc and Mauzac, picked as late as January when the grapes are really raisined. It is utterly delicious, with honey, barley sugar and some hints of botrytis.

Jean-Louis Denois
Limoux 11300
www.jldenois.com

One of the key players in Limoux over the years has been Jean-Louis Denois. He is a *champenois* who studied in Burgundy and made wine in South Africa, helping to develop Cap Classique, the sparkling wine of the Cape. His first estate in Limoux, Domaine de l'Aigle, now belongs to Gérard Bertrand. He then developed more vineyards, a large part of which he has sold recently to the *négociant* Badet Clément. Tasting with Jean-Louis is always an exciting experience. He has the ability to surprise and enjoys some confrontation. He fell foul of the French authorities for planting Riesling and Gewürztraminer in Limoux long before they were accepted in the Languedoc. His current bone of contention is the fact that you cannot make any sparkling wine in Limoux other than Limoux, which he considers to be too prohibitive, arguing that Kriter is made in Burgundy and Veuve du Vernay near Bordeaux. He also complains about the restrictive percentages of grape varieties in Limoux, particularly that Pinot Noir should not exceed 20 per cent.

He is the only *vigneron* I know who produces three completely different wines from the same vineyard, a plot of Syrah at St Paul de Fenouillet in the Haute Vallée d'Agly, one of the cooler parts of Roussillon. The first picking makes a crisp *blanc de noirs* sparkling wine, while the second picking ten days later produces Bulles de Syrah Rosé d'Une Nuit, which, after a night on the skins, is a pretty pink. The fermentation is stopped, leaving natural sugar for the second fermentation, so the wine is fruity with less acidity. The remaining grapes are picked three weeks later, to make a classic Syrah, with firm, peppery fruit. Over the years Jean-Louis has made some distinguished Pinot Noir, energetically defending the quality of Pinot Noir from the Languedoc which he feels has yet to be recognized. His Crémants de Limoux continue to be exemplary, including a classic *cuvée*, and Bulles d'Argile Extra Brut, from Chardonnay and Pinot, which includes some barrel fermentation in old wood.

Domaine de Baronarques

St Polycarpe 11300
www.domaine-de-baronarques.com

This estate was bought by Philippine de Rothschild of Château Mouton-Rothschild back in 1998. It was originally Domaine Lambert and comprises 43 hectares in production near the village of St Polycarpe, but it dates back to the seventeenth century, with a château built at the end of the nineteenth century. I met Vincent Montigaud, who had run the estate from 2001 until he was replaced in 2017 by Augustin Deschamps, whose background is in working for Bernard Magrez in Bordeaux. I quizzed Vincent about the Rothschild interest in Limoux. He told me that they wanted to play a part in the resurgence of the Languedoc, with its great *terroir* just waiting to be developed. Limoux was not known for its reds, as the appellation was only created in 2003, and yet the potential is enormous, situated as it is on the climatic crossroads of the Atlantic and the Pyrenees with the advantage of relatively high altitudes and cool vineyards. Initially they formed a company with the Limoux cooperative Sieur d'Arques to give themselves time to learn about Limoux and in 2003 they became independent and the estate made its first wines. They have done a considerable amount of replanting, concentrating initially on red wine, both *bordelais* and Mediterranean varieties, with Merlot accounting for half their red vineyards, plus Cabernet Sauvignon, Cabernet Franc, Malbec and some Syrah, and two quality levels, La Capitelle and Grand Vin. They made their first Chardonnay, of which they now have 11 hectares, in 2009.

Limoux celebrates its eightieth anniversary in 2018 and there is no doubt that it has much to celebrate. Its originality is Mauzac, sometimes distinctively pure, and often tempered by Chardonnay and Chenin Blanc. The vineyards are well managed, with a high percentage of growers working organically, or with Terra Vitis, the organization for *lutte raisonnée*. There is an energy among the younger wine growers, but they need to do more to develop the image of their appellation and not allow it to be lost in a sea of sparkling wines.

6

CORBIÈRES WITH BOUTENAC

Corbières is still the largest appellation of the Languedoc, and indeed the fourth largest appellation of France, after Bordeaux, Côtes du Rhone and Champagne. The vineyards cover a large expanse of hilly land to the south-west of the city of Narbonne. In the north, they are limited by the Aude valley and the Canal du Midi, and touch the appellation of Minervois. To the south, the departmental boundary with the Pyrénées-Orientales separates Corbières from Côtes du Roussillon. Vineyards of the much smaller appellation of Fitou are interspersed in some of the Corbières villages. The countryside is wild and dramatic, and the terrain is harsh so that only vines and olive trees, as well as the vegetation of the *garrigue*, will grow there. Two mountains dominate the skyline, the Montagne d'Alaric in the north and Mont Tauch to the south. The name Corbières not only describes the wine but also the hills that are really the first foothills of the Pyrenees. Those are never far away, especially on a clear day when the snow-capped peaks form a dramatic backdrop.

There is much to explore in the Corbières. Lagrasse is a picturesque village, with narrow, cobbled streets, a Roman bridge over the Orbiel, an old market hall, and a Benedictine abbey. The magnificent Cistercian abbey of Fontfroide is worth a journey, as the Michelin guide would say, for its cloisters and rose garden, and it also produces wine. Ruined Cathar castles, Aguilar, Quéribus and most majestic of all, Peyrepertuse, built on inaccessible hills, dominate the countryside as imposing reminders of the land's troubled past.

Corbières was recognized as a VDQS in 1951, but did not become an appellation until 1985 when the area was delimited to encompass 20,000 hectares in 87 villages, or *communes*, between Narbonne and Gruissan. Illogically, for reasons of local politics, Gruissan, on the edge of the Massif de La Clape, was deemed part of Corbières rather than La Clape but that situation is in the process of being rectified. Corbières is firmly red, with rosé accounting for 9 per cent of the appellation, and white a mere 3 per cent. The usual five grape varieties are used for red Corbières, with a minimum of two in the blend, and with Carignan the dominant variety. Corbières is where Carignan produces some of its finest results, illustrating its suitability to the climatic conditions of the Languedoc. As for white varieties, most common are Marsanne, Roussanne Vermentino and Grenache Blanc, but not yet Grenache Gris, as well as Bourboulenc and Macabeo.

Most will agree that the particularity of Corbières is the diversity of its *terroir*, for both soil, which is mainly clay and limestone, and climate, ranging from Oceanic in the far west to a warm Mediterranean climate on the coast. Altitude varies from zero to 600 metres. With such variations, it is no surprise that there is also much variation in the blends. Mourvèdre likes the coastal areas whereas Syrah performs better in cooler, higher inland sites. The prevailing winds also have a significant effect on the microclimates. The cers is a harsh, drying northern wind while the marin is a gentler wind that comes from the sea and may bring rain. As a result of these differences, the appellation was divided into 11 different *terroirs* back in 1991 and, although they were very valid, with significant differences, they never really took hold and were eventually dropped. However, a group of energetic estates worked on the *cru* of Boutenac, which came to fruition in 2005, and has more restrictive regulations than Corbières itself. With the success of Boutenac, there are other possible *crus* in the pipeline, namely Alaric, Corbières-Maritimes, Durban and Lagrasse, but as yet nothing concrete.

With so many producers of Corbières, it is impossible to cover them in any great detail, so what follows is a small selection of highlights and personal favourites, with a focus on some of the newcomers and those who have developed their wines in this century, as well as some longer-established names. First of all, I visited producers of the *cru* of Boutenac.

The ruined Cathar castle of Aguilar

BOUTENAC

The *cru* of Boutenac covers a small part of Corbières, namely the area on either side of the Massif de la Pinède, about 15 square kilometres, including ten *communes* from St Laurent to Boutenac, with Lézignan, Luc, Ornaisons, St André, Montséret, Ferrals, Fabrezan and Thézan. You can take a dirt track past Fontsainte and the chapel of St Siméon, to a viewpoint at 350 metres and look down on a patchwork of vineyards, with the Montagne d'Alaric in the distance. The soil is clay and limestone, *calcaire aggloméré*, poor friable rock which they call *pouding*. Very much less of Boutenac is actually declared than the area officially recognized. For most producers, it is their top *cuvée*, the icing on the cake of Corbières. The first vintage of Boutenac was 2005. So why has Boutenac been successful in achieving *cru* status when others have so far failed? The answer has to be the human element: after spending an afternoon with some of the producers of Boutenac, you sense an energy and a cohesion for a common cause.

Producers

Château la Voulte Gasparets

Boutenac 11200
www.lavoultegasparets.com

I first went to Château la Voulte Gasparets in the mid-1980s and met

Jacques Bergès. His grandson, Laurent Reverdy, now runs the estate, making his first vintage in 1997. They have 60 hectares of vineyards, including 9 hectares for their flagship wine, Cuvée Romain Pauc, which is a Boutenac. They could produce more Boutenac but they only want to make the one *cuvée* of the *cru*. The estate was one of the first to bottle in the area, back in 1974, and has subsequently established a firm reputation. Laurent makes a convincing range of wines, a vat-aged white from Vermentino, Grenache Blanc and Macabeo, as well as a barrel-aged white, Paul and Louise, after his children, from the same varieties. The composition of his red vineyards is 50 per cent Carignan, 25 per cent Grenache, 15 per cent Mourvèdre and 10 per cent Syrah, with the characteristics of the various wines determined by the age of the vines, the selection of different plots, and the *élevage*, in wood or not.

Laurent considers Carignan to be their *fer de lance*, or spearhead, and continuing to follow the original advice from Marc Dubernet, it is always vinified by carbonic maceration. Jacques Bergès tried a classic vinification but found carbonic maceration more interesting and certainly the wines combine the spicy character of Carignan with the sturdiness of the Corbières. Jeunes Vignes is just that; Cuvée Réserve always comes from the same plot and spends six months in wood. Romain Pauc, named after Laurent's great-great-grandfather, who planted the vineyards, is a blend of Mourvèdre and Syrah, which are only 20–30 years old, with Grenache and Carignan between 60 and 120 years old, grown on stony south-facing slopes. It spends 12 months in wood, of which 20 per cent is new, and the average yield is just 20–25 hectolitres per hectare. The palate is nicely rounded with a firm backbone and good mouthfeel. Une Fois de Plus, almost pure Mourvèdre with some Carignan, is firm and structured with 12 months' *élevage*. The tasting room with various vinous artefacts is welcoming, opening onto the adjoining barrel cellar, and nearby is the chapel of Gasparets, with its cypress trees.

Château les Aiguilloux
Thézan-des-Corbières 11200
www.chateau-aiguilloux.com

Château les Aigoulloux is another old-established estate. Marthe Lemarié, and her husband François, bought the property in 1981 and made their first wine the following year. They have 30 hectares of vines, of which 8 hectares are classified as Boutenac, although only 4 are actually sold as such. Although she was born in Paris, Marthe is Martiniquaise. She studied chemistry and worked as a teacher on the Ivory Coast, where she met François, and a chance meeting with Eric Latham of Château Ste Estève brought them to the Corbières. Marthe is bright and vivacious; she has done various *stages* and laughed about going to Aix-en-Provence to learn about rosé, back in 1987, when she was not only the only non-white person but also the only woman and even the only person from an independent cellar on the course. How things have changed. Her son, Georges, is a qualified chef, which made for a delicious lunch after our tasting, under the shade of the parasol pines. Again, they favour carbonic maceration for Carignan, but it does depend on whether there is enough juice. If the grapes are too small, there is too much vegetal matter and insufficient juice. Their Boutenac is half Carignan and half Syrah, given 12 months' *élevage* in old oak. It was nicely mouth-filling with a tannic streak. For Marthe, the typicity of Boutenac is the force of the tannins of the Carignan, combined with the elegance of the other varieties; freshness is not necessarily a characteristic of Boutenac.

Château de Luc

Luc-sur-Orbieu 11200
www.famillefabre.com

Louis Fabre, of Château de Luc in the eponymous village, was one of the pioneers of organic viticulture in the region 20 years ago. These days 30 per cent of the Corbières vineyards are farmed organically. Château de Luc has a long history, dating back to the fourth century, with a Visigoth sarcophagus bearing a vine leaf emblem. Louis XIII destroyed the original château but it was rebuilt. Altogether the Fabre family have five properties, with 350 hectares, including Château Fabre-Gasparets, la Courtade near Béziers and a Minervois estate, la Bergerie de Rieux. Louis took me to a viewpoint, La Roche Trouée, with sweeping views over La Clape, Fitou and the Corbières. You could see the Caroux and the Pic de Vissou, the Canigou and the emblematic Corbières hills of Alaric and Mont Tauch. 'All our wines are marked by wind,' enthused Louis. It was a windy evening. 'We get the cers and the marin; the wind carries aromas which are fixed in the taste of the wines.' Rosé accounts for 25 per cent of Louis's production. He makes a variety of wines, IGP, Corbières, and Boutenac. Boutenac Classique is a blend of 45 per cent each of Carignan and Mourvèdre, plus 10 per cent Syrah, with 12 months' *élevage*. It is firm and smoky with good fruit. Louis observed that it is silly to have what he called *un guerre de cépages*, a war of grape varieties. Carignan is always interesting, but not necessarily Mourvèdre. Louis began bottling his wine in the early 1980s, to which his grandfather's response was: 'Why do you want to become a grocer?' How things have changed!

Domaine Espérou

Boutenac 11200
www.domaine-esperou.fr

There are newcomers to Boutenac, such as Cécile Bonnafous who has wine in her genes. Her great-great-grandfather, Victor Espérou, worked at Château les Ollieux; her grandfather made wine for sale *en vrac* and she and her husband Eddy took over his vineyards. They have 8 hectares, of which 7 are classified as Boutenac, but they make just 4,000 bottles of the *cru*. The first vintage of Corbières that they bottled was 2007 and for Boutenac, 2011. Their Corbières Cuvée Romarin is a blend of 50 per cent Carignan, 30 per cent Syrah and 10 per cent each of Grenache and Mourvèdre, all made by carbonic maceration, as her grandfather did. Cuvée Etienne, Boutenac, from 50 per cent Carignan, with Syrah softening the rusticity of the Carignan, is aged in vat. Cécile does not like wood, and her wines are supple and elegant, rather like their maker. She is quietly making her mark on Boutenac.

Domaine St Jean de la Gineste

St André de Roquelongue 11200
www.saintjeandelagineste.fr

Marie-Hélène Bacave is bright and vivacious, but with a streak of sadness as she was widowed a few years ago. Her daughter now helps her run the estate. The first vintage came in 1991. She has a welcoming tasting room, with various vinous sayings scattered around the room by people like Georges Brassens: '*Le meilleur vin n'est pas nécessairement le plus cher, mais celui que l'on partage*' ('The best wine is not necessarily the most expensive, but the one that you share'). I quite agree with my favourite French singer. Marie-Hélène has 20 hectares, mostly classified as Boutenac, though she makes very little of it, preferring a broader range of Corbières. She looks for elegance and finesse, observing that it is a question of temperament: 'I am not going to get worked up.' She makes a Vieilles Vignes, which includes Carignan that is over 100 years old, as well as Grenache planted 70–80 years ago. Velours Noir is based on Mourvèdre, which Marie-Hélène likes making best, enjoying the variety's challenges, although Syrah is much easier in both vineyard and cellar. A more traditional blend, Crépuscule is sturdier and more concentrated, but with supple tannins.

CORBIÈRES

Producers

Cave de Castelmaure et d'Embrès
Castemaure 11360
www.castelmaure.com

Cooperatives play an important role in Corbières and there is one that has consistently maintained its quality ethic since I first visited Corbières in the mid-1980s, namely the Cave de Castelmaure et d'Embrès, which was founded in 1921. In the late 1970s this was one of the first producers to work with Bordeaux *barriques*, using a selection of the best plots, to make Cuvée Pompadour. The now ruined Château de Castelmaure was owned by a family called Pompadour, and there is no connection with Mme de Pompadour, the mistress of Louis XV. The director, Bernard Pueyo, has been there since 1983. It was his first job, when he was fresh from studies in Toulouse, Montpellier and Bordeaux. As a student, he did *stages* with the Vignerons du Val d'Orbieu and with the oenologist Marc Dubernet, but he has never been tempted to move on, with so much to retain his interest at Castelmaure. He quickly realized that their natural handicaps of low yields and a multitude of steep vineyard sites, making mechanization difficult, could be put to their advantage, and that they needed to develop their sales in bottle.

The development of the technique of carbonic maceration, a method much favoured by Marc Dubernet, had a fundamental impact on quality. Back in 1983, Carignan accounted for 90 per cent of the vineyards, but the creation of the appellation led to the planting of more of the so-called *cépages améliorateurs*. However, for Bernard Pueyo, 'Carignan is the king here,' even if it may only account for a maximum of 50 per cent of a blend. He is an ardent defender of Carignan, and practises carbonic maceration for virtually all his Carignan, believing the technique really improves the variety, but he is not so sure about

Syrah, half of which is fermented by carbonic maceration and the rest destalked. Grenache Noir is a complicated variety and is all destalked, as the stalks are too thick and woody. They have very little Mourvèdre, as it is not a good area for that tricky grape variety. Mechanical harvesters are impractical on this terrain and, in any case, for carbonic maceration the bunches must be hand-picked.

The cooperative now has 400 hectares, mainly around the village, in the heart of the Corbières hills. There are 65 members, of whom 18 earn their living from their vines and account for 85 per cent of the production. They make Corbières, and a little Vin de France, but no IGPs or Fitou. When the appellation of Fitou was first suggested, the village was simply not interested.

Bernard looked back on the development of the cooperative. In the 1980s they improved their winemaking facilities, and then in the 1990s they looked at their vineyards, examining the *terroir*. They have schist towards Fitou and hard limestone towards Tautavel in Roussillon, both of which limit yields naturally. They practice *lutte raisonnée* but will never be organic because it is too complicated for a cooperative, but they do try to reduce the chemical treatments and encourage their members to till instead. They have developed a system of vineyard selection, linking a specific vineyard to a particular wine. Unusually for a cooperative, their members are paid by the hectare, rather than by weight, ensuring that they are guaranteed their remuneration. This means that they resist the temptation to pick too early. For the past few years they have been working with the INRA on the conservation of old vine varieties, creating an inventory of grape varieties, of which there are about 50, including a couple that were completely unknown. They are increasing the plantings with cuttings, ten cuttings of each. Carignan has thrown up some 100 different variations, out of which they have selected 20, which they are multiplying, with a consideration of what to plant in ten years' time or so.

They still have the original solid concrete vats, dating back to 1921, but they modernizing their facilities, investing in new cooling equipment and in *foudres* for *élevage*, which are especially suitable for Grenache Noir. They have 800 *barriques*, of which a quarter are replaced each year, and are also experimenting with a couple of eggs for *élevage* but without any positive conclusions so far. Bernard is very aware of the importance of oenotourism and has turned the *quai de réception*' into a restaurant on weekend evenings during the summer months, with an opportunity for visitors and villagers to enjoy the local wines.

The tasting room is equipped with an oenomatic wine dispenser, to ensure that the wines are served in the best condition, and at the appropriate temperature. Corbières Blanc comes mainly from Grenache Blanc with Vermentino and Macabeo, with a cheerful 4L, the classic car of the *vigneron* in the 1980s, on the label. Vermentino lightens the Grenache, while Macabeo is relatively neutral, and the wine is fresh and crisp. Corbières Rosé is mainly Grenache Noir, with a little Carignan and Cinsaut and a splash of Syrah, with rounded raspberry fruit.

The first vintage of Cuvée Pompadour, from some of their best vineyards, was made by Bernard's predecessor in 1978. It is classic Corbières, with 50 per cent Carignan, as well as Grenache Noir and Syrah, following their first experiments with carbonic maceration in 1976. Bernard observed that over the years it has lost its concentrated extracted quality to become more drinkable and less powerful. The Carignan gives a fresh drinkability, with ripe red fruit and supple tannins. Seventy per cent of the blend spends 11 months in barrel, and it is bottled in January.

Grande Cuvée was first produced in 1995 and is a blend of Syrah and Grenache, but no Carignan, with a classic vinification. The ageing includes some new wood and the wine is ripe with tannin and oak and a rounded finish. No 3 is so-named as it is the third *cuvée*, after Pompadour and the Grand Cuvée; additionally it is made from three grape varieties, and by three people, the cooperative, with Dominique Laurent and Michel Tardieu, two Burgundians, who used to advise them. The Syrah component goes into barrel, of which 50 per cent are new, while the Carignan and Grenache goes into older wood, and future vintages will include ageing in *foudres*. The wine is firm and structured, ripe and rich with a tannic streak and a warm powerful finish.

We talked about the important economic role of the cooperative in the fabric of village life. It employ ten people as well as providing an income for its members. Bernard is optimistic for the future. They sell all the wine they produce. He talked about climate change, and how that has improved the quality of Carignan. In 1983, it was difficult to ripen Carignan properly, even at 12.5% abv. These days it is more likely to be 14.5% abv with the same vintage date, and the flavours benefit from being fully ripe. I asked about the *cru* of Durban. The INAO has agreed in principle but they need to visit the vineyards. The profile of the *cru* would be Cuvée Pompadour, with the emphasis on Carignan. The cooperatives of Cascastel and Tuchan are also involved as well as some independent producers. To show just how well their wines can age, Bernard opened Cuvée No. 3, 2004. It was maturing beautifully in the summer of 2016, with a rich nose and some leathery notes on the palate. I left with the impression of a cooperative that is working well for its area, and has a strong sense of pride in its wines. To prove the point, their labels say: 'Cooperative since 1921'.

Domaine Ste Croix
Fraisses-des-Corbières 11360
www.saintecroixvins.com

Jon and Liz Bowen are the English owners of Domaine Ste Croix. Liz explained how they came to make wine in the Corbières. A degree in agriculture and agricultural economics, but nothing particularly related to wine, led her to work in finance. Jon read history and worked in various wine shops, and then realized that it was winemaking rather than sales that really interested him. In 1996, he did the first full-time winemaking course at Plumpton College in Sussex before spending several years doing contract winemaking in France with various organic wine producers, and also in California and Australia. Then, after working with Pierre Clavel (see p.268) near Montpellier for a couple of years, they decided the time had come to buy something for themselves.

So they looked for old vines, namely Grenache Noir and Carignan, and limestone, and in the Languedoc because vineyards there are affordable. Someone suggested the Corbières and that is where, in 2004, they found limestone with volcanic outcrops in the village of Fraisses-des-Corbières, 15 hectares, now reduced to 12, with a functioning cellar. They have been organic from the beginning, but that can be complicated if your neighbours are not, and no one else in the village is. Over the years, however, they have managed to create about six islands of vines where there are no neighbours, by buying, swapping and selling vineyards.

Half of their vineyards are old Carignan planted in 1900 and 1905 and they also have some Grenache Noir and Syrah, as well as Grenache Blanc and Grenache Gris, from the 1940s, mixed up together, on two distinct vineyards, one of limestone and one of schist. For the moment, Grenache Gris is not recognized in the Corbières because it is deemed to be a mutation of Grenache Blanc and is therefore not considered as a separate variety. Five kilometres further south, in Roussillon, it is recognized as a different variety. Such are the intricacies of French wine legislation.

Liz enthused about Carignan, which is still very much the grape variety of Corbières, even though the maximum percentage is fixed at 50 per cent in the vineyards. I also asked her about the putative *cru* of Durban. For her it really only concerns the cooperatives, Embrès et Castelmaure and Cascastel; there are not enough independent producers to give it any weight and they don't really need it.

We talked about organic and natural wine. They have gradually moved to minimal sulphur for some wines, and none for others. They began by using cultured yeast, as initially it was safer, but since 2009 everything has been fermented with natural yeast. They practise minimum intervention in both cellar and vineyard, which entails a lot of time checking to see to see what needs to be done. They may use a little sulphur at harvest, depending on the condition of the grapes and the weather, and maybe a little at bottling, especially for the export market, with uncertain transport conditions. Liz does not really see a big difference between organic and natural wines. You choose a wine by its flavour, not by the principle. White wine should not look like lemonade, she laughingly observed. Nor are they biodynamic in the vineyard. She is interested, but there is a lot to learn. It is very time consuming, with several constraints, and needs to be done properly. Sulphur dust is one of the cheapest ways to treat the vines and is used by most people in the village. Weed control is the most difficult thing; they leave the grass to grow, which encourages the bees, and cut it once it is dying down anyway.

Jon and Liz make a varied range of wines. La Serre is a Vin de France, from Grenache Blanc, Grenache Gris and Terret Gris, all planted in 1960 and grown on schist and on limestone. The wine is fermented in stainless steel and kept on its lees to add some weight, with lovely herbal and mineral notes, and good acidity from the Terret. Pourboire Nature is a blend of 73 per cent Carignan with 27 per cent Syrah. There is too much Carignan for it to be Corbières and anyway it is atypical, with no sulphur. They pick quite early to keep the freshness, and the acidity reduces the need to add sulphur. The colour is vibrant, with fresh red fruit, some acidity and a streak of tannin. There is no legal definition of natural wine; it is up to each individual producer.

They make two different Corbières. Le Fournas, from 45 per cent Carignan with 28 per cent Grenache Noir and 27 per cent Syrah, accounts for half their production, with fresh youthful fruit. Magneric is a similar blend and comes from older vines. Half of the juice is put into larger barrels, mainly *demi-muids*, but none new. I liked their back labels, with bullet points to convey the essentials: • living soils, • limestone, • Carignan, • Grenache, • *terroir*, • full tannins, • elegance, • delicious dark fruit, • Syrah, • 100-year vines, • passion, • wild herbs. That summed the wine up very nicely.

Carignan, Vin de France, from vines planted in 1905 with 8 per cent Grenache from 1968 is aged in wood for 18 months. Liz explained that the Grenache fills in a couple of holes in the palate, making a lovely example of the rustic elegance of Carignan, with some red fruit. Another Vin de France, Celèstra, is mainly Grenache Noir with 20 per cent Mourvèdre (they have just one plot of Mourvèdre), given 20 months' *élevage*, with rich liqueur cherries balanced with a streak of tannin. Finally, there was La Part des Anges, a late harvest Carignan with some Syrah, that is not made every year; it all depends on the weather. It is wonderfully original, with tannin and acidity and some ripe, red fruit. Carignan raisins better than Grenache and retains acidity, and Liz mentioned that in this area traditionally everyone made a late harvest wine. There were some large glass *bonbonnes* in a corner, indicating that they were working on a *rancio*.

Domaine Xavier Ledogar

Ferrals-les-Corbières 11200
xavier.ledogar@orange.fr

Xavier Ledogar in the village of Ferrals-les-Corbières can only be described as a Carignan enthusiast. Altogether he has 20 hectares, in Ferrals, Boutenac and Villerouge, in 33 different plots, farmed organically, including three plots of Carignan that are 80, 60 and 40 years old. He and his brother Mathieu are fourth generation growers. His great-grandfather had some vines and his grandfather was a founding member of the village cooperative in the 1930s. His father really wanted to make his own wine, but could not extract the family vines from the cooperative until 1998. Xavier began working with his father and in 2003, inspired by Didier Barral in Faugères, did his first vinification without cultured yeast. His winemaking tends towards the natural in that he uses as little sulphur as possible. He makes his wine in an old *bâtisse* in the heart of the village. We talked about natural winemaking, with Xavier saying that he was not really much in favour of progress, but it has allowed for improvements in natural wine, notably with hygiene and temperature control.

Our tasting included a Macabeo Pays d'Aude with firm, stony acidity and a Carignan Blanc, with firm, nutty notes and some minerality. Xavier observed that whites from the Languedoc could be greater than the reds. He is working on a small nursery of indigenous old white varieties, such as Terret and Listan. Rouge Clair Vin de France is a blend of Carignan and Mourvèdre, with 48 hours on the skins, so that it is light red in colour with juicy, refreshing fruit. Mariole is usually a pure Carignan, made with a short maceration, with some *sympathique* rustic tannins and fresh red fruit. Corbières la Compagnon is a blend of 60 per cent Syrah with equal parts of Grenache and Carignan. Xavier admits to being less enthusiastic about Syrah, which he ferments at a cool temperature to retain the aromatics, with a long maceration and an *élevage* in a concrete tronconic vat. It was fresh and peppery. His Corbières Boutenac is a blend of 50 per cent Carignan with 30 per cent Mourvèdre and 20 per cent Grenache, blended around the harvest, with 18 months' *élevage* in barrel, making for well-integrated oak and some underlying richness. Finally, Tout Nature! is a Vin de France made from equal parts of Carignan and Mourvèdre, without any added sulphur, with some rounded, ripe fruit.

Domaine Olivier Mavit
Roquefort-des-Corbières 11540
www.oliviermavit.com

Wine for Olivier Mavit is a second career and he is, as I write in 2017, the newest arrival in the Corbières, making his first wine in 2015. He had worked in printing but realized he really wanted to be a farmer. Although his great-grandfather had made wine, it was agriculture that interested him originally; wine came later, and he acknowledges a great debt to Jean-Philippe Padié in the village of Calce in Roussillon who helped and encouraged him. He recuperated the family vines, just 4.5 hectares, from a *fermage* agreement. For the moment, he only has red varieties, the usual Languedoc quintet, but he has pulled up some Mourvèdre and is replanting with Macabeo and Grenache Blanc. His vineyards are in the course of conversion to organic viticulture. He favours natural yeast and natural practices, and avoids using any products, but he does not like the term *nature*, preferring the term *vin libre*.

Olivier makes an extraordinary variety of original wines from his small estate. Joseph is a pure Grenache Noir Pays de l'Aude, with some fresh fruit. Boire Mavit du Bon Côté is an appealing interpretation of Carignan, with a fresh finish. Olivier described the vinification as semi-carbonic in that he puts whole bunches, with some juice, into the vat. A Corbières, Némorin, is a blend of Grenache Noir vinified traditionally, and Carignan and Syrah, with carbonic maceration and aged in wood. There is a touch of oak with some fresh fruit and a rounded palate. Ma Capricieuse is a pure Syrah, so called because it is the vineyard that has caused the most problems: 'I spend my life there,' Olivier lamented, but the wine has some peppery fruit after nine months in oak. The Taste of Titou is a Corbières made from Carignan, Syrah, and Grenache. He uses carbonic maceration for the Carignan and Syrah, and ages the Syrah in oak for nine months, so that the wine has rounded fruit and spice. Magic Tételle is a pure Macabeo, given nine months' ageing, with a ripe nose and fresh stony acidity. Finally, Ma Vie en Rose is a pure Mourvèdre, for a rosé to be drunk with food. Olivier has a sense of fun, as the names of his *cuvées* suggest, and he is thoughtful, observing that people do not have confidence in their region. He is particularly enthusiastic about Carignan, discovering it with Jean-Philippe Padié. He describes his typicity as '*sur le fruit*'. I would not disagree with him.

Domaine la Cendrillon

Ornaisons 11200
www.lacendrillon.fr

This is another estate where a son has returned to the family land, but on a different scale. Robert Joyeux explained how Domaine la Cendrillon has been in his family since 1750. He is the seventh generation, but his father was not particularly interested in the vineyards and only ever sold his wine *en vrac*, whereas Robert realized that he really wanted to make wine – great wine. Having initially worked in management he knows how to organize things. He began working on the estate in 1993 and his father 'gave him the keys' soon afterwards. After working to improve the vineyards and modernize the cellar, he bottled his first vintage, the 2008.

The property includes 40 hectares of vineyards, planted mainly with red varieties: Grenache Noir, Mourvèdre, Syrah, as well as a little Carignan, Cinsaut, Marselan and Merlot. Currently there are just 2.5 hectares of white, but Robert is planning more, with Grenache Blanc and Gris, Marsanne, Roussanne and, more unusually, Verdejo, Petit Manseng and Albariño. His first white vintage was 2014. He enthuses about the region, the variety of soils, with an old river bed and several terraces containing quartz and limestone. The Languedoc is a region of *assemblage*, of blending with variations in *terroir* and grape variety. His winemaker, Julien, is encouraged to do lots of microvinifications, identifying the characteristics of the various different plots. The average of the vines is between 20 and 30 years old, with about 15 hectares replanted over the past decade, including white varieties.

Nuance, Vin de France, is an original blend of all their white varieties, namely Petit Manseng, Albariño, Verdejo, Grenache Gris and Blanc, Marsanne and Roussanne. One-third of the blend is fermented and aged in *demi-muids*, mainly the Petit Manseng and Grenache Blanc component. The nose is exotic and intriguing, with honey, pineapple and citrus notes, and the palate has fresh acidity with some saline mineral notes. It should evolve beautifully.

Minuit, Corbières Rosé, is a blend of Grenache Noir, Mourvèdre and Cinsaut, with a rounded palate. There are three different red Corbières. Corbières Cuvée is a blend of 40 per cent Syrah and 30 per cent each of Grenache and Carignan, with quite a long *élevage* in vat rather than barrel. They do a first blend after the malolactic fermentation and then adjust the blend later in the year. It has some dry, leathery spice, with nicely integrated tannins. Corbières Inédite is a blend of 50 per cent Syrah, with 40 per cent Grenache and just 10 per cent Mourvèdre and some of the wine is fermented in the large tronconic vats. The grapes come from slightly higher vineyards and half of the blend spends 18 months in *foudres*. It has firm, peppery fruit and a structured palate. Corbières No. 1 is a blend of 60 per cent Mourvèdre, with some Grenache and Syrah from higher vineyards, all vinified in tronconic vats and blended after a three-year *élevage*. It is only made in the best years, with 2008 the first vintage. The 2011 was ripe and fleshy, with a rounded, concentrated mouthful of flavour, and a long life ahead of it.

Clos de l'Anhel

Montlaur 11220

www.anhel.fr

The heavens opened just as we reached the little village of Montlaur and the narrow streets quickly turned to gushing streams. Montlaur seems to economize on street signs, and Sophie Guiraudon on cellar signs, but eventually we found her and it proved well worth persevering.

Sophie talked about the creation of Clos de l'Anhel, with Philippe Mathias. Their first vintage at Clos l'Anhel was 2000. He was and still is the *régisseur* at nearby Château Pech Latt, but is no longer involved with Clos de l'Anhel. They took over 6 hectares from a cooperative member, with vines in the villages of Ribaute and Lagrasse, and converted them to organic viticulture. Sophie's first solo vintage was in 2009 and she now has 9 hectares. She studied oenology at Toulouse, and worked at the Dubernet laboratory in Narbonne, but she really wanted to follow the entire viticultural cycle and not have a boss. Initially, Sophie only had red grape varieties but she has since rented some 60-year-old vines of Grenache Blanc and Grenache Gris, to make a Vin de France, which spends seven months' ageing in a concrete egg.

I am always intrigued by wine names and asked for an explanation of Lolo de l'Anhel. Lolo is the milk for a baby and *anhel* is a lamb, or *agneau*. Sophie said she liked *velours dans la bouche*, velvet in the mouth, and sometimes finds the tannins of Corbières a little rustic. She wants elegant tannins. She keeps her pressed wine separate and does not mix it with the free-run juice, so that all her pressed juice goes into Lolo, and there is none in her other wines. I found it quite solid and sturdy, with ripe fruit and fresh tannins. Les Terrassettes is her principal *cuvée*, mainly from Carignan, with Grenache and Syrah and a little Mourvèdre, with some firm, sturdy fruit on the palate, and with rich, concentrated flavours. The *élevage* is in vat; she only uses wood for a *rancio*. Les Dimanches is the best wine of the year; it might be Syrah, but the vintage I tasted, the 2013, comes from 80-year-old Carignan, accounting for 80 per cent of the wine. It was concentrated and tannic with good fruit. Afterwards as we drove through the dramatic gorges de Congoust at the southern foot of the Montagne d'Alaric, the clouds had cleared, and we stopped for a quick look at Sophie's vines outside Lagrasse.

Château Trillol

Cucugnan 11350
www.sichel.fr

The countryside of the Hautes Corbières is wild and dramatic, featuring the ruined Cathar castle of Quéribus and the strategic fortress of Peyrepertuse. Cucugnan features in Alphonse Daudet's *Les Lettres de Mon Moulin*, with his story about the *curé* of Cucugnan, who looked for his congregation in heaven, only to find them in hell. The village boasts one of the best bakers in France, and an old windmill dominates the skyline, as well as a statue of the virgin. Thirty years ago, there were three local cooperatives, with Rouffiac and Duilhac as well as Cucugnan. They initially pooled their resources, but none the less failed to survive, making a sorry, but not uncommon, story. These days, the village lives from tourism and *la chasse,* rather than wine.

Peter Sichel, who was an eminent member of the British Bordeaux wine trade, first came to the Corbières in the late 1980s and fell for a *bergerie* at the foot of Peyrepertuse, which he bought as a holiday home. He then realized that there was terrific potential in buying vineyards, and the first wines were made in 1990. Sadly, Peter died in 1998 before he could achieve the full potential of the project, but Château Trillol is now part of Maison Sichel, and has been run by Henri and Martine Guiot since 1995.

This part of Corbières is not an easy place to grow vines. Although essentially Mediterranean, the climate is extreme and the wind is a problem as it can reach speeds exceeding 100 kilometres per hour. The vineyards, a mixture of clay and limestone, lie at an altitude of 300 metres. Altogether there are 40 hectares, in about 65 different parcels, in two main plots, close to Quéribus and towards Peyrepertuse, now cultivated organically. The grape varieties are the classics of the Languedoc, mostly about 30 years old, as they replanted extensively when the vineyards were bought, and for whites, Roussanne and some 100-year-old Macabeo. The cellar is functional, a large shed with the usual concrete and stainless steel vats and *barriques*.

La Dame d'Argent, Corbières Blanc, is a blend of Macabeo and Roussanne, with a slow fermentation in vat, lasting one to two months. Henri observed that Roussanne has a tendency to develop aromas that make you think it has been in oak, with a certain tannic quality, so it does not need oak, and three months on the fine lees adds some texture. The rosé is mainly Grenache with some Cinsaut, that is *saignée* after a few hours, making for a nicely vinous palate.

They make three levels of red Corbières. Le Fruité, from 50 per cent Grenache, 30 per cent Syrah and 20 per cent Carignan, with 20 per cent carbonic maceration, usually for the Carignan, is just that – red fruit with some supple tannins, intended for early drinking. Château Trillol also comes from Grenache, Syrah and Carignan, of which half the blend is aged in wood (one-third new) for ten months. The wine has ripe fruit with some well-integrated oak and a harmonious finish. The *élevage* is in 350-litre barrels, from various different coopers, mostly from the south-west, such as Boutes in Narbonne and St Martin in Buzet. The Cuvée Prestige is a selection from the best plots, so that the percentages of Carignan, Syrah and Grenache may vary. They are looking for wine with more depth and ageing potential and that is what they have achieved. Quizzed about the typicity of Carignan, Henri talked of *fraîcheur*, which comes from the altitude, and elegant tannins, with depth and structure, but not weight.

Domaine d'Aussières

Narbonne 11100
www.lafite.com

Domaine d'Aussières represents more *bordelais* interest in the Corbières, this time from the Lafite branch of the Rothschild family. The baron Eric de Rothschild was apparently considering investing in a Mediterranean property, possibly in Tuscany, but instead had a *coup de coeur* for the abandoned property of Aussières. That was back in 1998, since when the property has undergone enormous investments. The neglected vines – they had not even been pruned – were pulled up and replaced with Mediterranean varieties to make Corbières, and *bordelais* varieties along with Chardonnay for Pays d'Oc.

Aymeric Izard, who runs the property – his family estate is Domaine Lerys in Fitou (see p. 96) – took us for a drive through the vineyards. They are in a cooler part of the Corbières, in a small hollow, with north-east to north-west facing slopes that make for slower ripening. The property totals 600 hectares altogether, and includes a viewing point where you can look towards the étang de Bages and the Massif de La

Clape, and see the Pyrenees on a clear day. There is wind 300 days of the year, and for 100 days it reaches over 50 kilometres per hour, making for healthy vines. They practise what Aymeric described as *lutte raisonnée plus*, using mainly organic products. He observed that they can take more risks here than in Bordeaux, because the financial consequences of a mistake would be significantly less. Wild boars are a problem, so they protect the vineyards with electric fences. As you would expect, the cellars are efficient and streamlined, well equipped with stainless steel and concrete vats and there is a smart barrel cellar.

Aymeric Izard with his foreman (on the phone), Domaine d'Aussières

Essentially the core of their range consists of two Corbières, Blason d'Aussières and Château Aussières, following the *bordelais* pattern of a *grand vin* and a second wine. Syrah is the dominant variety, with some Mourvèdre and Grenache, as well as some Carignan in more recent vintages. They blend in the autumn before putting the wine in barrel. All the *grand vin* is aged in barrel, for about 18 months, 50 per cent new and 50 per cent in barrels of one fill, and *barriques* only. They have not been convinced by their experiments with *demi-muids*. Aymeric treated us to a mini-vertical tasting, including 2008, with some leathery notes with black fruit and tapenade. The 2010 was drinking beautifully in September 2017; this is what we hope for every year, observed Aymeric, with textbook weather. The wine was elegantly balanced, with rich flavours. They are working on extraction and tannin, to enhance the finesse of the wine, and they practise some carbonic maceration for Syrah and Mourvèdre, as well as for Carignan, but not Grenache Noir because the stalks can be green. The 2012 was a more complicated vintage, with a small yield, with some smoky, cedary notes on the palate and a youthful balance. The 2014 completed the range, with some young, ripe fruit. Their methods have gradually evolved, with the ageing of the vines also helping to improve quality. Blason d'Aussières is 20 per cent aged in barrel and, as you would expect, is younger and fresher. They make 30–40,000 cases of it, as opposed to 10,000 cases of the *grand vin*. Aymeric is optimistic about the future, though he admitted that esca is a problem, especially for the Mourvèdre, although the young Carignan is doing well. As for the typicity of Corbières, that is difficult to define, because the area is so varied, but here he favours freshness and elegance.

Château la Baronne

Moux 11700
www.chateaulabaronne.com

I first visited this estate in the mid-1980s for an earlier book, *French Country Wines*, when it was run by André and Suzette Lignières. At the time they were among the pioneers of Corbières, and now the next generation, Jean, with his wife Anne, and brother Paul, has taken the reins, maintaining and improving the quality and concentrating on natural wine.

Altogether they have 110 hectares, with Domaine la Baronne and neighbouring Domaine las Vals, while a separate property, Domaine du Plo de Maorou, is joint venture with the Jackson family in California, and only sold in the USA. The vineyard soil is clay and limestone, but very mixed, with four geological eras within about 4 kilometres. They were certified organic in 2010. Their oldest vineyard is Carignan, which was planted in 1892; Carignan accounts of 40 per cent of their vineyards. Paul is particularly partial to that variety, liking its elegance and length and finding it a very good expression of the *terroir*. The Montagne d'Alaric, which dominates the skyline, acts as a *régulateur de l'eau*; it is a limestone mass and operates like a sponge. Its altitude is between 270 and 300 metres, creating a microclimate, with the prevailing wind coming over the mountain, cooling the air, and making ultimately for more acidity in the wines. The wind, which can blow in the Aude, is '*notre grand copain*', our great friend.

Back in the cellar, concrete eggs and amphorae, minimal use of sulphur and natural yeast are essential aspects of their winemaking. They are careful about extraction, with Paul adamant that they do not want to make heavy wines, and they have certainly succeeded, producing wines with true finesse. For the red wines, there are three levels at la Baronne, namely les Lanes, les Chemins and a selection of different *terroirs*. Les Lanes is a blend of Grenache and Carignan. The wine spends 12 months in cement tanks, on the fine lees, with some *bâtonnage* and is neither filtered nor fined. It has rounded fruit, with spicy berry flavours, with some tannin. Les Chemins is a blend of Carignan, Grenache and Mourvèdre, from different *terroirs*, partly aged in vat and partly in barrel. On the nose, it seems sturdier, but more elegant on the palate, with spicy fruit.

The selection of *terroirs* includes Alaric, from 60 per cent Syrah with some Carignan and Grenache, aged mostly in barrel, but not new wood. Pièce de Roche is an IGP Hauterive, rather than Corbières, as it is a pure Carignan from 4 hectares of vineyard that were planted in 1892. The *cadastre viticole*, which records what was planted and where, did not start until 1905, so they do not know exactly what was planted after phylloxera and before 1905. La Pièce describes the best vineyard of the estate, and the yield is tiny, about 20 hectolitres per hectare. The wine, aged in barrel and amphorae, has the characteristic freshness of Carignan, balanced with spice, acidity and tannin. Les Chemins de Traverse is a blend of Cinsaut, Carignan and Grenache, vinified in tronconic vats, followed by six months' *élevage*, with an elegant palate, with fresh cherries and silky tannins. Les Vals rouge, IGP Hauterive, is a pure Mourvèdre, kept on its lees for 12 months, with depth and elegance.

As for white wines, Vermentino NW, Vin de France is fermented in amphorae or stainless steel vats, with an *élevage* partly in an egg and partly in vat, making for stony, mineral fruit and good acidity. Las Vals, Vin de France, a pure Roussanne grown on the foothills of the Montagne d'Alaric, is fermented in both amphorae and eggs, with white blossom and a rounded textured palate. There is a touch of tannin from the stalks, with refreshing acidity. Le Grenache Gris de Jean, a Vin de France, is orange-pink in colour, the result of a fermentation and then maceration on the skins, for as long as six months, followed by *élevage* in an amphora for another six months, so that the wine has a structured palate, with tannin as well as acidity, texture and weight, and an intriguing finish. Although la Baronne is within the appellation of Corbières, the wines are very individual and do not really conform to the appellation, and you are left with a feeling that nothing stands still. In an outhouse was a museum piece, an old lorry, a Berliet from 1919, which Paul's great-grandfather had driven to deliver barrels. It reached a speed of 13 kilometres per hour and, curiously, the steering wheel is on the right-hand side.

Château Vieux Moulin

Montbrun 11700
www.vieuxmoulin.net

Château Vieux Moulin is built around an attractive courtyard near the village of Montbrun and has belonged to the They family for the past 200 years. The present incumbent, Alexandre, is bright and articulate, and sports an impressive beard. He studied law but took over running the estate for the 1998 vintage after his grandfather died, and immediately began putting the wine in bottle. His grandfather had only ever produced wine for sale *en vrac*. Altogether there are 30 hectares, in 23 plots around Montbrun, on clay and limestone terraces, which have been officially registered as organic since 2010. It is a windy area, drier than nearby Lézignan, with an average rainfall of 300–350 millimetres. Alexandre makes both Corbières and Vin de France, observing that you can be much more creative, and work with fewer constraints with Vin de France.

We chatted as we tasted. Alexandre has learnt his winemaking gradually, with various *stages*, and Claude Gros advises. His entry-level Corbières is a blend of 60 per cent Carignan and Grenache with 40 per cent Mourvèdre and Syrah, aged in vat, with some spicy fruit and firm tannins. Vox Dei is firmer and more structured, with 70 per cent Syrah and Grenache, and 15 per cent each of Mourvèdre and Carignan, aged in wood and including a pre-fermentation cold maceration. It was ripe and dense, with a fresh finish. Les Ailes is one-third each of Carignan, Grenache and Mourvèdre, again with a maceration before fermentation. The malolactic fermentation takes place in wood, in new 400-litre barrels, in which the wine stays for 14 months. It is rich, with black fruit and well-integrated oak. Alexandre does not like his wine to be marked by wood, so he favours light toasting, to avoid any vanilla notes, and the malolactic in wood also calms any oak. To show how well Les Ailes ages, he opened the 2000. It had developed some tertiary aromas, with leathery notes, but was still very fresh, elegant and nuanced. Vin de France Terre d'Eoile is a Carignan and Cabernet Sauvignon blend and he has also made a Syrah fermented in an open barrel that was destalked by hand. He enjoys experimenting and aptly described the Languedoc as *un grand laboratoire* – a big laboratory!

Château Haut Gléon / Vignobles Foncalieu
Villesèque-des-Corbières 11360/Foncalieu
www.hautgleon.com; www.foncalieu.com

It seems simplest to cover Foncalieu, or to give the company its full name, Les Vignobles Foncalieu, under Corbières because that is where their property, Château Haut Gléon, is situated. They bought it at the end of 2012, for the simple reason that they wanted a flagship estate. Haut Gléon already had a reputation for its white wine, which is unusual in the Corbières, and Foncalieu has continued to work on that. Domaine Haut Gléon is a blend of Sauvignon, Bourboulenc and Chardonnay, while Château Haut Gléon is made from Grenache Blanc, Marsanne and Roussanne. There are two rosés, Domaine Haut Gléon Gris, an IGP from the Vallée du Paradis made from Grenache Noir, Cabernet Sauvignon and Cabernet Franc, while Château Haut Gléon comes from the Languedoc varieties of Grenache Noir and Syrah. There are three red wines. Again, the Domaine red is an IGP, including some Grenache Noir and Syrah, as well as Cabernet Franc and Cabernet Sauvignon, while Château Haut Gléon is a Corbières from Syrah, Grenache Noir and Carignan, aged in barrel with some firm, black fruit. Notre Dame de Gléon, after the tiny chapel on the estate, is a selection of the best grapes and again a blend of Syrah, Grenache and Carignan.

As for Foncalieu, it was created in 1967, with the fusion of several cooperatives and the name comes from: *Fon*tiès d'Aude; *Ca*pendu, *Al*zonne and Montol*ieu*. Altogether they work with 5,100 hectares of vines in three regions, namely Gascony, the Rhône Valley and the Languedoc, and cover 20 appellations and IGPs. Two things stand out: they have a very strong quality motivation and they are also very innovative. They were the first to plant Sauvignon Gris in the Languedoc and now make both a white and a rosé from that grape variety. They also have some Albariño, and Piquepoul Noir for rosé, and also make a rosé that is a blend of 80 per cent Syrah and 20 per cent Viognier (the two grape varieties being co-fermented, with early-picked Syrah and late-picked Viognier).

They have developed their Atelier Prestige range, beginning in 2008, with the first real vintage in 2009. The winemaker Isabelle Pangault talked about the way they chose the vineyards for these wines. Obviously, the *terroir* must be good, with vines in particularly favourable sites, but much also depends on the human approach. They work with a very small number of winegrowers for each of the four wines, people who are possibly more daring and certainly more willing to take extra care of their vines. Their aim is to show that it is possible for a cooperative to make high-quality wine in the Languedoc. The wine growers are paid by the hectare, so the yield is not a significant issue for them financially. There are two growers making Le Lien in the Minervois: La Lumière is a Corbières; Les Illustres comes from the Coteaux d'Ensérune, a blend of 60 per cent Syrah, 30 per cent Cabernet Sauvignon and 10 per cent Malbec, made by the Languedoc's oldest cooperative at Maraussan. Finally, there is a St Chinian, Apogée, from Syrah and a little Grenache Noir, grown on clay and limestone. Foncalieu is also known for Le Versant, a range of Pays d'Oc, with three whites, namely Viognier, Chardonnay and Sauvignon Blanc, a rosé Grenache, and four reds, namely Pinot Noir, Cabernet Sauvignon, Merlot and Syrah.

The new president of Corbières, Daniel Sendrous, who is also president of the Lézignan cooperative, le Chais des Vignerons, is optimistic about the future. He is ambitious for what he called the collective spirit of the region, with a new young generation of energetic wine producers, as well as newcomers investing in the appellation. The *cru* of Boutenac is well established and there are other crus in the pipeline, which will help to enhance the reputation and quality of a diverse appellation.

7

FITOU

Fitou is an appellation divided in two: the *côté montagne* and the *côté mer*. The appellation covers just nine villages, four high in the wild Corbières hills, namely Tuchan, Paziols, Villeneuve-les-Corbières and Cascastel, while the other five are close to the sea, with Fitou itself, Leucate, Lapalme, Treilles and Caves. The name Fitou originates from *fita*, or frontier, with reference to the fact that the village was close to the frontier with Catalonia. The castles of Fitou and Leucate are now ruins, but Salses on the other side of the border in Roussillon is worth the detour to admire its solid fortifications and impregnable walls.

Fitou prides itself on being the oldest red table wine appellation of the Languedoc, recognized in 1948, and a contemporary of white Clairette du Languedoc. Any earlier appellations such as nearby Rivesaltes are for fortified wines; neighbouring Côtes du Roussillon was not recognized until 1977, and Corbières not until 1985. These days, with the move towards creating a hierarchy of appellations in the Languedoc, Fitou might be seen as a *cru* of Corbières, well ahead of the established *cru* of Boutenac. Some of its producers do also make Corbières and Rivesaltes, but I suspect that it prefers to stand alone. However, the early development of Fitou relates to Rivesaltes, as these were the nine villages of the department of the Aude that also made Rivesaltes, and still do. At the time, the market for vermouth and *vins doux naturels* was flourishing, but far-sighted wine growers also saw the potential for red wine.

Fitou is only red, not even rosé, and unlike some other southern appellations, there is no move to create a parallel white appellation. Any white or rosé wine produced in the area is either AOP Languedoc,

Corbières or an IGP Vallée du Torgan. The grape varieties are essentially the same as for Corbières, but with the exclusion of Cinsaut, which was eliminated 15 years ago, as it was deemed to lack colour and alcohol, whereas today the problem can be the opposite, with other varieties providing too much of both. Consequently, there is a move to reinstate it, as well as a definite move towards indigenous varieties, with Carignan coming into its own again. Ask any grower what accounts for the typicity of Fitou and they are very likely to reply Carignan, which is appreciated for its freshness.

Producers

Domaine Bertrand Bergé

Paziols 11350
www.bertrand-berge.com

We followed the valley of the river Berre up into the hills, heading for Paziols, where our destination was Domaine Bertrand Bergé, to meet Jérôme and Sabine Bertrand, who immediately took us up into their vineyards. Altogether they have 36 hectares, which are cultivated organically. Jérôme has some very old vines; he does not know exactly how old, but pre-1906, before detailed records were kept. The soil at Paziols is *galets roulées*.

The scenery is spectacular, with the snow-capped Pyrenees in the distance, the Cathar castle of Aguilar and the lookout tower of Tautavel, in Roussillon, and one can just make out the spectacular fortress of Peyrepertuse. Across the valley is Mont Tauch, one of the two large hills of the Corbières, which dominates the vineyards of the surrounding villages.

Winemaking chez Bertrand Bergé is meticulous. 'We only ferment what we would eat.' They have a sorting table and do a final check by hand, with Jérôme explaining: 'The healthier the grapes, the less sulphur dioxide you need'. His cellars are scrupulously clean. We tasted in the barrel cellar, with *foudres* and *demi-muids* as well as *barriques*. His white wine, La Boulière Blanche, the name of the vineyard, is an IGP Vallée du Torgan, a blend of old Macabeo and Grenache Blanc and Gris, planted in 1956 and fermented together, partly in new wood and partly in stainless steel, with no malolactic fermentation. As he pointed out, it was their first real white wine; they have made Muscat for years, but this was ground-breaking for them. It has some rich fruit, well integrated oak and firm acidity. Previously these grapes had been used for Rivesaltes. One challenge was deciding on the picking date, as the harvest would be much earlier for table wine, in late August, as opposed to the beginning of October for the *vin doux naturel*.

The first vintage they bottled was 1993, with La Cuvée d'Origine. Originally, they only had Carignan and Grenache but then in 1996 they planted some Syrah, and Mourvèdre followed in 2008. This *cuvée*, however, remains a blend of 60 per cent Carignan and 40 per cent Grenache, aged only in vat. Jérôme described it as *ma perle friandise*, my delicacy of a pearl. It is redolent of black fruit, with a streak of tannin. Mégalithe is made from his oldest Carignan vines, *complanté* with Grenache Noir; he has gradually replaced dying Carignan vines with Grenache Noir so that it accounts for about 10 per cent of the blend. The palate is sturdy and dense. La Boulière Rouge is a blend of 50 per cent Mourvèdre with equal amounts of Carignan and Grenache, aged for 18 months in *foudres*. It is more restrained, influenced by the Mourvèdre, with firm mineral, tannic notes. Ancestrale is a blend of all four varieties, about 30 per cent each of Syrah, Grenache Noir and Carignan with 10 per cent Mourvèdre, and is nicely concentrated. Syrah dominates the flavour, but Jérôme observed that it can mask the *effet terroir*. Finally, we were treated to three vintages of Jean Sirven, named after Jérôme's great-great-grandfather, who planted vines in the village in the 1880s after phylloxera. The wine was sold in barrel in Amiens in northern France, having been taken by cart over the hills to the nearest station, Estagel, from where it went by train to Amiens. The blend of 45 per cent each of Syrah and Carignan with 10 per cent Grenache is given 18 months in new barrels. In the young wine the flavour was sweet and rich. The 2006 had developed some leathery, peppery notes, with some freshness from the Carignan, while the 2000, the second vintage of the *cuvée*, had evolved into a wonderfully complex bottle, with spice and length.

Domaine Sarrat d'en Sol

Tuchan 11350
famille.brassou@wanadoo.fr

Nicolas Brassou is a new wine producer in the village of Tuchan, making his very first wine in 2010, with 5 hectares of vines. His father still has vines at the Tuchan cooperative; Nicolas did other things before returning to wine. He has several different plots, at an altitude of about 400 metres, planted with 60 per cent Carignan, 30 per cent Grenache and 10 per cent Syrah. The name of the estate means 'small hill in the sun'.

First, we tasted some vat samples and Nicolas talked about his winemaking. He too has some 100-year-old Carignan, which he destems, and gives a pre-fermentation cool maceration for ten days in order to extract more fruit and colour. A vat sample had some fresh cherry fruit balanced by a streak of tannin. His first experiments with wood were for the 2015 vintage, and he has just six barrels, from a couple of different coopers. His 2015 Fitou promises well, with a tannic backbone and good depth of flavour. For Nicolas, Carignan provides the typicity of Fitou, while Grenache fills out the flavour and Syrah adds a floral note. He is planning a white wine, a blend of Macabeo, Grenache Blanc and Gris, once those vines have been extricated from the cooperative. He also has some Muscat but that would be '*un peu* too much' in the blend. I thought that Nicolas had made a very convincing start in his new career.

Domaine Lerys
Villeneuve-les-Corbières 11360
www.domainelerys.com

This is one of the old, established estates of the village of Villeneuve-les-Corbières, with 60 hectares of vines, run by Alain Izard and his son Alban. They took me to a viewpoint outside the village, where I admired gnarled old vines planted on schist. The schist was glinting in the sun and, though the wind was ferocious, the views towards the Pyrenees were breathtaking. There was some 100-year-old Carignan (they do not know the exact age) and they replace the vines by *marcottage*, so that some of the vines have an additional thick trunk going back into the soil. There was a flock of sheep and also some Jersey cows, performing a useful service eating the ground vegetation and also manuring the vineyards. We talked about the problems with wild boars; the hunters try to keep them at bay but also provide extra food for them, which exacerbates the problem.

Their Cuvée Tradition is a blend of 60 per cent Carignan with 40 per cent Grenache Noir, all vinified by carbonic maceration and given an *élevage* in vat. The Cuvée Prestige from one-third each of Carignan, Grenache and Syrah is aged in vat for 18 months, with some solid red fruit and a sturdy streak of tannin. Belor is a blend of 80 per cent Carignan with 20 per cent Syrah, which spends nine months *sur marc*, on its skins. After nine months, the skins fall back into the juice and then the wine is aged in old Burgundy barrels for six months. It was redolent of ripe berry fruit, with nicely integrated oak. Cuvée Adrienne, named after an aunt, is 80 per cent Carignan with 10 per cent each of Grenache Noir and Syrah. Part of the Carignan is fermented by carbonic maceration, but most is destalked and given a pre-fermentation cold maceration. It was ripe and nicely structured, with a fresh finish; 'the effect of the schist,' observed Alban.

The following morning, I was shown the *terroir* of Fitou Maritime, by Christophe Jaulent from the cooperative of Leucate. All the vines of the village are on a plateau that is essentially surrounded by water, either the sea or the étang de Leucate. As Christophe explained, the village lives on oysters, tourism and wine. He has 25 hectares on the stony plateau, including some 100-year-old Carignan, and some Mourvèdre planted as early as 1984, as well as some almond and peach trees. He pointed out a typical walled garden, with its *coin de repos*, vegetable plot and fruit trees. There is a small group of organic vineyards within the Leucate cooperative, and experiments with pheromones have proved successful, so that 800 hectares of vines on the plateau are now protected against pests in that way. We looked at a plot that was being cleared for planting. This required getting rid of the bigger stones and then breaking up the smaller ones, before analysing the soil to ascertain the appropriate rootstock for so much calcium. A flock of long-legged sheep come for the winter grazing amongst the vineyards.

Mas des Caprices

Leucate 11370
www.mas-des-caprices.com

Pierre Mann comes from Alsace and is related to the Alsace grower Albert Mann. He was in the hotel and restaurant business but, after feeling it was time for a change, in 2005 he moved to Leucate, bought vines and learnt to make wine. Originally, he had considered Provence but found the milieu too closed; Leucate offered a maritime influence that he liked.

First, we were greeted by his splendid hound, Carignan, and then Pierre showed us round his cellars. He has *jarres*, or amphorae, from Castelnaudary, eggs as well as cement vats and some stainless steel tanks. A white Corbières is a blend of 30 per cent each of Grenache Blanc and Gris, 40 per cent Macabeo and a drop of Muscat. All the vines are *complanté*, in a very stony vineyard on a cliff by the sea. The wine was firm and mineral, with very good acidity. Pierre talked about his eggs; they provide a natural *bâtonnage*, adding weight to the wine, while the amphorae make for a wine that is tighter, with tension and purity. A Corbières rosé, Ozé, is a blend of Mourvèdre and Grenache, picked and vinified together, with some firm acidity and dry fruit. A pure Grenache Gris is a Pays d'Oc, as Grenache Gris is not allowed in the appellation. The wine was the palest of pink, and riper and more rounded than Ozé. RAS, Rouge à Siroter, comes from Grenache with 40 per cent each of Carignan and Mourvèdre, with a short maceration and no *élevage*, which means that it is Pays d'Aude rather than Fitou – Fitou requires *élevage* since it cannot be sold until 1 May after the harvest. This had lovely fruit.

Three Fitou followed, the entry level, Ze Fitou, based on Mourvèdre, with Carignan and Grenache, was the lightest of the three with some fresh fruit, following a short maceration. Retour aux Sources, with Carignan, Grenache and Mourvèdre, grown on schist, aged partly in vat and partly in *foudres*, was rich and concentrated with a firm, stony finish. Anthocyane, from Pierre's oldest vines, Mourvèdre, Carignan and some Grenache, on north-facing slopes, aged in *foudres, demi-muids* and *barriques*, was perfumed with some oak and spice. We finished with a Grenat Rivesaltes, a pure Grenache aged in vat and barrel, which was rich and raisiny with nutty notes and a hint of liquorice. It was almost lunchtime so I allowed myself to spit internally, as they say!

Château Champs des Sœurs

Fitou 11510
www.champsdessoeurs.fr

Laurent Maynardier from Château Champs des Soeurs made his first wine in 1999. However, his family arrived in the region after the Revocation of the Edict of Nantes in 1685. His uncle makes wine at Château Abelanet. The name Champs des Soeurs derives from the best *terroir* of his great uncle, called Camp de la Source. Laurent took us to see his vineyards in the hills above Fitou, where he has 17 hectares. The soil is a mixture, with schist and limestone in Fitou and clay and schist in the adjoining village of Treilles. This is one of the driest parts of France with an annual rainfall of just 350 millimetres. Storms can be a problem as can the winds: the tramontane from the north-west, the grégal from the north-east, the marin from the south-east, from the south the sirocco, straight from the Sahara, and the ponent from the west. Until the Second World War the area was known for its sheep as well as vines, with as many as 800 *capitelles* in the hills, with the remains of old terraces.

Back at Laurent's neat cellar in the village we tasted his range. Unusually for a Fitou estate, one-third of his production is white. Bel Amant, a Corbières Blanc and a blend of 70 per cent Grenache Blanc with Roussanne, was nicely rounded, with white blossom and good acidity. A second *cuvée* la Tina, a blend of 60 per cent Grenache Blanc with Roussanne, is aged in *demi-muids* for six months, making it firm and structured. As for Fitou, for which he has stopped using any sulphur, there is Tradition from younger vines, mainly Carignan and Grenache, with a little Syrah. Bel Amant comes from older vines, at least 30 years old, with ripe black fruit. La Tina is 80 per cent Carignan, destemmed, with whole bunches of Mourvèdre, with intense flavours and good ageing potential. For Laurent, the typicity of Fitou is the freshness that comes either from the higher altitudes of the hills or from the proximity of the sea. Carignan too gives freshness, whereas Grenache can be too heavy, while Syrah and Mourvèdre add a note of complexity. However, by the sea Mourvèdre is more successful than Syrah, which he deems 'complicated'. I was left with an impression of a thoughtful and focused winemaker.

Domaine Jones
Tuchan 11350
www.domainejones.com

Katie Jones is one of the few wine producers to have vineyards in both Roussillon and the Languedoc, which she admits is an administrative nightmare. Côtes Catalanes declarations are made in Perpignan, for Fitou she goes to Narbonne, and Vin de France is run from Paris. After starting her career in the UK wine trade, Katie came to work for the large cooperative in Tuchan in 1993 where, as its Export Sales and Marketing Director, she really helped to put its wines on the map. She left in 2009, but without any burning ambition to make wine. However, the opportunity to buy a vineyard presented itself. Initially she planned to stay small and use her marketing expertise to run a consultancy business, but then her cellar was vandalized and a vat of Grenache Gris poured down the drains. That was the trigger to demonstrate that she could become a serious and successful winemaker. For this she has enormous support from her *compagnon*, Jean-Marc Astruc, who has his own vines and is a former president of the Tuchan cooperative. Katie has a cellar in Tuchan, in what was once the old train depot. A train used to run between Narbonne and Tuchan, the end of the line, as the last village before the department of the Pyrénées-Orientales. It took four hours to reach Narbonne and at Lézignan the line linked up with the route to Bordeaux.

Katie Jones, Domaine Jones

Katie's very first vintage was 2009, beginning with a 2.5 hectare vineyard in Maury. She had four varieties from which she made three wines, Grenache Gris, Grenache Noir, with a little Carignan, and some sweet Muscat. In 2010, she bought a Fitou vineyard in Tuchan, which is why she fits most comfortably into this chapter, and she has gradually added vineyards. Now she has at least 20 different plots, mostly around Tuchan, and she makes Fitou, Côtes Catalanes in Maury and various tiny *cuvées*, her best wines, as Vin de France, les Perles de Jones, which is completely contrary to French wine hierarchy. She particularly looks for small plots of old vines and is the only person I know of who produces a varietal Carignan Gris, of which she has just one-third of a hectare. There is very little Carignan Gris; it is such a late ripener, usually in the middle of October, that the cooperative does not like it. As for flavour, it is textured and understated, with stony notes and good acidity. There is also a Grenache Gris, of which a very small percentage is fermented in oak. Again, there is texture and mouthfeel, some herbal, nutty notes and ageing potential. Les Perles de Macabeo is a little more exuberant, with a hint of pineapple, while les Perles de Grenache Gris is vinified in barrel and has more weight, with buttery notes. Côtes Catalanes rouge from Grenache Noir has the fragrant, perfumed fruit of the grape, while Perles de Carignan has a structured palate with rounded red fruit and silky tannins. It is an elegant Carignan, with Katie successfully avoiding the rustic notes that you often find with Carignan. Finally, her Fitou is a blend of 30 per cent each of Grenache Noir and Syrah, with 40 per cent Carignan. Part of the Syrah and Carignan is aged in barrel, but never the Grenache, and there is spicy fruit on the nose and palate with supple tannins and a ripe but elegant finish. There is no doubt that Katie has successfully risen to the challenge of becoming a *vigneronne*.

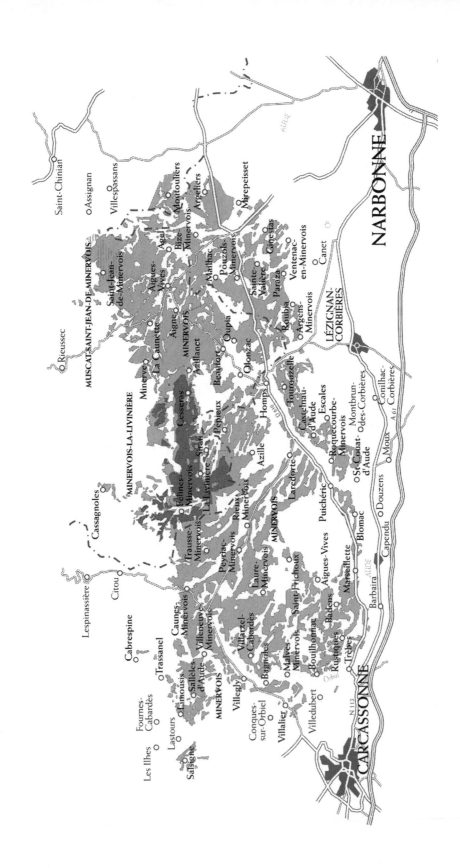

8

MINERVOIS WITH MINERVOIS LA LIVINIÈRE AND ST JEAN DE MINERVOIS

Minervois is separated from Corbières by the valley of the Aude and the Canal du Midi, with the vineyards of Minervois lying on the foothills of the Massif Central between the medieval city of Carcassonne and the Roman city of Narbonne, facing those of Corbières on the first slopes of the Pyrenees. Minervois is a much smaller appellation, with about 4,000 hectares.

The wine takes its name from the village of Minerve which perches in what seems to be an unassailable position, on steep cliffs above the confluence of the Cesse and the Brian. If you approach the village from the west, you are rewarded with dramatic views of the Canyon de la Cesse and the cliffs continue toward the village of La Caunette. In summer, the rivers diminish to a mere trickle, but with heavy winter rain they can turn into raging torrents overnight. Minerve takes its name from Minerva, the Roman goddess of wisdom. The ramparts of the village were built in the twelfth century, for it played its part in the Albigensian crusade as one of the last strongholds of the Cathar heresy, and many Cathars died at Minerve after a successful siege by Simon de Montfort in 1210. These days Minerve has been much restored, with little shops and cafés, making it a tourist destination. The village of Rieux-Minervois boasts an awe-inspiring Romanesque church and Caunes-Minervois is known for its abbey, and the Hotel d'Alibert, with its beautiful renaissance courtyard. Its marble quarries provided stone for the columns of the palace of Versailles.

The appellation of Minervois was created in 1985, for white and rosé, as well as red wine. White accounts for only 3 per cent and rosé 13 per cent. The grape varieties are those common to most other appellations of the Languedoc. The *cru* of La Livinière is well established, with others in the pipeline, namely Laure and Cazelles and there is also talk of La Causse between Minerve and La Caunette, with those names replacing other earlier suggestions that never came to fruition. There are also growers who are slightly isolated, whose wines do not fit into a *cru*, for whom a local *lieu-dit* may be recognized, such as Terres de Georges in the village of Castelnau d'Aude, adjoining Corbières.

MINERVOIS LA LIVINIÈRE

The *cru* of La Livinière was recognized in 1999, and granted retrospectively for the 1998 vintage. The current aspiration, soon to be realized, is a stand-alone *appellation communale* La Livinière, without any mention of Languedoc or Minervois on the label. Whether this will help the reputation of the wines remains to be seen. Most wine growers think it will, but the average consumer might be more geographically challenged than they realize. La Livinière covers the vineyards of six villages, about 350 hectares, but is for red wine only. The distinctive silhouette of the church tower of La Livinière forms an effective logo on the capsule of each bottle. The geology is based on limestone and clay, but it is climate more than geology that is the unifying factor. Cliffs run at an altitude of about 140 metres at the foot of the Montagne Noire between Caunes-Minervois and La Livinière, so the vineyards are all south-facing and protected from the prevailing north winds, though nights can be cool. The scenery is wild and dramatic, and the soil so stony you wonder that anything will grow. The regulations are stricter than those of Minervois, with an emphasis on Syrah and the possibility of 5 per cent of *anciens cépages*, such as Ribeyrenc, Terret and others. The minimum *élevage* is for 15 months, in vat, barrel or bottle.

The wine producers insist on freshness, the effect of the Montagne Noir, accounting for the typicity of the La Livinière so that the wines are a combination of elegance and richness, with supple tannins. La Livinière is more elegant than Minervois, silkier and less rustic. However, no one makes La Livinière alone, and most of the estates with a reputation for La Livinière also produce some serious Minervois. There are well-established estates, with a reputation already established in the past century, such as Clos Centeilles and Ste Eulalie, and then there are newcomers to the region, or even newcomers to wine who have bought vineyards, or a new generation who have taken the family vines out of the cooperative, as is the same all over the Languedoc.

Producers

Domaine Borie de Maurel

Félines-Minervois 34210
www.boriedemaurel.fr

Michel Esclande boasts a wonderful head of curly hair and somehow the unruly hairstyle complements his personality. He and his wife, Virginie, are based in the village of Félines. Michel has been making wine since 1989. He is one of the enthusiasts of the appellation and a generous host in the tasting room, especially when he broaches the subject of older vintages. Our tasting began with Gypse, a Pays d'Oc Chardonnay, which was quite fat with a streak of acidity, and then came A la Belle Aude, a pure Marsanne, with white blossom, and a perfumed Belle de Nuit, from Grenache Noir. Charivari is also a pure Grenache, for easy drinking. Minervois Esprit d'Automne is a Minervois, and next came three Minervois La Livinière: La Féline, a blend of Syrah with some Grenache and Carignan, Maxime, based on Mourvèdre and Scylla, based on Syrah. Michel also makes a pure Carignan, Vin de France.

Michel talked about the evolution of his winemaking. He has given up using oak barrels, observing that you do not need oak if you want fruit and, after an initial false start, has returned to organic viticulture. He proved how elegantly his wines aged – vintages of Scylla from the last century had notes of tapenade and leather – noting that 'people do not think about selling older vintages in the Languedoc; it is not usual and there is no real tradition of mature wine in the region'. Attitudes need to change.

Domaine Ste Eulalie

La Livinière 34210
www.chateausainteeulalie.com

Isabelle and Laurent Coutale arrived at Ste Eulalie from Bordeaux in 1996 and are still referred to as *les bordelais* in the village, such is the conservatism of rural France with regard to outsiders. We went for a windy walk in the vineyard. The soil is very stony, with chunks of limestone, which perform a useful role in absorbing heat and then reflecting it back onto the vines. The drainage is good, with reserves of water underneath, so the vines are not stressed. However, Isabelle is aware of the effects of climate change, noting: 'Fortunately, we do have Carignan, whereas Syrah is more worrying and less resistant to drought.' The wine they are best known for is la Cantilène, after the very first poem in French dated 881AD, *la Cantilène de Ste Eulalie*, about the saint's martyrdom. Syrah is the dominant variety, with some Carignan and Grenache Noir, aged in barrel.

Since 2009 they have made a more serious Grand Vin from Carignan planted in 1910 and some Grenache from 80-year-old vines. The wine is aged in both vat and barrel for two years, for Isabelle wanted to show that you can make good wine without *barriques*; scorning what she called *maquillage*, or make up, she wants the original fruit. We were treated to some mature vintages of Cantilène that were showing beautifully, notably a spicy, cedary 2004.

Clos Centeilles
Siran 34210
www.closcenteilles.com

Patricia Domergue at Clos Centeilles has been a friend since she and her husband Daniel made their first vintage together in 1990. Sadly, they have gone their separate ways and Patricia is now helped by their daughter Cécile. She is an enthusiastic exponent of some of the lost grape varieties of the Languedoc, such as Ribeyrenc, Terret and Piquepoul so a tasting *chez* Patricia begins with C de Centeilles Blanc, Côtes du Brian, from Araignan Blanc, Ribeyrenc Blanc and Gris and some Grenache Gris for some original southern flavours. C de Centeilles Rouge is equally eclectic, from Piquepoul Noir, Ribeyrenc, Oeillade and Morastel Noir à jus blanc. Patricia's wines rarely conform to the regulations for Minervois but it is what is in the vineyard that counts. So Carignanissime is a pure Carignan and a delicious example of the variety, and Patricia is also particularly enthusiastic about Cinsaut, for red as well as for rosé, arguing that Cinsaut deserves to be taken seriously and treated carefully in both vineyard and cellar. Campagne de Centeilles is mainly Cinsaut while Capitelle de Centeilles is a pure Cinsaut, which is surprisingly age worthy. In contrast, Clos de Centeilles, her Minervois La Livinière, is a more conventional blend of equal parts of Grenache Noir, Syrah and Mourvèdre. The vineyards at Centeilles surround the small medieval chapel with its unusual fresco of a pregnant virgin.

Château Mignan
Siran 34210
www.chateaumignan.com

Christian Mignan of Château Mignan took over some of his grandfather's vines in time for his first vintage of 2003. His grandfather had been a grocer with a few vines, and after the vines froze during the excruciatingly hard winter of 1956, he joined the local cooperative. Christian's father and uncle duly followed. After working for some years selling wine, Christian realized that he really wanted to make it. He has built a cellar and converted the 15 hectares, of which 9 hectares are La Livinière, to organic viticulture. He is passionately enthusiastic but, as he says, 'passion is not enough, you need faith or conviction too'. For commercial reasons, he makes two *cuvées* of La Livinière, Les Trois Clochers and L'Oeil du Temps, with varying blends of Syrah, Grenache and Carignan, but with Syrah always the dominant variety, and with a high proportion of oak ageing in 400-litre barrels. The differences between the two are not so great, both exuding rich tapenade fruit, balanced by supple tannins.

Château Maris
La Livinière 34210
www.chateaumaris.com

'Come and see my vegetal roof', or *toit végétal*, was an invitation I could not possibly refuse! It came from Bertie Eden of Château Maris. He has built a brand new cellar on the outskirts of La Livinière off the road to Caunes-Minervois. Not only is the roof green, but the bricks are made of hemp straw and the whole cellar, apart from the concrete floor, could be recycled.

Bertie talked about the bricks. Building material in France must be authorized, so that its parameters are recognized, as to how much weight the bricks can bear and so on. Hemp is not a recognized building material, but wood is, so there had to be a wooden frame joining the bricks, which are made from hemp straw mixed with lime, put in a mould and dried. The bricks are extraordinarily light. Ordinary straw is very similar to hemp straw, but with one big difference: hemp straw breathes, so it redistributes air and consumes carbon dioxide at a rate of 44 kilos per square metre per year. Temperature control in the cellar happens naturally and the floor is concrete for reasons of hygiene and weight bearing. An alternative would have been lime, but that can crack, leading to potential problems with bacteria. As for the vegetal roof, it is bought in rolls by the metre, like turf for a lawn. Bertie is also considering a vegetal covering for the outside walls. In the cellar, there are barrels and tronconic vats, equipped with a *chapeau flottant*, so that they have a dual purpose, fermentation and *élevage*, and also unlined cement vats and concrete eggs. Bertie had wanted concrete vats without metal supports, and the way to achieve that is with eggs. He has compared Grenache from a barrel and from an egg and found the wine from the egg to be more lively and fresher.

Bertie now has 47 hectares of vines all around La Livinière. His first vintage here was 1997. He has had vineyards in other parts of the Languedoc, but these days concentrates on the Minervois. He realized he wanted to be a winemaker after he was expelled from Stowe School for making beer, so he went to Australia to work for Len Evans at Rothbury; he spent time at Castello di Rampolla in Chianti Classico, and with Becky Wassermann in Burgundy and Christopher Cannan in Spain. When the time came to be his own boss he looked in the Languedoc and really liked what he saw in the Minervois. Bertie's vineyards range in altitude between 180 and 250 metres and he has been certified biodynamic since 2004. Asked about the typicity of La Livinière, he suggested that it was a delicate subject, and a difficult question to answer. Every vineyard is individual; it depends on the grower.

As for his wines, there is a textured Grenache Gris, Vin de France and a range of Minervois La Livinière. La Touge is 60 per cent Syrah, 40 per cent Grenache Noir, with a drop of Carignan; les Anciens is mainly Carignan aged in 50-hectolitre *foudres* for 15 months. Bertie enthused about Carignan: 'It is a noble variety here, and it can stand up to the seasons.' This had the elegant rusticity that is the benchmark of good Carignan, with some firm red fruit. For Las Combes, Grenache is the dominant variety, from 80-year-old vines, with *élevage* in an egg.

CAZELLES

There is talk of other areas being recognized as *crus*, namely Cazelles and Laure, with the appropriate dossiers submitted to the INAO in 2016. Take Cazelles first, which groups a cluster of vineyards and villages, on a limestone plateau south of St Jean-de-Minervois, around the eponymous hamlet, with eight estates cultivating about 180 hectares, which could develop with some replanting to about 300 hectares. It is all about personalities. La Livinière was the result of the right people at the right time, and the same can be said for Boutenac and explain the lack of other *crus* in the larger appellation of Corbières.

Producers

Domaine Sicard

Aigues-Vives 34210
www.ledomainesicard.fr

Philippe Sicard in the village of Aigues-Vives explained that Cazelles has a precise geological unity, determined by its soil. It is also affected by the cool winds coming off the Montagne Noire, with the vineyards at an altitude of 120–250 metres making for freshness. The name Cazelles is Occitan for *capitelles*, the stone shelters, while *caze* is *une petite maison en pierre*, a small house in stone. Philippe's great grandfather created the family estate in 1920 and his grandfather was one of the founders of the Vignerons du Val d'Orbieu, with which he no longer works, feeling that they are not sufficiently interested in quality. First, we looked at his vineyards. He has old Carignan vines and has even planted some more. 'It is the emblematic variety, our identity and the variety best adapted to our *terroir*'. He has an old village cellar with indestructible concrete vats and works by gravity, favouring carbonic maceration for his red wines, except for the Grenache Noir because its stalks can sometimes make for greenness. Carignan is particularly suitable for carbonic maceration, as Philippe's Cuvée Sicarignan demonstrates, made only from old vines, with red fruit, a hint of liquorice and juniper and a firm finish. Cuvée Jean-Claude Dreyfus, an homage to the actor, would be his Cuvée Cazelles, from 80 per cent Syrah with some Carignan and Grenache Noir, given 18 months' ageing in new 400-litres barrels. The new oak impact is quite strong, but there is fruit behind the oak, with ageing potential. It promised well for the potential *cru*.

Domaine Cazelle-Verdier

Cazelles 34210

jpverdier20@gmail.com

Jean-Paul Verdier arrived at our appointment wearing a T-shirt saying 'Challenge Accepted'; maybe the challenge is the creation of the *cru* of Cazelles. We tasted in his tiny barrel cellar in the centre of the village. He explained that the family property dates back to 1713, with wine always their principal activity. His father was never a cooperative member but sold wine *en vrac*, and Jean-Paul began bottling his wine in 1991. His father had vineyards of Aramon, Terret and Carignan which he has replanted with Chardonnay, Mourvèdre and Syrah, and he also has Grenache and Carignan. Our tasting started with his Chardonnay, a buttery Pays d'Oc with good acidity and an elegant finish. He confided that Anne Gros, his Burgundian colleague, likes it! A Minervois Tradition was fresh and spicy with red fruit. His first organic *cuvée* from the 2014 vintage, a blend of Syrah, Grenache and Carignan, was rounded with black fruit. The next wine is called Le Marchand de Poivre in recognition of his grandfather who spent 20 years in Indochina at the beginning of the twentieth century before returning to the village to take up winemaking, causing the people in the village to call him Le Marchand de Poivre, or pepper merchant. Les Pierres qui Chantent describes the stones on the plateau of Cazelles, and is a blend of Syrah, Carignan, Grenache and a little Mourvèdre, with 60 per cent aged in wood for six months. It is structured, with some firm fruit. Finally, le Chemin des Croisades comes from a vineyard called La Croix, a reference to the Cathar crusades. The *élevage* includes a 9 hectolitre American oak barrel and there was a strong note of vanilla on the palate. Jean-Paul is also experimenting with a pure Syrah, which he intends to put into a 7 hectolitre amphora.

Domaine Anne Gros

Cazelles 34210

www.anne-gros.com

It is fascinating to compare the Burgundian approach with that of the Languedoc. Anne Gros and her husband, Jean-Paul Tollot, have fine reputations for their respective family estates in the Côte d'Or but they had never worked together, so they decided to look for vineyards in the south, arriving eventually at Cazelles. Anne enthused; they felt *une énorme emotion*, but it was so far from Burgundy, a five-hour drive. Their first vintage in the Minervois was 2008, beginning with 8 hectares, which have grown to 16, with Cinsaut, Grenache, Carignan and Syrah, but no Mourvèdre. They planted Marselan, about which Anne is surprisingly enthusiastic, and Vermentino for white wine, and also some Pinot Noir. She had hesitated about Pinot Noir, initially thinking it would be too hot in Cazelles, but then she realized that was not the case, and that the soil was suitable.

Paul and Jean-Paul Tollot of Domaine Anne Gros

The vineyards are beautifully tended, with barely a weed in sight. 'Grass provides competition for water, a *concurrence hydrique*, which will detract from the quality.' They use no weedkiller, but are not organic. 'Copper is even worse than chemicals,' which degrade, 'copper does not.' The main problem is *vers de la grappe* and also occasionally oidium. Anne sings the praises of Cinsaut, comparing its elegance with Pinot Noir; it is also much easier than Syrah, which needs a lot of work. Cinsaut can produce very large grapes, which can look like tiny footballs, but do not have a lot of juice, unless it rains heavily. Good aeration is essential. They do an *ébourgeonnage*, a debudding, in May, which is usual in Burgundy, but not in the Languedoc, and they remove leaves and tiny *grapillons*.

Anne talks with enthusiasm about a mosaic of different soils, and her love of Carignan. 'That is what is keeping us here, with its structure.' She has some very old Carignan, a vineyard with stone walls on three sides, and vines that are a venerable 104 years old, and another plot that is 102 years old. Three of her wines are named after the vineyard, and as a Burgundian she was particularly excited to buy a plot called Les Combettes. Everything is hand-picked by a team from Béziers, who are paid by the hectare, rather than by the weight of the grapes, which is the usual practice in the Midi.

Back at her cellar we settled down to a comprehensive tasting of bottles, a range of single vineyards, as is customary in Burgundy. Her wines were initially all Vin de France, but now she tends to use the local IGP, Côtes du Brian, and two of her vineyards will be Cazelles, namely Ciaude and Carrétas, as soon as the name is accepted. Her labels are a distinctive orange, inspired, she said, by the colour of Carignan leaves in the autumn. La Cinso, a pure Cinsaut, is fresh and fragrant. The principal wine, le 50/50, referring to the partnership with her husband, is a blend of Syrah, Grenache and Carignan, aged in vat with some spicy cherry fruit. L'O de la Vie, Minervois, is mainly Syrah with some dry, peppery fruit. Another Minervois, Les Fontanilles, a blend of Grenache and Cinsaut, kept in tank, and Syrah and Carignan in barrel, is rounded with elegantly ripe fruit. La Ciaude, from old Carignan, with some Syrah and Grenache is structured, with red fruit and les Carrétals from Carignan, planted in 1909, all aged in wood, has lovely fruit with a streak of tannin. La Grenache 8, Côtes du Brian, is rich and ripe and very *gourmand* and Les Combettes, Marselan, had rich black fruit, but lacked the hallmark elegance of Anne's other wines. The 2008 Fontanilles, from her first vintage, had some subtle, leathery, mature notes, and supple tannins.

Clos du Gravillas

St Jean-de-Minervois 34360
www.closdugravillas.com

I always enjoy visiting Nicole and John Bojanowski in the village of St Jean-de-Minervois, as they are never short of an opinion or two. John is American but has embraced life in the Languedoc, following Nicole in her ambition to make wine, based on limestone and altitude, from Syrah and Cabernet, inspired by the iconic estate of La Grange des Pères. They bought a house in St Jean-de-Minervois in 1999, with initially just 1 hectare of vines, half of it Carignan planted in 1911, and the other half Grenache Blanc. They now have 8 hectares with 15 different varieties, and are planning a new cellar for the 2018 harvest. At the moment everything is rather higgledy-piggledy, with vats of varying sizes to which John has given names, often with a literary association. The largest is called Shakespeare; next in size is Chabal, a ferocious French rugby player, and others include Tolstoy and Hemingway.

John is behind the Carignan Renaissance movement and Nicole makes an exemplary version, Lo Viehl, from the vines planted in 1911. They favour other old varieties. Emmenez-Moi au bout du Terret, a play on the words of a Charles Aznavour song, is, as you might expect, a pure Terret, with firm, stony mineral notes. Their Minervois Blanc l'Inattendu, made from Grenache Blanc and Gris as well as Macabeo, is tight and stony. Sous les Cailloux des Grillons is a blend of Syrah, Cabernet Sauvignon, Carignan, Grenache, Counoise and Mourvèdre. Rendez-vous sur la Lune will be Minervois Cazelles, a blend of Carignan and Syrah, with some rounded fruit. Then there is a range of wines based on Muscat, of which more on page 121. Suffice to say that having saved Carignan, John is now intent on saving Muscat, but meanwhile he is also optimistic about the *cru* of Cazelles, feeling that it has a more homogenous identity than La Livinière. The decree just needs a signature. He is also optimistic about Minervois. It is a young, dynamic appellation, with new, young wine producers, unlike St Chinian which is still dominated by the old families.

LAURE

From Cazelles I drove across the Minervois, along la Minervoise, as the road is called, with splendid views of the Pyrenees in the spring sunshine, to the village Laure-Minervois. The potential *cru* of Laure will include about fifteen to twenty growers around the village, near the dried-up lake of Marseillette, with the identifying and unifying feature of sandstone, which makes for subtle tannins. The original name was les Balcons d'Aude, but that has been dropped in favour of Laure.

Producers

Domaine La Tour Boisée

Laure-Minervois 11800
www.domainelatourboisee.com

Jean-Louis Poudou is genial and welcoming, with a good head of white hair, and his cellar is on the edge of the *circulade* village, which was fortified in the Middle Ages, with four gates. Bousquet means little gate, and the Tour Bousquet stands behind his cellar. Altogether he has 70 hectares of vines, all organic, half in Minervois and half in Coteaux de Peyriac, which he prefers to Pays d'Oc, which he considers to be too big and international, whereas Peyriac reinforces the image of the family estate.

Jean-Louis makes an eclectic range of wines. He is the first member of the family to put wine in bottle; his father-in-law sold in barrel and he showed me a card that advertised the wines of the estate: 'Vins de Minervois, Vins de table pour clientèle bourgeoise'. A white Minervois includes six different varieties, Marsanne, Roussanne, Vermentino, Grenache Blanc, Macabeo and Muscat à Petits Grains. They are all picked together and fermented together in early September. He describes himself as non-interventionist. 'It is the vintage that decides, not us,' and the wine is left on the fine lees until it is bottled in January. The flavours are fresh with herbal notes, white peaches and white blossom. A Minervois rosé is a blend of Grenache Noir and Grenache Gris. Grenache Gris is now allowed in the appellation, but originally when the appellation was created in 1985, no one wanted it because it lowered the alcohol level. There was fresh raspberry fruit and good acidity on the palate. 'I am not making a copy of Provence,' asserted Jean-Louis.

Unusually Jean-Louis still has some Alicante vines, which he blends with Malbec, and a vineyard that was planted in 1905 that contains 23 different varieties, some unknown and others more commonly found in the Minervois. He usually picks everything together about two-thirds of the way through the harvest and the wine is a Vin de France, with a deep colour, some spicy berry fruit, firm tannins and a certain freshness. A Carignan from vines planted mainly in 1955 had some fresh berry fruit and elegant concentration. His red Minervois, Histoire de Famille is mainly Grenache Noir and Syrah, with spicy fruit. More serious *cuvées* include Marielle et Frédérique, named for his daughters, with greater depth of flavour, and Marie-Claude (for his wife), which is a blend of equal parts Syrah, Grenache and Carignan, aged in wood. Our tasting finished with 2005 Minervois Jardin Secret, which had developed beautifully, amply illustrating the ageing potential of good Minervois.

Château la Grave
Badens 11800
www.chateau-la-grave.net

Jean-François Rousquette is Jean-Louis Poudou's nephew, although only two years younger, and they share a keen enthusiasm for the region and its wines. Jean-François's estate is in Badens, in the most southern, and one of the driest, parts of the Minervois. Corbières is just 5 kilometres away, where they have more Carignan and Grenache. He described Corbières as 'more rustic, more animal, with more muscles', while Minervois is 'more elegant with more finesse'. His parents bought the estate in the 1970s, when the vineyards consisted of Aramon, Alicante Bouschet and Carignan. They have kept the old Carignan and replanted the other vineyards, with Merlot and Cabernet for IGP and Syrah and Grenache Noir for Minervois, and unusually they have a high proportion of white wine. There was Macabeo and Grenache Blanc, and they have added Sauvignon and Chardonnay. The Minervois Blanc contains a high proportion of Macabeo which Jean-François described as '*mon cépage chéri*', defending it fervently. His 60-year-old vines are blended with Vermentino and Marsanne to make a wine with fresh acidity and stony fruit. Privilège is a blend of old Macabeo and Grenache Blanc, fermented and aged in wood. The Macabeo makes for good acidity and the wine has a satisfying texture. As for red Minervois, he uses Syrah, Carignan and Grenache for his Minervois Classique, as they are most representative of the appellation. Mourvèdre is at its limit here, and difficult to ripen. However, Privilège including one-third Mourvèdre with Syrah and Grenache Noir, with more powerful fruit and well integrated oak, will be his future *cru* Laure. The local IGP is Haut de Badens, a sub-division of Coteaux de Peyriac, which he uses for Chardonnay, Sauvignon, Marselan, Cabernet Sauvignon and Merlot.

Jean-François's other passion is Cartagène. When the growers took their grape skins to the distillery, they were given pure alcohol in return, as a privilege, and in deciding how to use their alcohol, each family developed its own recipe for Cartagène. It was the very first alcoholic drink that Jean-François touched, and originally was not offered for sale but drunk with friends and family. These days you have to buy the alcohol and the legislation is so complicated that many people have abandoned it, so he fears that the tradition will be lost. The origin of the name comes from the original concept, the addition of one-quarter of spirit to three-quarters of wine; it has nothing to do with the town in Spain. The older it is, the better it is, so he has a solera system entailing the addition of this year's wine to last year's and it will continue to improve in bottle. I thought it was utterly delicious; sweet and rich with a subtle kick of alcohol.

Domaine Pierre Cros

Badens 11800

dom-pierre-cros@wanadoo.fr; www.vinparleur.net/-Pierre-Cros-58-

Pierre Cros is based in the village of Badens, with 27 hectares planted with the five Minervois varieties, as well as Nebbiolo, Pinot Noir, Touriga Nacional, Alicante, Aramon, Piquepoul Noir, Ribeyrenc, Morastel, Petit Verdot and Cabernet Sauvignon. For white wine, he has Vermentino, Grenache Gris and Blanc and Piquepoul Blanc, from which he makes eleven or twelve different wines each year. Some of the vines date back to the 1920s and 1930s. As he laughingly admitted, 'I am always trying something new.' He made his first wine in 1978, for sale *en vrac*, and bottled his first wine in 1987. His vineyards are organic, but without any mention on the label, and his cellar is equipped with lots of small concrete vats and Burgundy barrels. He is not convinced by larger barrels.

As you might imagine, tasting with Pierre is a roller-coaster of flavours, and enormous fun, with pertinent observations sprinkled with humour. His rosé Partouse is a blend of Aramon, Picpoul, Morastel, Ribeyrenc, Cinsaut and Grenache, the grape varieties that can cope with a lack of water – '*les anciens* weren't stupid' – and as most of those varieties were not included in the appellation, Pierre developed his *cuvée* Les Mal Aimés from the same varieties. It has supple fruit and tannin, with peppery spice and a fresh finish. Pierre believes that there are no bad grape varieties, only bad wine growers, and people did not do anything serious with these varieties because they were so despised. He planted Nebbiolo, defying the administrative challenge, quite simply because he loves Barolo, for its finesse and freshness. I drank his wine once alongside a Barbaresco and it held its own. His Pinot Noir is elegant and fresh. Touriga Nacional, the result of a visit to Portugal, had the characteristic liquorice notes of the variety.

Pierre makes some serious Minervois. Cuvée Tradition, from the five classic varieties kept in concrete and tronconic vats, has ripe spicy fruit. Entre la Vigne et la Mer is a blend of 75 per cent Syrah with Mourvèdre, with ripe fruit and a fresh lift on the finish. A Minervois Vieilles Vignes comes from vines that are at least 100 years old, from Carignan and Grenache Noir *complanté*, with some white vines. Les Aspres is mainly Syrah aged in new wood, and Les Costes is a white Minervois based on Vermentino with some Grenache Blanc, Piquepoul and a drop of Muscat, blended at fermentation, with a nicely rounded palate.

Château St Jacques d'Albas

Laure-Minervois 11800
www.chateaustjacques.com

The purchase of St Jacques d'Albas in 2001 represented a complete career change for Graham Nutter, after a previous life in international finance. About three-quarters of the vineyards were planted with Carignan that was delivered to the local cooperative with an average yield of 130 hectolitres per hectare, so there was much to be done to transform the property. Most of the vineyards have been replanted and the yields of the remaining vineyards reduced to a more serious level of 45 hectolitres per hectare, with strict pruning and efficient trellising. Graham now has 27 hectares in production on a 90-hectare estate that includes the remains of a ruined chapel (just the tower remains). He follows the Cousinié protocol, ascertaining what the soil is lacking, specifically potassium and manganese, and remedying the deficiencies, particularly with the application of mulch and humus. The vines are now organic and better able to withstand drought and resist disease. Since the beginning, Graham has employed a down-to-earth Australian, Richard Osborne, as his winemaker.

Graham makes a very logical range of wines. The rosé, Domaine d'Albas, is half Grenache and half Mourvèdre, with fresh fruit and acidity, from a slow-cool fermentation. He planted Viognier, Roussanne and Vermentino for white wine in 2010, Viognier for the palate, Vermentino for the bouquet and Roussanne for the finish. Vermentino is becoming more popular in the Minervois: 'It is the new Piquepoul and it works well in drier areas,' he says. He also thinks that white wine has a great future in the Minervois and is using stainless steel barrels to retain the freshness. There is no evaporation, and they can last for 25 years; they cost €1,200, as opposed to €600 for an oak barrel that might only be used for three years. The white wine is a Coteaux de Peyriac because Viognier is not allowed in the appellation of Minervois, and it accounts for 60 per cent of the blend, with 10 per cent Roussanne and 30 per cent Vermentino. Domaine d'Albas Rouge is the entry level, from 60 per cent Syrah and 20 per cent each of Grenache Noir and Mourvèdre, aged in vat. Château de St Jacques d'Albas comes from older vines, predominantly Syrah with 12 months' *élevage*, with some Grenache that is kept in vat. It has fresh, peppery fruit with youthful tannins. La Chapelle d'Albas comes from older vines, 55–60 years old, 95 per cent Syrah with a drop of Grenache, with 18 months' *élevage*, making a ripe wine, with black fruit and spice. Graham is very aware of the draw of wine tourism and organizes a series of concerts during the summer months.

MINERVOIS WITHOUT A CRU

Producers

Domaine Terres Georges
Castelnau d'Aude 11700
www.domaineterresgeorges.com

Roland and Anne-Marie Coustal work out of a back street in the village of Castelnau d'Aude, which is one of the most southern villages of the Minervois, with the Corbières village of Escalles just 2 kilometres away. They have taken over Anne-Marie's father's vines, which were originally in the village cooperative, becoming *vignerons independents* and making their first wine in 2001. For Roland, this represents a career change; at the age of 30 he realized that he did not want to spend his days in front of a computer screen. They are the only independent producer of Minervois in the village, and they are deemed to be quite mad, in an area dominated by cooperatives that prefer to concentrate on high yields, instead of Minervois. They have 14 hectares in Castelnau and the neighbouring village of Tourouzelle and explained that, unlike their neighbours, they do not irrigate their vines but do a green harvest and hand-pick. Anne-Marie's father had produced 1,000 hectolitres from 12 hectares; in contrast, they make 600 hectolitres from 14 hectares.

They have Syrah, Grenache Noir, Mourvèdre, and Carignan, and for white wine, Vermentino, Roussanne and a tiny amount of Muscat d'Alexandrie. Their first vintage of white will be in 2019.

They believe fervently in their area, and explained how they perceive the typicity of Castelnau. The soil is predominantly clay, making for freshness and acidity in the wines, and the climate is Mediterranean. They practise *lutte raisonnée*, but are not yet organic. They make four red wines. Et Cetera comes from equal parts of Syrah, Grenache and Carignan, aged in vat, with dry spice and red fruit. Racine is pure Carignan, a Vin de France, with a 30-day *cuvaison*, from 60-year-old vines, with fresh, structured fruit. Caméléon, a Pays d'Oc, is based on Merlot with 30 per cent Syrah, partly aged in wood, with some rounded cassis fruit. Quintessence is 80 per cent Syrah with some Grenache, which spends eight months in oak, with fresh, peppery fruit and a structured palate.

Roland and Anne-Marie talked openly about their initial problems. They depended upon bank loans, which covered floors, vats and a tractor, but not bottles. In 2001 the Languedoc was hit by a viticultural crisis and the price of a litre of wine dropped to 30 euro cents as opposed to 65 cents today. They had thought that they would be able to sell to the *négoce*, but that did not happen. They consequently took the decision to bottle some wine and presented it for the Concours Agricole, where it was well received, as it also was by the *Guide Hachette* and the magazine *Le Point*. It was a heartening example of how good luck can come out of a setback. Roland observed that if people go to a *vigneron artisan*, they want something typically Languedoc, and not a varietal wine. These days there is much more emphasis on the appellation, 'and we have grown up, and matured'. They have learnt from experience and realize they no longer want 'hyper-extraction or *bêtes à concours*, competition winners, but *buvabilité*' and certainly that is what they have achieved with a very convincing range of wines.

Domaine Pierre Fil

Mailhac 11120
www.domaine-pierre-fil.fr

Pierre Fil officially retired in 2007, so I met his son Jérôme, who explained that he is the seventh generation and began working with his father in 2000. They have 28 hectares altogether, mostly around the village of

Mailhac in the southern part of the Minervois, half IGP Pays Cathar and half Minervois. The first bottlings were at the end of the 1980s.

The originality of the estate lies with the predominance of Mourvèdre, with 8 out of 14 hectares planted with that variety. Pierre visited Bandol in the early 1980s and, looking to improve the quality of his own wines, realized that Mourvèdre could work in his part of the Minervois, which is nearest to the sea. Consequently, his Minervois include a higher than average percentage of Mourvèdre. Heledus is 25 per cent each of Mourvèdre, Carignan, Grenache and Syrah, all vinified by carbonic maceration – his father began working with Jean-Henri Dubernet, father of Marc Dubernet and one of the earliest pioneers of technique, back in 1968 – and the wine is rounded and spicy. For Jérôme, in this instance, the Mourvèdre provides spice, Carignan black cherry fruit, Grenache sucrosity and Syrah tapenade. Orebus contains 60 per cent Mourvèdre with 20 per cent each of Grenache and Syrah, with a proportion of barrel ageing. Jérôme points out that carbonic maceration gives powerful tannins, but they are well integrated. Dolium, a reference to a nearby archaeological site, where buried *dolia* or amphorae were found, comprises as much as 60–70 per cent Mourvèdre. The fermentation is finished in barrel, and the wine stays in barrels for 12–18 months, with one-third new wood. The result is rich and powerful, with plenty of ageing potential. Then in 2015 Jérôme made a pure Mourvèdre, M2015, observing that 'Mourvèdre is our house speciality'. The wine is bottled young so that it ages in bottle, a much slower process than ageing in barrel, and it is a Vin de France, as 80 per cent is the maximum percentage of any one variety for the appellation. The wine is structured, ripe and elegantly opulent.

Domaine la Tasque
Mailhac 11120
www.domainelatasque.com

Across the rue Tasque from Jérôme is a fellow Master of Wine, Juliet Bruce-Jones, and her husband, Simon, at Domaine la Tasque. Juliet arrived in the Languedoc in 2004, but did not buy her first vines until 2011. Originally, she had no intention of making wine, but she could not resist a hectare of Syrah just outside the village, and then she was offered the plot of 60-year-old Carignan next door. She initially thought she would send her grapes to the cooperative, but in 2011 she made just

300 bottles, in her garage, and a little more in 2012, and events took over. As an MW, she knows the theory of winemaking, but she had to learn the practical details, not to mention how to drive a tractor. So, in 2014, she and Simon vinified the grapes of 2 hectares and made about 3,000 bottles, with two wines, both Pays d'Aude. A Carignan with 10 per cent Syrah has ripe berry fruit, after a three-and-a-half week *cuvaison*, pressing with a small basket press, and a small percentage spends nine months in barrel. A Syrah with a drop of Carignan, fermented in an open wooden vat, was ripe with good acidity and a rich finish. Juliet is now buying more Carignan vines, and also some Grenache Noir, and would love some white vines. She has made a great start.

MUSCAT DE ST JEAN DE MINERVOIS

It is curious that there is an enclave of Muscat in just one village of the Minervois. No one is really quite sure why. Muscat has been grown there since the eighteenth century and the vineyards were developed between the two world wars, when Muscat fetched a higher price than Minervois. The appellation was created in 1950. These days the demand for Minervois is much greater than for Muscat. The village cooperative, with 150 hectares, has almost given up making sweet wine to concentrate on dry Muscat and there are a handful of wine growers, accounting for about 30 hectares, who make sweet Muscat. However, things may be about to change.

Producers

Clos du Gravillas

We talked earlier to John Bojanowski (page 112). He has set himself a mission: to save Muscat. He describes it as 'a rare pearl, coming from a secret garden; a sleeping beauty'. His wife Nicole talked of how the women in the village of St Jean-de-Minervois believe in Muscat, but they simply do not know how to sell it. Their enthusiasm is irrepressible. John proved his point with three different wines and three completely different interpretations of Muscat. First came Jour du Teuf, the name being a play on words and an example of French slang, from Jacques Tati's film, *Jour de fête*. Fête in French means 'party' but if you say the word in reverse, it creates the word '*Teuf*'. The wine is what John calls a Pét Nat, a naturally *pétillant* wine, made without any sulphur, and chilled to leave enough sugar, 15 grams per litre, for it to start fermenting again. It is bottled with a beer cap at the end of September. By Christmas it is lightly fizzy and by March fully fizzy, and tastes fresh, grapey, and honeyed. Next came an orange wine, À fleur de peau, fermented on the skins for 15 days, with regular *pigeage*. The colour was quite golden, with sweet orange notes on the nose, and an intriguing palate, with dry orange, tannin, acidity and an underlying sweetness. 'Who decided that white wine should be made without its skins, and red wine with its skins?' questioned John. The final wine of the trio was more conventional, a Muscat de St Jean-de-Minervois, with honeyed, grapey flavours, with 125 grams per litre residual sugar and 15% abv. In 2015 John also made a dry wine, and in 2016 a late harvest wine that was still fermenting in June 2017. It would seem that diversity is the way forward.

Domaine Barroubio

St Jean-de-Minervois 34360
www.barroubio.fr

Barroubio is an attractive little hamlet close to the village of St Jean-de-Minervois, with Domaine Barroubio run by Raymond Miquel. The population of the village totals just twelve, including some Miquel cousins and one other family. It dates back to the fifteenth century. Raymond's house bears the date 1632 and his rather cramped cellars have a beam with the date 1740. You feel slightly as though you are in a time warp, but Raymond has kept abreast of modern vinification methods. He explained that there is a distinct difference in the soils for Minervois and Muscat à Petits Grains; there is no Muscat d'Alexandrie here. The vineyards are on a very stony limestone plateau that runs across the *commune*, facing south at an altitude of about 300 metres. The limestone pebbles absorb the heat and reflect it back onto the grapes to ensure that they ripen fully, and the pebbles also retain moisture underneath, ensuring that the vines do not suffer from drought. In contrast, the red grapes for Minervois are planted in clay and limestone soil.

Domaine de Barroubio totals 29 hectares, 18 of Muscat and 11 for Minervois, including some very old Carignan planted between 1903 and 1907. Raymond makes a range of Minervois, with Cuvée Jean Miquel, after his father, from 90 per cent Carignan with some Grenache, with some sturdy fruit, following 15 months of oak ageing. Cuvée Marie-Thérèse, for his mother, is mainly Syrah and Grenache and also aged in oak for 15 months. It is, of course, Muscat that provides the originality of the estate. Raymond was less optimistic about the future of Muscat than John, but none the less produces a very convincing range of wines. Muscat Sec Pays d'Oc is fresh and pithy. The grapes are picked in late August and the vinification is simple, with a cool fermentation and no malolactic fermentation, as that would make the wine too heavy. Le P'tit Dernier is another Pays d'Oc, with some residual sugar balanced by some acidity for easy drinking.

The grapes for Raymond's range of sweet wines are picked later, from the middle of September. Grain d'Automne, Vin de France, is a selection of grapes, picked in late November or early December with a potential abv of 20%, to finish at 14% abv with 70 grams per litre residual sugar. It is elegantly honeyed without being heavy or cloying. Then came a variety of interpretations of Muscat for the appellation. The classic Muscat de St Jean-de-Minervois, in contrast, has 128 grams per litre residual sugar, with an abv of 15.3%. It is gently honeyed and rich, while Cuvée Bleue spends 12 to 15 months on the lees and is more intense, with some rich flavours. Raymond observed that the lees must be kept in suspension as otherwise they can develop undesirable aromas. Cuvée Dieuvaille, named after the chapel in the hamlet, is a late-harvest wine for which Raymond chooses the best plot, never the same each year, with the grapes picked at the end of October. With 12–18 months' *élevage*, the wine is rich, rounded and unctuous, with 140 grams per litre residual sugar and 15% abv. His wines ferment as slowly as possible at about 10–11°C to fix the aromas. He noted that Muscat can be very expressive and then suddenly collapse, and he therefore wants his wines to last. The final wine is Cuvée Nicolas. The grapes are picked in December and whole-bunch fermented like a carbonic maceration. Raymond then stops the fermentation by adding the alcohol and presses the grapes. His other Muscats are *muté sur jus*, rather than *sur grains*, and the fermentation is warmer, with a higher potential of residual sugar. The aim is a wine that will last and the flavour profile was quite different, with orange marmalade and apricots. It was deliciously intense and very original.

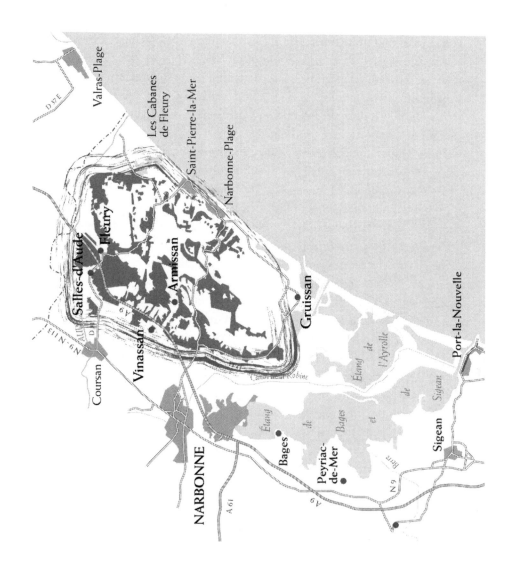

9

LA CLAPE

The Massif of La Clape is a spectacular rocky outcrop rising out of the coastal plain, close to the city of Narbonne, that was actually an island until the river Aude changed its course in the Middle Ages. It is often described as a *montagne vallonnée*, a mountain with several valleys between the hills and rocks, which reaches 214 metres at its highest point at Pech Redon. The road around the mountain is spectacular, as the scenery changes sharply from mountain to sea, with the blue water contrasting vividly with the *garrigue* covered hillsides and the parasol pines. There are vineyards, about 750 hectares altogether, some high up in the hills, and others closer to the sea and the lagoons, but all enjoy a maritime influence to a greater or lesser extent. La Clape may have unfortunate connotations in English, but in Occitan, the derivation is *clapas*, or stones, and the Massif is indeed a rocky, stony, limestone mass.

La Clape was recognized as a VDQS in 1959 and then elected to be part of the Coteaux du Languedoc, rather than Corbières, with the exception of the village of Gruissan, which is illogically in Corbières. However, that is about to change, and La Clape became an appellation in its own right, for white and red wine, in 2015. Any rosé is AOP Languedoc. The grape varieties for red and rosé are the usual Languedoc quintet, but Mourvèdre is more important here than in other regions, thanks to the proximity to the sea. In many respects, although it only represents a small part of the appellation, the white wine is more original. The main grape variety is Bourboulenc, otherwise known as Malvoisie, but not related to any other Malvoisie or Malvasia. It may be blended with Grenache Blanc, Marsanne, Roussanne, Vermentino, Clairette, Macabeo, Piquepoul, and also Viognier, but only in tiny amounts, as it must not dominate the blend. Bourboulenc is a late-ripening grape, which resists drought well and provides wines with structure and texture, and also some ageing potential. The reputation of white La Clape was already established in the 1980s, by Jean Ségura from the former estate of Domaine la Rivière-Haute, which today is part of Château d'Anglès. I remember a 1986 that was rich and rounded, with flavours of nuts and honey, and all without any oak. It was quite unlike any other white wine from the Languedoc at the time. Pure Bourboulenc is not allowed in the appellation, and to my knowledge there is only one example of it as a pure varietal – from Christophe Barbier at Domaine de Simonet in the village of Fleury d'Aude as an IGP Cotes de Pérignan – and delicious it is too.

Producers

Domaine Pech Redon

Narbonne 11100
www.pech-redon.com

The Bousquet family bought this estate in 1988 from Jean Demolombes, one of the early pioneers of the Languedoc, who experimented with *élevage* in wood in the early 1980s and, as a *négociant* in Narbonne, was a talented blender. Meanwhile Christophe Bousquet had studied oenology, but his family vines were committed to the cooperative at St Saturnin. They were sold to purchase Domaine Pech Redon, inspired by the reputation of Jean Demolombes, as well as Jean Ségura at Château la Rivière-Haute and the Chameyrac family at Château Mire l'Etang.

You immediately sense that Christophe is a very thoughtful winemaker and as president of the appellation he cares passionately about La Clape and its future. Tasting with him is an immensely rewarding experience for the wealth of insights he gives you about his wines and his region. L'Epervier Blanc, 'sparrowhawk', is a blend of 60 per cent Grenache Blanc and 40 per cent Bourboulenc, aged in vat on its lees, but without any lees stirring, as Grenache Blanc has sufficient weight not to need it. La Centaurée, a local flower, the star thistle, is a blend of 80 per cent Bourboulenc, fermented in 500-litre barrels, with 20 per cent Grenache Blanc, given 12 months' *élevage*. Christophe observed how the conditions in his vineyards are quite different from those at sea level, with much cooler nights, so that he finds freshness, salinity and minerality. Bourboulenc is interesting for its mouthfeel, with its thick skins providing a texture that other white varieties do not have.

Les Cades is a simple Languedoc, a blend of young Syrah and old Cinsaut vines, with the aim of fruit and drinkability, and that is just what Christophe has achieved, with a peppery note that is typical of Pech Redon. When he arrived at La Clape, Grenache Noir was an important variety, but these days Syrah is dominant. L'Epervier red is a blend of 60 per cent Syrah, from 25-hectolitre *foudres*, and 40 per cent Grenache Noir, kept in vat. Christophe uses concrete vats for the fermentation and pointed out that he was one of the first to use *barriques* for La Clape. He has gradually increased the size of his barrels, 300, 400, 500 litres, and now finds that 25-hectolitre *foudres* are best of all. His wines spend two winters in barrel before bottling. Christophe wants freshness in this wine, and that is what I found, with appealing fresh fruit and wild *garrigue* notes. L'Epervier ages well, as illustrated by a comparison of 2011 and 2012, and also the 2006, with some red spice and a youthful tannic streak. The style was different, stemming from the *élevage* in barrel rather than *foudres*. Christophe remembered that Jean Demolombes had called the estate a real *terroir* for ageing, and observed that his own winemaking has changed, with a move away from extraction to lighter, more elegant wines.

L'Éperon, 'spur', named after the plot, which is in the shape of a spur, is a pure Carignan Vin de France, from 60-year-old vines. Again, Christophe looked for fresh rather than powerful tannins and without any oak *élevage* the wine has some lovely fresh fruit, and a crunchy character. I thought it was delicious. La Centaurée is mainly Mourvèdre, with some Grenache and Syrah, given 30 months' *élevage* in 500-litre barrels. The three varieties are all fermented together in cement vats, with the Syrah picked first, then the Grenache, and then the Mourvèdre, over about a week. The Syrah is kept cool, so that the fermentation does not start before the other varieties are added, and the flavours are very satisfying, combining structure and power, with tamed tannins and elegance. Lithos is only made in the good Syrah years, for the blend is 85 per cent Syrah with Grenache Noir, aged in vat rather than barrel, to make for some youthful, firm, peppery fruit, with a profile more characteristic of the northern Rhône than the Languedoc.

Finally came les Genêts, a blend of one part Viognier to two parts Chardonnay, kept in barrel on its lees for six years, without any topping up. I wasn't quite sure what to expect. Christophe said it was for people who like very sweet, *liquoreux* wines but who do not like sugar. It was dry and nutty, but with an underlying richness as well as some acidity and made a fascinating conclusion.

Château d'Anglès

St Pierre sur Mer 11560
www.chateaudangles.com

This estate has enjoyed a resurgence since the Fabre family arrived from Bordeaux in 2002. Eric Fabre had been the technical director of Château Lafite but he wanted his own estate and chose La Clape because he was particularly interested in the potential for Mourvèdre, seeing similarities with Bandol. Eric has reunited the two estates of Château Rivière Haute and Château Rivière Basse, and called them Anglès after a local landowner, Barthélèmy Etienne d'Anglès, whose family owned both estates for over a hundred years after the French Revolution. Their vineyards are less than 2 kilometres from the sea so there are always some cooling sea breezes. The cellars have been modernized and you can sense a *bordelais* approach, with a Cuvée Classique and a Grand Vin for their red and white wines.

On my last visit, I tasted with Viannay Fabre, who studied oenology in Bordeaux and then worked for Bollinger for five years before joining his father in 2007. Classique is 40 per cent Syrah and Grenache with 20 per cent Mourvèdre, given 18 months' *élevage* in vat. They do an initial blend after the harvest, and a second blend 12 months later. The Grand Vin includes 55 per cent Mourvèdre with 25 per cent Syrah, 20 per cent Grenache and 5 per cent old Carignan, given 12 months' *élevage* in one-year-old Lafite barrels. Viannay enthused about Mourvèdre liking the sea, the limestone, the sun and the wind, which are all the key components of the *terroir* of La Clape.

Classique rosé, AOP Languedoc, comprises 80 per cent Mourvèdre, from young vines as well as 10 per cent each of Syrah and Grenache. The grapes are picked at 6 a.m. when they are cool, and pressed immediately, making for greater freshness. They want a *terroir* rosé with a saline note and some *garrigue* herbs.

Classique Blanc includes 50 per cent Bourboulenc, 30 per cent Grenache Blanc and 10 per cent each of Roussanne and Marsanne.

Viannay described Marsanne and Roussanne as the salt and pepper; Bourboulenc provides freshness and can be quite tannic, while Grenache gives some weight and exotic fruit. The wine is kept on lees for five or six months, and contrasts satisfyingly with the Grand Vin, which comes from Jean Ségura's 80-year-old Bourboulenc vines, with some 60-year-old Grenache Blanc, aged in old barrels. A 2006 showed just how well the Grand Vin will age; at ten years old it was remarkably youthful, with structure and fruit and the benchmark saltiness of the appellation. The flavours evolve, and Viannay allowed himself to enthuse: 'This is a wine that has three or four different stories to tell over dinner'.

Château Rouquette-sur-Mer

Narbonne-Plage 11100
www.chateaurouquette.com

I met Jacques Boscary on my very first visit to La Clape in the mid-1980s, so this is my third book in which he has featured. His is an estate that I always enjoy visiting, most memorably for a *ballade vigneronne*, the annual Sentiers Gourmands, when all the *vignerons* of La Clape get together to provide a wonderful experience of wine, food and walking. Rouquette-sur-Mer totals 360 hectares, including 58 hectares of vines, on the seaward side of La Clape, just outside Narbonne-Plage. There are wonderful views of the coast, from Cadaques to Sète on a clear day, or as Jacques eloquently observed, from Salvador Dali to Georges Brassens. Jacques always suggests a tour of the vineyards, with numerous small plots surrounded by *garrigue*, and with the thirteenth-century ruined château. It was abandoned when the vineyards shifted towards the sandier coastal area, owing to the realization that phylloxera could not survive in sandy soil, and was badly damaged by the Germans during the last war. It is now a picturesque ruin.

Back at the nineteenth-century château, we adjourned to the tasting area. Jacques makes two white wines, Cuvée Arpège and Cuvée Henry Lapierre, from different proportions of Roussanne and Bourboulenc. Arpège sees no wood, while a proportion of Henry Lapierre is fermented and then aged in new wood for six months, with some regular *bâtonnage*. There is an extensive range of red wines, including L'Esprit Terroir, from 30 per cent each of Syrah and Mourvèdre, with 20 per cent each of Grenache and Carignan, all kept in vat, with some black fruit and tapenade. Cuvée

Amarante is the same blend but with some *élevage* in oak. Henry Lapierre is a blend of Syrah and Mourvèdre, aged for 12 months in *demi-muids*. Le Clos de la Tour is from a selection of different plots, with 60 per cent Syrah to 40 per cent Mourvèdre, also aged in *demi-muids* and is rich and intense. L'Absolu represents, as the name implies, Jacques' attempt to push the winemaking to the extreme. He makes just 3,000 bottles, from Syrah and Mourvèdre, from a selection of plots. The vines are leaf-plucked to expose the fruit, so that it is as ripe as possible, with the wine aged in *demi-muids*, making for rich, dense, chocolatey flavours. The first vintage, 2007, was still very youthful when it was almost ten years old.

Château Négly
Fleury d'Aude 11560
www.lanegly.com

Chateau Négly is the family property of Jean Paux-Rousset, who has renovated both the vineyards and cellars. Didier Lecreu has made the wine for him since 2007, with Claude Gros as the consultant. As well as 75 vineyards in La Clape, both at Négly, and the adjoining estate of la Boède, they have 10 hectares of land in the Hérault, at St Pargoire, including the iconic 3.5-hectare Clos des Truffiers. However, the grapes are brought to Négly in a refrigerated truck for vinification, so a tasting with Didier includes wines from both areas. La Brise Marine is a refreshing blend of Bourboulenc and Roussanne, picked and chilled for two days, and then pressed early in the morning. It is mainly free-run juice, with selected yeast for a cool fermentation, followed by two or three months on the lees, to develop a fresh saline note from the Bourboulenc, while the Roussanne adds a little more weight. They decide when to pick simply by tasting the grapes, with Didier asserting that Bourboulenc must be ripe. Oppidum, from 30-year-old Chardonnay vines, upsets my prejudice about not liking Languedoc Chardonnay, and La Falaise, from 70 per cent Marsanne as well as Roussanne, grown both in the Hérault and on La Clape is fresh and lightly buttery from 12 months' ageing in *demi-muids*.

For red wines, there is Le Pavilion, an easy-to-drink IGP, from 70 per cent Cinsaut and 30 per cent Syrah, with appealing fruitiness. La Côte includes a high proportion of Carignan, with some Grenache, Mourvèdre and Syrah, with a six-month *élevage* in tronconic vats, and with firm fruit and an aromatic note from the Carignan. La Falaise is 55 per cent Syrah with some Grenache and Mourvèdre, with some rounded spice and a firm tannic streak, and Les Grès is a blend of 60 per cent Syrah and 40 per cent Grenache, grown on sandstone. The range is completed by what they call three treasures, namely L'Ancely, from 80 per cent Mourvèdre and 20 per cent Syrah, aged in 15-hectolitre barrels; la Porte du Ciel, from Syrah with a drop of Grenache; and then one of the most expensive wines of the Languedoc, Clos des Truffiers, from Syrah with some Grenache Noir. The flavour is dense and concentrated. Monsieur Rousset's father planted Clos des Truffiers in 1963, and for 30 years the Syrah went into the cooperative vat at St Pargoire. It is yet another sign of the changes in the Languedoc.

Domaine Sarrat de Goundy

Armissan 11110
www.sarratdegoundy.fr

Olivier Calix at Domaine Sarrat de Goundy is an example of the new generation of wine producers in the Languedoc. He studied history of art and museum studies, and worked at the Guggenheim in Bilbao and then at a museum of contemporary art in Barcelona. Meanwhile his parents were cooperative members, selling their grapes to the Vignerons du Val d'Orbieu and, as Olivier put it, they were very good *viticulteurs* but did not know how to make wine. He came back to the family property in 2000 and bottled his first wine in 2003, having done some basic wine studies, and has since learnt on the job. He has an enquiring mind and you sense that he is really enjoying his new situation, finding it a rewarding challenge.

Sarrat means summit in Occitan and the vineyards are on a long plateau between two valleys, in the hills above St Pierre, near Camplazens, at an altitude of 190 metres. It was certainly not practical to build a cellar there, so Sarrat de Goundy's cellars are conveniently situated next to a roundabout outside the village of Armissan. There is a welcoming tasting vault, or *caveau*, and shop as well as a restaurant, La Table de la Vigneronne.

Le Marin Blanc is a blend of 70 per cent Bourboulenc, with some Grenache Blanc, Macabeo and a little Viognier, aged on the lees for six months with regular *bâtonnage* to give a rounded palate with a mineral finish, while the Viognier adds a peachy hint. Part of the Bourboulenc is picked later, when it is very ripe and the berries almost orange, which adds extra complexity.

Cuvée du Planteur is named for Olivier's father, who was indeed a great planter of vines, with the tool for making holes in the soil for the vine portrayed on the label. It is a blend of 50 per cent Bourboulenc with Grenache Blanc and some Roussanne, fermented and aged in wood for nine months, and comes from slightly riper grapes to make a wine that is firmer and more structured, with ageing potential. To complete the white range there is a Vin de France, a blend of Grenache Blanc and Viognier vinified in wood, with an *élevage* in vat, combining oak and peachiness on the palate, balanced with good acidity.

Le Moulin Rouge is a blend of Syrah and Grenache with some Carignan and Mourvèdre, from younger vines and aged in vat, with some fruity spiciness. La Cuvée Planteur from young vines of Syrah with some Grenache and Mourvèdre is more substantial, with 12 months' ageing in wood, but not new barrels. Combe des Louvres, meaning a valley of she wolves, comes from the oldest vines, 50-year-old Mourvèdre, as well as some Syrah, Carignan and Grenache, planted by Olivier's grandfather, aged in wood for 14 months. The Syrah and Mourvèdre give elegance balanced with power and structure.

The final wine, Cuvée Sans Titre No 6, a pure Mourvèdre, aged in terracotta *jarres* or amphorae for nine months, was very appealing, with its spicy nose and combination of elegance and richness. The taste somehow seemed even more powerful than the preceding wine, with Olivier explaining that some evaporation had concentrated the flavour. He talked about working with *jarres*, which he obtains from Castelnaudary. They are difficult to clean because you must avoid any bacterial contamination, but give some fascinating results. There is more evaporation than with a barrel so they provide some oxygenation, but without any oak impact. Next, he would like to try Bourboulenc in a *jarre*.

Mas du Soleilla

Narbonne 11100
www.mas-du-soleilla.fr

Peter Wildbolz is a qualified oenologist. He trained in Bordeaux and ran the Staatskellerei outside Zurich before he and his wife Christa looked for pastures new. After managing another La Clape estate, Château Laquirou, for four years, he decided to buy his own vines in the area. He realized that if you buy an estate, you are also buying its history, and so he looked for vines and found the 8-hectare plot of Clos de l'Amandier, in the heart of the Massif of La Clape. However he could not build a cellar there and needed somewhere to live. At the time, Jacques Ribourel was selling Domaine Ribourel, two-thirds of which became Château l'Hospitalet, while Peter bought the other third to create Mas du Soleilla. His first vintage was 2002. He talked of a voyage of discovery as he had no expectations; he needed to observe and every year has been different. The climate is increasingly unstable and unpredictable, and the weather forecast is never right. Rainfall is decreasing. There used to be much more water on La Clape; the Romans called it an island of lakes, but the old river beds are now dry. However, Peter is philosophical: 'We are in a relationship with nature, which has mind of its own.' His vineyards have been organic since 2008 and now he is working biodynamically, resulting in a more intimate relationship with his surroundings. He would not be averse to some irrigation – observing that Jacques Boscary, as president of the *cru*, says we should live with the *terroir*, 'but we also have to survive and increasingly smaller yields become uneconomical'.

Peter Wildbolz, Mas du Soleilla

Our tasting began with les Chailles, the name of the plot, meaning silex or flint. The wine is mainly from 40-year-old Grenache vines, with some Syrah, and with an *élevage* in vat. There is spice, elegant concentration and a warm finish. Peter is looking to make lighter wines, but the climate of La Clape does not always allow that. Les Ammonites, after the ammonites found in the vineyard, comes from vat-aged Grenache Noir and barrel-aged Syrah, with some juicy fruit and elegant spice. Peter has a range of what he calls Cuvées Ephémères, named by lot number, when a wine is particularly good. We were able to taste Z11, some Grenache Noir that was picked a little early so that it was fresh and elegant, with flavours of ripe kirsch. Les Bartelles is mainly Syrah aged in larger oak, with 20 per cent Grenache Noir, with firmer fruit than the Grenache-based wines, and more tannin and concentration. Clos de l'Amandier is mainly Syrah, aged in new wood, with a balance of fruit and tannins, and elegant concentration on the finish. Our tasting finished with his white wine, from 70 per cent Bourboulenc and 30 per cent Roussanne, half fermented in tank and half in barrel. It has a rich nose and intriguing herbal notes, with layers of flavour, but for my taste buds is slightly atypical because the oak masks the usual salinity of La Clape.

Château l'Hospitalet

Narbonne 11100
www.gerard-bertrand.com

It is difficult to know where to fit Gérard Bertrand into the Languedoc, as his wines feature in so many different appellations. However, Château l'Hospitalet is his flagship estate, even if the original family estate was Domaine de Villemajou in the Corbières, which I first visited with Gérard's father, Georges, in the mid-1980s. That is where Gérard participated in his first harvest at the age of ten. He bought L'Hospitalet in 2002 and has gradually developed the property. There are three levels of red La Clape: Classique, Grand Vin and a single plot, Hospitalitas. A welcoming visitor centre has one of the smartest wine shops I have seen in the Languedoc, as well as an elegant restaurant and a small hotel. Further purchases have followed, Domaine de l'Aigle in Limoux, Domaine de Cigalus for IGP Aude Hauterive, Domaine de Sauvageonne in the Terrasses du Larzac, Domaine de la Soujeole in the Malepère, Domaine Aigues-Vives and Domaine le Viala in the Minervois and, most recently, two estates in Cabrières, Domaine du Temple and Domaine des Deux Rocs. Altogether Gérard owns 750 hectares, in 14 estates, which will all be farmed biodynamically by 2020. There is a *cuvée* Bee Friendly, entailing beehives in the vineyards and considerable care about the use of anything that might disturb the bees. Another *cuvée* is Prima Nature, a wine made without the use of any sulphur. Cap Insula is an ecological cellar, on the outskirts of Narbonne, for their *négociant* activity.

My most recent tasting included a selection of rosés from the simplest Gris Blanc, to Prima Nature Grenache and then Grand Vin rosé from Domaine de la Soujeole in the Malepère, of which a percentage spends six months in oak, supporting the idea that rosé can age. The final wine was Château la Sauvageonne, la Villa, a blend of Grenache Noir and Mourvèdre, with a tiny proportion of white grapes, Vermentino and Viognier, with six months in wood, so that it is nicely structured and quite atypical.

Château de Villemajou Grand Vin Corbières Blanc illustrates how well white wine is developing in the Languedoc. It is a blend of Marsanne, Roussanne and Vermentino, fermented in wood, with some nicely integrated oak on the palate. Château l'Hospitalet Grand Vin La Clape Blanc is a blend of Bourboulenc, Roussanne, Vermentino, and Viognier, fermented and aged in oak. It is well made and nicely textured but lacks the salty notes that I look for in white La Clape. There was an elegant Chardonnay from Limoux, with some leesy notes. As for red wines, Cigalus, IGP Hauterive, followed because the blend includes *bordelais* varieties, planted by the previous owner, as well as Mediterranean varieties. It is quite sturdy with dry spice and cassis. A Pinot Noir from Domaine de l'Aigle, Haute Vallée de l'Aude, was fresh with raspberry fruit. L'Hospitalitas, the single vineyard from Château de l'Hospitalet, is warm, spicy and intense, with Syrah and Mourvèdre. Le Viala, Minervois La Livinière, provides an immediate contrast, as it is cooler than La Clape, giving a different expression of Syrah, with more elegant, spicy fruit. La Forge, Corbières Boutenac, is a blend of Carignan and Syrah, with Gérard working on selections of Carignan. This has dry spice on the palate, with freshness on the finish.

Clos d'Ora is a recent addition to the range, a blend of Grenache Noir, Syrah, Mourvèdre and Carignan grown in a 9-hectare plot within Minervois La Livinière. Attention to detail is meticulous, with diligent work in the cellar and barrel ageing for 12 months. The taste is impressive, with ripe tapenade, rich oak and supple tannins, making a serious wine, with with balance, polish and considerable aspirations.

However to my taste buds it does not have the sense of place of some of Gérard's other wines. Clos d'Ora is currently the most expensive wine in the Languedoc and Gérard is adamant, that 'we must not be afraid of selling at a higher price'. It comes from a micro-*terroir* that happens to be Minervois, but that is not the point. 'What is the appellation of Grange, the iconic Australian wine created by Penfolds' legendary winemaker Max Schubert?' There is no doubt that the Languedoc needs people like Gérard Bertrand, who have a thoughtful approach combined with dynamic energy and a broader vision of the place of the Languedoc in the world of wine.

10

QUATOURZE

Quatourze is the westernmost *terroir* of the former Coteaux du Languedoc with vineyards almost touching the suburbs of Narbonne. It is a compact area, limited by Narbonne in the west, the étang de Bages in the south and protected from the sea on the eastern side by the Massif de La Clape. The vineyards are on a plateau that rises just 17 metres above sea level. The soil is stony with clay and *galets roulées*, like those of Châteauneuf-du-Pape, for the vineyards are on what was the old delta of the Aude, before it changed its course. Consequently, the *terroir* is quite different from nearby Corbières or La Clape. This is one of the driest parts of the Languedoc, lying in a corridor between the Pyrenees and the Massif Central, with an average rainfall of about 450 millimetres a year.

There are two theories about the origin of the name Quatourze, both based on the fact that the word means fourteen in Occitan. With such low rainfall, the wine here can be strong and alcoholic, often reaching a natural 14% abv. An alternative story says that during the Middle Ages, most of the land belonged to the Bishop of Narbonne, and would normally be taxed at one-tenth of its revenue, but as the land was so poor and arid, the bishop only took a fourteenth.

Producer

Château Notre Dame du Quatourze

Narbonne 11100
www.ortola.fr

I first visited Quatourze in the mid-1980s, when Yves Ortola at Château Notre Dame du Quatourze was the mainstay of the appellation. He was a fourth generation Algerian who bought an abandoned property in 1965, and developed the vineyards extensively. On my next visit, I met his son Georges, an energetic man who was busy defending the position of Quatourze, fighting against the urban sprawl of Narbonne and hoping that other wine producers would join him. These days he is now more concerned with ecological packaging and it is his son, Nelson, who is now responsible for the estate, or rather three estates; the family's vineyard holdings have grown, to include Château de Lunes and Château Tapie, as well as a recent purchase of Château Ymys, totalling about 100 hectares. The only other Quatourze producer is the cooperative of Narbonne.

Nelson shares his father's energy and is highly articulate. He took us for a drive through the vineyards on a rather hot afternoon, with his sheep dog, Darwin. You do feel wonderfully isolated from the city. We admired the *galets roulées* and Nelson explained that they have farmed organically for about ten years and are now working biodynamically. 'The soil must be alive; it is the basis of our work.' Sheep graze in the vineyards during the winter. Mildew is not a problem, with the ferocious tramontane wind. The massif of La Clape blocks any sea breezes so the vineyards are in a corridor of wind, with very little humidity. They also irrigate the vines, with Nelson pointing out that they want the grapes to ripen properly and not just produce alcohol.

Poignantly, Nelson showed us the statue of the virgin that his grandfather had brought with him from his village in Algeria. When he was looking for an estate, the name Notre Dame du Quatourze seemed like destiny, and there were also olive trees, which he loved. The cellars are large and functional, with concrete vats of varying sizes, and a barrel cellar. We tasted a selection of wines, starting with a white from Vermentino with a little Viognier and Grenache Blanc, which was fresh and rounded. They have also planted some Roussanne and make Sauvignon Blanc and Chardonnay for IGP. The rosé is fresh and light, from Syrah, Grenache and Cinsaut. Their Quatourze, which is red only, comes from blends of Syrah, Grenache and small amounts of Carignan and Mourvèdre, with three different *cuvées*, Tradition, Nautica, with a small percentage of oak ageing, and Black Reserve, all aged in oak, and riper and more intense. The differences depend on the selection of vineyards, with a variation in the age of the vines. They are working on more plot selection, with greater precision in the cellar. Nelson cited an example of the renaissance of Carignan. When Quatourze first became a VDQS in 1951, Carignan was the sole grape variety and subsequently a replanting programme introduced Syrah and Mourvèdre, but now he has just planted a new vineyard of Carignan.

Asked about their typicity, Nelson replied, 'fruit, and wines with tension'. The estate is part of the producers' group Vinadeis, which was formerly Vignerons du Val d'Orbieu, and benefits from the advice on vineyard and cellar work, as well as help with sales. As for the future of Quatourze, it seems that a status quo has been reached. As long as the Ortola family continues to farm their vineyards and make their wine, the name will continue, as a distinctive part of the Languedoc vinous landscape. It would be sad if it were to suffer the fate of other former *terroirs* of the Coteaux du Languedoc, such as Vérargues or even La Méjanelle, that no longer feature on a label.

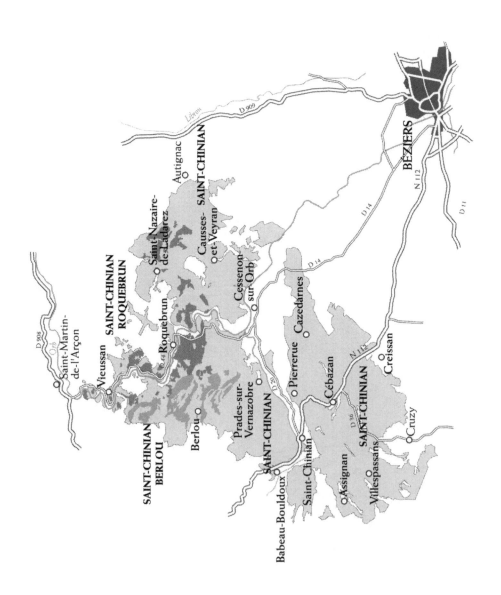

11

ST CHINIAN WITH ROQUEBRUN AND BERLOU

St Chinian is an attractive little town nestling in the valley of the Vernazobre. There is a large square, lined with tall plane trees, providing refreshing shade in the midday sun. Sunday is market day, when it is nicely animated and filled with colourful stalls. In one corner, you will find the Maison du Vin, which provides a welcoming shopfront to the appellation. Here you can buy and taste wines from virtually all the producers of the appellation, with some expert guidance. Once a year, at the end of July, St Chinian hosts a *fête du vin* and the square becomes even more lively, with stands for the wine producers mixed with the regular market stalls, and tasters and shoppers jostling in the crowd.

The appellation of St Chinian was recognized for red and rosé in 1982, two years before Coteaux du Languedoc, and then incorporated into that appellation, but it has always stood alone, in that there was no requirement to mention Coteaux du Languedoc, or Languedoc, on the label. It includes 20 villages and hamlets, of which Berlou and Roquebrun were recognized as *crus* in 2005. A white appellation also followed in 2004. The vineyards, about 3,000 hectares, lie in the foothills of the Cévennes, and are divided in two by the river Vernazobre, with quite different soils on either bank. To the north and west, the soil is based on schist and includes St Chinian itself, as well as Berlou and Roquebrun, while the southern part of the appellation is a mixture of limestone and clay. Consequently, perceived wisdom states that you could detect two different styles of St Chinian. In theory, the wine from schist is lightly fruity and supple, with flavours of the *garrigue*, ripe fruit and liquorice, and destined for relatively early drinking, while the wines from clay and limestone are more substantial, with more marked tannins, and benefit from longer ageing. In reality, it is not as simple as that. Cyril Bourgne from Domaine la Madura would argue that the *terroir* is much more complicated, and much depends on the individual wine producer's methods and practices.

There are several long-established estates in and around St Chinian, such as Clos Bagatelle, which has been in the hands of the same family since 1623 and today is run by a brother and sister team, Luc and Christine Simon. Château Coujan outside Murviel-les-Béziers, was where François Guy was one of the pioneers of the Midi in the 1980s. Château La Dournie, just on the outskirts of the town of St Chinian, with its beautiful park with mature trees, has belonged to the Etienne family for six generations. Château Viranel outside Cessenon claims a winemaking history that goes back to 1551 and the Jougla family at Domaine des Jougla in Prades-sur-Vernazobre can trace their family back to at least 1595. All of these featured in an earlier book, so I have preferred to focus on some of the newer producers in the appellation.

ROQUEBRUN

Roquebrun is a pretty village perched above the Orb river, with a botanical garden, and a ruined castle dominating the skyline. There is a friendly restaurant, the Cave St Martin, which describes itself as an *épicerie, bar à vin nature*, and in the summer you can eat on the terrace looking over the Orb.

Wine production in Roquebrun is dominated by its cooperative, which was founded as recently as 1967, and works well for the village. However, in contrast with Berlou, it seems that the individual producers of the village, such as Thierry Navarre, Mas d'Albo, Domaine Boissezon-Guiraud and Domaine Marquise des Mûres, prefer not to make Roquebrun and take a more independent approach to their labelling.

Producers

Domaine Thierry Navarre

Roquebrun 34460

www.thierrynavarre.com

Thierry Navarre has his cellar just at the entrance to the village before the bridge over the Orb. He is a great enthusiast of the old forgotten grape varieties of the Languedoc, like Ribeyrenc Noir and Blanc, and even Gris, which disappeared after phylloxera. Tasting with him shows just why the Languedoc should reconsider the potential of these old varieties and incorporate them into the appellations. Instead they are humble Vin de France. Thierry feels very strongly that the diversity of the Languedoc has been considerably reduced, with a serious impact on agriculture and the environment.

Thierry Navarre

His family were never members of the cooperative. His grandfather bottled wine in the 1960s, and sold Muscat and Grenache Noir, *vin doux*, but with no added alcohol, as did most small *vignerons* at the time. That was very much the tradition of the region, and Thierry feels it is a shame that the appellation does not remember this old tradition for Grenache and Muscat. His grandfather also produced Vin Rouge, Carignan des Coteaux, which was initially sold *en vrac* before he began to bottle it. He also made white wine from Servant, which can also be a table grape. Thierry's first vintage was 1988. He is dismissive of the *cru* of Roquebrun – 'that is for competitions' – and the cooperative does perform particularly well in competitions, concentrating on Syrah – 'which is a stupidity; it comes out like Indian ink'. The challenge is to produce fresh wine in a hot climate and that is what he does. All Thierry's back labels say 'Tchin tchin' (or cheers!), demonstrating an engaging sense of humour.

Lignières Blanc is a blend of Ribeyrenc Blanc, Clairette and Grenache Gris, which he considers to be very much better than Grenache Blanc, which tends to be rather flat. The wine has a floral nose and some mineral notes with fresh acidity on the palate. He obtained the Ribeyrenc vines from the INRA; you cannot buy them from a nursery. 'I wouldn't plant Chardonnay,' Thierry says. He feels that the *vignerons* 'are ashamed of their region' and that is why they plant international varieties rather than the old indigenous vines of the region. The vineyards of the Languedoc once comprised one-third Ribeyrenc, one-third Oeillade and one-third Piquepoul. Carignan and Grenache Noir arrived from Spain in the nineteenth century and were planted after phylloxera.

Terret Gris is fermented on the skins, making it an orange wine, with original flavours of orange and honey, and with good acidity and texture. Oeillade has the advantage of being ripe at 11.5% abv, so that his Vin d'Oeillade has some lovely fresh fruit.

His Ribeyrenc Rouge is equally low in alcohol, at 11.5% abv, with some appealing fresh cherry flavours. As far as I know, there are only four *vignerons* with Ribeyrenc in the whole of the Languedoc, namely Patricia Domergue at Clos Centeilles, François Henry and Damien Coste in St Georges d'Orques and Thierry, who has just 1.75 hectares as well as 2 hectares of Oeillade. He described Ribeyrenc as his baby. It must be grown up in the hills, never on the plain. Thierry has also planted some Piquepoul Noir; apparently there is a *lieu-dit* in Roquebrun called Piquepoul.

Next came a couple of St Chinian. Le Laouzil, meaning schist in Occitan, is a blend of Carignan, Grenache Noir and Syrah, with spicy fruit. Cuvée Olivier, St Chinian, comes from his oldest vines: 30-year-old Syrah and 80-year-old Carignan, and Grenache Noir, with ripe, supple fruit.

Thierry's other project is a vineyard of just 1.3 hectares, of Syrah, Merlot and Cabernet Sauvignon, planted by friends up in the hills at

600 metres, at the highest point of the *commune* of Roquebrun. The vineyard is surrounded by woods, with a three-week delay in ripening in comparison to the lower vineyards of Roquebrun and the soil is clay rather than schist. The wine is called La Conque after the *lieu-dit* and represents a complete change of register in the taste spectrum, with elegant cassis fruit and tannin. An old farmhouse nearby serves as an ageing cellar, as it is so much cooler up in the hills.

The finale to our tasting was a Vin de Grenache, for which the fermentation is stopped by chilling after about five or six days of maceration. Aged in barrel, the wine has flavours of figs and dried fruit.

Domaine la Lauzeta
St Nazaire de Ladarez 34490
www.domainelalauzeta.com

For my compatriot Tom Hills, Domaine la Lauzeta represents a complete career change. When we met in September 2017, Tom had just completed his third harvest, having arrived in the village of St Nazaire de Ladarez in May 2015. He has had a varied career, including a degree in Russian, teaching in St Petersburg, banking in London and sugar trading in South America. Then he decided he wanted to do something with wine. A chance meeting with Adam Deakin, who specializes in vineyard sales, introduced Tom to the Languedoc so he came to explore and saw its enormous potential. You are free to experiment here and he tasted wines new to him that he really enjoyed. He also liked the idea of starting from scratch, citing La Pèira in the Terrasses du Larzac as an example to follow. The name of his estate comes from a song from the twelfth century troubadour Bernart de Ventadorn, *Can vei la lauzeta*, or when the skylark sings.

The schist in St Chinian attracted Tom and, with the help of the SAFER, the organization that controls vineyard purchases, he found a 23-hectare property, with 20 hectares in one block, close to the appellation of Faugères. He vinifies 7 to 8 hectares while the rest go to the Roquebrun cooperative. Tom took us to see his vineyards on the one grey day of September. The main block is at an altitude of 200–320 metres, on schist, facing mainly east or north-east. The vines were in good condition when Tom took over, with 10- to 35-year-old Syrah and 30- to 55-year-old Grenache. There is also old Carignan and a bit of Cinsaut, but no Mourvèdre, and for the moment no white varieties.

Back at the cellar in the village, we tasted Tom's first vintage, which he had recently bottled. First was a rosé, Jauzimen, a blend of 45 per cent Cinsaut, 40 per cent Grenache and 15 per cent Syrah, with a pale colour and fresh fruit. Then came Mezura, a blend of 70 per cent Syrah with Carignan; half the Syrah goes into new oak, accounting for 40 per cent of the blend, and the wine is fresh and peppery, and already quite approachable, with a hint of oak and some tannin and black fruit. La Lauzeta is a blend of 60 per cent Grenache with 40 per cent Syrah. All the Syrah goes into *demi-muids* while the Grenache is kept in stainless steel tanks, making for some ripe cherry spice with nicely integrated oak. Tom follows the advice of his oenologist, Claude Gros, paying great attention to detail and favouring gentle extractions. As he says, he is learning winemaking by doing it and his first vintage promises well for the future.

Domaine Lanye Barrac
Ceps 34460
www.lanye-barrac.plugwine.com

From St Nazaire, we took the scenic route to Ceps, up the Orb valley, to meet Mélanie and Bernhard Backhaus of Domaine Lanye Barrac. The cellar under their house in the heart of the pretty little village makes a snug vaulted tasting *caveau*, where we sat and chatted. Although he was born of German parents, Bernhard was brought up in France, on Corsica and in the Dordogne. After a successful career as a sommelier the time came for a change because the lifestyle is not compatible with family life. After studies in Montpellier, he looked for vineyards. Corsica was not an option; people tend to keep their vines, and unplanted land is too expensive. Also, it would have taken too long to start from scratch, planting vines and building a cellar, and so he looked in the Minervois, St Chinian and Faugères and found one large plot of 25 hectares, on slopes facing south and south east, with 18.5 hectares of vines, mostly within the *cru* of Roquebrun. On the other land he has cows, donkeys and pigs. He made his first wine in 2014, from just three hectares; the rest are with the cooperative of Cessenon, and he is gradually increasing his holding, so that in 2017 he vinified 12 hectares. The *lieu-dit* of his vineyards is called Barrac but that sounded rather harsh, so they have added Lanye, Mélanie's nickname.

Bernhard is particularly enthusiastic about schist: 'I adore schist; it is our signature' and so, appropriately, his first St Chinian is called Eclats de Schists, from Grenache Noir, with 30 per cent Syrah and 10 per cent Carignan, from free-run juice and intended for early drinking. It was fresh with some ripe black fruit and a streak of tannin. Le Rabidote is the name of another *lieu-dit* where the animals are and they all feature on the label, as they contribute to the wine. Apparently, donkeys are brilliant at pre-pruning as they eat the long tendrils of vine shoots, stopping at the point where the wood becomes too hard, making the job of pruning much simpler. They also provide excellent organic manure – or, as the back label puts it, 'our animals graze, pre-prune and work our land'. La Rabidote is a blend of 60 per cent Syrah with 30 per cent Mourvèdre and 5 per cent each of Carignan and Grenache, given 18 months in oak.

L'Infini is a pure Carignan, Pays de l'Hérault; 'our favourite variety', enthused Bernhard. They have 4 hectares of old vines, planted between 1910 and 1942, on south-facing slopes of schist. Bernhard selects the best small plots for this wine, which enjoys a long semi-carbonic maceration. He does not add any extra carbon dioxide and the weight of the grapes gradually liberates the juice, so that he only uses the free-run juice. The flavours are redolent of fresh red fruit, with an elegant finish. You sense that Bernhard has an enquiring mind and he promises what he called an outsider – a new *cuvée*, an experiment – each year. For 2016 it was les Bellandes, a blend of Grenache Noir, vinified as a white wine, with some Muscat, with just 8 grams per litre residual sugar, making for a rounded, fruity wine. He made his first Roquebrun *cuvée* in 2017, mainly from Syrah and Mourvèdre, aiming to give it 24 months in oak, and was also considering a natural wine. Bernhard and Mélanie's enthusiasm promises well for the future.

BERLOU

Berlou is a little village, not really on the way to anywhere, on a narrow road that eventually leads to Vieussan in the Orb valley. You really have to want to go there, and these days there are good reasons to do so. The cooperative of Berlou was one of the pioneers of the appellation, with an energetic president, Georges Dardé, who encouraged his members to plant the *cépages améliorateurs* and work on the quality of their vineyards. It was a pacesetter in the 1980s and largely responsible for the creation of the *cru* at a time when it was virtually the sole producer in the village. Things have changed. From 550 hectares, the co-op now controls 230 hectares, with just twelve members. The current president, Bernard Roger, is optimistic that they are recovering from their financial difficulties and sales are going well. Indeed, they have a smart shop, just as you arrive in the village, and make a sound range of wines, though the Berlou co-op is also criticized for its lack of ambition in comparison to the cooperative of Roquebrun. Their flagship wine, Château des Albières, Cuvée Georges Dardé, is an appropriate recognition of the man who said 'On est condamné à faire de la qualité' which translates roughly as 'We are condemned to make quality'. There is a plaque in his memory on the cooperative's cellar wall.

Producers

Domaine Rimbert
Berlou 34360
www.vinsdomainerimbert.fr

The inadequacies of the cooperative have resulted in the development of some exciting independent estates in Berlou. Jean-Marie Rimbert made his first wine in Berlou in 1996 and was the first new estate in Berlou after the creation of the cooperative in 1965. He arrived in the Languedoc from the Luberon, where there were family vines, working first at Château de Flaugergues outside Montpellier before following a suggestion from Pierre Clavel and looking for vines in Berlou. He liked what he saw, what he called the quality of the silence and the *côté assez sauvage*, the wild side. The vines are on hillsides, at an altitude of 200–250 metres. He now farms 26 hectares, half of which he owns, observing, 'I am from a farming family, *une famille de paysans*, and we like to pass on our land'. However, these days Jean-Marie is concerned about the low yields, the result of the summer heat. In the 20 years he has been in Berlou, 15 have been years of limited rainfall. He is also pessimistic about what he called the '*côté conformist*' of the appellations, with the new generation showing little interest in the appellation itself and concentrating on their own wines, irrespective of the appellation.

Tasting with Jean-Marie is fun. He is highly articulate and tastings are interspersed with pertinent observations. He makes two white wines, identical blends of 40 per cent each of Clairette and Vermentino, and

10 per cent each of Grenache and Roussanne, but one is aged in vat and the other in acacia, with lots of lees. The comparison is fascinating. With acacia, the nose was less pronounced, but the palate more rounded, and slightly nutty, but a different nuttiness than with oak, while the wine in vat, which I preferred, was more herbal with firm, stony mineral notes. Jean-Marie is very involved with the Carignan Renaissance group and makes three different Carignans. One, which he calls Jarrignan, is fermented in vat and aged in amphorae or *jarres* with ripe cherry fruit. Two *jarres* give him just 300 bottles. There is a simple Carignan fermented in vat with natural yeast, making for ripe fruit with a cheerful rustic note. For Carignator the grapes are not destemmed and the wine is kept in old wood, so that the structure is quite different, sturdier with a fresh finish. Les Travers de Marceau, named for his son, is a blend of Syrah, Carignan, Mourvèdre and Cinsaut, with some rounded, supple fruit and a streak of tannin. His St Chinian Berlou is quite supple, but with more body.

Domaine de Cambis
Berlou 34360
www.cambis.fr

Martin Pérolari's parents bought their vineyards in 2002. His father is a dentist turned winemaker and his mother went back to school to study winemaking, and now he is making the wine. He is fun and friendly, with a nice sense of humour. First, he took me to see the building site of their new cellar on a hillside outside the village. The view over the surrounding countryside is stunning and Martin admitted that it had taken five years to get planning permission. Everything will work by gravity, as they have cut into the hillside and have a wall of schist that will help with insulation. The Vallée de Cambis is behind Berlou, going towards the village of Prades. Altogether they have 15 hectares of vines, in 25 plots, including some 80- and 110-year-old Carignan, and they are aiming to be biodynamic in about five to ten years. However, an *intercep*, which makes mechanical weeding between the rows possible, is simply not practical with very old vines, so grass management is a problem.

Barocco Vin de France is a pure Cinsaut, with cherry fruit and a streak of tannin. Martin also makes a pure Carignan, as well as a St Chinian from Carignan, with some Grenache and Syrah, the *coeur de la gamme*, with some spicy fruit after a gentle extraction and *élevage* in vat.

His St Chinian Berlou is mainly Syrah with some Grenache Noir and Carignan, and has spent 12 months in *demi-muids*, so that it is more solid, with greater depth. Calyop is his white wine, from Grenache Blanc, Roussanne and Vermentino, with fresh, herbal fruit. Martin described Berlou as a hidden gem. I am inclined to agree.

Domaine les Terrasses de Gabrielle

Berlou 34360

www.lesterrassesdegabrielle.fr

Olivier and Fabienne Pascal make wine both in Berlou and at Capestang near the Canal du Midi for Pays d'Oc and Pays de l'Hérault. Gabrielle is the name of Olivier's grandmother and also the couple's daughter. We met for what turned out to be a hugely enjoyable and unusual tasting in Fabienne's mother's kitchen in the family house in the centre of Berlou. The family bought vineyards in Berlou in 1993, which they removed from the cooperative in 2008, from which they make two *cuvées* of St Chinian and one of Berlou. Un Jour au Cirque, after the song by Alain Bashung, is a blend of Grenache, Carignan, Syrah and Mourvèdre, with some supple fresh fruit. Et Moi et Moi et Moi, after another song, by Jacques Dutronc this time – my knowledge of French singers soared – is a blend of Syrah and Lledoner Pelut, with 24 months *élevage*, with rounded fruit and a streak of tannin. They are moving towards bigger containers, 500 litres rather than 225. Their Berlou is based on their best plots of Syrah and Mourvèdre, rather than Carignan, with 24 months in *demi-muids*, with some attractive spice and greater depth than the St Chinian.

More unexpected was the range of other varieties that they grow in Capestang, such as Counoise, Sangiovese, Braquet, Altesse and Assyrtiko. The last two were only permitted as recently as November 2016 and have only just been planted. They also wanted Verdelho, but were sent Verdejo, and also some Godello, but that is not yet officially allowed. Although the *cru* of Berlou is only red, they have planted more conventional white varieties, such as Viognier and Roussanne. Their white St Chinian is a blend of Viognier, Grenache Blanc, Roussanne, a little Vermentino and also a drop of Chenin Blanc and Petit Manseng, for extra acidity. It has the refreshing sapidity of the Vermentino with a hint of dry honey. A Roussanne in an acacia barrel was floral and rounded; a rosé de Nielluccio was fresh and structured; Braquet, which you find in Bellet, was fresh and lightly floral. Counoise was ripe and textured; a pure Cinsaut was fragrant with lovely fruit; a Cabernet Franc had some fresh ripe cherry fruit. Fabienne's father had grown Aramon in that vineyard, with a yield of 300 hectolitres per hectare!

Domaine la Grange Léon
Berlou 34360
fernandez.berlou@wanadoo.fr

Joël Fernandez is one of the wine growers who left the cooperative in 2008, even though his grandfather Léon had helped to create it and his father had remained a member. Joël is self-taught, with 12 hectares. He was busy emptying a vat when I arrived at his cellar on the outskirts of Berlou. Our tasting began with a cheerful rosé, followed by a white Pays d'Oc from Viognier and Sauvignon Blanc, an intriguing blend with some peachy fruit, with the Sauvignon restraining the Viognier. Sacré Madeleine, after Léon's wife and his grandmother, is also a Pays d'Oc, a blend of Grenache Blanc, with 20 per cent each of Vermentino and Viognier. Joël never knew his grandmother, but he does have good memories of Léon, who lived to the age of 92.

There is a range of reds. L'Insolent, with a silhouette of the young Léon on the label, from Grenache, Syrah and Carignan, has some fresh peppery fruit. L'Audacieux, which depicts Léon with his fishing rod, is a blend of Mourvèdre and Grenache, with the elegant structure of Mourvèdre. 'J'adore Mourvèdre,' Joël announced. It works well in Berlou, and does not need to see the sea. He does a strict green harvest, leaving just four bunches per vine, so that the grapes ripen well. D'Une Main à l'Autre is a St Chinian Berlou, from Syrah, Carignan and Grenache, which spends nine months in 500-litre barrels, making for rich, supple fruit with a touch of vanilla. L'Infidèle contains a very high percentage of Mourvèdre, and is so-called because Mourvèdre can be very fickle and does not perform well every year. This was smoky and elegant with a long finish, after 24 months in *demi-muids*, making an original glass of wine. For Joël, the typicity of Berlou is the schist, which gives spicy fruit, with Carignan made by carbonic maceration. He may have new *cuvées* in the pipeline, admitting that he likes things that are out of the ordinary.

We adjourned to Le Faitout, the village restaurant, which is well worth the journey, for some local flavours and a wine list that concentrates on the closest appellations.

ST CHINIAN

Producers

Domaine les Païssels
Babeau-Bouldoux
www.paissels.fr

Les Païssels is a new estate in the village of Babeau-Bouldoux. Vivien Roussignol and Marie Toussaint met studying in Montpellier and made their first wine in 2011. A *païssel* is a supporting pole for a bush vine, and they only have bush vines, 7 hectares, all on schist. We went to see them in the early autumn sunshine, with the vines just beginning to change colour. They have Mourvèdre, Carignan, Syrah and Grenache for their red wine, Cinsaut for rosé, and have planted some Grenache Gris, of which the first crop was 2017. It is not yet allowed in St Chinian, but Vivien had liked what he had tasted in Maury. Altogether they have ten plots in three groups all around the village, including an old vineyard of 50 ares with as many as 16 different varieties, some of which I had never heard of, such Danugue, which comes from Algeria, and Petite Bouschet, as opposed to Alicante Bouschet, as well as more usual varieties such as Muscat, Oeillade and Carignan, both Blanc and Noir.

The rosé is a pure Cinsaut, Vin de France, from 60-year-old vines. Le Banel is a blend of two-thirds Carignan to one-third Grenache, combining the fruit of Grenache and the freshness of Carignan. The Grenache vines are 20 years old and the Carignan was planted in 1951. Les Païssels itself comes from a blend of approximately one-quarter each of Carignan, Syrah, Grenache and Mourvèdre, of which one-third is given 10 months' ageing in barrel. There is a satisfying combination of spice and structure, with rich fruit and a fresh finish. Les Jalouses comes from old Carignan and the other old vines, but not the Muscat. The first vintage was 2016, just 1,000 bottles with an *élevage* in vat, to see how it works. The wine had structure and freshness on the palate and promises well. Vivien treated us to a mini-vertical tasting of Les Païssels. The 2013, when the harvest was late, had rich, chocolatey notes and ripe fruit; 2012 was more elegant, with some dry spice; and 2011 was still rich and concentrated, with a lovely balance. Maybe he will make a pure Carignan next, and he wants to see how the Grenache Gris turns out.

Left: A vineyard carpeted with
wild rocket, with the Château
de Cassan in the background.
Its wines are made by a local
cooperative.

Below: Summer vineyards
with the village of Caux in the
far distance.

Above: A vineyard at Domaine d'Aussières in the Corbières, in one of the windiest parts of the Languedoc.

Left: A wonderfully gnarled 100-year-old Muscat vine.

Below: Old vine Carignan ready for harvest.

The grapes at Domaine d'Aussières in Corbières are always hand harvested, and by the same team.

Above: Pumping juice and grape skins.

Left: Whole bunches of hand-harvested grapes fall into the harvest trailer.

Below: Frothing young wine leaving the vat.

Right: The hallway of the new offices of Domaine de l'Hortus in the Pic St Loup. Stylish, modern architecture is increasingly replacing the traditional cellar designs of the Languedoc.

Below: The Pic St Loup in autumn sunshine. The vines have almost lost all their leaves.

Pruning in winter sunshine. Battery-operated secateurs facilitate the task.

Above: The medieval city of Carcassonne, with winter vines.

Below: Old bush vines in winter with a dramatic backdrop of the snow-capped Pyrenees.

Above: Vineyards in winter; such a thick covering of snow is unusual in the Languedoc.

Left: A frosty vineyard in Limoux, one of the coolest parts of the Languedoc.

Domaine la Madura
St Chinian 34360
www.lamadura.com

Cyril Bourgne is one of the more thoughtful and analytical winemakers of St Chinian and very committed and focused. He worked in Bordeaux, running Château Fieuzal for a number of years, before developing his own estate in St Chinian, and making his first wine in 1999. He now has 12.5 hectares of vines and has recently built a smart new cellar outside the town of St Chinian, just in time for the 2015 vintage.

For Cyril, there is no doubt: the specificity of St Chinian is the variety of *terroirs*, which complement each other, as well as the effect on each grape variety. There is a world of difference between Grenache grown on clay and limestone and Grenache on schist. With clay and limestone, the wine has more colour and tannin, with less exuberance on the nose, while on schist it is very aromatic, but with less colour and acidity. The same differences are apparent with Syrah. Cyril was also adamant that he wanted four grape varieties, with sizeable holdings of Grenache and Carignan, as well as Mourvèdre and he admits to being frightened by what he called the '*uniformisation*' of Syrah. He likes the freshness of Carignan and Mourvèdre. 'You have to be careful as both Grenache and Syrah can be too heavy. *Élevage* is important too. New wood here is an aberration; it is merely make-up and adds to uniformity. The grape varieties have sufficient expression and character not to need extra make-up.'

Cyril talked about his work in the vineyard. 'The deeper the roots, the more freshness you obtain.' He wants maximum aeration, and maximum leaf exposure, so that the vines are less sensitive to rot and disease. If the leaves are in the shade, they consume energy, and create a negative effect. He limits treatments. Work in the vineyard pays off in difficult years, but it is rare to have a week of bad weather. We broached organic viticulture. Cyril questions some of the treatments – with *bio* you may not use synthetic chemicals, but you can use copper and sulphur, which are also harmful. He would rather use synthetic products, but in the tiniest quantities. In any case, prevention is better than treatment. He is a little cynical about the commercial value of *bio* – a combination of marketing and political correctness. 'I am against political correctness. There are people who don't want to hear the truth about *bio*, as it disturbs them.' He prefers the criteria of Haute Valeur Environnementale, an organization created in 2007 that works on the management of water and the need to reduce the carbon footprint, with a respect for the diversity of the soil.

Cyril's range of wines is very logical, following the *bordelais* pattern with a Classic and a Grand Vin for both red and white. An innovation since my previous visit is the addition of Piquepoul, just half a hectare to see how it performs. It is a local grape variety, and a late ripener, which is good in an area where everything tends to ripen early. The first vintage was 2013 and it was 'a lovely surprise'. Classic Blanc consists of 40 per cent Piquepoul to 60 per cent Sauvignon Blanc, with the Piquepoul grown on schist and the Sauvignon on clay and limestone, and the wine is kept in vat, on its lees, with no malolactic fermentation, or *bâtonnage*. It is fresh and stony with good acidity. The Piquepoul really does complement the Sauvignon. The Grand Vin has slightly less Piquepoul and both varieties are fermented in old barrels, making a wine with more texture and mouthfeel, with balancing acidity. Cyril feels that the old grape varieties that are disappearing, such as Morastel and Ribeyrenc, should be reinstated because they are really adapted to the climate.

The red Classic, a blend of four varieties, but mainly Carignan and Grenache, is fresh and elegant. Syrah and Mourvèdre are given some *élevage* in wood on their lees and blended after two winters in the cellar. The Grand Vin is mainly Mourvèdre and Syrah with a little Carignan and Grenache. The oak is well integrated and the palate richer and more powerful than the Classic, with great ageing potential. It is a lovely glass of wine.

Borie la Vitarèle

Causse-et-Veyran 34490
www.borielavitarele.fr

I cannot completely ignore some of the longer established estates of the appellation. Jean-François and Cathy Izarn made their first wine at Borie la Vitarèle in 1990, a year which coincided with the birth of their daughter Camille, who is now helping her mother run the estate. Very sadly, Jean-François was killed in a tractor accident in 2014. They now have 18 hectares, all farmed organically. The land, in a lost valley outside the village of Causse-et-Veyran, came originally from Cathy's parents. You feel as though you are driving into the middle of nowhere. Cathy took me to a viewpoint, and showed me the village with its Romanesque church in the distance, and vineyards surrounded by *garrigue*, at our feet. At 350 metres, her vineyards for white wine, with

Clairette, Vermentino and Bourboulenc, all *complanté*, are amongst the highest in the appellation. The house next to the cellar, which they use as a tasting room, is what Cathy described as '*du show-off*', with a very elegant façade but with very few narrow rooms. It was used by wealthy *biterrois*, from Béziers, as a weekend country retreat.

The range of wines has evolved over the years. Out tasting began with le Grand Mayol, a white Languedoc. As Cathy does not have Roussanne or Marsanne, it cannot be St Chinian. Mayol means young vineyard in Occitan and the harvest begins with Vermentino, then Clairette, and finally the Bourboulenc two weeks later. This is a serious white wine, first made in 2012, with texture and body, and ageing potential after some *élevage* in *demi-muids* for the Clairette.

La Cuvée des Cigales, Coteaux du Murviel, is a blend of Merlot and Grenache, with a drop of Syrah. Les Terres Blanches is the easiest drinking of their St Chinian, a blend of Syrah, Grenache and a little Mourvèdre, with some spice and ripe fruit. The vines are grown on clay and limestone. Schistes, from Syrah and Grenache, grown as the name implies on schist, has ripe, peppery fruit with a tannic streak. The grapes are hand-picked and destemmed, spending three weeks on the skins. Les Cres, from 80 per cent Syrah with Mourvèdre, includes 20 per cent whole bunches, with 12 months' ageing in *demi-muids*. It is fresh and peppery, with good structure. Midi Rouge, St Chinian Roquebrun, comes from three *terroirs*; the principal varieties, Syrah and Carignan, are grown on schist; the Grenache on clay and limestone; and the Mourvèdre on sandstone. All are given 18 months' *élevage* in *demi-muids*. It is ripe, rounded and fleshy, concentrated and tannic. The name recalls the wine growers' demonstrations of 1907. The final *cuvée* is Hommage, in memory of Jean-François. However, our tasting finished with a lovely comparison of Schistes and Les Cres, from the particularly good vintage of 2001, demonstrating the ageability of the Languedoc, with which Cathy served some delicious homemade pâtés.

Mas Champart
Villespassans, St Chinian 34360
www.mas-champart.com

Mathieu and Isabelle Champart are from northern France, she from Paris and he formerly a farmer in the Aube. They first came south to St Chinian on holiday in 1976, and simply stayed, creating the 16-hectare estate of Mas Champart. They made their first wine in 1988, and their range has gradually developed, so that their wines are amongst my favourite St Chinian. You sense that Isabelle is thoughtful and a little self-effacing, but with hidden depths, rather like her wines. Mathieu is the balance to her discretion.

For their white wine, they have some of the oldest vines of the *commune* of Villespassans, about a hectare planted in 1902, mainly of Terret Blanc, with several other varieties such as Cinsaut, Bourboulenc and Clairette all mixed up in the vineyard, and there is a plot of old Carignan nearby. Their white wine, currently Pays d'Oc though it may be changing to Vin de France for a different image, comprises 70 per cent from the old vineyard of Terret, with 30 per cent Grenache Gris, with some picked early to enhance the minerality and some slightly overripe Terret, so that harvest takes place over about three or four weeks. Eighty per cent of the wine is fermented in 500-litre wood barrels and aged for six months. It is quite delicious, firm and fresh with stony minerality and a long finish. The white St Chinian is a blend of Grenache Blanc, Bourboulenc, Roussanne, Marsanne, Clairette and Viognier. Apparently, replanting with Bourboulenc is not permitted, so they have planted Clairette instead. Forty per cent of the wine is kept in old wood and the palate is nicely rounded with fresh minerality. They are worried by the irregularity of the rainfall and are looking to plant later-ripening varieties which give more aroma. They cool the grapes for their white and rosé before pressing, which helps preserve the flavours.

A red Pays d'Oc comes from Cabernet Franc, from a plot planted in 1988, with just 10 per cent Syrah. It has fresh fruit and vivacity. Côte d'Arbo includes all five red varieties of the appellation, grown on clay and limestone, and aged in concrete vats. They blend gradually, or they may ferment a couple of varieties together, Grenache with a little Carignan, depending on the ripening times, but they also like playing with the blends. This is a lovely glass of wine, with spice and elegance. Causse du Bousquet is a blend of Syrah with Grenache and some Mourvèdre and Carignan, grown on the limestone plateau nearby, with two-thirds aged in barrel. The wine is elegantly smoky, with a long finish. The final wine of their range is Clos de la Simonette, which is predominantly Mourvèdre with some Grenache and Carignan, including some that is very old, with all except the very old Carignan aged in 600-litre barrels.

The Mourvèdre is grown on clay and the Grenache and Carignan on limestone – they are looking for riper grapes, with red fruit. The wine has ageing potential, with a long, elegant finish.

Isabelle talked about the changes she has seen in St Chinian. The new estates are young and competent, and she thinks that the older estates have improved, with wines that are powerful and balanced, but retain their freshness. There is a diversity in the *terroir* and that makes for great variety in the wines, with plenty of personality. We left her on an optimistic note.

Mas des Dames
Murviel-lès-Béziers 34490
www.masdesdames.fr

Lidewij van Wilgen is a bright, young Dutch woman who has, almost single-handedly, developed a new estate outside the village of Murviel-lès-Béziers on the edge of the appellation of St Chinian. Her first vintage in 2002 represented a complete career change, from life as an advertising executive in Amsterdam. Each time I see Lidewij, I am filled with admiration for her energy and courage. Life as a *vigneronne* on your own, in what is still a man's world in the Languedoc, is not always easy. The last time we met, she related how the *pépiniériste* (vine nurseryman) had taken her for a ride, selling her his worst quality vines, and then tried to blame her for their failure to grow.

Lidewij now has 14 hectares of vines and 24 hectares of land in what seems like a lost corner on the way to nowhere. She has worked organically since 2009 and is moving towards biodynamics, in vineyards that include 70-year-old Carignan and 100-year-old Alicante Bouschet. The leaves were glorious red in the autumn sunshine. Lidewij has a new vineyard within the appellation of St Chinian but she prefers simple AOP Languedoc. Some of her land is also eligible for the putative appellation of Fonséranes but this will mainly cover the flatter lands around Béziers and, in any case, is 'very political'. Lidewij prefers to keep her distance. She has a neat cellar, with red and cream concrete vats and observed that her sorting table is the most important thing. 'I wouldn't make a pie with rotten apples, so I don't want rotten grapes in my wine.' She has also bought a concrete tronconic vat, and added some smaller vats, so that she can vinify several different plots separately and play with the blending.

Lidewij van Wilgen, Mas des Dames

Her range consists of a Mas des Dames blanc, Pays d'Oc, from Grenache Blanc, 'my favourite variety,' she enthused. 'The appellations always want blends. I've tried them but don't like them,' so she makes a pure Grenache Blanc and gives 50 per cent of it an *élevage* in wood. The nose is delicate and the palate structured, with firm fruit and ageing potential. Diva Blanche represents one particularly good barrel, from older Grenache Blanc, with textured layers of flavours, balanced by good acidity. 'More Burgundian than *languedocien*,' thought Lidewij. Five years ago, she would never have dared use all new oak. Diva Rosé comes from Grenache Noir and Mourvèdre, fermented and then aged for three months in oak, so that it is rich and vinous with a dry streak. La Dame is a blend of Grenache, Syrah and Carignan, aged in tank, with spice and an elegant finish, while La Diva, Coteaux de Murviel, comes from 60 per cent Syrah aged in wood, 25 per cent Grenache Noir and 15 per cent Alicante Bouschet aged in vat. It could be St Chinian if it were not for the Alicante, but Lidewij is very attached to her Alicante, which makes for a wine with ripe spice, a youthful tannic streak and elegant freshness on the finish.

12

FAUGÈRES

The vineyards of Faugères lie at the foot of the hills of the Espinouse. Two magnificent viewpoints provide a perfect introduction to the area. The Pic de la Coquillade displays Faugères at your feet, with the village of Caussiniojouls in the immediate foreground, Cabrerolles, and then Autignac and Laurens in the distance. On a clear day, you can just make out the silvery streak of the Mediterranean. The other point is the site of Les Trois Moulins above the village of Faugères itself, which provides a wonderful idea of the topography of the appellation, the undulating hills and valleys that twist and turn as they fall away to the sea. The terms *balcons de schist*, or balconies of schist, is very apt, for the *terroir* of Faugères is schist, and only schist. That is what has defined the appellation, limiting it to just seven villages and a couple of hamlets. The grape varieties are the usual five red varieties, with Mourvèdre compulsory in the vineyards, but not necessarily in the wine. For the tiny amount of white wine, the permitted grapes are mainly Marsanne, Roussanne, Vermentino and Grenache Blanc. The schist makes for a distinctive freshness that distinguishes Faugères from neighbouring Pézenas. The differences between the closest vineyards of St Chinian, also on schist, are less marked. However, at Château de Ciffre, which is the only estate to include both appellations, you can see a very distinctive faultline demarcating the two.

I have to admit to having a soft spot for Faugères. It is close to my French home and consequently was the natural choice for my previous book. Choosing which producers to include and which to omit has proved more difficult than for the other appellations, simply for reasons of familiarity, but, as elsewhere in this book, although I have written about some of the more established wine growers, I have favoured the most recent arrivals, including the most newly established, who arrived after the publication of *The wines of Faugères* in 2017. The Languedoc attracts outsiders; not only foreigners, but French from other parts of the country, and it seems that Faugères lures more than its fair share to settle in this enchanting part of the Languedoc.

Producers

Mas d'Alezon

Faugères 346000
www.alezon.fr

Catherine Roque, Mas d'Alezon

Catherine was already making wine at Domaine de Clovallon, outside Bédarieux, when she discovered Faugères in 1997. She had heard that *un vieux monsieur* who sold wine *en vrac* to the *négoce* was retiring, and thus she came to buy 7 hectares at Montfalette outside the village of Soumartre. She was not able to make Faugères immediately because she had no Mourvèdre, so she sold her first two vintages to the *négoce* while she got to know her vineyards. She admits it was quite a steep learning curve. At Clovallon she could invent everything, while in Faugères she had to adapt to the appellation, which was quite a challenge. Clovallon is limestone and north-facing; Faugères is schist and south-facing. In 1999, she bottled her first wine, as Coteaux du Languedoc. In 2003 (by which time she had acquired some Mourvèdre) she made her first Faugères. She now has three plots of vines, in three different zones: Caussiniojouls, Soumartre and Faugères itself, including some very old Carignan. However, she is not at all enthusiastic about the variety: 'I have a problem with Carignan!' On the other hand, Mourvèdre is much better: 'People were wrong when they said it would not ripen.' So, Catherine's Faugères has evolved into two *cuvées*: Montfalette, which is Mourvèdre and Syrah, with Grenache Noir providing the link between the two characterful grape varieties, and Presbytère, which is mainly Grenache Noir with some Mourvèdre.

Catherine has progressed over the past 20 years from *lutte raisonnée* to organic and now biodynamic viticulture. She uses no sulphur dioxide in the cellar, so hygiene must be meticulous. Nothing is destemmed as she favours a traditional vinification *des anciens*, in an open vat. The grapes are pressed after three weeks. She would love to make more white wine, and suggests that Faugères Blanc should include Clairette and Carignan Blanc. The potential is enormous. As for *élevage*, Catherine favours larger barrels rather than small *barriques*, and is adamant that vine age is a quality factor. In 2014, she made rosé for the first time, from a new plot that includes some Cinsaut. When asked about typicity, she talks about the wines she likes: '*aerien, profondeur*, you can drink them young or old. Faugères is not immediately generous; there is a certain austerity that gradually reveals its character.'

Domaine Ollier Taillefer

Fos 34320
www.olliertaillefer.com

This is one of the long-standing estates of Faugères. Marcel Taillefer worked to create the appellation or, more precisely, the VDQS (the category below an appellation) just after the war and, in 1961, his daughter Nicole married Alain Ollier, a farmer from Lodève, who joined the family business. All the wine was sold *en vrac* until 1976, when Alain took the then pioneering step of putting some wine in bottle, just one pallet's worth. It took a good ten years for them to reach the stage of selling all their production in bottle. Alain began with 7 hectares outside Autignac and then cleared *garrigue* and planted vines in the pretty village of Fos, so that they now have 36 hectares altogether. Fos is also where you will find their tasting *caveau*, as well as a smart new cellar, used for the first time in 2014.

These days it is the next generation running the estate. Luc makes the wine and his sister, Françoise, is responsible for sales. Together they make a good team: Luc is a thoughtful and sensitive winemaker, while Françoise is bright and vivacious with a keen sense of humour. She always conducts a cellar visit with great enthusiasm and it has become one of my favourite cellars to visit, for the repartee as much as for the wine. Les Collines is their entry-level traditional Faugères, for which I have a soft spot. It is sunshine in a glass, everything that good Faugères should be, fruity and fresh, but uncomplicated. The blend includes a high proportion of Grenache Noir with some Carignan and Syrah, and some young Mourvèdre, all aged in vat. Grande Réserve comes from a selection of the oldest vines, namely Carignan, Grenache and Syrah, which give structure, tannin and perfumed fruit, but with more concentration and depth than Les Collines. Then there is Castel Fossibus, which is aged in oak and again benefits from some bottle age. Le Rêve de Noé, a blend of Mourvèdre and Syrah, is a new *cuvée*, made for the first time in 2013. Essentially, they have made just one barrel of each variety, aged in new oak, to provide 800 bottles and 60 magnums. It was rich and concentrated, with ageing potential, and illustrates how each generation makes its mark. Allegro is their white Faugères, a blend of Vermentino and Roussanne, with the Vermentino providing some natural freshness and herbal notes, while the Roussanne fills out the palate with a touch of white blossom. Finally, Baies de Novembre, their dessert wine, comes from Grenache Noir picked in November. They leave one bunch per vine, and, if the birds, the weather and the tourists are restrained, the grapes are picked when they are fully raisined. The juice is fermented in oak very slowly until the summer and the wine stays in oak for a couple of years to develop the oxidative character of the Grenache. Needless to say, it is not made every year. Fine de Faugères completes their range.

Domaine des Trinités
Roquessels 34320
www.trinites.com

One of the rising stars amongst the newcomers is Domaine des Trinités in Roquessels. Simon Coulshaw is British, while his wife, Monica, comes from Barcelona. Simon had always enjoyed wine, but started his working life in IT. In 2004, when it was time for a change, he elected to do the two-year course at Plumpton in East Sussex. He even thought about buying land in Sussex, but southern reds are his real passion and so he began the search for vineyards and a cellar in the Mediterranean, considering Spain as well as the Midi. He had very precise ideas as to what he wanted, and with the one hundred and seventh property he visited, in the village of Roquessels, in the heart of Faugères, he found it. Above all, he wanted an interesting *terroir*, not vineyard land on the plain; he was looking for unrealized potential, and what is now called Domaine des Trinités fulfilled those criteria. The vineyards now comprise 17 hectares of Faugères around the village of Roquessels, and 9 hectares of the newer *cru* of the Languedoc, Pézenas, around the tiny village of Montesquieu.

I always enjoy a tasting with Simon, not just for his wine, but because he is full of ideas and opinions, which he expresses with articulate enthusiasm. I asked him about the typicity of Faugères. He was in no doubt: 'It is freshness that sets Faugères apart. There is a natural lift, you get wonderful aromatics, notes of the *garrigue*, with fruit and spice from the schist. It is not heavy or concentrated. Faugères is about schist. Do not mess around with it.'

As well as Faugères and Pézenas, he makes two Pays d'Oc whites, from Viognier and Roussanne. Simon is particularly enthusiastic about his Roussanne, which he now ferments on its skins, observing: 'It is so much more than a blending wine, which is how it is often used in the Midi. Orange is the future!' The 2017 spent three weeks on skins and has wonderful rich flavours. A recent addition to the range is L'Étranger, which is mainly Cinsaut with a splash of Syrah, given a long maceration with a daily *pigeage* making for gentle extraction. The result is some lovely perfumed fruit on both nose and palate.

Simon makes two *cuvées* of Pézenas, Le Pech Mégé and la Devèze, and three Faugères, Le Portail, Les Mourels and, occasionally, Cuvée 42. Le Portail, the entry-level Faugères, is a blend of 60 per cent Syrah with some Grenache Noir, Carignan and a little Mourvèdre, while Les Mourels is mainly Mourvèdre with 20 per cent Grenache Noir, with an *élevage* in vat. His Mourvèdre is particularly successful as it is planted on a good south-facing slope. He is not alone in observing that people often have Mourvèdre in quite the wrong place. His flagship wine, produced in tiny quantity, is Faugères, Cuvée 42. Why 42? If you have read *The Hitchhiker's Guide to the Galaxy*, you will know that 'It's the Answer to the Ultimate Question of Life, The Universe, and Everything'. It represents a serious labour of love, the production of three different biodynamic vineyards, a hectare each of Grenache Noir, Syrah and Mourvèdre, which are co-fermented and then spend 18 months in 500-litre barrels. The wine is rich and concentrated, but with a fresh finish. 'Cinnamon and spice, and all things nice' comes to mind.

Simon Coulshaw, Domaine des Trinités

Domaine de Sarabande
Laurens 34480
www.sarabande-wines.com

Paul Gordon first discovered wine while working in London for Terence Conrad. He comes from Sydney and, when he went back to Australia, he studied winemaking and then worked a vintage with various Australian estates and in New Zealand, at Isabel Estate in Marlborough. Isla was backpacking in New Zealand at the time and turned up at Isabel Estate looking to earn some money in order to continue travelling. They spent five years together in New Zealand but then it was time to come to Europe. They first looked in Spain, in Priorat, but the land was too expensive, so they shifted their attention north of the Pyrenees and realized that Faugères ticked all the boxes: 'It's close to the mountains, close to the sea, has very good soil and great wines, nice villages and it is not too busy.' They looked for vineyards to rent and someone offered them 5.5 hectares, in two blocks just outside the village of Autignac. Then they found a house in Laurens with a large garage that was perfect for some small vats and a few barrels.

Paul and Isla took over their first vines in March 2009, just in time to prune them and they now have 8 hectares, which are farmed organically, with minimal use of sulphur and copper. Unusually for France, Paul bottles all his wine with a screw cap as most of his sales are overseas, and, even more revolutionary for a French appellation, he puts the grape variety blend on the front label, rather than on a discreet back label.

Paul talked about typicity. Above all he wants freshness in his wine: 'You get very good acidity from the soil in Faugères. In other parts of the world, if you wait until the grapes taste ripe, you need to add tartaric acid. Natural acidity is so important for the fresh fruit character.' He does not use any cultured yeast or malolactic culture. Nor does he fine or filter. He makes his wine as naturally as possible, but does use some sulphur.

The range has evolved over the years and currently includes four different Faugères, with variations on the blends. Misterioso is based on Grenache, with Syrah and Mourvèdre; Les Espinasses is predominantly Syrah with a little Mourvèdre; Les Rabasses is a blend of Syrah with Grenache and Mourvèdre, while Bousigue is a new *cuvée*, which is predominately Mourvèdre with some Syrah. Their aim is to make serious wines with ageing potential, but Paul is not afraid to experiment and you sense that things will never stand still.

Domaine de Cébène

Faugères 34600
www.cebene.fr

Brigitte Chevalier arrived in the Languedoc in 2004 and made her first Faugères in 2008. She comes from Bordeaux, where she worked for a couple of *négociants*, but she really wanted to make her own wine. The variety of the *terroir* and the choice of grape varieties attracted her to the Languedoc. 'Here you have a wonderful impression of liberty, compared to Bordeaux where you are weighed down by tradition.' Cébène takes its name from the goddess of the Cévennes, the mountains that form a backdrop to the vineyards of Faugères. She now has a new cellar outside the village of Faugères, buried in the schist, with views across the valley to the village and the Pic de Tantajo.

Brigitte Chevalier, Domaine de Cébène

Brigitte has always looked for cooler sites, so that her grapes have a long, slow ripening time, and her estate now consists of 11 hectares in two large plots, divided into smaller vineyards, around her new cellar. She also makes a Pays d'Oc, Ex Arena, from her very first vineyard in the village of Corneillan, outside the appellation of Faugères, from 85 per cent Grenache Noir with some Mourvèdre. Altogether she makes three Faugères. First is Belle Lurette, a name that comes from the expression '*il y avait une belle lurette*', or 'once upon a time', for this is mainly old Carignan, 70 to 100 years old, with a little Grenache Noir and Mourvèdre. Les Bancèls, '*les balcons de schiste*', is mainly Syrah, with some Grenache Noir and Mourvèdre, and a little Carignan, and no oak ageing, while Felgaria, '*les caprices de la terre*', is predominantly Mourvèdre with some Syrah. Asked about typicity, Brigitte looks for elegant drinkability. She likes what she calls the *côté digeste*, the digestibility of Faugères: *douceur* or sweetness, and finesse, with elegant tannins. Mourvèdre is her favourite variety because it has an original aromatic range, with sweet spices, and is not aggressive. When she was looking for her vineyards, she sought out schist above all else, as well as altitude and north-facing vines. You sense, tasting with Brigitte, that she is a very meticulous and observant, not to mention talented, wine grower. She now has, she says, a much better understanding of her vines, and that shows in her wines. She will go far.

Newcomers

Faugères has seen many new producers establishing themselves during recent years. For instance, 2014 saw the emergence of four new wine estates, namely Domaine Epidaure, Domaine de l'Arbussèle, Mas Nicolas and Mas Lou, each with quite a different story and background.

Domaine Epidaure

Fos 34320
j.vialla@hotmail.com

Jérôme Vialla's grandfather had a family estate in Mauguio, which was sold for inheritance reasons; his father is the *régisseur* at Domaine Valensac in Florensac and makes Pays d'Oc, so Jérôme found himself a *fils de vigneron*, but without any family vines. He studied viticulture and winemaking at Carcassonne, and then worked at Domaine de la Pommière, on the plain, which he describes as a factory, as they produced 25,000 hectolitres from 200 hectares of vines. He wanted to get away from the plain, so he bought a small house in Fos in 2012 and met his next-door neighbour, Jean-Pierre Grippal, who was approaching retirement and had no children interested in his vines. So Jérôme has rented Jean-Pierre's vines on a long-term contract, 20 hectares, mainly of Syrah, Grenache Noir and Carignan, with a little Mourvèdre and Cinsaut, in the villages of Fos and Roquessels. He has started cautiously, making wine for sale *en vrac*, and increasing the quantity in bottle gradually. He had to build his cellar, which was completed just in time for the 2014 harvest. With his first vintage he made a rosé, a white and three reds. His white is a fresh, lively Carignan Blanc, and the rosé a blend of the usual five varieties, but mainly Syrah and Grenache Noir. His entry-level red, again from all five varieties, makes for easy drinking with dry spice. Next comes a blend of Syrah, Grenache Noir and Carignan, with some sturdy, youthful fruit. The barrel-aged wine is a blend of Syrah and Grenache Noir, with some red fruit and a tannic streak. And why the name Epidaure? Jérôme's wife is a chemist and the town of Epidaurus was an important centre of ancient Greek medicine.

Domaine de l'Arbussèle
Fos 34320
www.domainelarbussele.com

Sébastien Louge has also taken an interesting path to Fos. He comes from Tarbes in the Hautes-Pyrénées and, after studying agriculture, turned to viticulture and oenology at Bommes in Bordeaux and worked in Ste Croix du Mont. More studies followed, in Toulouse, and then a couple of *stages* at Château Montus in Madiran and Domaine de Montredon in Châteauneuf-du-Pape. Next, he spent a year in Virginia, USA, at Cross Keys vineyards, helping them create their cellar. Back in France he worked at Château Guilhem in Malepère, and then at Domaine de la Grange outside Gabian. Finally, he found 10 hectares of vines in Fos and Laurens for sale, mainly Syrah and both old and young Carignan, as well as an old tractor shed which only needed a small amount of work to turn it into a functioning cellar.

My conversation with Sébastien focused on the hurdles you have to go through to qualify for financial help as a young wine producer. You must be between 18 and 40, with the appropriate qualifications. There are forms galore to complete, as your project is checked to ensure that it is viable. He called it a '*parcours de combatant*', an obstacle course, and he made a good start with his first vintage. There was a crisp rosé, Envol, a blend mainly of Grenache Noir, with some Syrah and a little Mourvèdre. Envol Rouge is Sébastien's entry-level wine, with 45 per cent Syrah, 30 per cent Carignan and 25 per cent Grenache Noir, with an *élevage* in vat. The aim is fruit, and that is just what he has achieved, with a mineral note and youthful freshness. Authentique comes mainly from old Carignan, with some Grenache Noir and a little Syrah, again aged in vat. The name is a reference to the fact that Carignan was the original variety of Faugères. It was nicely structured with a pleasing rusticity balancing the fruit. The final red, Révélation, of which there were just two barrels, is a blend of Grenache Noir with 20 per cent Carignan and 15 per cent Syrah. It had some ripe liqueur cherry fruit, balanced with a streak of tannin and promised well.

Mas Nicolas
Cabrerolles 34480
www.vin-masnicolas-34.com

Nicolas Maury's father, Philippe, is currently president of the cooperative, as was his grandfather, so viticulture is in his genes. However, he is the first member of his family to make his own wine. He has rented 4.5 hectares from his father, plots that could be released from the contract with the cooperative. He learnt his viticulture from his father, but realized he really wanted to make his own wine and that simply to continue as a cooperative member would not be very rewarding. He now has a small cellar on the family estate of Coudigno, on the road to Aigues-Vives from Lenthéric. As 'Coudigno' is the name of one of the cooperative's *cuvées*, Nicolas has decided on 'Mas Nicolas' for the name of his wines.

I asked about subsidies for a young *vigneron* and Nicolas explained that you have to have a minimum of 10 hectares in order to qualify, as well as a viable vineyard holding and cellar, with your own tractor and so on. He felt that this was far too much to ask of a beginner. When I quizzed him as to whether his father had given up the best plots, he pertinently observed that they did not actually know how their wine would taste because all the grapes had been going into the cooperative vat. He has vines at Caussiniojouls: some Carignan, Grenache Noir, Syrah, Cinsaut and just ten rows of Mourvèdre, and also some Viognier. For his first vintage, he made a red wine from 40 per cent each of Grenache Noir and Carignan, with some Syrah, which had fresh cherry fruit and a streak of tannin. The wine from the 100-year-old Carignan was in barrel and showed good fruit with some sturdy tannins, while a Syrah had some peppery notes and the spice of the *garrigue*. The Viognier was elegantly peachy, with subtle varietal character. Nicolas's label is illustrated with a quince flower, as '*coudou*' in Occitan is a quince, and '*coudougno*' means a place where quinces grow. As Nicolas remarked: 'I have everything to discover.' It will be a great adventure and he is not afraid, especially as he has a lot of support from his family.

Mas Lou
Faugères 34600
www.mas-lou.com

Olivier Gil and Adèle Arnaud have bought Catherine Roque's old cellar in the heart of the village of Faugères. Olivier comes from a family of *vignerons*; he studied oenology at Montpellier where he met Adèle, who does not come from a winemaking family but describes her parents as '*grands amateurs*', or great wine enthusiasts. More studies took them to Dijon and to Toulouse. They worked first in South America and then in Collioure, which gave them a different experience of schist, and then they knew that they wanted to go it alone. Pierre Alibert from Domaine Ste Cécile, an estate that sold mainly bulk wine, was retiring and so they took over his vines in Fos on 1 January 2014, calling their new estate Mas Lou. There are 8.3 hectares, in seven plots, with the usual five varieties. The vines are in good condition, with some newly planted vines, some 45-year-old Mourvèdre, some old Grenache Noir, and some 100-year-old Carignan.

The names of their various *cuvées* relate to their stay in South America. The rosé, Selva, for the Amazonian forest, is a blend of 80 per cent Mourvèdre with some Grenache Noir, with some fresh acidity and red fruit. The first red, Angaco, is a blend of old Carignan with some Grenache Noir and a smaller amount of Lledoner Pelut, with some ripe cherry liqueur fruit, fresh acidity and balancing tannins, with an appealing drinkability. Aksou is a blend of 60 per cent Syrah with Grenache Noir, of which almost half is aged in wood, giving some peppery fruit and nicely integrated oak. Tio, of which there are just three barrels, is a pure Syrah from one plot in Fos on a steep slope at 320 metres; it was redolent of black fruit and pepper. Olivier said that he was looking for elegance and concentration, and for supple tannins, and that is certainly what he has achieved. He sees himself as a traditionalist and wants wines that represent the appellation, staying within the classic Faugères framework of finesse and *fraîcheur*.

Domaine Florence Alquier
Faugères 34600
www.domaine-florence-alquier.com

Gilbert Alquier was one of the pioneers of Faugères, one of the first to plant Syrah and Mourvèdre, and to age his wine in barrel and put it in bottle. His two sons, Jean-Michel and Frédéric, took over their father's vines and divided their inheritance into two estates. Jean-Michel continues to make exemplary Faugères but, sadly, Frédéric died in 2015. Ten hectares of his vines have been rented by Frédéric Desplats, who has also bought another 10 hectares in Roquessels with a partner, Denis Degros. They have appropriately taken the name of Frédéric Alquier's widow, Florence, for his estate and describes it as a 'retirement project'. It is all very much in the early stages, with their first wines made in 2017: a white Le Village, from Marsanne, Roussanne and Grenache Blanc, and a rosé Plô des Figues, with Cinsaut and some Grenache. So far there are also two reds: Renaissance, from predominantly Grenache, with some Carignan, Mourvèdre and Syrah, and Puech Mourié, from Carignan, with some Grenache and Syrah. An oak-aged red is also in the pipeline. I have as yet to taste the wines and it will be interesting to watch the progress of another newcomer to Faugères.

Domaine Montgros
Lenthéric 34480
www.montgros.fr

It can be challenging for a young, aspiring wine producer, without any family land or connections, to set up their own wine estate. This is where the enterprising Ludovic Aventin has been able to help, with his company Terra Hominis. He had already developed Domaine Montgros and Mas Angel, with a cellar outside the hamlet of Lenthéric, with numerous associates who own the vineyards. Now he has passed on these two estates to two young wine growers. Maxime Secher, who used to run Pierre Gaillard's estate, Cottebrune, is now responsible for Domaine Montgros, where he made his first wine in 2017. Maxime explained that his 6.6 hectares of vines are rented from 130 rugby players, all friends and associates of Ludovic's, who have invested in the vineyards for fun. Then there is the company that makes the wine, of which Maxime is the majority shareholder, and is responsible for all the work in vineyard and cellar. He also has a 60-ares plot of Syrah of his own, from which he made Les Princesses for the first time in 2014. The princesses were all the friends who helped to pick the grapes, and the wine had some lovely rich, peppery fruit. Ultimately Maxime hopes to find a separate cellar. Meanwhile, for Montgros, Maxime is continuing to make the same *cuvées* as Ludovic, a rosé from Grenache and Syrah, Première Ligne, from 70 per cent Cinsaut with some Carignan and Grenache, with some perfumed fruit, and sturdier, oak-aged Elite, from Syrah and Grenache Noir.

Mas Angel
Lenthéric 34480
www.faugeres-masangel.fr

Meanwhile Alexandre Durand has taken over Mas Angel. His family had vines in Bergerac, and he moved to Faugères, with his Italian partner Sybil Baldassarre, in January 2014, initially to run both Mas Angel and Montgros. However, in 2016 they decided to concentrate on the former. He is setting up his own company as a young farmer and, like Maxime, has 130 vineyard partners, for 8 hectares, with as many as 15 different plots. He was particularly taken by the 50-year-old bush vines, of old varieties, and aims to vinify each plot separately. As well as Faugères he makes Les Balinières, Vin de France, from the old varieties. Clin d'oeil de Balinières is a blend of Oeillade and Cinsaut, with perfumed fruit; Aramon has more body and weight; and the Carignan has some dry spice. Alex works as naturally as possible, using indigenous yeast, with a month's maceration of destalked grapes, but no *remontages* or *pigeages*, an *élevage* in vat, and no filtering. He simply allows the *cuvée* to infuse. The flavours are fresh and intriguing. The top Faugères of Mas Angel is named Marius, after the man who came to Faugères, fleeing from Mussolini, and planted the vineyards in the 1950s. The eponymous Angel is his son, who sold his father's vineyards to Ludovic Aventin. The wine is made from Syrah, with just 10 per cent Grenache Noir, given 12 months in wood, with some red fruit and tannin, while Prestige, from 70 per cent Carignan with some Grenache, also all aged in wood, is more accessible. You sense that Alex has very definite ideas as to what he wants to make and also what he likes drinking. He is very much his own man.

La Grain Sauvage

Caussiniojouls 34600
sybil.wine@gmail.com

Alex's partner Sybil Baldassarre is a vivacious Italian, who studied oenology in Milan and Turin and worked with Luc de Conti, one of the stellar winemakers of Bergerac, and that is where she met Alex. She really wanted to make her own wine, rather than working with Alex, and so has acquired 2.5 hectares of white varieties, mainly Vermentino, Roussanne, Marsanne and Grenache Blanc in high vineyards at an altitude of 430–450 metres. Like Alex, she has vineyard associates, 123 of them, and a small cellar in Caussiniojouls, where she made her first wine in 2015. Altogether she produces four wines. Vermentino, Vin de France, is elegant and stylish, sappy with good acidity. Lutz, meaning *grande lumière*, is a blend of Roussanne and Marsanne, kept in concrete, including a tulip-shaped vat, and is rounded and textured with notes of white blossom. Her Faugères Blanc, Rocalhas, including Grenache Blanc as well as Marsanne and Roussanne, has more weight and structure, again with benchmark acidity and no oak. Riserva dei Soci, for her associates, is an oak-aged wine, with more weight, but I preferred the refreshingly elegant and understated fruit of the unoaked whites. There is no doubt that Sybil has made a great start.

Domaine les Serrals

Faugères 34320
www.serrals.com

Frédéric Almazor and Chloé Barthet made their first wine in Faugères in 2016. Frédéric explained how the project has matured over about ten years. Chloé comes from Paris and had worked in the London wine trade, while he is a Breton and worked in the construction industry. They began looking for vines around les Dentelles de Montmirail, but vineyards in Gigondas are five or six times more expensive than in Faugères. Tautavel in Roussillon was a possibility until they saw an advertisement for five hectares in Faugères, near the Chapelle de St Etienne. The decision was taken and they started pruning their vines in January 2016. There are some 50-year-old Carignan and Cinsaut plants, as well as some mature Mourvèdre and Syrah. The vineyards were already organic and they have progressed to working them biodynamically. Frédéric admitted to a steep learning curve. Finding a cellar was not easy, and they are renting space from Jérôme Rateau of Château Haut Lignières.

As they have no white varieties, they made a white wine from Grenache Noir, le Vilain Petit Grain Noir, a *blanc de noirs*, Vin de France, which was delicate and fresh, with a small part vinified in wood to add a little weight and structure. They would like to plant some white varieties, with Frédéric wondering about Bianco Gentile from Corsica to complement Vermentino. The rosé, Pimprenelle, a flower that you often find in the vineyards, is a blend of equal parts of Grenache Noir and Mourvèdre, with fresh fruit and firm acidity. The first red, Sur le Zinc, a blend of Syrah and Carignan, is fresh and peppery, and intended for easy drinking. Côte à Côte, from two slopes, with Syrah and Carignan, as well as Mourvèdre and Grenache, is the heart of the range, given a long maceration, with a small proportion aged in barrel. It is classic Faugères. The final wine, Aquilae, is mainly Mourvèdre, aged in a 500-litre barrel, with a little Syrah and Grenache.

You sense that they are very excited by their arrival in Faugères, and already very committed to the area and its wine. Frédéric pertinently observed, 'In 30 years' time, we shall be surprised by the evolution of Faugères.' I have no doubt that he is right.

13

PÉZENAS

Pézenas is one of the most charming of all the towns and villages of the Languedoc. It may have given its name to a *cru* of the Languedoc, for red wine only, in 2007, but it really prides itself on its association with Molière. France's most famous playwright and actor was invited to Pézenas by the Prince de Conti in 1650, and Pézenas has never forgotten it. There is a Molière festival every summer, and no prizes for guessing the name of the local wine cooperative. Pézenas's other claim to fame is its association with Lord Clive of India and its twinning with the Shropshire town of Market Drayton. Clive, who was born in Market Drayton, spent the winter of 1766 at nearby Lignan-sur-Orb. With him, he brought his Indian cook, who developed a recipe for what are now known as *petits pâtés de* Pézenas, sweet and savoury little pies. No baker's window in the town is complete with a tray of them.

The historic centre of Pézenas is a pedestrianized area of cobbled streets and substantial town houses. Look through doors into courtyards and you will see wonderful galleries, vaulted arches and hidden nooks and crannies. There are medieval doorways, statues and carvings and much to draw the eye. Like so many French towns, Pézenas really comes to life on market day, which is Saturday morning.

The aspiring appellation of Pézenas covers fifteen surrounding villages, of which Nizas and Caux are the most important. However, it is difficult to see what really accounts for its typicity. Jacques Bilhac, owner of Domaine de l'Aster and the current president of the *cru*, suggested the basalt that you see all over the area, but there are other soils too. The vineyards are on gentle hillsides, none higher than 300 metres, and there is a climatic unity for this is one of the drier areas of

the Hérault. It is a place of independent wine growers and, as Jacques put it, no big locomotive for the appellation. For others, there are so many different *terroirs* that it is difficult to define Pézenas. It almost seems to be an amalgam of villages that do not fit anywhere else and are conveniently close enough to Pézenas to be able to take advantage of its name. Christine Bertoli Mouton from Domaine Ste Cécile du Parc is quite dispassionate: 'There is no typicity; Pézenas is simply a geographic administrative area, with the advantage of the name that is known for Molière.' Domaines Paul Mas produce Côté Mas, a blend of wines not only from Domaines Mas, but from other contributing producers. Jean-Claude Mas himself is optimistic about the future of Pézenas: it is true, he says, that they need to create a specific style of wine, with a coherent message, but it has the potential to be a convincing appellation with an excellent image and reputation.

Producers

Prieuré St Jean de Bébian

Pézenas 34120
www.bebian.com

Karen Turner, award-winning winemaker at La Prieuré St Jean de Bébian

This is one of the oldest estates of the area. I first visited it for an earlier book back in the late 1980s, when it was the property of the maverick winemaker Alain Roux. He claimed that the soil was the same as that of Châteauneuf-du-Pape, with its distinctive *galets roulées*, and had planted all thirteen varieties of that appellation. When I suggested that they did not all feature in the regulations for Coteaux du Languedoc, he told me firmly that *'ça n'a pas d'importance!'* Alain sold Bébian in 1994 to Jean-Claude Le Brun and Chantal Lecouty, French wine journalists, who introduced various changes that refined the wines, and employed the talented Australian, Karen Turner, as their winemaker. Then in 2008 they sold to Russians Dmitry Pumpyansky and his son, Alexander, who have invested heavily in the vineyards and built a state-of-the-art new cellar, with a tasting room designed for visitors and an oenomatic machine. They have also restored the twelfth-century chapel, which is beautiful in its simplicity, and a restaurant will open in the summer of 2018.

They have 25 hectares of vines, in 42 different plots, on limestone *galets roulées* and also some basalt and *villefranchien* gravel, all farmed organically and planted with Grenache Noir and Blanc, but not Gris, as well as Syrah, Cinsaut, Mourvèdre and a little Cabernet and Merlot. For white wine there is Roussanne, Clairette, Viognier and Vermentino. The other varieties of Châteauneuf-du-Pape are lost in the blend. For both red and white wine, they make three qualities, la Croix de Bébian, Chapelle de Bébian and Prieuré de Bébian, with a fourth red wine 1152, from Syrah grown on basalt, blended with Grenache and Mourvèdre. There is also one rosé, les Poupées Roses, a reference to the Russian matryoshka dolls. They select their own yeast, which sometimes entails a more complicated fermentation but undoubtedly makes for wines with more personality. Prieuré Blanc is a blend of 70 per cent Roussanne with 15 per cent each of Grenache Blanc and Clairette, all vinified in oak, of which 25 per cent is new. Red Prieuré comes from 50 per cent Syrah, 30 per cent Grenache and 20 per cent Mourvèdre; in contrast la Croix and Chappelle have more Grenache, which Karen never puts in oak, as she wants to emphasize its perfumed fruit in the more accessible wines.

Domaine les Aurelles

Nizas 34320
www.les-aurelles.com

Domaine les Aurelles was established in 1995, by Basile St Germain, with Karl Mauguin, who has since gone on to pastures new. Basile comes from Lorraine, where he had trained as an architect and landscape gardener before turning to wine and spending two years as a *stagiaire* at Château Latour in the mid-1980s. As he says, it was a great apprenticeship. His wife Caroline comes from Cognac and for a while he worked there, before settling in the Languedoc in 1995. He has 9 hectares of vines, with a spacious cellar, built in 2001, just outside the village of Nizas.

Basile's red wines are original in that they see no oak; instead they are aged in stainless steel vats for four years before bottling. The vats are shallow and wide, allowing for a large cap of grape skins and natural extraction. Basile follows the methods that he learnt in Bordeaux, favouring minimum intervention, maybe a few *remontages*, and long macerations. The range consists of Déella, a blend of Carignan and Grenache Noir, and the more serious Solen, which is also based on Carignan and Grenache Noir. Basile calls Solen his homage to Carignan, observing that he wanted Carignan in his vineyards as culturally it is the grape variety of the Languedoc. He also described the Languedoc, very aptly I thought, as a sleeping beauty. He does not want to make a pure Carignan because the focus of the Languedoc lies in blends, but Carignan should be the dominant grape variety. Then there is Aurel, for which Mourvèdre is the principal grape variety, with 20 per cent Syrah and 15 per cent Grenache Noir.

The red wines are good, but it is Basile's white wine that I really enjoy. It is indisputably one of the great white wines of the Languedoc, a pure Roussanne that is aged in 350-litre barrels for 12 to 18 months. Perhaps unusually for the Languedoc, Aurel undergoes a malolactic fermentation. Basile explained that Roussanne is very tricky; the yields are tiny, as the grapes are small and do not provide much juice, which makes it complicated to vinify. The only skin contact is in the press and he does some *bâtonnage*, not for more body, but to keep the lees in suspension and to avoid adding any sulphur. He does not have any Marsanne; in the south, it does not have the elegance that it has in Hermitage and its yields are pretty high. Roussanne is so much more complex and the ageing potential is considerable. A 2001 drunk when it was 11 years old could only be described as sublime, with subtleties and nuances galore.

Domaine le Conte des Floris

Pézenas 34320

www.domainelecontedesfloris.com

This is another estate of fine white wine. Journalist-turned-winemaker Daniel le Conte des Floris studied in Burgundy in 1996 and then came south to the Languedoc in search of affordable vineyards, making his first vintage here in 2001. Initially he worked from a cramped cellar in the village of Caux, but now has a more spacious one on the edge of the town of Pézenas. As for vineyards, he now has 7 hectares in seven plots in six villages, farmed biodynamically, and for white wine focuses on Carignan Blanc, Roussanne and Marsanne, making three different wines, Lune Blanche, Lune Rousse and Pleine Lune, respectively. They may be pure varietals or blends. Daniel has also planted a small plot of 20 ares with an assortment of grape varieties, including 'all the things I love', Chenin Blanc, Petit Manseng, Riesling, as well as more *languedocien* varieties, such as Clairette, Terret Blanc, Muscat and Viognier, with the idea of adding such a small amount of that blend to mask the *côté cépage* with the *côté terroir*.

Daniel is particularly enthusiastic about Carignan Blanc, acknowledging that it was Olivier Jullien (see p. 223) who introduced him to it. He had not even known that it existed until he came to the Languedoc and at the time Olivier was the only one to vinify it on its own. The vine nurseries do now offer a Carignan Blanc clone, and there is also Carignan Gris, but only in Roussillon, not in the Languedoc. Tasting with Daniel is always fun as his enthusiasm is infectious. In 2016, he made four separate pickings and vinifications of Carignan Blanc, at one week intervals from the middle of September to 10 October, and naturally we had to try each of them. The first was firm and stony with very fresh acidity; the second was a little more rounded on the palate; the third fairly similar but with more weight, while the last picking had hints of honey and was rounded with very good acidity. 'I have tamed it!' Daniel asserted. Pleine Lune, which previously was called Ares Blanc, is based on Marsanne and is savoury and rounded; Lune Rousse, a blend of Roussanne with some Carignan Blanc, is elegant with southern notes of white blossom. I particularly liked the 2015 Lune Blanche, a pure Carignan with very good structure and mineral fruit. 'The Chablis of the Languedoc,' I mused. Daniel observed that there is too little white wine in Pézenas to qualify for a white version of the *cru*. Then, to show just how well Carignan Blanc ages, he opened a 2010, with some petrolly notes, an exotic 2009 and an intriguing 2005, also with notes of petrol, not unlike mature Riesling.

Two of Daniel's red wines are named according to the soil, so that *Villefranchien* is based on Grenache Noir, with some ripe cherry fruit and Carbonifère is mainly Syrah, with fresh spice and pepper. The third,

Homo Habilis, from Mourvèdre, aged in barrel for two years, is firm and structured. Daniel has started fermenting whole bunches, which he finds gives more elegance, enhancing the acidity and freshness of the wine.

Next came a Vin Orange made from Carignan Blanc with 10 per cent Roussanne, which spent six weeks on the skins fermenting gently and was then put into an amphora above ground, and subsequently aged in wood for 12 months. We tried a barrel sample of the 2015, which was very intriguing, with tannin, salinity and perfume. To finish, Daniel insisted that we try his Cartagène, his latest passion. The white is made from Carignan Blanc, Roussanne and Marsanne and aged in barrel for a couple of years, so that it is rounded and nutty, ripe with a long sweet finish. The red is made reductively from Grenache Noir, so that it tastes of fresh ripe cherries, not unlike a young Maury. Next came a 10-year-old solera, Cartagène de Solera, from Carignan Blanc, from between 2003 and 2013, as well as some Roussanne, Marsanne and Grenache. It was not unlike a *vin santo* from Tuscany, and very intriguing and long.

Things do not stand still chez Daniel. He has planted some Cinsaut, saying that he looking for *légèreté*, or lightness, because he is tired of wines that are too powerful. He is planning a new *cuvée*, Cinsaut blended with Mourvèdre, an unusual combination that I shall be curious to try in a few years' time.

Château La Font des Ormes
Caux 34720
www.fontdesormes.fr

Château La Font des Ormes lies off the road between Nizas and Caux. Guy Cazalis de Fondouce is one of the many people in the Languedoc who have come to wine after a successful career in another field, in his case child psychiatry, in both France and La Réunion. His family comes from the Languedoc, with an estate near Villeveyrac, but he wanted land of his own and bought La Font des Ormes in 2002, since when he has gradually bought more vineyards, replanting some and retaining old vines of Carignan and Terret Blanc. He began working with Claude Bourguignon, a soil specialist, who advised on the purchase of a particularly fine plot of old Carignan on basalt. In fact, most of Guy's appellation vineyards are on basalt, for there is an extinct volcano nearby. As well as Carignan, Guy has Grenache Noir, Syrah and Mourvèdre, and is replanting some Cinsaut. There are Merlot and Marselan for IGPs, grown in sandier soil, as well as Terret Blanc, for a first white wine with the 2017 vintage. There was a lot of work to do at the beginning; the grapes were fit for the local cooperative, but not much more. These days Guy makes a range of three red wines, and has a flexible arrangement with the cooperative in Adissan, which takes any grapes, such as those from young vines, that he does not want. The property now comprises 20 hectares, with 17 hectares of vineyards, 14 of which are currently in production. The first serious vintage that he put in bottle was 2011.

The cellar is a splendid old Languedoc barn, dating from the eighteenth century. Originally there were several 200-hectolitre concrete vats. These days one functions as a small office, while the others have been replaced by stainless steel and smaller tronconic cement vats. Three enormous stone vats have been knocked into one and now function as a barrel cellar.

The range comprises firstly a Pays de Caux, a blend of 45 per cent Marselan and 55 per cent Grenache Noir, intended for easy drinking. The AOP Languedoc is a blend of 45 per cent Grenache, with 25 per cent Mourvèdre, 15 per cent Syrah and 15 per cent Carignan and is more serious, with the wine spending a year in vat, followed by a year in *demi-muids*. Guy asserted that basalt gives elegance to a wine; and elegance is what he is looking for. For his winemaking, Guy is advised by Jean Natoli and he favours short extractions, with quick *remontages* and, above all, does not want what he called 'violent' tannins. For that reason, although he first bought *barriques*, he has moved onto *demi-muids*. Finally, there is a Pézenas *cuvée* with 40 per cent Grenache Noir to balance 30 per cent each of Syrah and Carignan. This is given a longer ageing in *demi-muids*, making for more depth than the Languedoc, with some appealing spice and fruit.

The year 2016 was marked by a lack of water but Guy told us that Claude Bourguignon has been advising him on rootstocks that send out deep roots in search of water, so that his vines have not suffered from water stress. The vineyards were certified as organic in 2016, but 'that is not complicated enough' so now they are working on biodynamics. A viticulturist who worked with Anne Leflaive in Burgundy advises them.

We discussed sales opportunities, with Guy making the pertinent observation that 'we are *méconnu dans un region méconnu*', 'an unknown estate in an unknown region'. But that is sure to change.

Domaine Ste Cécile du Parc

Pezenas 34120
www.stececileduparc.com

Domaine Ste Cécile du Parc, outside Pézenas, backs on to the enormous walled property of le Parc, which is enclosed by a large wall and dates back to the Middle Ages. If you are looking carefully, you will see two sets of open gates on either side of the road between Caux and Pézenas.

Christine Mouton Bertoli and her husband Stéphane made their first wine in 2005, and now have 15 hectares of vines, of which 12 are in production, planted with Grenache Noir, Merlot, Cabernet Franc, Syrah and Sauvignon Gris as well as Blanc, and also some olive trees. The Cabernet Franc, for which Stéphane has particular enthusiasm, and the Grenache Noir are recent plantings, replacing vineyards of Aramon. They have carried out a lot of soil analysis; they have limestone and clay, some *villefranchien* and a little sandstone. Their work in the vineyard is meticulous, paying attention to the shading and aeration of the bunches, and there is some drip irrigation for the young vines. They were officially registered organic in 2013.

The previous owner sent his grapes to the Caux cooperative, so they needed to build a cellar, a spacious streamlined building, which was ready for the 2011 vintage. There is a brand-new basket press, and cement vats of varying sizes, as well as wooden tronconic vats, stainless steel tanks and a couple of concrete eggs, in addition to barrels.

As Ste Cécile is the patron saint of music, all the names of their wines have a musical association. Notes Pures is a blend of Sauvignon Blanc and Sauvignon Gris, vinified in tank and then aged in *demi-muids* to add some creaminess. Notes Frivoles is a blend of Syrah, Grenache Noir, Carignan and Cabernet Franc, a pretty, pale rosé, with some crisp fruit. Like the white, it is a Pays de Caux, which they prefer to Pays d'Oc because it is more original, even if less well known. Several reds follow. Notes Franches is a blend of Cabernet Franc and Merlot, with some luscious ripe fruit; Notes d'Orphée is Syrah with 15 per cent Cabernet

Franc, which adds freshness; Sonatina, Pézenas, is a blend of 75 per cent Syrah and 25 per cent Cinsaut, aged in *barriques* and *demi-muids*; and Mouton Bertoli is 80 per cent Cabernet Franc and 20 per cent Syrah, aged partly in new oak and partly in second-fill barrels. The 2011 was the first vintage of this wine. We tasted the 2012, which was smoky with some oak, a touch of pepper and a fresh finish, promising to turn into a very satisfying bottle. And why so much Cabernet Franc? Quite simply, Stéphane loves Château Cheval Blanc!

Domaine Monplézy

Pézenas 34120
www.monplezy.fr

Anne Sutra de Germa's family has been involved with wine for six generations. A great-great-grandfather was a *négociant* in Bordeaux; her grandfather bought vines outside Pézenas in the 1930s; and her father sent his grapes to the cooperative. However, when Anne took over Monplézy in 2000, she decided to make her own wine, helped first by her husband, Christian, and now their son, Benoît. His first vintage here was 2013, after working in both California and Provence, and he is gradually making his mark and introducing new wines from their 23 hectares of vineyards just outside Pézenas.

As well as Pézenas, they also make the local IGP Côtes de Thongue. Their vineyards have been registered organic since 2012 and Anne is adamant that organic viticulture adds an extra dimension of expression to their wines, in particular enhancing the freshness and elegance. All their labels carry the outline of a hoopoe, a bird with a distinctive voice that you often see and hear in the vineyards. Their label Le Canon Huppé is a play on words, for *huppé* refers to the bird and also means posh, whereas a *canon* is the slang for a glass of wine. With his experience in Provence, Benoît is making elegant rosé, with Le Plaisir based on Cinsaut and Emocion based on Grenache Noir. The white wines include Le Canon Huppé, a pure Viognier, for Benoît likes single varieties, as well as Felicité, a blend of Marsanne, Roussanne and Viognier, and Emocion, an unusual blend of Sauvignon and Viognier. As for red wines, Canon Huppé is pure Cinsaut; Plaisirs is a spicy blend of Grenache Noir, Carignan, Cinsaut and Syrah; Emocion is mainly Syrah with just 5 per cent Carignan, aged in wood for 14 months; and

Felicité is their Pézenas, a blend of Grenache Noir, Carignan and Syrah, also aged in oak for 14 months.

The last time I visited Monplézy, Anne treated me to a small vertical tasting of Felicité, from 2015 back to 2011. The 2015 was young and structured; 2014 beautifully balanced with cassis fruit; 2013 was tighter in comparison; 2012 a wetter vintage, with supple fruit; and the star was 2011, which had developed some attractive tertiary aromas of dry spice and *garrigue* and was just reaching its plateau. The final red wine was a new *cuvée* for Anne's grand-daughter, Gabrielle, born in 2013. Grenache de Gabrielle has lovely ripe cherry fruit on the palate, while Délice is just that, made from Grenache Noir picked at the end of October and aged in wood for two years. It is rich and sweet with ripe cherry fruit. All that was missing was some dark chocolate to accompany it!

Mas Gabriel
Caux 34720
www.mas-gabriel.co.uk

Deborah and Peter Core learnt their winemaking in New Zealand after leaving high-powered jobs in London, as a solicitor and accountant respectively, but eventually it was time to return to Europe. They spent two years looking for the right vineyards, between Perpignan and Nîmes and even in the Rhône Valley. The Languedoc appealed as it offers great opportunities, with a growing reputation. Their criteria were north- or east-facing vineyards, on *coteaux*, or gentle slopes, with Mediterranean varieties planted on interesting soil, and if possible already farmed organically. And that is pretty much what they found in the village of Caux. They bought 5 hectares, with Syrah, Carignan and a little Grenache, and some bare land. Now they have just over 6 hectares in production and have added Carignan Blanc, Vermentino and Grenache Gris, on a variety of soils – basalt, *villefranchien*, and limestone. Their first vintage was 2006.

Their range has gradually evolved so that they now make two white wines, Clos du Papillon, from Carignan Blanc with 20 per cent Vermentino, kept only in vat, with some nutty herbal notes, and Champs des Bluets, from 70 per cent Vermentino with Grenache Gris. The Vermentino is aged in vat, while unusually they ferment and age the Grenache Gris in acacia wood. The flavours are elegant and herbal. Fleurs Sauvages, from equal parts of Carignan, Cinsaut and Grenache Gris, is an elegant rosé with delicate raspberry fruit. They make two red wines. Les Trois Terrasses, Pays de l'Hérault, is a pure Carignan, and as the name suggests is grown on three different adjoining terraces. It is firm and structured with good fruit and a fresh finish, and as a vertical tasting showed, capable of development in bottle. The 2009 at nearly eight years old had filled out to develop some rounded, supple leathery notes. Clos des Lièvres, Pézenas, is based on Syrah with 20 per cent Grenache Noir, aged in 500-litre barrels. The young wine is firm and peppery, while the 2012, tasted when it was five years old, was richer and more chocolatey, with some ripe tannins. Although Peter and Deborah only make one wine that is Pézenas, they are very positive about the future of the area.

Deborah and Peter Core, Mas Gabriel

Domaine Lacroix-Vanel
Caux 34720
www.domainelacroix-vanel.com

This estate has recently changed hands. It was bought from Jean-Pierre Vanel by Marc-Olivier Bertand, who arrived in Caux just in time for the 2016 harvest. Marc-Olivier comes from Alsace and, after studying agriculture and then oenology, worked in Limoux and the Côtes de Provence for a number years. However, he really wanted to do his own thing. He saw Jean-Pierre Vanel's vines were for sale and liked what he saw and tasted, so with the help of Ludovic Aventin from Terra Hominis he acquired 130 co-owners for his 8.5 hectares of vineyards and set up his own company for the production of the wine. The vineyards were already farmed organically, which was an important factor in his decision.

Marc-Olivier Bertrand of Domaine Lacroix-Vanel

We went to see them on a sunny autumn day. After some rain the previous week, there was vegetation in the vineyard, contrasting sharply with the neighbour's across the road, without a single blade of grass in sight. Marc Olivier talked eloquently about sowing *engrais verts*, or green fertilizer, and maintaining humidity and life in the soil. Back in his small cellar in the village we tasted some vat samples of the 2017 vintage. The range will stay the same as Jean-Pierre's, all Pézenas, with Fine Amor, mainly Grenache; Mélanie, predominantly Syrah; and Ma Non Troppo, principally Mourvèdre. The bottled wines are still inevitably Jean-Pierre's but the vat samples promised well. Marc-Olivier opened the 2014 Fine Amor, with some elegant perfumed fruit, and then the 2010 Mélanie, pointing out that 'this is the wine that convinced me to buy the estate'. It had some satisfying notes of evolution with supple tannins and a fresh finish. You sense that he will follow successfully in Jean-Pierre's footsteps.

ROUJAN

My own village of Roujan comes within the *cru* of Pézenas. When we first arrived, its viticultural activity was dominated by a rather lacklustre cooperative, which concentrated on selling wine in bulk to the *négoce*. Subsequently they have done what so many other cooperatives have done, that is join up with neighbouring cooperatives to share the overheads. They do bottle some wine, but it is certainly not worth seeking out. However, things are looking up, with the development of three new small wine estates, so Roujan may yet earn its place on a map of the Languedoc's finest. Although Pézenas is only part of their offering, this is the most logical chapter in which to place them.

Producers

Domaine Picaro's

Roujan 34320
cvioche@orange.fr

Pierre Rouillé comes from a long-established Roujan family. His grandfather had the traditional Languedoc cellar with large *foudres*, while his father preferred to put his vines into the Roujan cooperative. Pierre studied oenology at Dijon and then he and his wife, Caroline, went to work in Chile, in the Maule valley, for three years. When they returned to France, they wanted to create something from the family vines, and their first *cuvée* was born, Amano, a blend of Syrah and Grenache, handmade, as the name implies, with meticulous attention to detail, aged partly in barrel and partly in vat. From 2015 it was Pézenas.

They have 11 hectares altogether and ten different grape varieties but only produce wine from 4 hectares, with the other 7 in the Roujan cooperative. Meanwhile, Pierre is director of the Marseillan cooperative, which has a sound reputation for its Côtes de Thau. From Amano their range has developed and they made a white wine, Princesse, for the first time in 2016. It is a blend of 60 per cent Grenache Blanc in vat and 40 per cent Chardonnay aged in *demi-muids*, with six months' *bâtonnage* for both. They wanted a wine with good body and ripe flavours, and that is what they have achieved, with structure and some tension. Eclosion, Pays d'Oc, is almost pure Carignan, softened by a touch of Syrah, vinified in whole bunches, with some rounded fruit. Caroline, who makes the wine, likes Syrah a lot. It ripens well, and she wants to avoid any hard tannins, so that it has a peppery freshness. And why *éclosion*, which means hatching? They found a bird's nest in the vineyard. Plurielles AOP Languedoc is mainly Syrah with some Grenache Noir, with some appealing spice.

For the moment, they do not make a rosé. Caroline sees it as too technological. It is a *vin de soif*, and they simply do not have the space to make any large volumes but she admits that she is tempted, after trying Domaine la Sauvageonne's barrel fermented La Vila.

Domaine des Abournières
Roujan 34320
Tel: + 33 (0)6 85 02 92 91

Philippe Gallart works in a somewhat chaotic cellar in his modern house on the hill opposite the chapel of St Nazaire. Following a career with IBM he bought his vines in 2000 and until 2010 sent his grapes to the Neffiès cooperative. Altogether he has eight plots totalling 4 hectares, from which he makes three wines, all Vin de France, from Syrah, Grenache Noir and Merlot. Philippe is very much his own man. He admits to learning a lot from David Astruc of Domaine de la Reclauze in Neffiès and was inspired by some of the wines of nearby Domaine Brescou and now 'follows his nose'. He is a saxophone player, hence the instrument on his labels, and also played international rugby, notably at Cardiff in 1994. As for his wine, the Grenache is made into rosé and he was planning a red with it in 2017. The Merlot was ripe and rounded with a streak of tannin and the Syrah was fresh and peppery. Both are given a long maceration in fibreglass tanks, and there is no oak, which Philippe does not like. He is happy with his 4 hectares, observing that wine, like music and rugby, is a great vector for communication.

La Grange de Bouys

Roujan 34320
www.grangedebouys.fr

The third newcomer to Roujan is La Grange de Bouys. Again, this represents a change of direction. After a successful career in international finance, it was time for Stéphane Monmouseau and his wife Florence to leave Paris. Their initial purchase was land without vines, but Stéphane has wine in his genes. He is part of the Monmousseau family who make wine in the Loire valley, and despite the fact that Florence was adamant that she was not going to be a farmer's wife, they bought vineyards and now have 7 hectares of vines in one large plot outside Roujan. We went for a walk early one summer's evening and admired young plantings of Clairette and Vermentino as well as the dry-stone walls that Florence has beautifully restored around the vineyards.

Adjoining their house is one of the classic Languedoc cellars, with the enormous *foudres* that are now part of the history of the region. Consequently, Stéphane has the luxury of space and his small stainless steel vats are dwarfed in comparison. He is also proud of his one Stockinger barrel. The range has gradually evolved since their first vintage in 2014, beginning with just two different red wines, and currently two whites, both from Grenache Blanc and some Clairette, one oaked and the other not, and a fresh rosé, Pays de l'Hérault. As for reds, Le Vin des Amis is an intriguing blend of Syrah with a little Grenache Blanc, following the practice in Côte Rôtie of adding Viognier to Syrah, and it is fresh and spicy. A Carignan Vieilles Vignes is nicely structured with fresh red fruit and Cuvée St Andrieu, AOP Languedoc, is mainly Syrah, with some Grenache Noir and Carignan, co-fermented and partly aged in oak. The oak is nicely integrated and the flavour fresh and peppery. After a year studying in Burgundy, Stéphane has a clear idea of his winemaking style, making balanced wines emphasizing one grape variety. He does not want overly extracted wines and uses as little sulphur as possible. The vineyards are being gradually converted to biodynamic viticulture. In many ways, he is very characteristic of the many small wine growers who have come to the area as a result of a change in career and direction.

14

CABRIÈRES

Cabrières was one of the original *terroirs* of the Coteaux du Languedoc and has fiercely maintained its independence, despite suggestions that it might join the neighbouring appellation of the Terrasses du Larzac, or the *cru* of Pézenas. Ultimately it would like the status of *appellation communale*, without any specific reference to Languedoc on the label. The next stage is to submit the appropriate dossier to the INAO, probably sometime in 2018.

There is a well-founded feeling that Cabrières is quite individual. The village is surrounded by hillsides, giving it a very precise delimitation and the vineyards are dominated by an extinct volcano, the Pic de Vissou, which rises to 480 metres. It makes a challenging and rewarding walk. The appellation will cover not only red but also rosé, as Cabrières has a historical reputation for its rosé, with a reference to *vin vermeil* in the archives of Montpellier, dated 1357.

As the name implies, the original vocation of Cabrières was pastoral. I was told that at the beginning of the nineteenth century there were as many as three or four thousand sheep and goats in the village. Today all the goats have long since gone – the last goatherd died in 1984 – and viticulture is the main occupation. The cooperative of Cabrières accounts for about half of the production of 500 hectares and in addition there are a handful of other estates, of which two, Domaine du Temple and Domaine des Deux Rocs, have recently been purchased by Gérard Bertrand. Clos Romain is a small estate with some original wines, that also produces olive oil, while Domaine Valbrune, although it has vines in Cabrières, has its cellar in nearby Tressan.

The geology of the village is intriguing. There were copper mines here in the third millennium BC, which makes them the oldest in France, if not Europe, and mining continued until the middle of the nineteenth century, when it became unproductive. The vineyards lie on the band of schist that runs from Berlou, covering the northern part of St Chinian and the whole of Faugères. However, you will be told that the schist of Cabrières is different from that of its neighbours.

Producers

Caves de l'Estabel

Cabrières 34800
www.estabel.fr

The cooperative of Cabrières is one of the more successful cooperatives of the Languedoc and works well for its area. The director, Luc Flache, is all too aware of its importance to the village economy. Quite simply, without the cooperative, the vineyards would have returned to *garrigue*. It was founded in 1937, and after the Second World War took the then very forward-thinking decision to start bottling its wine, realizing this was a way to maintain the flourishing viticultural activity in the village. The brand L'Estabel was created, named after a spring that runs occasionally from the nearby hills. The spring was last seen in 1996. Currently there are 60 members, of whom 20 account for 85 per cent of the production. For the rest, their vines are a hobby – a weekend job and a connection with the land.

These days rosé accounts for half the production of the cooperative, notably L'Estabel Grande Cuvée, which is a blend mainly of Cinsaut with some Syrah and Grenache Noir. The grapes are picked at night and pressed for a cool fermentation. The wine is fresh and rounded, with light raspberry fruit. Cuvée Fulcrand Cabanon, after the village priest who was attributed with presenting Cabrières to the court of Louis XIV, benefits from a *sélection parcellaire*, with more Syrah and Grenache, so that the wine is more structured, with a fresh finish. There is also a satisfactory range of red wines, mainly based on Syrah and Grenache. Mourvèdre does not perform so well in Cabrières. Champs des Cistes, from two-thirds Syrah to one-third Grenache, has the spice of the *garrigue*, with a streak of tannin, while Cantate des Garrigues, from one-third Syrah and two-thirds Grenache, is rounded and supple.

Château de Cabrières, with some ageing in barrel, is more structured, and Luc described Prieuré des Crozes, a blend of 70 per cent Syrah with Grenache Noir, as *la crème de la crème* because it enjoys a *sélection parcellaire* and some ageing in new wood, with structure and ageing potential.

Asked about the typicity of Cabrières, Luc suggested that it was more powerful than Faugères. Schist gives body, with an underlying suppleness. As for the future, he sees the creation of the appellation as a long-term ambition, observing that the French have a very strong sense of place, not just for wine, but for so many other products – cheese, olive oil and so on. The Languedoc is at the beginning of its identification of appellations: 'We have barely started.' He is confident that Gérard Bertrand's involvement will help the development of the appellation, as is Jean Attard at Mas Coris, who observed that his marketing power would help make Cabrières better known.

Mas Coris

Cabrières 34800
www.mascoris.com

The other significant estate in the village is Mas Coris, again the result of a career change, this time from journalism. After spending 25 years writing for diving magazines, Jean Attard explained that he wanted a name with a link to the sea, and Coris – or to give its full name *Coris julis* – is a girelle, or rainbow fish. It also has a satisfyingly memorable ring about it. His old university friend Jean Natoli helped him find vineyards in Cabrières and he has gradually developed the estate to total 5 hectares in eight plots, mostly at the foot of the Pic de Vissou. Jean recalls that Jean Natoli told him when he was looking for his vineyard land that there are three criteria: namely, a small area, a beautiful spot, and plenty of motivation. Jean now has an old cellar in the centre of the village and made his first wine in 2010. His grapes are all hand-picked, with the help of friends, and his labels acknowledge this with a very *sympathique* mention: Jean et Véronique et leurs amis. He uses a small basket press and sorts the grapes in the cellar after they have been destemmed so that only perfect grapes go into the press.

His range is all Cabrières. Atout Pic is from Syrah with some Cinsaut, with some appealing easy fruit. Bouteilles à la Mer is his principal *cuvée*, from Syrah, Cinsaut and Grenache, including just 5 per cent Syrah aged in wood, with some dry, spicy fruit. Pic de Vissou, from Syrah and Grenache, is also aged in wood, with sturdier fruit. The final wine in the range is Tethys, from Cinsaut, Syrah and Grenache, aged half in vat and half in barrel, with some spicy, leathery notes. It is not made every year; it all depends on the quality of the Cinsaut. Jean is particularly enthusiastic about Cinsaut, considering it a magnificent grape variety. To use it just for rosé is to do it a gross disservice. Our tasting concluded with a delicious *bonne bouche*, a Cartagène de Clairette, from late harvested Clairette, with the flavours of honey and raisins.

15

CLAIRETTE DU LANGUEDOC

Clairette du Languedoc was the earliest white table wine appellation of the region, with its decree signed in 1948. The appellation stipulates Clairette Blanche but does not allow Clairette Rose, although, happily, the vinification methods were not defined, which allows for considerable variations of flavour, from young and fresh to mature, and variations of sweetness, from late harvest and *rancio*. The area covers a small group of villages between Pézenas and Clermont l'Hérault. Today, while there is renewed interest in the potential of Clairette as one of the indigenous grape varieties of the Languedoc, with its ability to withstand heat and drought, the appellation of Clairette du Languedoc has few producers The cooperatives of Adissan and Cabrières are the biggest; Domaines Paul Mas buys wine from two other cooperatives; and Charles-Walter Pacaud at Domaine la Croix Chaptal is the lone protagonist amongst the independent wine growers. No one can make a living from Clairette alone, and Charles-Walter also makes a range of red wines, as the southernmost estate of the Terrasses du Larzac, close to St André de Sangonis.

Producers

Domaine la Croix Chaptal

St-André-de-Sangonis 34725
www.lacroixchaptal.com

I went to see Charles-Walter on 14 September 2017, which, as it happened, was the day that he was picking Clairette, three weeks earlier than usual. Out of a total of 18 hectares, he has 2 hectares of Clairette Blanche, and also some Clairette Rose, all 50-year-old vines, with the rose *complanté* with the blanche. We walked in the vineyards and could see that the grapes were dark pink, as opposed to the pale pink of a *gris* variety. Charles-Walter considers Clairette to be the white grape variety of the Languedoc. It is a later ripener and resists drought giving a wine that is rich and rounded at 13% abv. He finds the white version of Clairette quite rustic, whereas the rose is more elegant, and he has planted more of it, but for the appellation Languedoc Blanc, which allows up to 10 per cent Clairette Rose. Apparently, the possibility of an appellation for Clairette du Languedoc was considered as early as 1936, with the designated area agreed, but the *bordelais* objected to the name Clairette, claiming that it would cause confusion with claret.

Charles-Walter treated us to a vertical tasting of his Clairette, going back to 2007, explaining that he gives the wine a long *élevage*, partly in barrels and partly in vat, with some initial *bâtonnage*, but he just leaves it to rest gently after the first five or six months. There is a little skin contact while he is filling the press; essentially his method is *à la bourguignonne*, with lees contact in the barrel. The *élevage* gives greater complexity and longevity. The 2015, which he was just about to bottle in September 2017, was honeyed on both nose and palate, with hints of quince, texture and acidity, and a long finish. There were subtle nuances with each vintage, but dry honey was the common theme, and also an element of bitterness on the finish, which is a qualitative factor. No wine was made in 2011 following a devastating hail storm, and while the 2009 was quite evolved, the 2007 was extraordinarily fresh and herbal. I had no idea that Clairette could age quite so well. Our tasting finished with a 2010 Rancio Vendange Tardive. The grapes were more botrytized than *passerillé*, and picked in November. Rancio dictates a minimum of three years' ageing in barrel, while Charles-Walter prefers five to seven years. He observed that with a *rancio* wine 'you control absolutely nothing'. You need an Indian summer after some rain in October, so that mornings are damp and the afternoons dry. Clairette is quite thick skinned, so it can cope with humidity, and it is quite susceptible to botrytis. The only thing you can decide is the moment to pick. The wine had extraordinary acidity and freshness as well as honeyed, nutty notes and a smooth finish with a firm bite.

Caves de l'Estabel

Cabrières 34800
www.estabel.fr

The cooperative in Cabrières has about 30 hectares of Clairette du Languedoc, from which they make three styles of wine, *sec, moelleux* and a *vin de liqueur*. The dry version, Cuvée Fulcrand Cabanon, is given a slow fermentation and an *élevage* on the lees so that the wine is rounded and textured, with a slightly salty finish. They are considering some barrel ageing for a second wine. *Moelleux* implies about 40 grams per litre residual sugar. These grapes are the last to be harvested, when the potential alcohol level is about 14% abv, and the wine is fermented very slowly and centrifuged at the appropriate moment to remove any remaining yeast. The flavours are elegantly honeyed with a fresh finish. Luc Flache, the director of the cooperative, observed that the tradition of Clairette is for *moelleux* rather than dry wine. Occasionally, about every five or six years, they make a *vin de liqueur*, which is fortified like a *vin doux naturel*, with an alcohol level of about 17% abv. The wine is kept for four years in barrel and develops dry, nutty notes, with a hint of honey, with orange and almonds, and a firm bite on the finish. It is very gratifying that a village cooperative continues to maintain what is potentially a dying tradition.

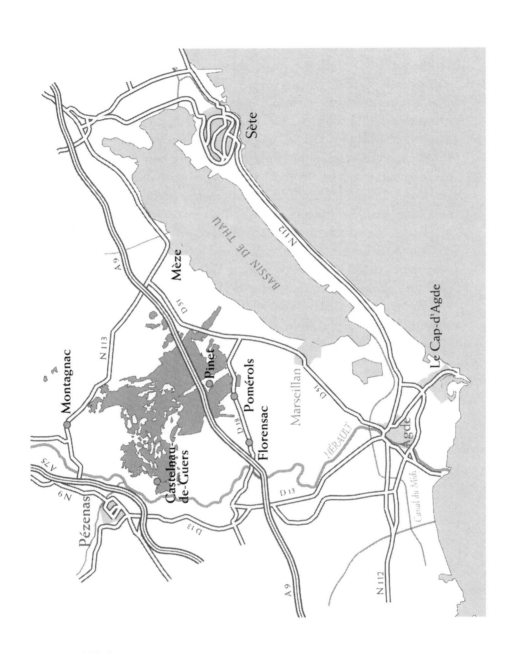

16

PICPOUL DE PINET

One of my favourite Languedoc moments is lunch on the waterfront at Bouzigues, at Le Grand Bleu. If you have a table upstairs, you are able to look out on the oyster beds of the étang de Thau while you eat oysters or mussels that probably came of out of the étang that morning or the previous day. And you are sipping the perfect accompaniment, the fresh, dry white wine that is Picpoul de Pinet. All is right with the world, the sun is shining, the water is sparkling in the sunlight, and the wine is delicious, with a lemony saline note to complement the oysters.

Picpoul de Pinet has enjoyed an enormous surge in popularity in recent years. Gérard Bertrand even suggested that it was the Pinot Gris of the Languedoc! There is hardly a restaurant wine list in London that does not include it. People now order Picpoul de Pinet much in the same way as they order Chablis or Côtes du Rhône, paying scant attention to the wine grower's name. They know that the quality is reliable and the flavours enjoyable. Yet not so long ago Picpoul de Pinet was in the doldrums.

The original history of Picpoul de Pinet is based on the vermouth, notably Noilly Prat, which is produced in nearby Marseillan. Piquepoul, as the variety should be spelt, was once a relatively common grape, grown all over the south of France, but was gradually abandoned, only to remain around the étang de Thau, but principally for the vermouth trade. Terret Blanc was more popular for its bigger berries and resistance to disease and by the early 1970s there was very little Piquepoul left. However, with the development of the seaside resorts and the tourist trade in the 1970s, its fortunes began to revive. As Guy Bascou, of Domaine Condamine l'Evêque (see p. 326), who was until recently the very articulate president of the syndicat of Picpoul de Pinet, put it, 'there was an explosion in technology', particularly for white wine, with more gentle pressing, cool fermentations and the prevention of oxidization, all aspects of winemaking that we take for granted these days. Also, Piquepoul has a considerable advantage in the Mediterranean climate; it retains its acidity.

The export market for Picpoul de Pinet is currently very buoyant, with the United Kingdom the biggest customer. Joël Julien, the very able director of the cooperative of Pomerols, talked about the success of Picpoul. When he arrived at the cooperative in 2009, there was no demand at all for Picpoul and they did not know how to sell it. However, they were lucky. First they found a solid partner in London, the wine shippers Liberty Wines, and then in 2010 they began supplying the supermarket giant Tesco for their 'Finest' label, for which the turning point was winning the accolade of Best White Wine of the Languedoc in the annual Top 100 tasting competition. This gave an enormous boost to Picpoul de Pinet, establishing its reputation, and helped pave the way to the establishment of the appellation. Picpoul de Pinet was recognized as an appellation in its own right, without any supporting mention of Languedoc on the label, in 2013.

The delimited appellation of Picpoul de Pinet covers 2,400 hectares, of which about 1,500 are actually planted with Piquepoul, covering six villages, Pinet, Pomerols, Montagnac, Florensac, Mèze and Castelnau-de-Guers. It seems that the *délimitation parcellaire*, determining exactly which vineyards were to be included, was quite problematic, with vineyards being eliminated that merited inclusion or indeed vice versa. Vineyards that are not Picpoul de Pinet are classified as IGP Côtes de Thau, and most wine producers make both.

So, what determines the appellation? The altitude is low, with vineyards barely above sea level on gently rolling land rather than completely flat plains. The climate is influenced by the proximity to the sea, with vineyards generally facing east, looking towards the étang de Thau for the sea breezes. Rainfall is a significant factor in the summer; the southern part of the appellation below the motorway and the Via Domitia is more exposed to drought than the northern part. The soil is predominantly limestone, with some sandy deposits.

Producers

Cave Coopérative les Costières

Pomerols 34810
www.cave-pomerols.com

Although four cooperatives make Picpoul de Pinet, there are two for whom it is their flagship wine, namely Pomerols and Pinet. A visit to the cooperative in Pomerols entails a walk through a forest of stainless steel tanks, past a state-of-the-art bottling line. Since 2000 they have invested €20 million (US$24.7 million), one-third of which was EU subsidies. The technology has improved enormously in recent years and so has the work in the vineyards. Half of their members, of which there are 300, cultivating 1,750 hectares of vines, including 450 of Piquepoul, practise what they call *lutte biologique*, which entails abandoning the use of weedkiller and using an *intercep* to deal with weeds between the vines. These practices are not fully organic, but it helps to build the image of the appellation and they are generally much more respectful of the environment. They are also very aware of their proximity to the étang de Thau, with its fragile ecosystem and oyster beds.

Where once they made just one Picpoul de Pinet, they now make a whole range of different wines, depending on vineyard selection and variations in vinification, including *élevage* on the lees, which may affect acidity and weight. Beauvignac is their principal brand, a fresh stony wine, benefiting from a simple vinification and a little lees stirring. Cuvée Anniversaire comes from older vines, entailing more work with the lees and a longer *élevage*, to make for a wine with more weight. Cap Cette, with a more detailed selection of vineyards, is richer and more exuberant. They also have a Picpoul *fût de chêne*, with solid, oaky flavours, and a Picpoul Brut, *méthode traditionnelle*, as well as a *moelleux* made by stopping the fermentation to leave about 35 grams per litre of residual sugar. That is Côtes de Thau rather than Picpoul de Pinet. They make a range of Côtes de Thau, including a particularly successful rosé from a blend of Grenache Noir, Cinsaut, Carignan and a touch of Merlot, as well as various varietal wines, both red and white.

Cave de l'Ormarine
Pinet 34850
www.cave-ormarine.com

Cyril Payon, the bright director of the Pinet cooperative, is very aware of the success of Picpoul de Pinet, and also of its possibly precarious position. He attributes its success to a series of circumstances; Muscadet in decline; people getting bored with Pinot Grigio; the excitement of a new appellation with an appealing identity and a very good *rapport qualité–prix*, as the French so succinctly describe wines of good quality that are reasonably priced. Back in 2000 they produced 14,000 hectolitres of Picpoul de Pinet, which was difficult to sell. They now make 33,000 hectolitres, which they have no problem in selling. Currently, one-third of it goes to the United Kingdom; it remains to be seen what the effect of Brexit will be. Although the recognition of the appellation brought a reduction in the vineyard area, there has actually been an increase in production, as Piquepoul has replaced other varieties. The cooperative at Pinet has links with the cooperatives in Villeveyrac, where they make red wine, and also Cournonterral, which includes St Georges d'Orques, and most recently with nearby Vias, as well as St Hippolyte-du-Fort in the Gard, but their focus at Pinet is on Picpoul. They favour concrete vats over stainless steel because the temperature changes are less dramatic, and have several different sizes of presses, which gives them flexibility at harvest time. The vintage is inevitably fairly concentrated, usually occurring between about 10 and 25 September. They too are very aware of the ecological repercussions of their proximity to the étang de Thau. Two-thirds of their members follow Terra Vitis, the organization for *lutte raisonnée*, and Cyril hopes that by 2018 they will all be practising *lutte raisonnée*. The next step would be organic viticulture, but many of the vines are not suitable for the use of an *intercep*. He also points out that the carbon footprint can be higher with organic viticulture because tractors tend to be used more. In addition, they are erecting *nicheoires*, or nesting boxes, for bats.

Taste in their caveau and you will immediately become aware of the diversity of Picpoul de Pinet. Carte Noire is fresh and lemony, with good acidity. Duc de Morny comes from riper grapes and older vines. A Picpoul *sur lies* amply illustrates the benefit of *bâtonnage*, with a selection of better vineyards and lower yields, making for some firm mineral flavours. L'Effet Mer is a blend of Duc de Morny and Picpoul *sur lies*, combining the best of both. Esprit Libre was an experiment in 2016, using no sulphur, which received mixed reactions as the colour was very golden and the flavour quite unlike traditional Picpoul. A sparkling wine, *méthode traditionnelle*, was remarkably successful, with fresh, salty fruit, and in some years they make a late-harvest wine.

Château St Martin de la Garrigue
Montagnac 34530
www.stmartingarrigue.com

One of the most important producers of Picpoul de Pinet is Domaine St Martin de la Garrigue. I first visited this property in the 1980s when it was owned by the Henry family, who sold it to an Italian, Umberto Guido, with the talented Jean-Claude Zabalia as his manager and winemaker. François Henry in the meantime has gone on to make highly original wines in St Georges d'Orques. In 2011 it was sold again, to a Russian, Boris Pukhunov, who also has vineyards in southern Russia as well as a distillery, and a wine estate in Bulgaria, and also Domaine St Louis in the Corbières, at Boutenac. In Mr Pukhunov's absence, the estate is very ably run by Jean-Luc Parret, who lived in Moscow for 20 years. The Château of St Martin dates back to the sixteenth century, and is now beautifully restored. A tenth-century chapel with faded wall paintings adjoins the château and there are some elegant gardens.

The winemaker is Jean-François Farinet, who amongst other places, spent ten years with Delas in the Rhône Valley, and worked with Luc Sorin in Burgundy. Jean-François talked about making Piquepoul, which can be quite a neutral grape variety, but if handled correctly, indeed imaginatively, it becomes much more original, with a greater depth of flavour. He favours a later picking, as much as ten days later than many of the cooperative members, who tend to pick early because it is a fragile variety, at risk of rot from the humidity of the sea breezes. A little skin contact and a fermentation at a low temperature enhance the aroma. For Jean-François, Piquepoul should always have a lemony note, and some fresh salinity, with a slightly bitter note from the skin contact. He wants complexity, even with a *mono-cépage*, observing that the impact of vinification is greater on a *mono-cépage* than on a blend. The bitter note gives tension, and that is what he seeks in his wine.

They make a range of other wines at St Martin de la Garrigue. Bronzinelle Blanc, AOP Languedoc, is a blend of 55 per cent Grenache Blanc, giving the wine body, with 15 per cent Marsanne and 20 per cent Roussanne, which provide aroma, and just 10 per cent Piquepoul, giving a citrus iodine note. Bronzinelle Rosé comes from Grenache Noir and Cinsaut, all pressed, with minimum skin contact, while Bronzinelle Rouge comes from 50-year-old Syrah vines, with some Grenache Noir and Mourvèdre. Two-thirds of the wine is aged in oak and they are gradually shifting from *barriques* to larger *demi-muids*. The wine is redolent of spice and they consider it the most characteristic of the *terroir* of St Martin.

In contrast, they think their *cuvée* of Grés de Montpellier represents their savoir-faire, as it comes from their oldest vines with the lowest yield. Their 18 hectares of Grés de Montpellier are in the most western part of that appellation, adjoining the north-western corner of Picpoul de Pinet. In fact, they are the only estate to make both appellations. The Hérault valley separates the appellation of Grés de Montpellier from that of Pézenas, even though the soil is similar. The wine is a blend of 45 per cent Syrah, 25 per cent Mourvèdre and the balance is Grenache Noir, coming from older vines, given 12 months' ageing in 500-litre barrels, of one to five fills. Jean-François is looking for silky tannins; he does not like new oak and avoids over-extraction, and the result is rich with powerful elegance and ageing potential.

Domaine La Croix Gratiot
Montagnac 34530
www.croix-gratiot.com

This is an estate that has successfully changed direction under the direction of Anaïs Ricome, who works with her father, Yves. He explained how the estate has evolved. His father and grandfather had vines in the cooperative at Mèze and he has been growing grapes since 1982, initially with his brother, who now concentrates on melons. They used to farm conventionally, but five years ago converted to biodynamic viticulture and are thrilled with the results. They have 8 hectares of Picpoul de Pinet while the other 27 hectares are Pays d'Oc or Pays de l'Hérault. Situated around the cellars, in about ten different plots, they comprise an eclectic range of grapes, including Chardonnay, Viognier,

Sauvignon Blanc, Muscat, Roussanne, and, for reds, Syrah, Cabernet Sauvignon, Grenache Noir, Mourvèdre and Pinot Noir. The planting of Grenache Noir and Mourvèdre allowed them to make their first *cuvée* of AOP Languedoc in 2017.

Yves explained how they make two different Picpoul de Pinet. For the simpler wine, there are two pickings; for the first they use only the free-run juice, which makes for a wine with refreshing vivacity, while a second picking, a week later, is given some *bâtonnage* and the two wines are blended together to make a fresh, sappy wine, with distinctive Picpoul flavours. The more complex Brechallune, after the song by Nicolas Jules, spends six months on the lees, with regular *bâtonnage*. It is a much more serious wine, quite rich and solid, with good acidity and an almost bitter salty finish, presenting a fascinating comparison of two contrasting styles of Picpoul. In addition to Picpoul de Pinet, they make a varied range of IGP, various white wines and some Pinot Noir and Syrah, as well as sweet Doux des Zazous, a dessert wine from frozen grapes.

Domaine Félines-Jourdan

Mèze 34140
www.felines-jourdan.com

This is the largest of the independent growers of the appellation, with a total of 95 hectares, of which 45 are planted with Piquepoul. Félines is the *lieu-dit*, close to the étang de Thau. Claude Jourdan explained how she has three large plots of vines, the largest near her cellars at Félines, a second plot, Les Cadastres, to the north of the motorway and the third, La Coulette, close to St Martin de la Garrigue.

I asked Claude how she would describe the typicity of Picpoul de Pinet, to which she asserted '*un vin des amis*', a refreshing and easy to drink wine that you share with friends, maybe with your feet in the sea. The advantage of Piquepoul is that it is very accessible and easy to explain as a single varietal. She ferments her wine in stainless steel, without any skin contact, apart from the 40 minutes or so that it takes to bring the grapes from the vineyards. They pick at night by machine, when the grapes are cool. She looks for concentration, but wants to keep the acidity. Piquepoul must not be too ripe. However, it could age without changing its typicity. As for the wine, it has a firm, salty nose, while the palate is firm and stony with fresh acidity and a little weight, the result of a blend of the three vineyards. The climate between the three can vary. The motorway is a barrier and Montagnac is wetter than Félines, which is more moderate in temperature. In a recent storm, Montagnac received twice as much rainwater, which affects the vines and the size of the berries, though at Félines the maritime humidity helps the grapes to ripen.

Féline comes from a separate plot that is usually riper, so that the wine will last a year or two longer, belying the idea that you should always drink the youngest wine available. Claude separates the last juice of the press so that there is free-run juice, as well as a first and a second *taille*. The pressed juice gives more concentration and tannin, so in contrast her basic Picpoul has less pressed juice. *Bâtonnage* every couple of weeks adds weight and structure to Féline, so that the taste was very pure, salty and lemony, with very good depth. Claude is going to see how it ages in a magnum. She has also experimented with Piquepoul and oak, but simply did not like it. She looks for concentration, noting that 'You must retain the acidity and it should not be too ripe, and oak has absolutely nothing to do with Picpoul de Pinet.'

Claude's other wines include a white AOP Languedoc, a blend of 95 per cent Roussanne with just 5 per cent Piquepoul. She explained how Roussanne must be fully ripe to express itself, so that the wine has some appealing floral notes. Her two IGP Coteaux de Bessilles, les Fruités, are just that, a blend of Chardonnay, Roussanne and Sauvignon for the white, and Grenache Noir and Syrah for the red. I was left with an impression of a quietly talented and very successful wine producer who has known how to evolve since she began working with her mother in 1995.

I certainly agree with Claude about the oak and her opinion was endorsed by Guy Bascou, who considers that oak deforms the grapes and makes the wines all taste the same. For him, the next generation of Picpoul de Pinet will depend upon lees ageing, giving more length on the palate, with more finesse. 'It is an original grape variety in a world of grape varieties.' Piquepoul is not allowed in Pays d'Oc and there are moves to remove it from Côtes de Thau, thereby making the appellation an almost unique example of the grape; that is a rare thing in the Mediterranean, a variety with an acidic finish, and a characteristic hint of bitterness, which must be retained at all costs.

17

TERRASSES DU LARZAC, WITH ST SATURNIN AND MONTPEYROUX

The Terrasses du Larzac covers a large area, from the village of Octon in the west to Murles in the east, from Pégairolles in the north-west and Moulès-et-Baucels near Ganges in the north-east to St André-de-Sangonis in the south. Think of them as the Upper Circle or the Gallery of the amphitheatre of the Languedoc, nestling under the *causses*, the plateau, of the Larzac, with some of the coolest and highest vineyards of the whole region. It is an area that has attracted enormous interest over the past 20 years. In my book *The Wines of the South of France* (2001), I gave it little more than a cursory mention, merely acknowledging its existence as a proposed new *terroir* of the Coteaux du Languedoc. Things moved fast, so that it was recognized as an appellation in its own right in 2015, with a retrospective use for 2014, and incorporated both St Saturnin and Montpeyroux.

However, it can be argued that the area is quite different from Montpeyroux and St Saturnin, in that it is usually much wetter and not so hot, with cool nights even in August, which greatly benefits the grapes, making for ripeness without any loss of freshness. The common thread of the seemingly diverse 32 villages of the Terrasses du Larzac is the cool wind coming off the plateau onto vineyards with an average altitude of about 100 metres, but in some instances much higher. A very precise *délimitation parcellaire* has been carried out, excluding valley bottoms and any inappropriate *terroir*. However, there is a variety of different soils, including schist, clay and limestone. The wines are only

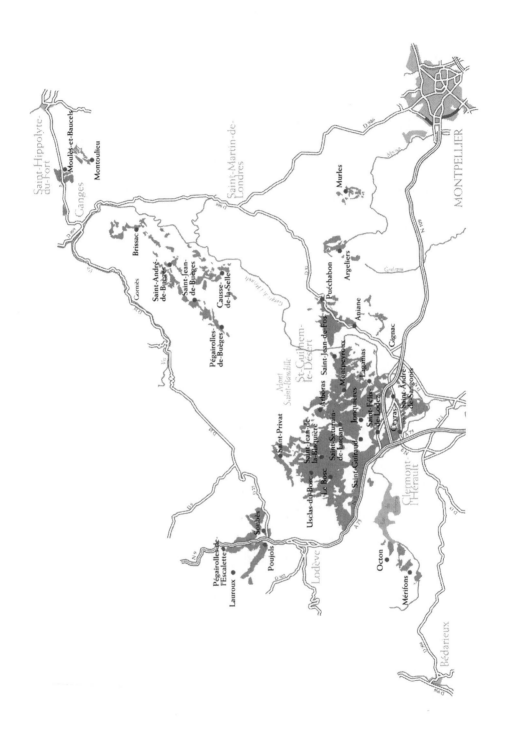

red, a blend of three varieties, with a minimum *élevage* of 12 months, in recognition of the ageability of the wines of the area.

Another defining factor, but one shared by other appellations of the Languedoc, is the strong move towards organic viticulture, including as many as 65 per cent of the wine growers; those producers who are not organic are likely to practice *lutte raisonnée*, or sustained viticulture. As Eric Ajorque, the new president of the appellation, commented: 'At the very least, everyone should stop using herbicides.'

There are about 80 independent wine growers, many of them recent arrivals in the region, accounting for about 70 per cent of the production, plus four cooperatives, and also *négociant* properties, such as Jeanjean at Causse d'Arboras, Domaines Paul Mas at Crès Ricards and Gérard Bertrand at La Sauvageonne. Les Grands Chais de France has just bought one of my favourite estates, Plan de l'Homme.

There are numerous highlights. I have travelled circuitously from east to west, and feature each estate in the village where the cellar is, rather than the vineyards. I began in the pretty village of Octon, by the *lac de* Salagou.

Producers

Mas des Chimères
Octon 34800
www.masdeschimeres.com

Guilhem Dardé has lived in Octon all his life. He talked about life in the village and compared it with neighbouring Salasc. There is a big difference; Salasc is a richer village as it has water, so that agriculture there is more successful, with people able to grow wheat. Octon does not have the fine houses of Salasc. It has suffered from rural depopulation, so that the school almost closed down, and it was a village of polyculture, with sheep as well as vines. Roquefort cheese was actually made in the village and transported to Roquefort for ageing. Guilhem remembered that his father was the first to buy a tractor in Octon in 1968 and two years later they sold their horse. They acquired a mechanical harvester and used it until Guilhem decided to leave the village cooperative in 1993. He has 23 hectares of vines, all around the village of Octon, in numerous small plots, on the characteristic *terres rouges* of the *lac de* Salagou. The Terrasses du Larzac vineyards of Octon are on basalt, while the red soil is on lower lying land.

Guilhem and Palma Dardé

On my last visit, I tasted in the small tasting *caveau* in the centre of the village, with Guilhem's friendly wife, Palma. They make a diverse range of different wines. Oeillade, Coteaux du Salagou, is perfumed and juicy, Cuvée Marie et Joseph, after Guilhem's parents – Marie was 92 in the summer of 2017, but she does not drink her wine – is a pure Carignan, with some fresh fruit. L'Hérétique is Merlot and Cabernet Sauvignon with just 4 per cent of Syrah, with an *élevage* in wood, for cassis fruit with a tannic streak. Guilhem remembers when subsidies were paid to pull up Carignan and replace it with Cabernet and Merlot. Nuit Grave is their Terrasses du Larzac, from Syrah, Grenache and Mourvèdre, with just a little Carignan and Cinsaut, with rounded spicy fruit. It contrasts with Caminarèm, named after a novella by Claude Marti and Jean-Pierre Chabrol, with one-fifth of each variety and more structured fruit. A white Coteaux du Salagou illustrates Guilhem's interest in old grape varieties, with a blend of Grenache Blanc, Carignan Blanc and Terret Blanc, with traces of Terret Gris and Noir in the same vineyard, as well as Chardonnay, Roussanne and a little Clairette. The wine was an intriguing combination of herbal notes and exotic fruit, with very good acidity.

Trois Terres
Octon 34800
www.trois-terres.com

Graeme Angus leads a double life, working as a GP three days a week and as a *vigneron* the rest of the week. Over ten years ago he took the decision to leave the rat race of the London medical world and settled with his family in Octon. His first vintage was 2004 and he now has 6.5 hectares of vines, across nine different plots, mainly in the two villages of Cabrières and St Jean-de-la-Blaquière.

At St Jean-de-la-Blaquière most of his vineyards are Grenache Noir, planted at 180 metres, benefiting from the freshness of the altitude. In Cabrières, Syrah on schist is the main variety, so that makes for two different *cuvées*, a Terrasses du Larzac based on Grenache and an AOP Languedoc based on the Syrah, with the grapes from Octon providing extra blending options. Sometimes he makes a little rosé. His tiny cellar is underneath their house in Octon, just along the road from Mas des Chimères. You sense that Graeme is quietly passionate about what he does, questioning it with a scientific mind, and he is ably supported by his wife, Alice. His winemaking is very simple, using natural yeast and some sulphur. Graeme used to keep each variety and plot separately but now that he knows his wines and vines better, he tends to blend earlier.

His range of wines has gently grown over the years. Le Petit Dernier is a pure Cinsaut, and Vin de France, for minimal administrative hassle, with appealing fresh fruit and acidity. Bagnaloup comes from Grenache and Carignan planted in 1968. There should be a third variety for Terrasses du Larzac but Graeme does not want to add any Syrah, considering Carignan to provide sufficient support for the Grenache. The vines are on an exposed plateau near the abbey of St Michel de Grandmont, with views all around from the Pyrenees to the Mont Ste Claire, 'with armies of wild boars', Graeme added ruefully. The taste is very Grenache, with ripe cherry liqueur fruit. Le Saut du Diable is a blend of Grenache, Carignan and Syrah from vineyards at St Jean-de-la-Blaquière, with an *élevage* in 350-litre barrels, with some brambly fruit. Cuvée Moderne is an AOP Languedoc with 70 per cent Syrah and 30 per cent Grenache Noir, from vineyards at Cabrières, with some fresh peppery fruit. The final wine is a Terrasses du Larzac, La Minérale, from 80 per cent Syrah with a little Cinsaut and Grenache. More mature bottles over lunch proved just how well both Graeme and Guilhem's wines age.

Clos des Clapisses

Octon 34800

www.masdusalagou.com

Bruno Peyre works for Jeanjean but also owns vineyards at Octon, where he took me to an old *mazet* by the lac de Salagou, close to most of his vines. There are old crosses around Octon, 24 in all, including a damaged one by his *mazet*, the Croix du Précepteur, dating from the sixteenth or seventeenth century. The original family vineyards were expropriated in 1966 when the lac de Salagou was created so that they lost 11 out of 13 hectares. There is a photograph in Bruno's cellar of the last harvest; he is in the picture as a baby and you can see that where the family group is standing is now covered by water. The soil of Clos des Clapisses is basalt, with the characteristic red colour of the land around the lac de Salagou coming from iron oxide. Bruno's first harvest here was 2004 and he is passionate about old varieties, particularly Carignan, and also Cinsaut. All his grapes are hand picked and he keeps the stalks; they have anti-oxidant properties. His white Carignan Coteaux du Salagou, with some *bâtonnage*, and aged in vat, is lightly herbal with good acidity, sappy fruit and a firm, mineral finish. His rosé is a pure Carignan, a food rosé with some structure, and his red Carignan benefits from both carbonic maceration and a traditional vinification, with some fresh red fruit.

Bruno is full of ideas, with a lively mind. He talked about the village of Octon, which is more pastoral than viticultural. He feels that there is an argument for a subzone, Salagou-Mourrèze, which would include the surrounding villages. Apparently, there are moves afoot to rehabilitate the village of Celle, which was abandoned when the lake was created. Bruno's enthusiasm is infectious and I came away feeling even more positive than ever about the suitability of Carignan for the Languedoc.

Domaine du Pas de l'Escalette
Poujols 34700
www.pasdelescalette.com

Delphine Rousseau and Julien Zernott first came to the Languedoc in 2003. At the time Julien was making wine for Henri Pellé at Ménétou-Salon in the Loire Valley and Delphine was working for Les Vignerons du Val d'Orbieu.

They started with 8 hectares and now, after gradually buying vines, have 20, all cultivated biodynamically, in the villages of Lauroux and Pégairolles. It was this northern corner of the Languedoc that really captured their enthusiasm. There is a moment driving down the A75 when you come over the Pas de l'Escalette and you see vineyards at your feet, with dramatic cliffs behind. These are some of the coolest vineyards of the Languedoc. Their oldest vines are 80 years old and their vineyards comprise a multitude of old terraces, about 50 altogether, of which the largest is just 80 ares. They also have a vineyard in the adjoining valley of Lauroux, 50 ares of beautifully restored terraces. This is colder than the main valley, and consequently the grapes ripen later. The vineyards are at an altitude of 250–400 metres with the orientation of the vines north–south, as the valley slopes face east and west. Delphine observed that in winter, the village of Pégairolles is in shadow from 3 p.m. Their vineyards are well-drained, with soil that consists of *éboulies calcaires*, so predominantly clay and limestone.

Grenache Noir and Carignan are the principal varieties, along with some Syrah and Cinsaut, as well as Carignan Blanc, Terret Bourret, or Gris, and Grenache Blanc and Gris for their white wine. They have also planted some more Syrah, as well as some Marsanne and Roussanne. Delphine enthused about the growing conditions here. As one of the coolest parts of the Languedoc, a long, slow ripening season makes for beautifully balanced wines with good acidity. Possibly the main viticultural problem is the growing number of wild boars, against which they have had to install electric fences.

Back at the cellar, which they built in 2009, we admired the tronconic vats. It is a well-planned cellar, set into the hillside and partly underground, allowing for some natural insulation. If possible, they favour a co-fermentation of their wines, and certainly blend as early as possible. Les Clapas Blanc comprises 40 per cent each of Grenache

Blanc and Carignan Blanc, with 10 per cent each of Terret and Grenache Gris with good structure and mouthfeel. Les Petits Pas is their first red, from young vines, Grenache, Syrah and Carignan, including 50 per cent whole bunches, which they believe gives an extra dimension to the wine, with fresh, peppery fruit and elegant tannins. Las Clapas Rouge comes from Syrah with Carignan and Grenache, with whole bunches fermented in tronconic vats and some ageing in small *foudres*. Julien favours minimum intervention, and the wine is fresh and juicy, with lovely perfumed fruit. '*Nous sommes nordistes*', 'we are northerners', observed Julien; he does not like the sometimes heavier flavours of the south. Le Pas du D is half Carignan, with Grenache Noir and Cinsaut, aged in *foudres*, while Cuvée à Maman, created for Delphine's fortieth birthday, is the traditional blend of the valley, Grenache Noir, Carignan and Cinsaut, but no Syrah, with some lovely perfumed fruit. Le Grand Pas from their highest plot of Grenache at 450 metres, with some Carignan and Syrah, though sometimes they may use Cinsaut instead of Syrah, has elegant structure.

Cinq Sceaux, a pure Cinsaut from 35-year-old vines at 400 metres, from a vineyard they are calling Mas Rousseau, has intense, cherry fruit. The wine from terraced vineyard, Les Frieys – it was originally called Les Petites Terrasses and was made for the first time in 2015 – is a blend of Grenache Noir, Carignan and Mourvèdre, with more weight and tannin. Finally Julien opened a 2010 Le Grand Pas, from 70 per cent Grenache plus 15 per cent each of Carignan and Syrah, with an *élevage* in *foudres*, with some sturdy ripe fruit. For me it demonstrated just how well Julien and Delphine have fine-tuned their winemaking over the intervening seven years, with their younger wines displaying more freshness and energy. Julien thought this might be the effect of biodynamic practices. I think thoughtful winemaking also has an impact.

Domaine Caujolle-Gazet

La Vacquerie 34520
www.domainecaujollegazet.fr

There may be no vineyards at La Vacquerie, but there are two cellars and three wine producers.

I first met Alain Caujolle-Gazet when he was making wine in Montpeyroux, but life has moved on. He sold Domaine des Grécaux in

2011 and started afresh with vineyards outside the village of Lauroux, close to the Pas de l'Escalette. It is a stunning spot in the spring sunshine, with the cuckoo calling and views over the valley. In moving from Montpeyroux, Alain was looking for *fraîcheur* and humidity. He has Syrah, Carignan, Grenache Noir and Cinsaut for Terrasses du Larzac, as well as Merlot and Pinot Noir, and for white wine, some Chardonnay and Grenache Blanc, a total of 11 hectares in 11 plots mostly on the west side of the valley at an altitude of 400 metres. It is all farmed organically, and the soil is stony clay and limestone. Alain finds that the cool nights make for wines with more acidity and less power than in Montpeyroux. This part of the Terrasses du Larzac was originally excluded from the appellation of the Coteaux du Languedoc in 1985 because the commission from the INAO felt that grapes grown here simply would not ripen properly. Fortunately, the INAO has since seen the error of its ways.

Alain's cellar, a large shed, is on the outskirts of the village of La Vacquerie. The bricks are made from straw, covered with lime, making for very good insulation, and the cellar is equipped with cheerful bright orange concrete vats. Orfran, named after Alain's three children, Ortane, François and Antoine, is a blend of Chardonnay and Grenache Blanc. The Chardonnay is picked first and the Grenache Blanc added two weeks later, and fermented in vat. Alain does not like white wine in oak, and the flavour is fresh and herbal with good acidity and a mineral finish. A Merlot Pays de l'Hérault was ripe and rounded and a Pinot Noir, Andaino, was fresh with raspberry fruit and a streak of tannin, after spending 12 months in oak. La Petite Coulée, Pays de l'Hérault, is a blend of equal parts of Merlot and Grenache Noir; the Grenache softens the Merlot, making for a rounded mouthful of fruit. La Coulée Douce is a Terrasses du Larzac, a blend of 40 per cent Grenache with 30 per cent each of Carignan and Cinsaut, with 12 months' *élevage* mainly in vat, with some fresh, spicy, peppery fruit. The name is a play on words: *j'aime la coulée douce*, meaning 'I like a quiet life'. Alain did observe that as the years progress he works less on his wines, with less extraction. He feels that he is in a very individual part of the Terrasses du Larzac, the north-west corner, with vineyards facing north-east.

Mas Haut Buis
La Vacquerie 34520
www.mashautbuis.com

Olivier Jeantet is also based in the village of La Vacquerie, but again his vineyards are on the other side of the valley near Lauroux. He made his first wine here in 1999 and now has 13 hectares, with Syrah, Grenache, Carignan and Mourvèdre, and a recent purchase of Merlot, and for white wines, Chardonnay, Roussanne and Grenache Blanc, all farmed organically. He is self-taught, with winemaking in the family jumping a couple of generations. He commented that a great-uncle in Gignac used to make very good vinegar. Initially Olivier enjoyed his work in the vineyards, but in recent years he admits to being more interested in cellar techniques. He has changed his vats, explaining that, for *pigeage*, if you have straight walls, there is more force, whereas with tapered vats, there is less resistance and a natural extraction. Concrete reduces extremes of temperature. His red wines include Les Carlines, named after a variety of thistle that grows on the plateau. It is a blend of Grenache, Syrah and Carignan, given a classic vinification with whole bunches and then aged in tanks so that the flavours are ripe and peppery. Costa Cauda is a *sélection parcellaire*, with some 60-year-old Grenache and 80-year-old Carignan, blended at harvest and aged in *foudres*, to make for ripe spice with an underlying freshness. It ages beautifully, as a 15-year-old 2002 demonstrated, with leathery tertiary aromas. Les Agrunelles, Pays de l'Hérault, is a blend of Roussanne, Chardonnay and Grenache Blanc, aged in *demi-muids* and then concrete, with stony mineral notes on the palate. Olivier loves Chardonnay and would like to make a pure one. As I left, a trailer of Carignan grapes arrived; they were ripe, sweet and beautifully healthy.

Clos Maïa
La Vacquerie 34520
closmaia@hotmail.fr

Geraldine Laval is Olivier Jeantet's *compagne*, and mother of his children. Bright and energetic, she is deeply committed to the region, coming to it as an outsider from the Charente-Maritime. Taste is what initially interested her, rather than winemaking, but one thing led to another and after courses in Beaune and Bordeaux, and *stages* with various wine growers, including Chave, Leflaive and Château Brane Cantenac, she discovered the Terrasses du Larzac at Domaine du Pas de l'Escalette. Then, after a *stage* with Olivier Jullien, he convinced her that she was ready to start up on her own. She had by that time met Olivier Jeantet; fate led her to 2 hectares of high-altitude vineyards, at 380–400 metres, in Lauroux, and it was love at first sight. She found an old dairy in the village of la Vacquerie, which now makes a perfect cellar because it is three-quarters underground and consequently cool and damp.

Geraldine now has 6 hectares and makes two red wines. First, Le Petit Clos Maïa, is a Pays de l'Hérault, as she feels that it is a more distinctive classification than simple AOP Languedoc. It comes from Syrah, Grenache Noir and Carignan, blended at the harvest if possible, and vinified and aged in concrete vats. The Syrah grows in a vineyard at a lower altitude, not classified as Terrasses du Larzac, and the wine is elegant and rounded, with a fresh tannic streak. Clos Maïa is mainly Grenache Noir, blended with a plot of old vines, all *complanté* and including about ten vines each of Cinsaut, Carignan, Oeillade, Terret Noir, Alicante and Aramon, as well as Carignan Blanc and Terret, and even a couple that Geraldine does not recognize. They provide what she called the salt and pepper for the Grenache Noir, making a ripe, rounded wine with Grenache spice and elegance on the finish. Clos Maïa Blanc comes from approximately 30 per cent each of Chenin Blanc, Grenache Gris and Roussanne with 10 per cent Terret Bourret, fermented and aged in *demi-muids*, with rounded, perfumed fruit and fresh acidity. The hallmark of Geraldine's wines is undoubtedly elegance, and she admits to owing a lot to Olivier. She is a sensitive winemaker and observes that the hardest thing to do is to do nothing. 'You express your *terroir* through the vintage, merely accompanying the wine.'

La Traversée

Les Salces 34700
www.latraversee.fr

From La Vacquerie, I took a scenic route, a twisting road over the hills, passing close to Mont Baudile, to the tiny village of Les Salces to see Gavin Crisfield. You realize immediately that Gavin is a thoughtful, discursive winemaker. He related how a bottle of Rully St Jacques, when he was 12, was a turning point for him. At 19 he began working as a sommelier, but then realized that what he really wanted to do was make wine, so in 1995 he enrolled at Plumpton in East Sussex, becoming one of its very first graduates. Next, he did a *stage* at Domaine de Poujol near Montpellier with an Anglo-American couple, Robert and Kim Cripps, who have recently sold their estate. Then Gavin was offered two jobs, one in Argentina, the other at La Sauvageonne in the Terrasses du Larzac. He chose the latter, where he worked for eight years, until the estate was sold to Gérard Bertrand and the time was ripe to create his own estate. He is also a talented musician, a guitarist, and when we met had just released an album, *The Buckling Point*, an homage to his father who had worked on just that, calculating the buckling point on Concorde wings. Gavin's career could so easily have taken another direction.

Instead he bought his own vineyard, one 3-hectare block above St Jean-de-la-Blaquière. It is planted with Cinsaut, Syrah and Grenache, on volcanic *grès* and schist, called *ruffes*. He also has another plot of Syrah on limestone and some Carignan on schist, making a total of 4.5 hectares. His first vintage of La Traversée was 2009. Gavin's cellar is on the ground floor of a classic *maison de maître* in the centre of the village of Les Salces. He has concrete eggs, tronconic vats of both wood and concrete and small *foudres*. He enthused about the eggs. It all depends on fluid dynamics as the egg shape makes for movement, unlike a vat. It imitates an amphora, but is not as fragile as terracotta, and removes the need for *remontages*. Made from 15-centimetre-thick concrete, without any steel reinforcement, their other advantage is in concrete's ability to maintain a constant temperature, unlike stainless steel.

Gavin talked about the difficulty of choosing the right picking date, especially with the change in climate. With Cinsaut you can lose the right moment in just a day. He simply tastes the grapes, as he has done for the past 15 years, and picks when 'you get an emotion and your hair stands on end. It's a question of balance in the mouth.' Apart from a successful *négociant* business, which provides his bread and butter, he makes two wines under the La Traversée label. Asked if his winemaking has changed over the years, he says that he has learnt to do very little, at the right moment. It is a question of timing and of precision, and also of experience and confidence. There is a pure Cinsaut, which is elegant and fragrant, and a wine that is a blend of Cinsaut, Syrah, Carignan and some Grenache Noir. The Carignan and Grenache are usually fermented together. The 2015 that I tasted with Gavin the last time we met was fragrant and fresh, with some peppery tannins and elegant red fruit. The 2011 was a bigger vintage, 'my only bumper crop', with richer flavours and more concentration. Unfortunately, on my last visit, Gavin had completely sold out of his pure Cinsaut, and he admitted that he had to buy some Cinsaut in 2017, so short was he of grapes following the small harvest.

Clos du Serres
St Jean-de-la-Blaquière 34700
www.leclosduserres.fr

It is always fascinating to hear how people arrive in the Languedoc. After studying chemistry, Sébastien Fillon worked in computers, but soon realized that was not for him. He returned to college, this time for viticulture and oenology and, after a brief spell working in Beaujolais, he knew that he wanted vines of his own. He and his wife Béatrice started looking for somewhere south of Valence, and their search took them from Vinsobres in the southern Rhône down to Banyuls close to the Spanish border. Their criteria were simple: the area had to produce good wine, that they liked, and it had to be somewhere they would enjoy living, so not too isolated. Of course, it also had to be feasible economically, so that ruled out Châteauneuf-du-Pape, where the prices are now extortionate. In 2006 their search led them to St Jean-de-la-Blaquière, where the reputation of the Terrasses du Larzac was rising.

Things have evolved over the last ten years. They have moved from a cramped cellar in the back streets to a new, spacious one outside the village, and the silhouette on their label is the view from the cellar. Their range of wines now focuses very much on the different vineyards, in the Burgundian manner. To emphasize the point they have changed from Bordeaux to Burgundy bottles. Béatrice took us for a drive through the vineyards, pointing out the various differences. Essentially, they make five red wines, the village *cuvée* and four *sélections parcellaires*. The soil in St Jean-de-la-Blaquière is very mixed. There is schist, but not as old as that of Faugères, in the northern part of the village; some *galets roulées* from an old river bed; some red *ruffes*, old sedimentary soil, that is very poor with little organic matter; and on the plateau of the Larzac there is limestone, which is 7–8 million years old, as opposed to about 250 million for the *ruffes*. The scenery was breathtaking on a sunny morning and we could see the extinct volcano of Pic de Vissou in the distance.

There are dry stone walls everywhere, which are probably about 100 years old, and what Béatrice called *caveaux,* or tombs, that look like tiny chapels, surrounded by vines. Their vineyards have been organic since the beginning and they are now working on biodynamics. They have beehives in one vineyard.

Back at the cellar we tasted. Le Saut du Poisson, with a first vintage in 2011, is mainly Vermentino with Carignan Blanc and Grenache Blanc, partially aged in barrel, with a fragrant nose and some pithy fruit from the Vermentino. Béatrice observed that white wine in the region is *toute une histoire à reconstruire,* a complete story to rebuild, and it will take time. The village *cuvée,* including Grenache Noir and Oeillade as well as Cinsaut, has some spicy black fruit, with youthful tannins and a fresh finish. Ste Pauline, from Syrah and some Cinsaut and Carignan grown on *galets roulées,* fermented in tronconic vats and then aged in cement vats, has some fresh peppery fruit. Le Palas, from Syrah with some Grenache Noir and Carignan, grown on schist, is fuller-bodied with red fruit. Syrah may dominate both those wines, but the differences are immediately discernible. Les Maros, mainly Grenache Noir with Cinsaut and Carignan on schist, has elegant liqueur cherry fruit and l'Ancien Vagabone, from 100-year-old Carignan with some Syrah and Grenache, is fresh and elegant, with red fruit and a streak of tannin. Above all they are looking for drinkability.

Béatrice introduced us to other young wine producers in the village. Most established is Jean-Baptiste Granier, son of Jean-Philippe and related to Mas Montel in Sommières. He makes his wine in Béatrice and Sebastien's old cellar. Olivier Jullien led him to vineyards in nearby St Privat, so that in 2007 they made the first vintage of Les Vignes Oubliées and worked together until 2012 when Olivier suggested that 'now you are *grand* [grown up], go it alone'. His wine is a blend of Grenache, Syrah and Carignan, aged mainly in *demi-muids,* to make a rounded, full-flavoured wine.

Anne-Laure Sicard also has vines at St Privat and made her first vintage for Mas Lasta in 2016, from Grenache, Syrah and Carignan, just 7,000 bottles, with perfumed, peppery flavours. She acquired some Cinsaut for the 2017 vintage. She has worked elsewhere, including Australia, Bordeaux, Cornas, Niagara, Uruguay and Argentina, but chose the Languedoc when it was time to settle down.

Krystal Brot is making Le Clos Rouge from 8 hectares of vines in St Jean-de-la-Blaquière, 2 hectares of which she vinified in 2016, selling the rest to growers who had suffered from the hail in the Pic St Loup. Her 2016 Piccolo, Pays d'Oc, is a pure Cinsaut. She has a second wine, Babel, so-named because there were so many different nationalities amongst the pickers. It is a blend of Syrah, Grenache and Cinsaut, with more weight and spice.

There is undoubtedly a sense of cohesion and commitment amongst this small group of wine producers, who are hoping to take over the old cooperative building in the village, to use it for cellar space. It will also include the village restaurant, La Petite Fringale, for which the new owners have serious aspirations, but insufficient space.

Mas Jullien
Jonquières 34725
masjullien@free.fr

Olivier Jullien is one of the most philosophical of *vignerons*. You immediately sense somebody who is thoughtful, sensitive and perceptive. He talked of the '*étoile que je n'atteindrai jamais*', of the 'star that I will never reach', but he has inspired and encouraged many other *vignerons*. He always knew that he would work on the land, and started developing Mas Jullien while he was still studying, so that his very first harvest was in 1985, when he was 19. As he laughingly said: 'I did *stages* in my own vineyard.' Things have changed. He now has 20 hectares of vines, one-third at St Privat up in the hills beyond St Jean-de-la-Blaquière and the rest at Jonquières, where his cellar is. He talked about the differences between the two areas. At St Privat the vineyards are at 350 metres, whereas the highest vines at Jonquières are at 250 metres. There is a month's difference in the harvest dates, not so much because of the altitude but because of the cool exposition of the valley at St Privat. His work has changed; in 1999, he began working with *demi-muids* and has moved on to *foudres* of 50 and 22 hectolitres. The vineyards have also changed. In 1999, Grenache was the main variety, but now it is only in one wine, Carlan, from St Privat. He used to place more emphasis on Syrah, but now is working more with old Carignan and Mourvèdre.

Two wines come from St Privat. Carlan, a blend of 50 per cent Grenache Noir and 30 per cent Carignan, with some Cinsaut and Syrah, has fresh red fruit, supple tannins and plenty of nuance. Most of the grapes are blended during fermentation; the Carignan is added later, as it is the last to ripen. Lous Rougeos is a blend of 50 per cent Carignan, 40 per cent Syrah and 10 per cent Grenache, grown on limestone, with more structured fruit. Autour de Jonquières is a blend of several different vineyards, with 40 per cent Carignan, which provides the backbone, with acidity and length, and 40 per cent Mourvèdre, which gives depth, and breeding, with some Cinsaut and Syrah to tame the Carignan, given two years' *élevage*. Limestone provides the typicity of Jonquières, giving complexity and ageing potential. Olivier still makes a small amount of Etats d'Ame, one of the wines for which he was known in the early days, and enthuses about Carignan, which he has always liked for its refreshing quality.

Olivier talked of the pleasure he takes in going into his vineyards. If he does not like a vineyard, he will not like the wine. He is passionate about the Languedoc. It is extraordinary what has happened in the region: 'We have exceeded expectations; the Languedoc has come of age.' He talked about the Terrasses du Larzac, seeing four or five zones that are quite different and will be developed and recognized. He considers that, in the current era, the appellation is more important than the *vigneron*, whereas back in 1985 it was the *vigneron* that counted.

As for white wine, Olivier used to make two, Vignes Oubliées and La Mejeanne; nowadays there is just one white wine, from 70 per cent Carignan Blanc and 30 per cent Chenin Blanc. Olivier is particularly enthusiastic about Carignan Blanc, which he grows in Jonquières; and he has inspired others, such as Daniel le Conte de Floris in Pézenas, to plant it. Fermented in wood, with very good acidity, texture, salinity and minerality, it has an extraordinary depth of flavour. Chenin, from St Privat, adds a touch of honey, and is similar in structure to the Carignan. At the beginning, Olivier had no idea that white wines would be so successful: 'It is an unexpected surprise; we didn't even think about it.' His white wine is one of the most successful and original white wines of the Languedoc, with considerable ageing potential.

Château de Jonquières

Jonquières 34725
www.chateau-jonquieres.com

Château de Jonquières, in the centre of village of Jonquières, has been in the same family since the twelfth century. It has been an agricultural property since the thirteenth century, always with vines and sometimes wheat. The family name may have changed, but the property has never been sold. It is well placed, on the road to the Col du Vent at Arboras, connecting the north to the southern half of the Hérault. It has never been fortified and retains the stylish Italian Renaissance architecture from Bernardin de Latude, who was a pageboy to the mother of Louis XIV. They have a price list for Canada dating from 1870, including a wine from Jonquières, and a Muscat de Frontignan at the same price as a Sauternes, and they won a silver medal at the Paris Exhibition of 1889, the year the Eiffel Tower was built. The chapel of the château is still used by the villagers of Jonquières and although the original statues of lions at the bottom of the grand staircase were destroyed during the Revolution the villagers defended the château itself.

Since 2014, the viticultural part of the estate has been run by Charlotte de Cabissole, with her husband, Clément de Béarn. They have a logical range of five wines: three colours of Lansade, and a red and a white oak-aged La Baronnie. Lansade Blanc, Pays de l'Hérault, comes from 70 per cent 30-year-old Chenin Blanc vines and 30 per cent Grenache Blanc. The Chenin is picked a little earlier than the Grenache. The wine has a dry, honeyed nose, with an elegant palate, good acidity and some ageing potential.

We talked about the reasons for growing Chenin Blanc in this area when it is most commonly found in the Loire Valley. Apparently, the cooperative in the adjourning village of St Saturnin asked for Chenin Blanc as an experiment some 30 years ago, as they were looking for white varieties that would retain acidity, but Chenin was never accepted in the appellation. Other growers have it too, such Alain Chabanon, Domaine de Pountil, Cal Demoura and Olivier Jullien.

Lansade Rosé, Pays de l'Hérault, is Cinsaut with 10 per cent Carignan that was planted by Charlotte's great-grandmother 70 years ago. It has a nicely rounded palate. Lansade Red, Terrasses du Larzac, is a typical Languedoc blend with the usual five varieties, with as much as 40 per cent

Carignan, a high proportion of Cinsaut and just 10 per cent Mourvèdre. Carignan is now considered a principal, rather than a secondary, variety for the Terrasses du Larzac. The palate has dry spice, with firm, stony, mineral character and a certain freshness. La Baronnie Rouge, Terrasses du Larzac, is a blend of 40 per cent Mourvèdre, 30 per cent Syrah, 20 per cent Grenache Noir and 10 per cent Carignan, with firm, youthful fruit, integrated oak and ageing potential. La Baronnie Blanc, Pays de l'Hérault, is a blend of 50 per cent Grenache and 50 per cent Chenin Blanc, vinified in barrel, and given a little *bâtonnage*, before ten months' ageing on the lees, but without any more *bâtonnage*. The oak is nicely integrated, and the palate mouth filling, with good acidity and a long finish, making a lovely glass of wine, with ageing potential.

Cal Demoura
Jonquières 34725
www.caldemoura.com

In 2004 Vincent and Isabelle Goumard bought Cal Demoura, a property that had been created by Olivier Jullien's father, Jean-Pierre, when, encouraged by his son, he took his vines out of the cooperative. Vincent originally studied commerce and management, at that most demanding of business schools, INSEAD, and worked for Arthur Andersen. Deciding on a career change he went back to school, studying oenology in Beaune and Dijon, and was attracted to the Languedoc for 'the quality of life and the quality of the different *terroirs*, at affordable prices. It is a magical place. The Languedoc is in the middle of its revolution; Burgundy is too constrained. And it is open to outsiders.' Vincent was made president of the Terrasses du Larzac after just three years as a wine producer and was successful in achieving an appellation for the *cru* in a remarkably short time.

Vincent's enthusiasm and commitment are instantly engaging. You sense that he is utterly committed to the region and fervent about the need for all the producers to work together. With so many different areas and *terroirs* the Languedoc has no real reputation or identity, and the Vin de Pays d'Oc does not have a particularly good image, so they need to create one for the Terrasses du Larzac. The collective quality image is essential. Vincent does not lack for words; he is very articulate in expressing this ambition.

Vincent works very much *à la parcellaire*, with at least 11 different plots, including 2.5 hectares of white, with some Chenin Blanc, Grenache Blanc, Roussanne, Viognier and Petit Manseng. He has added Carignan Blanc, Carignan Noir and Mourvèdre, by massal selection, observing that the system does not encourage planting that way. If you use clonally selected vines, you receive between €8,000 and €10,000 (US$9,800–12,250) per hectare as a subsidy, but for massal selection you receive nothing. For his red wines, he favours destemming, and looks for gentle macerations with some *pigeage* and *remontages*, following each vat carefully, tasting regularly. His new cellar, built of Gard stone, helps with insulation, and the barrel cellar is furnished with Stockinger and also Taransaud, with some 24- and 30-hectolitre *foudres*. Asked about typicity, Vincent said that balance is the keyword; he wants finesse, precision, elegance and wines that are '*pleinement languedocien*', truly Languedoc in character. As for the typicity of the Terrasses du Larzac, it is a balance of the Mediterranean, wine with intensity, generosity and a supplement of freshness, with the different soils adding complexity.

Vincent's rosé, Qu'es Aquo, is a blend of one-third each of Cinsaut, Syrah and Grenache, with just a splash of Carignan and Mourvèdre. The Grenache and Syrah are pressed, and the other varieties *saignée*, to combine the freshness of the pressed wine with the weight of the *saignée*. It is rounded and ripe with balancing acidity. L'Etincelle is a Pays de l'Hérault, from a majority of Chenin Blanc, with some Grenache Blanc, Roussanne and Viognier, and just a drop of Petit Manseng. Half is fermented in *demi-muids* and half in vat, making for a dry, honeyed nose, with some peachy notes on the palate. The Carignan Blanc will add extra complexity and acidity when it comes into production in 2018. The second white, Paroles de Pierre, is a blend of 70 per cent Chenin Blanc with Grenache Blanc, and just a little Petit Manseng, with a year's *élevage*. The oak is more present in the young wine, with dry honey and ageing potential.

Terres de Jonquières replaces the previous L'Infidèle and is a blend of all five varieties and of all the various plots, to reflect the character of Jonquières, with two different soils, stony limestone, and clay and limestone, with 80 per cent matured in wood and the rest in vat. For Vincent, it represents his estate, with an expressive nose, rounded fruit and spice and an elegant finish. Les Combariolles now includes

25 per cent Carignan, when previously there was none, as well as Syrah, Mourvèdre and Grenache. Vincent feels that the Carignan gives freshness and energy to the wine, with some firm, sturdy fruit. Feu Sacré comes mainly from old Grenache Noir on limestone, with 20 per cent Carignan and 20 per cent Syrah, with restrained ripeness and elegant warmth. Finally, there was a new wine, Fragments, a blend of 70 per cent 35-year-old Syrah, with Carignan and Grenache planted on north-facing slopes, with fresh pepper on the nose and a ripe palate with a touch of vanilla. It all illustrates the diversity of the Terrasses du Larzac within the same domaine.

Les Chemins de Carabote
Gignac 34150
www.carabote.com

Jean-Yves Chaperon was a radio reporter and does indeed still present a weekly jazz programme. Although he comes from St Etienne, he had spent his childhood holidays in the Minervois and talked about having a vineyard until his *compagne* encouraged him to actually take the plunge. They spent a holiday looking at vineyards and found their vines in 2005, close to St André-de-Sangonis, abandoning their life in Paris in 2007 and building a small cellar in 2008. Jean-Yves has almost 8 hectares and produces an elegant range of wines with the help of Jean Natoli. His white, made for the first time in 2015, is an unusual blend of Chenin Blanc, Viognier and Riesling. And why those particular varieties? Quite simply, he wanted to try something out of the ordinary. The wine is lightly honeyed with good acidity and does not conform to any appellation, so it is a Pays de l'Hérault Mont Baudile. Jean-Yves is very enthusiastic about Carignan and is convinced that you can avoid its rustic characteristics; indeed, he has done just that with his pure Carignan, made partly through carbonic maceration, with the percentage depending on the characteristics of the vintage, and partly from the pressed and free-run juice of a classic vinification. For him Carignan is the grape variety that really displays its *terroir*, with some peppery spice and a fresh finish. You can smell the *garrigue* and feel the sunshine.

Chemin Faisant is a Terrasses du Larzac from 50 per cent Syrah with 35 per cent Grenache Noir and 15 per cent Carignan, aged in vat, with black fruit and tapenade. The grapes are destalked and given a 20-day maceration with some gentle *remontages*. Les Pierres qui Chantent, in contrast, includes 50 per cent Grenache to 35 per cent Syrah with the balance from Carignan and is given 18 months' *élevage*, with some ripe fruit and a firm streak of tannin, combining the *côté sauvage* and the *côté garrigue*. A pure Grenache, the late harvest Promenade en Novembre, was redolent of ripe fruit with a fresh finish.

Mas Conscience

St Jean-de-Fos 34150
www.mas-conscience.com

Eric Ajorque is one of the many newcomers to the Terrasses du Larzac, buying Mas Conscience in 2012. He studied marketing and commerce and ran his own business selling sports' accessories, selling it after 13 years. He and his wife, Nathalie, then spent two years in the south of India, which he described as a period of reflection, helping create a vocational training centre for children, to give them a useful skill for future employment. Meanwhile, they began to consider wine, liking the idea of working organically with the soil. Nathalie did a course in Montpellier and Eric has learnt *sur le champ*, on the job. We met on the day after he had finished his fourth harvest. Altogether the estate consists of 13 hectares in four plots, mainly towards Puéchabon and near the hills of Les Brousses. For red wines, he has the usual Languedoc quintet, including seven different plots of Syrah, some as much as 35 years old, which enables him to play with the blend. For white he has a veritable fruit salad of Grenache Blanc, Roussanne, Vermentino, Viognier, Petit Manseng and Sauvignon. For the moment, the appellation of the Terrasses du Larzac does not include white wine, but that is under consideration, though the INAO is not yet involved. The first thing is for the wine producers to decide on the possible grape varieties.

Eric has developed the range of wines from that of the previous owners, and all the names of his *cuvées* constitute a play on words, based on Conscience. The white wine L'In is a blend of Grenache Blanc, Roussanne and Vermentino, with some rounded white-blossom fruit and a firm, stony finish. A small amount of the juice is fermented in barrel. A pure Viognier is sometimes made. The range of reds starts with La Petite Prise, a blend of Grenache and Syrah, aiming for fresh, juicy fruit. A pure Cinsaut, Cieux, an IGP Saint Guilhem-le-Désert, is light and fragrant. Le Cas is a pure Carignan and an exemplary version of that grape variety, with structured red fruit. Finally, there are two Terrasses du Larzac. L'Eveil is a blend of equal parts Syrah and Grenache, with 10 per cent Cinsaut, all vinified together. The Syrah gives spice and the Grenache structure, with 12 months' *élevage*, making for some fresh, peppery fruit. Mahatma comes from Mourvèdre, Syrah and Grenache, given 12 months' *élevage* in tronconic vats, with some Mourvèdre spice, with firm, structured fruit and depth.

Eric talked about the future. As president of the syndicat of the Terrasses du Larzac he is concerned to integrate all the new arrivals, 25 since 2011, and to ensure that they share the same values. He talked about the need to '*valorizer*, to enhance the image of our *terroir*'. They are lucky in having three UNESCO sites within the appellation or nearby, namely the lac de Salagou, the dramatic Cirque de Navacelles and the awe-inspiringly beautiful abbey of St Guilhem-le-Désert.

Mas Combarèla
St Jean-de-Fos 34150
www.mas-combarela.com

This is one of the newer estates of the Terrasses du Larzac. Olivier Faucon is bright and keen, with a professional approach. He worked in market research for about 15 years, but agriculture was in his genes, with a grandfather farming in northern France. Deciding it was time for a change, he studied in Beaune before doing a *stage* at Cal Demoura, and then looked for vines in the south. He had originally wanted to buy an existing estate, but did not find anything suitable; however, he did find vineyards, 12 hectares, in three separate plots, in Arboras, between the Mont Baudile and the Rocher des Deux Vierges; close to Réserve d'O, near the chapel of St Genies, near Montpeyroux, and in St Jean-de-Fos in a spot called Combarèle, with lots of old Carignan, where he will eventually build his cellar. The vines were well cared for, but not farmed organically; as they came from a cooperative member, quantity had also been a consideration.

Olivier made his first wine in 2016, and when I met him in the spring of 2017 he had yet to put any wine in bottle so we tasted from vat, although the wines were almost ready for bottling. There was some Grenache

Blanc, which will be an IGP St Guilhem-le-Désert, and a refreshing rosé, with a certain structure, about which Olivier commented that he did not want to make a fashionable rosé. De Si et de Mi rouge is mainly Grenache Noir, with some rounded, spicy fruit. A pure Carignan, Les Vieux Mazets, IGP Saint Guilhem-le-Désert, has spent six months in a tronconic vat, and includes 20 per cent of carbonic maceration, making for rounded fruit with a fresh finish. Le Clos Secret is Cinsaut, fermented in a stainless steel tank and then transferred into an egg. Olivier did not want to spoil the fruit of the Cinsaut with any oak and it was deliciously fresh and fragrant. His Terrasses du Larzac is a blend of Syrah, Grenache Noir and Carignan, with more structure and weight. There is no doubt that Olivier has made a good start and deserves to do well.

Réserve d'O
Arboras 34150
www.lareservedo.fr

I went to see Marie and Frédéric Chauffray on a brilliantly sunny November morning. It was one of those days when the weather was too good to be true, when you are so happy to be alive. Marie took us up into her vineyards, which are in a magnificent position, lying at 300–400 metres above the village of Arboras and facing Mont Baudile. The Carignan leaves were golden in the sunlight, the herbs of the *garrigue* were pungent in the warmth, and the views were spectacular, looking towards Montpeyroux and les Cocalières, and far beyond. Altogether they have 12 hectares in three plots, with Roussanne, Grenache Blanc and Chenin Blanc for white wine, and Syrah, Grenache Noir and Cinsaut for red wines. They bought their vines in 2005 and have farmed them biodynamically since the beginning. Marie and Frédéric had a wine shop close to Paris, but with links with the Languedoc. They looked elsewhere, in no particular hurry, but had a *coup de foudre* for what they saw here. Arboras is a pretty little village, with a medieval castle and a population of just 80. There is no shop or café, but a pottery and tearoom are open in the summer. Their cellar is hidden at the bottom of the village – from the tasting room you can discern the coast, and on a very clear day you can see the Pyrenees.

Bilbo, AOP Languedoc, with fresh, perfumed fruit and a streak of tannin, is mainly Grenache Noir, plus some Cinsaut and Syrah, with 12 months' ageing in wood. Marie uses no sulphur during the vinification and very little at bottling. Her main wine, La Réserve d'O, Terrasses du Larzac, coming from 45 per cent each of Grenache and Syrah with a drop of Cinsaut, spends about 20 months in vat and has some fresh, peppery fruit, combining power and elegance. 'It represents our work, and also two-thirds of our production,' observed Marie. They want to keep the fruit, *un éclat de fruit*, and that they have certainly achieved. The Syrah gives structure and Cinsaut provides the link between the two main varieties, reining in the exuberance of the Grenache and softening the Syrah. Hissez O, from a song – it means 'raise the sails' – is another Terrasses du Larzac, with Syrah from a particularly stony vineyard, and some Grenache and Cinsaut. It spends two years in 400-litre barrels and is more structured than Réserve d'O, with well integrated oak. Finally, their white wine is a field blend of equal parts of Grenache Blanc, Chenin Blanc and Roussanne, fermented in barrel, with hints of honey, good acidity and an intriguing finish.

Marie described the typicity of the Terrasses du Larzac as 'concentration with finesse and elegance'. As the most recent past president of the *cru*, she is very optimistic about the future of the region. 'There is a good rapport between the growers, and a positive energy. It is very important that our wine corresponds to our *terroir*.'

Jeanjean at Domaine du Causse d'Arboras

Arboras 34150

www.jeanjean.fr

Jeanjean may be one of the big players of the Languedoc, and commercially linked to the enormous network of Advini, but above all it is a family business, run these days by the fifth generation, the energetic and very able Brigitte Jeanjean, with Matthieu Carliez as the thoughtful head winemaker. Brigitte is particularly keen to promote the family image. For an earlier book I had visited Bernard Jeanjean at Mas Neuf, in the appellation of Muscat de Mireval, but a more recent overview of their estates was provided by a helicopter ride, by way of escape from the hurly-burly of the annual Vinisud Wine Fair.

We set off from Montpellier airport towards the estuary of the Rhône, passing the medieval walled town of Aigues-Mortes, to Domaine le Pive, where Jeanjean produces a *vin gris*, Sable de Camargue. Nearby are the marshes and lagoons of the Camargue, with green patches of vineyards. Then the helicopter turned north towards the hills of the Larzac, heading for the newly acquired Domaine du Causse d'Arboras above the village of Arboras. The scenery quickly changes as you leave the coastal plain, with *garrigue*-covered hillsides. You could see the distinctive outline of the Pic de Vissou and the valley of the Hérault, with its narrow gorges above Aniane.

Next we turned south for le Devois des Agneaux and Mas de Lunès, two neighbouring Grés de Montpellier estates on the large limestone Aumelas plateau, eventually spotting the distinctive green-tiled tower of the Devois des Agneaux before landing at Mas Neuf, for a tasting.

Subsequently I have spent some time at Domaine de Fenouillet tasting Faugères and most recently I visited Domaine du Causse d'Arboras, which Jeanjean bought in December 2013. There are 16 hectares of vines, principally Grenache Noir and Syrah for red, with a little Mourvèdre and Cinsaut, and for a small amount of white wine, Vermentino, Roussanne and Marsanne. Mont Baudile, sometimes called la Sentinelle du Larzac, at 848 metres, dominates the vineyards, which lie at 300 metres.

Matthieu Carliez is particularly enthusiastic about the Terrasses du Larzac. 'You obtain ripe grapes without losing the freshness of the fruit and the temperatures are more temperate, with sharper diurnal differences. There is more rain, but the soil drains well.' A fault line separates them from Montpeyroux and les Cocalières. The cellar is efficient, though the building itself looks somewhat out of place, with an Italianate air. I tasted a selection of wines from the various estates. The white Causse d'Arboras comes from Vermentino, Roussanne and Marsanne, with some firm mineral notes and a tight-knit structure. Domaine de Fenouillet, Les Hautes Combes, Faugères, from Roussanne and Marsanne, with a small amount of oak, has white flowers on the palate and a rounded finish. Mas Neuf Dry Muscat Pays d'Oc is opulently Muscat, fresh and perfumed, with acidity. Domaine le Pive, Vie de Bohème, IGP Sable de Camargue, is pure Grenache Gris, which is indeed *gris* in colour, so the wine is a pale orange-pink, and the palate quite rounded and vinous. They make three red wines at Causse d'Arboras. Autochthone is their first experience of a Vin Nature, a pure Cinsaut and an IGP St Guilhem-le-Désert, with perfumed fruit.

Then there are two Terrasses du Larzac, La Sentinelle, from 40 per cent Grenache Noir and equal parts of Mourvèdre and Syrah, aged in vat with fresh, red fruit, while La Faille is 70 per cent Syrah with some Grenache and Mourvèdre, aged in *demi-muids*, with peppery fruit and well-integrated oak. There is no doubt that Jeanjean has made a good start at Causse d'Arboras. Next came Mas de Lunès, Grés de Montpellier, with ripe spice, and a new *cuvée* of Domaine de Fenouillet, MasoSchistes, (you need to be a masochist to work this land), with red fruit. Finally Domaine du Landeyran, AnarSchiste, from their estate in St Chinian, at St Nazaire-de-Ladarez, with more schist, was a blend of Syrah and Carignan aged in oak, with tapenade and supple tannins.

Domaine des Olivèdes
St Jean-de-Buèges 34380
domainedesolivedes@sfr.fr

We took a scenic road to St Jean-de-Buèges following the Hérault river up past St Guilhem-le-Désert to Causse de la Selle, and then down into the valley of the Buèges, to see Stéphane Canaguie at Domaine des Olivèdes. St Jean-de-Buèges is a picturesque village on the banks of the Buèges, dominated by its ruined castle, and provides the illustration for the cover of this book. Stéphane has 7 hectares of vines on the slopes of the Massif de la Séranne, at 300 metres, though 4 hectares are still with the cooperative of Corconne. He was encouraged by other local growers to take the plunge and make his own wine. From 3 hectares he makes two wines; his first vintage was 2014. The first is a Carignan and Grenache blend, SC, Vin de France, which may become IGP St Guilhem-le-Désert. It is fresh and perfumed after a vinification in vat. His Terrasses du Larzac is a blend of Grenache Noir, Syrah and a dollop of Carignan, with some *élevage*, making a substantial wine with good fruit. Stéphane is not interested in rosé, but would like to try his hand at white wine. He does have about 120 Carignan Blanc vines planted with his Carignan Noir, but they have always been declared as Carignan Noir and French bureaucracy would not contemplate a colour change! So, he will have to decide what to plant.

Domaine de Montcalmès

Puéchabon 34150

www.domainedemontcalmes.fr

Domaine de Montcalmès is a classic example of the new generation of wine producer in the Languedoc. The estate is run by a brother and sister, Frédéric Pourtalié and Muriel Fabre, with a cellar in the village of Puéchabon and 25 hectares of vines nearby, in Puéchabon, Aniane, St Saturnin and St Jean-de-Fos, with a variety of different soils, including limestone and *galets roulées*. The name Montcalmès comes from a nearby hamlet. Their father was a cooperative member but Frédéric wanted to make his own wine. He had learned from his father and gained experience with various growers such as Alain Graillot in Crozes-Hermitage and, closer to home, with Laurent Vailhé at La Grange des Pères in Aniane. They began converting to organic viticulture in 2012 and were officially registered in 2015.

They make three white wines. The first is a Vin de France, from Vermentino, Viognier and about 5–10 per cent each of Sauvignon Blanc, Chardonnay and Chenin Blanc as well as Gros and Petit Manseng and Gros and Petit Courbu, the grape varieties of Jurançon. The wine is fermented in wood with 12 months' *élevage* in wood, and 6 months in vat. With such a complicated blend, the flavours are nuanced and intriguing, with dry honey. A pure Chardonnay includes some bought grapes and here Frédéric explained the complication of French wine law. The bottle is labelled simply Montcalmès, rather than Domaine de Montcalmès, because the grapes are not theirs. However, if they make Vin de France, even from their own grapes, they cannot use the word domaine either! The Chardonnay is fermented in barrel, *demi-muids* and larger barrels, and the wine is elegantly buttery with fresh acidity. Frédéric observed that the altitude makes for acidity and they pick before the grapes become too ripe. The classic wine of the estate, a blend of equal parts of Roussanne and Marsanne, is fermented *demi-muids*, making for texture with balancing acidity.

For red wines, they make a pure Grenache Noir, Vin de France, with spicy red fruit, after an *élevage* in old *demi-muids*. Frédéric described Vin de France as the wine the *vigneron* wants to make, without any constraints, provided it is *loyal et marchand*, or drinkable and saleable. Le Geai, AOP Languedoc, from 70 per cent Grenache, with 25 per cent Syrah and a drop of Mourvèdre, with some fresh, elegant fruit, spends two years in wood. In 2014, they made their first Terrasses du Larzac from 60 per cent Syrah with equal parts of Grenache and Mourvèdre, from about 15 different plots comprising several different *terroirs*, including *galets roulées* and different types of limestone. The young wine has firm, peppery fruit, with underlying elegance, and will develop beautifully in bottle. This is undoubtedly one of the estates that has helped to create the reputation of the Terrasses du Larzac.

MONTPEYROUX

Montpeyroux is a pretty little village, lying at the foot of the Mont Baudile. There is an attractive market square, animated during the summer months by the tables of the restaurant, Terrasses de Mimosa, which has one of the better wine lists of the area. The outlying hamlet of Le Barry has an attractive deconsecrated church, which is used for exhibitions and concerts, and on the hills behind the hamlet stand the ruins of a medieval castle, Le Castellas. Montpeyroux really comes to life on the third Sunday in April, which is the occasion of Tous Caveaux Ouverts, when all the wine producers in the village join together to open their cellars. The village is festooned with purple balloons, looking like outsize bunches of grapes and there is a gentleman on high stilts animating the crowd. You buy a wine glass, which comes with a tasting booklet, and amble from cellar to cellar, tasting and maybe spitting. At lunchtime, copious quantities of *aligot* and barbecued sausage are on offer in the market square.

Montpeyroux may be part of the Terrasses du Larzac, but its growers aspire to the status of *cru* or *appellation communale*, so that Montpeyroux would stand alone on the label. Montpeyroux was recognized as a VDQS in 1958 and then as a *terroir* of the appellation of Coteaux du Languedoc in 1985. When I first visited the village back in 1987, the cooperative was the only producer of any note, and continues to function well and work effectively for its appellation. The director, Bernard Pallisé, is very aware of its importance and its impact on the economic fabric of the village, with the livelihoods of over 50 families depending upon it, in a population of about 1,200 people. Sylvain Fadat at Domaine Aupilhac, Alain Chabanon and Domaine de l'Aiguelière were just beginning to make their first wines at the end of the 1980s, and the village has continued to attract the development of new wine estates, so that Tous Caveaux Ouverts in 2017 saw 21 growers opening their cellars.

The vineyards of Montpeyroux are defined by the boundaries of the village, or *commune*, an administrative entity, so that the *vignerons*, with vineyards in neighbouring villages, will make AOP Languedoc, Terrasses du Larzac or the local IGP Mont Baudile. Montpeyroux can only be red, never rosé or white. It differentiates itself from Terrasses du Larzac with stricter yields; the grape variety mix is essentially the same, with the requirement of three varieties in the blend. Some observe that more religiously than others. The soil is quite varied, with more than one grower noting that in some ways the village lacks a distinctive typicity because of the mixture of soils. The higher vineyards, north of the village, such as Les Cocalières, are very stony and based on clay and limestone, whereas the lower vineyards have heavier soil, with more clay and with blue marl, which enables the vines to resist the stress of a drier year. As will be seen, there are palpable differences between the two in the glass.

Producers

Mas des Quernes

Montpeyroux 34150
www.mas-des-quernes.com

Jean Natoli has long worked as a consultant oenologist, beginning his career with Marc Dubernet, with 1983 his first professional harvest. He set up his own laboratory in 1992 and now employs 15 oenologists, with some 300 clients, concentrated in the Hérault, Gard and Vaucluse, and to a lesser extent in the Aude and Pyrénées-Orientales, but also in places as diverse as the Auvergne, Corsica, Morocco, Romania, Spain and Tuscany. In the Terrasses du Larzac, he has 20 clients, with five different oenologists following them. Jean would dispute any suggestion of uniformity, emphasizing that each oenologist has their own sensitivity. Since 2009, he has run his own estate of 15 hectares in the Terrasses du Larzac with his German partner, Peter Riegel. Although his cellar is in the village of Montpeyroux, for the moment he does not make any Montpeyroux because his vines are outside the delimited area. That may change if the area of Montpeyroux is extended.

Jean Natoli, Mas des Quernes

We walked through vineyards bathed in warm autumn sunshine, with a small *mazet* and series of small terraces. The oldest plot is Carignan planted in 1960, called le Blaireau, or badger. Grass is sown between the rows to give the vines some competition, but ploughed up in June to avoid any water stress in the summer. The name quernes is an invention from the English cairn. There are so many stones in the vineyards that they have built numerous small cairns and also dry-stone walls. There is a plot of experimental vines, with Piquepoul Noir, Counoise, Morastel, Muscardin and Vaccarèse, that you find in Châteauneuf-du-Pape, plus Sangiovese and Touriga Nacional.

Back at the cellar I was treated to a very comprehensive tasting, with several vintages of some wines and Jean talked about the recent developments in the Languedoc. For his own winemaking, he uses as little sulphur as possible, and favours cultured yeast. Highlights included Le Petit Travers, a blend mainly of Cinsaut and Syrah, with some spicy fruit. He makes two Terrasses du Larzac: Ruches, from Carignan, Mourvèdre and Grenache with some firm, structured fruit and spicy notes of the *garrigue*. La Villa Romaine is a similar blend, with less Carignan and more Mourvèdre, and some *élevage* in wood, making for more structure and concentration. Le Querne is the best of the vintage, whatever has performed particularly well. Often it is Grenache, but in 2015 Grenache suffered in the drought so the blend that year, labelled IGP Saint Guilhem-le-Désert, was 90 per cent Merlot with Syrah and Grenache, making for some ripe cassis fruit.

Domaine Alain Chabanon
Lagamas 34150
www.alainchabanon.com

Alain Chabanon was one of the pioneering wine growers of Montpeyroux, with a first vintage in 1990, at Domaine de Font Caude. He had a varied career before settling in Montpeyroux, studying in both Montpellier and Bordeaux and then working for Alain Brumont at Château Montus in Madiran, and at Domaine de Peraldi in Corsica. In 1987, he saw an advertisement in the *Midi Paysan* for 14 hectares of vines for sale in the nearby village of St Guiraud. He now has 17.5 hectares altogether, in about ten blocks, certified biodynamic since 2011, in the villages of St André-de-Sangonis, Jonquières, Lagamas, Montpeyroux and St Saturnin. Initially Alain made his wines in a cramped cellar in Montpeyroux, but then moved to larger premises outside the village of Lagamas. On my last visit I saw a state-of-the-art ageing cellar, with *foudres*, small stainless steel vats and eggs, and a welcoming tasting *caveau*. Alain has come a long way in 30 years and it has been fascinating to witness his progress. He has not used *barriques* since 2014, changing the ageing of his wines to include time in *foudres*, eggs and stainless steel. He has used eggs for ten years and finds them very efficient and only a little more expensive than new oak. They are easy to look after and the *bâtonnage* happens naturally, with a constant movement.

Alain now makes two white wines. He already had Chenin Blanc because there are pockets of it around St Saturnin and Montpeyroux, and planted Vermentino in 1999, vinifying it for the first time in 2002. Petit Trélans, Pays d'Oc, is a pure Vermentino, with the characteristic sappy fruit of the variety, while Trélans is a blend of equal parts Vermentino and Chenin Blanc, which has spent two years in stainless steel vat and a year in *foudres*. The wood adds body to the wine and the palate is a satisfying combination of weight and acidity, with dry honey.

Alain Chabanon

Alain's red wines are AOP Languedoc, rather than Montpeyroux or Terrasses du Larzac, apart from Esprit de Fontcaude, which comes from the 3 hectares of vines he has in the village of Montpeyroux. Campredon is a blend of Syrah with 10 per cent Grenache and 20 per cent Mourvèdre, aged in vat, with delicious fresh spicy fruit. Les Boissières is mainly Grenache Noir, given 36 months' ageing in stainless steel vat. Alain enjoys the elegance and purity of the Grenache Noir and the flavours are perfumed and spicy, so that it could almost be mistaken for a Pinot Noir. For him, Grenache, rather than Cinsaut, is the Pinot Noir of the Languedoc. Esprit de Fontcaude is a blend of 45 per cent Syrah and Mourvèdre with 10 per cent Grenache, aged in vat and *foudres*. Le Saut de Côte, named after the *lieu-dit* near the cellar, is predominantly Mourvèdre, given 36 months in eggs. It is rounded, rich and complex. As well as working with the classic Midi grape varieties,

Alain also makes some of the best Merlot of the south, with Le Petit Merle aux Alouettes and Le Merle aux Alouettes, both Pays d'Oc. The first is aged in vat and the second, with more depth, weight and rich plummy fruit, is kept in *foudres* for 24 months.

Alain is thrilled with his new cellar and believes it will greatly enhance the quality of his wines. Over the years he has become less interventionist with his winemaking: 'we do less and less', he says, yet he points out that the man is important too, not just the grapes. He considers elegance to be his typicity, observing that the wines have changed enormously and have become much more refined. Wines considered great 30 years ago, would today be criticized for having too much oak and alcohol. As for the typicity of Montpeyroux, it depends on its position at the foot of Mount Baudile, tucked under the Larzac plateau, making for cooler conditions with good diurnal differences.

Domaine du Joncas

Montpeyroux, 34150
www.domaine-du-joncas.com

Pascal Dalier and his wife, Christiane, at Domaine du Joncas feature amongst the relative newcomers to Montpeyroux. Their first vintage was in 2011. Winemaking was a complete career change for Pascal. He was a car *concessionaire* in Nancy, the elegant capital of Lorraine, with four showrooms, 120 employees and a €40 million turnover. Then the opportunity came for him to sell up and follow his dream. He worked with Alain Chabanon, and now considers Alain his guardian angel. He did some short courses and acquired 3 hectares of vines, and then a couple more, and now has a total of 9 hectares in three different plots: 5 hectares in Jurassic limestone high above Montpeyroux; 3 hectares in the nearby village of Jonquières; and another hectare of clay and limestone on the edge of the village. Joncas is the name of a canyon near the Mont Baudile, and describes a place where gorse grows, *ajonc* being the French for gorse. An early conversation with Pascal was about land prices. When he was looking for vineyards, land in Pic St Loup cost between €25,000 and €30,000 (US$31–37,000) per hectare as opposed to €10–15,000 (US$12,250–18,400) in Montpeyroux. He searched from Sommières to St Jean-de-Minervois and fell for Montpeyroux, observing that you do not find the precision and finesse of Montpeyroux in Pic St Loup.

Pascal built a cellar on the edge of the village, in time for the 2012 harvest. It is simple and functional, with small *foudres*, vats and some concrete eggs, and walls painted an elegant Burgundy red, for practical reasons! Pascal's range has gradually grown. His very first wine was Joia. As he said, he wanted to make *un vin joyeux*. It is 80 per cent Grenache Noir with some Syrah and for Pascal expresses the typicity of Montpeyroux with some fresh, elegant fruit. There are now two white wines. Alba, from just 40 ares of Grenache Gris, grown up in the hills and planted initially as an experiment is aged in an egg and has a satisfying structure, with firm acidity and minerality. Canta is most unusual. Pascal had a hunch that Riesling might work up in his highest vineyard, so he planted just 40 ares. It is quite unlike any other Riesling, but with recognizable varietal character, dry honey on the nose and steely acidity balancing the fruit on the palate.

As for the other red wines, Nèbla comes from the vineyards near Jonquières and is therefore a Terrasses du Larzac, with Syrah the dominant variety. It is richer and more structured than Joia. Obrà, another Terrasses du Larzac, again with Syrah as the principal grape variety, comes from the *causse* above Montpeyroux and is aged in both *foudres* and eggs for 12 months. It is rich and rounded, with concentration and also elegance. The latest addition to the range is Simpla. Pascal planted half a hectare of Mourvèdre, with a particularly fine clone, and another half hectare of Grenache with a low-yielding clone, which in 2015 he pruned tightly so that the vines produced one bunch per vine. The wine was aged in 10-hectolitre *foudres*. The 2016 tasted from *foudre* promised well, with depth and fruit while subtle nuances developed in the glass. In his winemaking, Pascal avoids using sulphur, except at bottling, and looks for elegance, freshness and minerality, which is what he has achieved. Our tasting finished with Nèbla rosé, a refreshing glass of wine made from one part Syrah to two parts Grenache Noir.

Mas d'Amile

Montpeyroux 34150
www.masdamile.fr

It all began when Amélie d'Hurlaborde, and her brother Sébastien, who works for Alain Chabanon, inherited a hectare of old Carignan vines from their grandfather. This led Amélie to make her first wine in 2007, a delicious Carignan, IGP Mont Baudile, that exhibited all the potential of good Carignan. Since that first vintage, the estate has gradually evolved, from making wine in her grandfather's garage to building a new cellar outside Montpeyroux. Amélie now has 7 hectares of vines, with nine plots altogether, planted with Grenache, in two different vineyards, some Carignan and small plots of Syrah, Mourvèdre and Terret Blanc, along with some Merlot that she uses for rosé, all farmed biodynamically since 2015. The altitude of her vines varies between 200 and 400 metres, on limestone soil.

Terret Blanc, IGP Mont Baudile, from 40-year-old vines was dry, mineral and salty. Her entry-level red, Le Petitou, Terrasses du Larzac, is a blend of 60 per cent Grenache and equal parts of Syrah and Carignan, aged in vat, for some fresh peppery fruit. The Carignan, from 80-year-old vines, is an IGP St Guilhem-le-Désert, rather than the more usual IGP Mont Baudile for Montpeyroux, because the vineyard is in the neighbouring village of Lagamas, which is not part of IGP Mont Baudile. The wine enjoys a classic vinification, as Amélie does not like carbonic maceration, with 12 months in old barrels for about 80 per cent of the wine. The flavours are perfumed and fresh, with a streak of tannin. Her Montpeyroux is a blend of approximately 50 per cent Grenache Noir, 15 per cent each of Syrah and Carignan and 20 per cent Mourvèdre, with some oak ageing, and some spicy flavours with a tannin backbone. It promises well with a little bottle age.

Villa Dondona
Montpeyroux 34150
www.domaine.villadondona.com

The village of Montpeyroux attracts more than its fair share of newcomers to wine. One example is Villa Dondona, created by a talented English artist, Jo Lynch, and her French husband, André Suquet, whose previous career was in medicine. Back in 1998 they bought 15 hectares of *garrigue*, just outside Montpeyroux, above the little hamlet of Le Barry, and in 2000 they decided to plant vines: Grenache Noir, Syrah and Mourvèdre. André particularly likes Syrah, and Jo Mourvèdre. Their first harvest was 2004, with just a tiny amount of wine, but none the less, and much to their surprise, they won a gold medal. Then a few years later they planted Vermentino and Roussanne, and acquired small plots of Grenache Blanc and Marsanne that were going to be pulled up and made their first vintage of white L'Espérel in 2010.

A drive through the vineyard reveals a dramatic site, with the ruined castle of le Castellas above. The plot is shaped like a fan, with several different soil types, including marl and red clay. The vines are trained low and planted close together, with 8,000 vines per hectare and 70 centimetres between the vines in each row. The Vermentino is grown on a pergola, to protect the grapes from the sun, and the direction of the rows is determined by the dominant wind. They have a small cellar carved out of the hillside, with stainless steel vats and some barrels of 300 litres, and also 270 litres, which apparently is the traditional size for the Languedoc. They come from a cooper in nearby Paulhan.

As well as L'Espérel, they make a rosé, Esquisse, which is a pure Cinsaut, and three different red wines, with a fourth in the pipeline. Dame Mourvèdre is, as the name implies, a pure Mourvèdre, aged in vat rather than barrel, and the bottle shape is unusual, a medieval shape according to Jo. There are two Montpeyroux, Villa Dondona, for which the blend is 40 per cent Mourvèdre and Syrah, with 20 per cent Grenache Noir, aged in vat, with some perfumed peppery fruit, and Oppidum, which is 60 per cent Mourvèdre and 40 per cent Syrah, aged in oak for a year, with denser, more powerful flavours. The last time I saw Jo and André, it was to taste a potential new *cuvée*, a pure Syrah, from two different vineyards.

Domaine d'Aupilhac
Montpeyroux 34150
www.aupilhac.net

Sylvain Fadat at Domaine d'Aupilhac has done more than most to develop the reputation of Montpeyroux. You will find him in the rue du Plô, one of the main streets of Montpeyroux, where he has a labyrinthine cellar, with vats and barrels, eggs and *foudres*, as well as a welcoming tasting *caveau*. Sylvain is friendly, articulate and full of ideas, on which he happily expounds during a tasting. Both his grandfather and father had vines and his first vintage was in 1989, from just 7 hectares planted mainly with Carignan. Consequently, Carignan has always remained an important element in his range, as a single varietal, Le Carignan. 'It is the grape variety of the Mediterranean that can withstand the hot, dry climate, and still retain its freshness. You must not put it in new wood.' Sylvain prefers *foudres* or *demi-muids*, and has never used carbonic maceration on it. Above all it must be ripe, and not be allowed to overproduce, and then it will age beautifully. In due course, Montpeyroux is likely to allow 60 per cent rather than the current 40 per cent Carignan.

Sylvain now has 25 hectares of vines in two areas of Montpeyroux. Aupilhac is a *lieu-dit*, south-east of the village, at an altitude of 120–150 metres, planted mainly with Mourvèdre and Carignan on blue marl. Les Cocalières is a spectacular vineyard at 350 metres, on the limestone *causses* above the village, which Sylvain cleared in 1998 to plant Syrah and Grenache, with a first harvest in 2003. The vegetative cycle here is longer and the grapes are ripe at 13% abv rather than the 14.5% abv at Aupilhac. La Boda is the marriage of the two vineyards, including the oldest Syrah of Cocalières and the oldest Mourvèdre of Aupilhac. Le Clos, a blend of Carignan and Mourvèdre, is not made every year. So, for Sylvain, there are two typicities within the village, but the key factor is that the vines do not suffer from drought because there is plenty of underground water and the proximity to the Larzac has a cooling effect.

Sylvain also makes some elegant white wines. Cuvée Aupilhac is a blend of Clairette, Ugni Blanc, Grenache Blanc and Vermentino, with some rounded white blossom, while Les Cocalières includes Roussanne, Marsanne, Grenache Blanc and Vermentino, aged in Stockinger *foudres*, with some satisfying weight and texture. The white wines must undergo a malolactic fermentation, which enables them to age. His two entry-level wines, a red and white, are labelled Lou Maset. He used to make a delicious pure Cinsaut, Les Servières, but unfortunately the wild boars kept eating all of the grapes.

Sylvain's winemaking has evolved over the years. Firstly, the basis of quality has always been ripe fruit; it has to be better than unripe fruit. He began working biodynamically in 2011 and was officially recognized in 2014. For him it is a question of details and he is convinced that his wine is fresher as a result. He keeps his sulphur levels as low as possible. He used to favour longer macerations, 32 days as opposed to the current average of 25 days, aiming for a much lighter extraction. He has also moved away from *barriques* to *foudres* or 600- or 700-litre *demi-muids*. He likes Stockinger for *foudres* because they do not *dénature* the wine.

It is important that his wines can age. Anyone can make good young wine, but the *terroir* of Montpeyroux allows for ageing, and that must be expressed. To prove his point, he opened a pair of 2003s, Les Cocalières and Aupilhac. Both had evolved beautifully; Aupilhac was rich and leathery, while Les Cocalières was more elegant and fresher, with some peppery fruit. A pair of 2006s followed, inviting a similar comparison, and then came La Boda with some ripe cassis and leathery fruit.

Montpeyroux is en route for promotion to the status of *cru*, hopefully within the next couple of years, as the dossier has been accepted by the INAO. Meanwhile, Sylvain remains optimistic about the future, while the annual fête symbolizes and underlines the economic importance of wine for the village.

ST SATURNIN

St Saturnin is a sleepy little village. There is a cheerful restaurant, Le Pressoir, and a small hotel, Le Mimosa, but no shop. The peace is broken by the regular chimes, every 15 minutes, of the church clock, twice, as is the custom in rural France, but otherwise there is very little to disturb the somnolent atmosphere. However, the village really comes to life on a weekend in late October when they celebrate the Fête du Vin Primeur. The small square is filled with stalls selling local produce and the cooperative offers the wine of the year. I once had a grandstand view from my hotel room of some sheepdog trials, not with sheep, but with obstreperous geese and ducks. The surrounding countryside is wild and rugged, especially from the viewpoint at the Rocher des Deux Vierges. The village is Roman in origin and was originally called St Saturnin-de-Lucian after a Roman notable who settled here. Later, the bishops of nearby Lodève used it as a summer residence. Little grows here apart from vines and a few olive and almond trees, so viticulture is virtually the sole activity.

Although St Saturnin is the neighbouring village to Montpeyroux and has a similar history in that it was recognized as a VDQS in 1958 and then as a *terroir* of the Coteaux du Languedoc in 1982, it has failed to develop the same dynamic wine culture. The reason for this is that membership of the village cooperative, which was founded in 1950, tied up its members' vineyards for 50 years. The only way to escape from the cooperative was to sell your vines, as did the Bousquet family, who now make very successful La Clape at Domaine Pech Redon. Consequently, there has been a firm brake on the development of wine estates.

Producer

Domaine Virgile Joly

St Saturnin 34725
www.domainevirgilejoly.com

It is no coincidence that Domaine Virgile Joly, which Virgile created in 2000, was the first new estate in the village in over two generations. Virgile has a small cellar on the village square, between the *mairie* and the church, and above the door the sign reads 'Virgile Joly, *vigneron depuis* 2000'.

Magda and Virgile Joly

I met Virgile fairly soon after his first harvest, which was the subject of a book, *Virgile's Vineyard*, by Patrick Moon, sympathetically describing the trials and tribulations of a young wine producer. He made his first wines from just 80 ares, and now has 15 hectares in 12 different plots.

All are worked organically. Virgile explained that the putative village *cru* of St Saturnin also includes land in the adjoining villages of Jonquières, St Guiraud and Arboras, but there are really only three producers who make St Saturnin: Virgile, the cooperative and another small estate, Mas d'Estelle. Other nearby growers who could be part of St Saturnin prefer to work with the Terrasses du Larzac. Even so, Virgile is optimistic that the INAO will eventually accept St Saturnin as a *cru*. The conditions will be stricter, with a yield of 42 hectolitres per hectare, as opposed to 45 hectolitres per hectare for Terrasses du Larzac. Rosé is a point of contention because the Terrasses du Larzac is only red, whereas St Saturnin also has a historic reputation for its rosé, and rosé accounts for a considerable proportion of the production.

Virgile was born in Avignon and studied in Montpellier and Aix-en Provence, both oenology and commerce, working in Chile and the Rhône Valley before coming to Montpeyroux. His grandparents had vines in the Côtes du Ventoux, but in 2000 the Rhône valley was too complicated and too expensive, and there was very good land to buy in Montpeyroux. Virgile has a broader vision than many of his colleagues. He talked about the financial realities of life as a *vigneron*. Wine estates vary enormously in size. It is perfectly possible for one person to live from a couple of hectares. By contrast there are investors such as Christopher Johnson Hill, a London solicitor, with whom Virgile was associated for a while. He bought his estate, Domaine des Cinq Vents, not to make a living from it, but for the pleasure of having a vineyard in the south of France. He has now sold his vineyards to Pierre Clavel (see p. 268). As Virgile asserts, 'Magda [his Polish wife] and I have to live from our vineyard; the realities are not the same, but the market does not see the differences and journalists, when they are waxing lyrically about an estate, should take its size into account.' Virgile certainly has a stronger commercial drive than some of his colleagues and he has developed a small *négociant* business alongside his vineyards.

The wine for which he is best known is the Le Joly Rouge, which is now paired with Le Joly Blanc. Both are easy to drink; the red is fresh and spicy with ripe cherry fruit, a blend of mainly Syrah and Grenache with some Carignan and Cinsaut, and the white comes from equal parts of Grenache Blanc and Roussanne, with some nicely rounded fruit. Saturne Blanc is Grenache Blanc with a little Roussanne, with some textured flavours, and Virgile Blanc is pure Grenache Blanc and consequently a Vin de France, which spends two years in barrel. Virgile now makes rosé, having ignored it for a number of years, observing that as president of St Saturnin and fighting for rosé, he should at least practice what he preaches. It is ripe and fruity with quite a deep colour; the colour range for rosé is measured from 1 to 5 and Virgile opted for between 3 and 4. Red Saturne comes from equal parts of Carignan, Grenache and Syrah, with fruit and structure, while Virgile is the same blend, a selection from the best plots, with 18–24 months' oak ageing, it has depth and elegance on the palate.

Asked if his winemaking has changed over the years, Virgile said he didn't think so, but observed that winemaking is the culmination of a multitude of details. His had perhaps become more 'soft' so that he is gaining in elegance and freshness, and making more accessible wines that are ready early, but will also age.

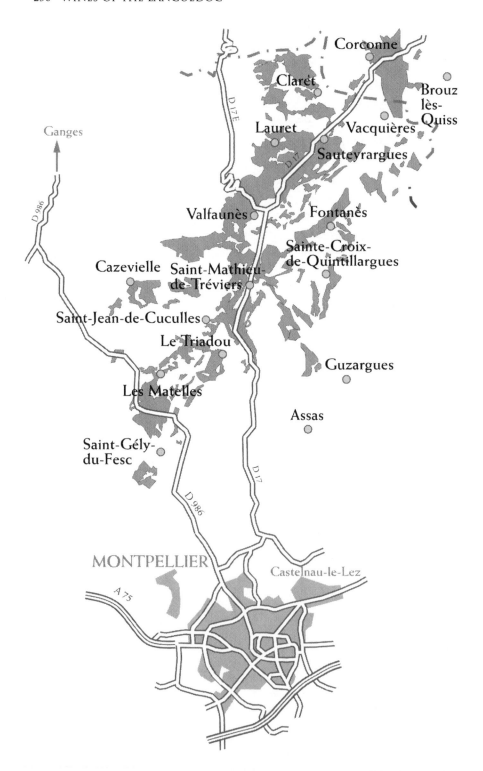

18

PIC ST LOUP

I have never forgotten my first view of the Pic St Loup. I took the road from St Martin-de-Londres, heading to St Mathieu-de-Tréviers. Turning a corner, it suddenly appeared, a pointed mountain with a sheer cliff, facing the Montagne de l'Hortus, with its own steep face, a dramatic juxtaposition of two high hills confronting each other. The Pic St Loup rises to 638 metres and dominates the surrounding countryside. Sometimes you see the gentler side of the Pic, with softer slopes, but from most places, the gradient is sharp. You would not think that you were so close to the bustling metropolis of Montpellier, for the southernmost *communes* of the Pic St Loup adjoin the city's suburbs. The growers in St Gély-du-Fesc and St Jean-de-Cuculles often feel that they are fighting a rearguard action against the property developers because some land is more valuable for construction than for vineyards.

Climb, as we did, to the top of the Pic St Loup on the first sunny Sunday afternoon of spring and you have *tout* Montpellier keeping you company, not just the young and the fit, but their dogs and children too. The view from the top is well worth the effort, for you look across the valley to the Montagne de l'Hortus and beyond. There is a small chapel dedicated to St Loup. Local legend has it that in the early Middle Ages a man called Loup from the village of St Martin-de-Londres fell in love, but he had two rivals. The three men decided to go on a crusade to prove their valour, but when they returned a few years later, the object of their affections had disappeared. Disillusioned, they each took the vows of a hermit and Loup settled on the nearby mountain.

Pic St Loup was recognized as a VDQS back in 1955 and then incorporated into the larger appellation of Coteaux du Languedoc.

In 1994, it achieved the status of *cru* with subtle differences to the Coteaux du Languedoc, and finally, after what seemed like years of negotiation and hassle, in 2016 it was recognized as an appellation in its own right, for a first vintage of 2017. The bone of contention had been the extension of the area of the appellation, with the acceptance of the inclusion of three new villages, on the eastern edge of the appellation, namely Assas, Guzargues and Vailhauquès, as well as more vineyards in Brouzet-lès-Quissac. The appellation is compact, about 18 kilometres long and 3 kilometres wide, on the east side of the Pic St Loup. About 1,000 hectares have been delimited, from 17 villages, all in the Hérault except for the most northern villages, Corconne and Brouzet-lès-Quissac, which are in the Gard. St Martin de Londres is well worth a visit for its Romanesque church, and another Romanesque chapel, Notre Dame d'Aleyrac, nestles in the vineyards.

The emphasis is very much on Syrah, with a minimum requirement of 50 per cent in the blend, and a minimum of two varieties, namely Grenache and Mourvèdre, as well as Carignan and Cinsaut, which are less important. The wine is only red or rosé, for the simple reason that very little white was being made when Pic St Loup was included in the original appellation of the Coteaux du Languedoc. Although there has been a considerable increase in the production of white wine, so that nearly everyone produces some, there is still no very clear idea of what is a representative white, with a choice of grape varieties and *terroirs*. Consequently, any white wine is either AOP Languedoc or Pays du Val de Montferrand, taking its name from a ruined château that sits on top of another small hill outside the small town of St Mathieu-de-Tréviers, which is the centre of the appellation.

You could wonder how it happened that the Terrasses du Larzac was recognized as an appellation so much more quickly than Pic St Loup. The answer lies within local politics. Pic St Loup had been working on its dossier since 2001, including the proposal to add vineyards from the three extra *communes*, using the argument that the geology is similar. However, that provoked a considerable outcry, with the accusation that the producers in those villages had not actually worked to create the appellation and therefore did not deserve to benefit from the new delimitation of the appellation. In addition, other producers of Pic St Loup would have their vineyards reduced as a result of the new detailed delimitation. As you can appreciate, it is a wonderful *histoire de clochers*, which has happily now been resolved.

So, what distinguishes Pic St Loup from other areas of the Languedoc? Most significantly, it is one of the more northerly parts of the Languedoc, and consequently it tends to be wetter, with as much as 1,000 millimetres of annual rainfall. The temperatures may also be a little cooler, with a good diurnal variation. Wind can have an impact, drying the grapes after any rainfall. As for the *terroir*, the soil is a mosaic of different limestone. Françoise Julien at Clos Marie observed that it lies between *la terre et la mer*. Travel 15 minutes in either direction and you reach either the hills or the sea. What follows are some highlights of the appellation, both long-established growers and newcomers, of which there have been several in the past few years.

Producers

Domaine de l'Hortus
Valflaunès 34270
www.domaine-hortus.fr

I have long had a soft spot for the wines of Domaine de l'Hortus, since my first visit to the estate back in the mid-1990s. The very first time I visited Pic St Loup in the late 1980s the sole producer of any significance was the cooperative in St Mathieu-de-Tréviers, which did much to encourage the aspiring wine growers of the area. Jean Orliac was among the first of that new wave of wine producers and these days the estate is run by his children, Marie, François, Yves and Martin, who share the responsibilities of 90 hectares of vineyards and also a *négociant* business. In addition, they have an estate in the Terrasses du Larzac, Clos du Prieur at St Jean-de-Buèges.

On my previous visit, Martin took me to see their vineyards, explaining that the typicity of Pic St Loup is *fraîcheur et matière*, with fruit and tannins. You can discern three different *terroirs* in the Pic St Loup: the southern part of the appellation around St Mathieu-de-Tréviers has less rain, with a smaller diurnal contrast; the central area has more rain, with bigger temperature differences; and the northern part of the appellations is much cooler, with even more rain. Their vineyards are between the two mountains and benefit from losing the afternoon sun quite early. The Syrah vineyard faces north, as it does not like too much sun, and the Mourvèdre looks to the south, which suits it. Martin talked about vine density, which is a key decision for grape quality, explaining that 4,000 vines per hectare is too little and makes for vines that are too vigorous so they have gradually increased to 7,100, 2 metres apart, with 70 centimetres within the rows. They have also invested heavily in the cellar in recent years, to good effect in their wines.

Yves Orliac, Domaine de l'Hortus, with the Pic St Loup in the background

Bergerie de l'Hortus Blanc is a Pays du Val de Montferrand from several grape varieties, namely Roussanne, Viognier, Sauvignon Blanc, Muscat à Petits Grains, Sauvignon Gris, Chardonnay and Petit Manseng, and is the result of various experiments. They could also have included Chenin Blanc, but do not find it very aromatic; nor are they very enthusiastic about Vermentino. The wine is intriguing, fresh and pithy, with notes of white blossom and more besides. Grand Cuvée Blanc, of which Chardonnay accounts for half the blend, with Viognier, Sauvignon Gris and Petit Manseng, is fermented in oak, with some rich buttery, nutty fruit. They make a small amount of rosé, but it is their red wine that excels. Bergerie Rouge is a blend of two parts Syrah to one part Mourvèdre with just a little Grenache Noir, aged mainly in vat to make for some rounded, spicy fruit with structure, length and a fresh finish. Grande Cuvée is a similar blend, given 18 months' ageing in *tonneaux*, 900-litre barrels. The grapes are riper and from higher altitude vineyards, and are given a longer *cuvaison* to soften the tannins, making for dry spice and elegant tannins. They are not looking for power but want rounded tannins and complexity. Finally came Clos du Prieur, from 70 per cent Syrah with some Grenache Noir and Cinsaut; the flavour register is different. The vineyards are higher and the climate more continental with hotter summers and colder winters, so that the wine is sunnier and riper. The harvest is always a little later than in the Pic St Loup. My visit finished with a very *sympathique* lunch *en famille* with a glass of a more mature vintage of Grande Cuvée.

Mas Bruguière
Valflaunès 34270
www.mas-bruguiere.com

Xavier Bruguière is the seventh generation, of a family that has made wine at Mas Bruguière since the Revolution. They have 20 hectares altogether, with the hub of the estate at the foot of the Pic St Loup, close to their cellar. Xavier explained that at the beginning of the nineteenth century this was an area of polyculture and the wine was sold to a broker. Then when the cooperative was created in 1920, a grandparent took the easy route. Xavier's father, Guilhem, took over in 1974 and remained a cooperative member until 1986, when he became one of the first independent producers to bottle his own wine. He bought a further 10 hectares in the northern part of the appellation, which he has gradually replanted since 1999. Xavier studied at Béziers and worked for a couple of years at La Liquière in Faugères under a system in which studies are alternated with practical cellar and vineyard work. He joined his father in 1999 and then Guilhem retired in 2004.

For red wine they have Syrah, Grenache and Mourvèdre, but no Carignan, and have recently planted Cinsaut for rosé, while for white wine, which is AOP Languedoc, they have Marsanne, Roussanne and Vermentino. Xavier believes that if you plant Carignan these days, you are planting for your children. Mourvèdre is tricky, *un cépage ingrate*; you cannot just plant it anywhere, and you need to work in the vineyard. The relatively new cellar is well conceived, so that everything works by gravity. Xavier uses natural yeast and has cement fermentation vats for his red wine and large tronconic oak vats for *élevage*, as well as some 600-litre barrels. Generally, he favours large containers rather than *barriques*. However, like most good winemakers, he believes that 80 per cent of the wine is made in the vineyards, which are farmed organically.

Guilhem Bruguière planted their white varieties in 1992 and the blend of Les Mûriers comprises 70 per cent Roussanne, 20 per cent Marsanne, and 10 per cent Vermentino, which is a more recent addition to the blend and was planted in 2008. Xavier had wanted to broaden the aromatic palate. He observed that later ripening varieties do better, and 30 per cent of the blend is vinified in small *foudres* of 12 hectolitres. He just uses the free-run juice and very first pressings. The nose is redolent of white blossom and the palate rounded and herbal, with very good acidity and a fresh finish. Rosé Pic St Loup, L'Arbouse, comes from equal proportions of Syrah and Mourvèdre, from a cooler vineyard site. The colour is a delicate orange pink and the palate rounded with some weight. As for red wines, there is Calcadiz, AOP Languedoc, from Syrah and Grenache, with some fresh red fruit. The first Pic St Loup L'Arbouse is 60 per cent Syrah with some Grenache, partially aged in cement vat and partly in tronconic vats, with the herbs of the *garrigue*, and a stony mineral nose. Asked about his typicity, Xavier replied: '*fruit, fraîcheur, finesse*', and you certainly find that in L'Arbouse, which is the fruit of the strawberry tree, or *arbousier*. La Grenadine is 80 per cent Syrah with a little Grenache and Mourvèdre and is more structured with some *élevage* in tronconic vats and *demi-muids* for 12 months, followed by six months in concrete vats. Our tasting concluded with Le 7me, named for the seventh generation, a pure Mourvèdre given 24 months' *élevage*, with depth and elegance. It makes a great tribute to a longstanding family of dedicated *vignerons*.

Clos Marie

Lauret 34270
clos.marie@orange.fr

Christophe Peyrus left the French navy to work on his wife Françoise Julien's family estate. The vines were extracted from the cooperative in 1992 and their first wine made in 1995. The estate is named Clos Marie after her grandmother, who died in 2008, aged 100. When I met her in 1998, a wizened old lady of 90, she insisted on telling me her age and that her own mother had reached the age of 103. Christophe comes from a family of wine producers in Cahors. Things have gently moved on since my last visit, with much fine-tuning in the cellar. They have small and large barrels, some tronconic vats, some eggs and two amphorae, as well as stainless steel vats and a sorting table. Eighty per cent of their red wines are destalked; the length of maceration depends on the *cuvée*, the vintage, the grape varieties and the weather. They are biodynamic, but are not labelled as such because they do not wish to pay for the label. The average age of their vines is between 30 and 40 years, and most are planted with a high density of 8,000 plants per hectare.

They were severely hit by the hailstorm of 17 August 2016, which destroyed virtually all of their crop, and so made just two wines in 2017, a red and a white, mainly from purchased grapes from the Terrasses du Larzac. We tasted the white, called Les Trois Saisons, as one season is missing. It is the same blend as for their own white wine, Manon, namely Roussanne, Clairette, Macabeo, Grenache Blanc and Gris, vinified in exactly the same way, making for good acidity, texture and fruit. They usually make a rosé and four red wines, namely L'Olivette, Simon, Métairie du Clos and Les Glorieuses, all from Syrah, Grenache, Carignan and a little Mourvèdre. Asked about their typicity, Françoise talked of freshness and minerality, with wines that take time to express themselves, making *vins de garde* that will last.

For Françoise, the Pic St Loup really established its reputation in the 1990s; that was the time when a lot of estates, such as theirs, were set up. It is now much more difficult to establish a place in the market – she talked of a terrible *engouement*, an infatuation of wine growers with the Languedoc, with so much planting and so many new estates.

Chateau Lascaux

Vacquières 34270
www.chateau-lascaux.com

Jean-Benoît Cavalier at Château Lascaux in the village of Vacquières has long been involved with the appellation. He took over the family estate from his grandfather in 1984 and made his first wine in 1990, having withdrawn the vineyards from the cooperative. He now has 55 hectares, all farmed organically. Jean-Benoît talked about the history of the area. The formation of the Pic St Loup was a repercussion of the creation of the Pyrenees. There is more *garrigue* than vineyard here, with the vines much more dispersed than in some other areas. There used to be flocks of sheep, which were taken up into the Cévennes during the summer months. Silkworms were important, too, at the end of the nineteenth century, because nearby Ganges was an important centre for silk. Polyculture was once the norm, but now the emphasis is on vines, and some olive trees. The soil is very varied, all based on variations of clay and limestone. Lascaux, the name of the hill outside the village where most of Jean-Benoît's vines are planted, means chalky stone in Occitan.

Jean-Benoît's new cellar is the fulfilment of a long ambition, a lifetime's project, he said, and will enable him to work much more efficiently. In its design, he focused amongst other things on the temperature for *élevage*, so the barrel cellar is underground, with an earthen floor to retain humidity, as well as an ecological green roof. He has moved from 225-litre *barriques*, to 300- or 600-litre barrels and small *foudres* of 15 and 30 hectolitres. *Élevage* is meant to help the wine develop, but not to add tannin or vanilla. He wants to be able to express the originality of each plot of vines. There are concrete and tronconic vats for red wine and stainless steel tanks for white and rosé.

We adjourned to his *sympathique* tasting *caveau* in the heart of the village, a vaulted cellar that dates back to the twelfth century. Jean-Benoît makes a logical range of wines, a red and white IGP, a red, white and rosé AOP Languedoc, and for Pic St Loup there is Carra and Les Nobles Pierres and three precise *lieu-dits*. Cuvée Garrigue AOP Languedoc is a blend of Vermentino, Roussanne, Marsanne, Grenache Blanc and a little Viognier, with an *élevage* in vat, to give an elegant, complex wine with plenty of nuance from the diversity of grapes. Les Pierres d'Argent is fermented in barrel with an *élevage* in small *foudres*, with more weight and body. Cuvée Garrigue Languedoc Rouge is 70 per cent Syrah, with Grenache Noir and a touch of Mourvèdre, kept in vat, because Jean-Benoît wants to concentrate on the aromatics, with tapenade and black fruit. The name Carra is a reference to the oak, the *kermess*, and a blend of 60 per cent Syrah with Grenache Noir, aged in vat with more black fruit and fresh tannins. Les Nobles Pierres, from 70 per cent Syrah with Grenache Noir, is riper, with more concentration after a 12-months *élevage* in wood. He has worked on wines from individual plots, first Bois de Tourtourel, from 60 per cent Syrah with Grenache Noir aged in barrel and *demi-muids* for 12–14 months and then two or three months in vat. Toutourel is a reference to doves and in this wine Jean-Benoît is looking for elegant concentration and red fruit with harmonious tannins. Madeleine is also on limestone, with concentration, black fruit and elegant power. The final *lieu-dit*, Patus de Musseu, was out of stock.

Bergerie du Capucin

Valflaunès 34270

www.bergerieducapucin.fr

Bergerie du Capucin was created by Guilhem Viau. The basis of the estate came from his ex-wife's family vineyards, which were taken out of the St Mathieu cooperative in 2008. The couple have now gone their separate ways, leaving Guilhem with 6 hectares, and he has rented a further 6. Ideally, he would like about 18 hectares, but it is difficult to find land, with the conflict between urbanism and viticulture. Building land costs €2 million per hectare, as opposed to classified vineyard land that needs clearing for planting at €50,000, but people do not want to sell. You also need planting rights, with an allowance of 1 per cent per annum, so as not to destabilize the market.

Guilhem's white wines are IGPs, good examples of Chardonnay and Viognier, and Dame Jeanne, a blend of Chardonnay, with two pickings, a week apart, with 15 per cent Viognier, which has some rounded peachy fruit. Rosé les Cent Pas is mainly Grenache Noir, with some Syrah, a fresh *rosé de piscine*, while Dame Jeanne Rosé, with 75 per cent Syrah plus some Grenache and Mourvèdre, is more substantial and vinous. Les 100 Pas AOP Languedoc is also based on Grenache, for easy drinking, while Dame Jeanne Rouge, based on Syrah, has some spicy fruit with a bit of pepper. This is Guilhem's principal wine. Larmenella red, from a selection of plots, is mainly Syrah with a little Grenache Noir, aged in 400-litre barrels for a year or so, with some fresh ripe fruit and tapenade notes. When I asked Guilhem about the typicity of the Pic St Loup, he laughed: 'The soil, the climate, the men.' People make choices, to decide how to make wines that illustrate the *terroir*. The climate allows for wines with supple tannins, while maintaining structure, with elegance and balance.

Mas Gourdou

Valflaunès 43270

www.masgourdou.free.fr

Mas Gourdou, outside the village of Valflaunès, has been in the hands of the Thérond family for several generations, at least since the Revolution. Benoît Thérond explained that originally they sold wine *en vrac* to the *négoce*, then his great-grandparents joined the cooperative, leaving his parents, who had other careers, to decide whether to sell or take over the vines when they inherited them. Benoît had studied tourism but knew that he wanted to return to the land. Meanwhile his parents had been gradually extracting their vineyards from the cooperative, a couple of hectares per year, to eventually reach 20, and Benoît made his first wine in 2013. The vineyards are very spread out, in the shadow of the Montagne de l'Hortus, at Valflaunès and at Sauteyrargues. A new cellar was built in 2015 from Gard stone, which is known for its insulation qualities, with a barrel cellar that has deep red walls and atmospheric lighting.

Benoît concentrates on Pic St Loup, with vineyards planted mainly with Syrah and some Grenache Noir and Mourvèdre. Les Roches Blanches, from 50 per cent Syrah, 35 per cent Grenache Noir and 15 per cent Mourvèdre is based on peppery fruit; Joseph Onésime is a similar blend, but with Mourvèdre and less Grenache Noir, blended and then partially aged in barrel for 12 months, with weight and nicely integrated oak. It is a homage to Benoît's two grandfathers; he affectionately called it the *cuvée des papis*. Pas du Loup spends 12 months in old wood, with some perfumed fruit from a higher proportion of Grenache Noir. He always blends before *élevage*, noting that you can always adjust afterwards. Divin Venin – 'alcohol can be divine or a poison' – spends 24 months in new oak, giving elegant concentration. The final wine is Le Grain par Grain, made with a *vinification intégrale*. The bunches are destalked and the wine fermented in small closed barrels, just one barrel each of Grenache Noir and Syrah, with an open bung to allow the carbon dioxide to escape, with a two-and-a-half-month maceration, to allow for a long, slow extraction. The wine is certainly oaky, but the oak seemed well integrated, with rich flavours and a sweet finish.

Benoît is a creative winemaker. He also has a more developed sense of wine tourism than most of his colleagues and would like to stand out from the mass. His labels featuring the outline of the Pic St Loup are certainly very recognizable on a wine shelf. As well as wine, he produces saffron, with a harvest later in the autumn, and the family also has olive trees. He deserves to do well.

Domaine Mirabel
Brouzet-lès-Quissac 30260
domainemirabel@neuf.fr

Samuel and Vincent Feuillade are in the northern village of Brouzet-lès-Quissac, part of which was originally classified as AOP Languedoc, or Coteaux du Languedoc, and which has benefited from the extension of the appellation to include all the village. The two brothers had their vines at the cooperative. Both sets of grandparents had been *viticulteurs*, but when the severe frost of 1956 killed the vines, they had lost their capital and it was impossible to remain independent. Their grandsons have now developed their own estate of 14 hectares. They took me on a drive through their vineyards on a rather grey November afternoon, explaining that *gravette* is the name of the soil here, a type of gravel based on clay and limestone, with iron and bauxite. The vineyards have been farmed organically since 2009. There are some dramatic cliffs above the neighbouring village of Corconne, with a chapel that you can visit. A ditch separates Corconne and Brouzet, but the soil is the same, and that was finally recognized with the extension of the appellation.

They have built a neat little cellar and make a small range of wines. I tasted Les Bancels, AOP Languedoc, and a blend of 50 per cent Syrah, 20 per cent each of Mourvèdre and Carignan, and 5 per cent each of Cinsaut and Grenache, aged in wood, with black fruit and tapenade and a fresh finish. Les Eclats, their Pic St Loup, with 50 per cent Syrah, 40 per cent Mourvèdre and a little Grenache and Cinsaut aged in 400-litre barrels and 35-hectolitre tronconic vats has ripe fruit and a firm tannic streak making for good ageing potential. A pure Syrah Grande Cuvée spends 36 months in a concrete vat – 'we did it for fun', they observed – and the wine is ripe and fleshy, with a fresh finish. They make just 400 bottles of it. All of their grapes are hand-picked, with the pickers given the instruction 'only pick the grapes you would eat'. They mentioned that 2014 was a difficult year because of rain during the harvest, so there was a lot of *triage* due to rot, with plenty of grapes that you certainly would not want to eat.

Mas Peyrolle

Vacquières 34270
jbpeyrolle@yahoo.fr

Jean-Baptiste Peyrolle in the village of Vacquières has broader horizons than some of his colleagues, for he has worked in New Zealand, at Ngtarawa in Hawke's Bay, as well as in California, in Australia at Michelton and in Morocco. He also spent time in Ireland as an importer and sommelier before the time came to go back to his roots. His father is from Vacquières and had bought land in the 1970s, with the grapes going to the cooperative at Sommières, only 17 kilometres away, as well as to nearby Corconne. Jean-Baptiste has gradually developed his estate, renting some vines from his father, buying a couple of hectares in 2003, and then in 2012 buying another 5 hectares from an uncle, so that he has Syrah, Grenache, Mourvèdre and Cinsaut. He also wants to plant some Carignan. 'It is the grape variety of the Languedoc and its bad press does it a gross disservice; it can cope with the lack of water, and with small yields on a hillside, and it gives very good results.' He is also intrigued by Counoise, which is allowed in the decree for the appellation.

Jean-Baptiste had interesting observations to make about the differences between the Pic St Loup and the adjoining vineyards of Sommières. Les Bois de Paris is a hill that provides a climatic limit between the two; the Pic St Loup is much wetter, with as much as 1,000 millimetres as opposed to 600–700 millimetres of rain, and has more marked differences in diurnal temperatures. However, the climatic shift over the past few years has changed things, with the cooler climate of Pic St Loup enabling successful white wine production, and more people making it, maybe in preference to rosé. Jean-Baptiste makes two *cuvées* of white wine, Finalement from Roussanne, Vermentino and a drop of Marsanne, with a nicely textured palate, and Nativo, from Vermentino with a little Roussanne, with a fermentation in oak and some *bâtonnage*.

We tasted in his barrel cellar, once an old stable, dated 1807. Esprit is a Pic St Loup, named after a grandfather in whose old cellar Jean-Baptiste made his first wines, with concrete vats from 1900. The blend is two-thirds Syrah to one-third Mourvèdre, with 12 months in *barriques*, making for ripe fruit with a fresh finish. Chante de l'Aire is almost pure Syrah with a little Mourvèdre and spends 15 months in a tronconic wooden vat, with some firm fruit and structure. Jean-Baptiste is very enthusiastic about Mourvèdre: 'It is a late ripener with ageing potential, but if September is wet, it can be problematic.' Mas Peyrolle is his *grande cuvée*, almost pure Syrah, with a splash of Cinsaut. He makes just four barrels, with black fruit, structure, and a fresh finish. He is looking for wines with body, but not weight, with fresh fruit, and no excessive alcohol or tannin. I enjoyed Jean-Baptiste's enthusiasm; he is young and keen and should go far. His wife is Italian, so he has planted some Nielluccio in Sommières.

Domaine de la Salade St Henri
St Mathieu de Tréviers 34270
www.chateaudelasaladesainthenri.com

Domaine de la Salade St Henri is on the outskirts of St Jean-de-Cuculles, where you are very aware of the urban encroachment. Anne Donnadieu was very dismissive of the village mayor: 'He is not interested in wine, only in start-ups.' The first thing I learnt was that a salad in this context was not a lettuce, but a particular Roman helmet without a visor. The name exists on the cadastre and the Romans were the first to grow vines in the area. For this reason, there is a visor on Anne's labels. St Henri comes from her grandfather and the other half of the property belongs to a cousin, who does not make wine. Anne is a chemist by training and her husband is a painter. She returned to the area in 2008 and recuperated the 15 hectares of vineyards from the cooperative, all of which are in one large plot around the estate buildings, and made her first wine in the old cellars. She bubbles nicely with enthusiasm. She remembers a childhood of Aramon and Carignan, and tasting Domaine de l'Hortus as a *jeune mariée* in the mid-1980s. 'Everything is in the head; you have the wine you want in your head and find it in the vineyards.' She works carefully, plot by plot; her key goal is healthy grapes, and she uses very little sulphur.

In the cellar, she does a gentle *pigeage*, aiming for silky tannins, and indeed that is what you find in her wines. Aérien is a blend of Syrah and Grenache, with elegant red fruit, 1803 comes from 40-year-old Syrah, 30-year-old Grenache and Mourvèdre, with a 12 month *élevage* in vat. It is rich with firm tannins and a fresh finish. For Anne, the typicity of Pic St Loup is '*force et finesse*; the appellation is evolving towards elegance, while keeping its concentration'. Aguire is 80 per cent Syrah with 10 per cent each of Grenache and Mourvèdre, given 12 months in wood, making a rich wine with a firm streak of tannin and youthful ageing potential. Anne has found her way after ten years and her daughter, Constance, has studied oenology, which promises well for the future.

Clos des Augustins
St Mathieu-de-Tréviers 34270
www.closdesaugustins.com

Frédéric Mézy made his first wine in 2003, having taken over his grandfather's vines; both of his grandfathers were called Augustin, hence the name of the estate. Altogether he has about 35 hectares of vines, all biodynamic, including some 45-year-old Syrah, outside the village of St Mathieu-de-Tréviers, with a wonderful view of the ruined château de Montferrand, with the Pic St Loup behind. This part of the Pic St Loup is cooler, with the Montagne de l'Hortus forming a barrier against the north winds. Frédéric talked about the *classement* for the appellation; he has had one vineyard declassified and others reinstated. His new cellar, built for the 2016 harvest using Gard stone, is very functional, with concrete tanks for red wine and stainless steel for whites, along with Stockinger *foudres* and *demi-muids* for *élevage*.

Altogether Frédéric makes five red wines, four white Pays du Val de Montferrand and two rosés. His labels are quite dramatic, designed by the painter Roger Bonafé. Highlights of our tasting included Les Bombins Blanc, a blend of Vermentino, Chardonnay and Roussanne, with a textured palate, with the Chardonnay aged in old wood. La Lueur du Jour is not made every year; it is Chardonnay with a drop of Roussanne and Marsanne, aged in barrel, with some nutty, textured flavour and depth on the palate. Les Bambins Rouge, Pic St Loup, is a blend of Syrah, Grenache and Mourvèdre, half aged in old wood, and half in cement, with ripe, spicy fruit. Le Gamin – Frédéric said 'that's me,' because he is the youngest of the family – comes from a selection of vines on higher slopes, with more limestone. It is 80 per cent Syrah, aged in *barriques* and *demi-muids*, with Grenache Noir in 40-hectolitre *foudres* and has some rounded fruit and a fresh finish. Sourire d'Odile, named after his grandmother, again from Syrah and Grenache, has more oak and a tannic backbone, while L'Aîné, referring to Frédéric's older brother who works in Paris, comes from different soil, and is mainly Syrah with some Grenache Noir, with quite dense but fresh fruit on the palate. Les Deux Rogers, after the painter Roger Bonafé and his father, who is also an artist, is a blend of Syrah and Mourvèdre, and is only made in a good Mourvèdre year, with an elegant concentration of fruit and tannin.

Chemin des Rêves
St Gély-du-Fesc 34980
www.chemin-des-reves.com

Chemin des Rêves, outside the village of St Gély-du-Fesc, is one of the most southern estates of the appellation. It was created by Benoît Viot, with a first vintage in 2003. Benoît has taken a convoluted path to winemaking, beginning his career in the pharmaceutical industry. He made his very first wine from a Boots winemaking kit when he was doing a *stage* with Boots in Nottingham and has always been intrigued by the chemical aspects of wine, and in particular the fermentation. His career took him to Venezuela, Spain, Paris and finally to Chile before he returned to France in 2000, encouraged by his cousins in the Médoc and at Château de Pibarnon in Bandol. He worked two harvests at Mas de la Séranne in the Terrasses du Larzac before first renting vines in 2003 and then buying vines in 2008. He now has 22 hectares of which 80 per cent are Pic St Loup. The rest are outside the appellation at Cambaillaux, for Grés de Montpellier, Vin de France or AOP Languedoc. All his vineyards are farmed organically. The name Chemin des Rêves comes from a path by his vineyard in Cambaillaux.

Abracadabra, his entry-level wine, comes in all three colours. The white is a blend of Vermentino, Grenache Blanc and Roussanne, kept in vat, with some fresh white blossom on the palate. Abracadabra Rosé is mainly Mourvèdre with some Syrah and is nicely vinous, while Abracadabra Rouge comes from Syrah, Grenache, Mourvèdre and Carignan, with some peppery fruit. A second white wine, La Soie Blanche, is a recognition of the heritage of his family, who came to Tours from Italy under François I and worked in the silk trade. It is an intriguing blend of five varieties, Vermentino, Grenache Blanc, Roussanne, Marsanne and Viognier. People are beginning to consider the possibility of a white Pic St Loup, maybe from Vermentino, Roussanne and possibly Grenache Gris. It is all up for discussion.

The Grés de Montpellier, L'Exubérant, was more perfumed and exuberant in comparison to Pic St Loup. As Benoît observed, Grés de Montpellier is nearer the sea, with sea breezes and milder nights, giving *douceur* and *rondeur*, softness and roundness, whereas the Pic St Loup enjoys the influence of the Cévennes, with more rain and greater temperature differences. Gueule de Loup, with some nicely integrated oak, is named after a red flower that grows in the vineyards in May. La Soie Rouge, from 55-year-old Syrah with some Grenache, is nicely structured and elegant. Above all, Benoît wants fruit and freshness, with supple tannins. Finally, Utopie is a Vin de France, from Cabernet Sauvignon, which he has always had in his vineyard, blended with a little Syrah. The proportions vary each year and the wine is aged in oak for 12 months, providing a contrast to the flavours of the south.

Traverses Fontanès

Fontanès 34270
contact@chateau-laroque.fr

We tracked down Cyriaque Rozier, winemaker at Château La Roque, outside the hamlet of Fontanès, where he is the *régisseur*. Château La Roque has recently changed hands and been considerably renovated since my last visit. Cyriaque worked for the previous owner, Jacques Boutin, and has stayed on under the new owners, Sylviane and Bertrand Barascud. Meanwhile he has developed his own estate, starting from scratch, buying 30 hectares of old olive groves, where the trees died in the 1956 frosts. He has planted 5 hectares by massal selection, 10,000 vines per hectare at 140 × 70 centimetres, *en echalas*. This makes for complicated viticulture, as you cannot use a conventional tractor and an *enjambeur* would be too high and too dangerous, although a small caterpillar tractor might be an option. A conversation about grafting followed. Cyriaque favours grafting *à l'anglaise* with a pointed graft, rather than *à l'omega*, in the shape of the letter, which can be done mechanically, but with a higher mortality rate. It might be a factor in the high mortality rate of Syrah. His vineyards contain the most extraordinary variety of vines: he has classic Syrah, and the clone Petite Sérine, from Côte Rôtie, and Hermitage; cuttings of Grenache Noir came from Châteauneuf-du-Pape; Mourvèdre from Bandol; Chenin Blanc from the Loire; and the Languedoc was the obvious source for Cinsaut, Carignan, Vermentino and Clairette. Then he has what he called *cépages rigolos*, 'fun' grapes, such as Aleatico, which came from the estate of Massavecchia in Tuscany; Assyrtiko, which he planted in 2016, and which came from Sigalas on the island of Santorini; and Malvasia d'Istria from an island off the Croatian coast near Split. He is looking for more southern varieties, being mindful of global warming, especially because he is firmly against irrigation.

Cyriaque's father has vineyards in St Véran in the Mâconnais and he worked as a consultant in Bordeaux for ten years. He arrived in the Languedoc because he has friends there and likes the wine; then his wife's work moved her to Montpellier. Cyriaque took us for a drive through the vineyards, which are on stony clay and limestone soil, surrounded by pine trees, and closed to protect them against the wild boars that are a growing problem in the area. It is a peaceful spot. All the vineyards are biodynamic, as are those of Château La Roque. Back at the château, where Cyriaque rents a corner of the cellar, we tasted.

His white Pays d'Oc is a blend of Clairette, Vermentino and Chenin Blanc, all fermented together in 12-hectolitre *foudres*, with honey, acidity and tannin. Sometimes he makes an orange wine that is fermented on the skins, and sometimes not. The grapes for his rosé, 35 per cent each of Cinsaut and Mourvèdre and 15 per cent each of Grenache and Syrah, are chilled for 36 hours down to 3°C before pressing so that the fermentation starts very slowly and gently rises to about 20°C. The flavours are vinous and supple, for a *rosé de table*. The first Pic St Loup is a blend of Syrah, Petite Sérine and Grenache Noir, with a small part *élevé* in 12-hectolitre barrels, making for spicy fruit, with brambly notes and a fresh finish. Pic St Loup Petite Sérine is just that, with a drop of Mourvèdre and Carignan, with whole bunch fermentation for a third of the blend. The stalks of older vines ripen better and they add structure and concentration. The wine spends 15 months in 12-hectolitre *foudres*. It was more concentrated than the first Pic St Loup. A Cabernet Sauvignon, Pays d'Oc, from 50-year-old vines was ripe and rounded. 'You don't need wood for this,' asserted Cyriaque. Finally, we tried an Aleatico Vin de France, which included a little Carignan, all vinified by carbonic maceration, inspired by the example of Massavecchia, with some lovely sweet cherry fruit and underlying acidity. Cyriaque should go far, making original wines, with a strong sense of purpose combined with enthusiasm, strong opinions and commitment.

Domaine Clavel

Assas 34820

www.vins-clavel.fr

I always enjoy seeing Pierre Clavel because he is irrepressibly full of fun and opinions, which he does not hesitate to express. Pierre is front of house; his wife, Estelle, is the talented winemaker behind the scenes. Their original vineyard was in La Méjanelle and they have ended a 31-year rental agreement to concentrate not only on Pic St Loup but also on a newly purchased vineyard in Montpeyroux, so that they now have 33 hectares, including a small plot close to the cellar at Assas, one of the new villages of the appellation. Pierre's very first harvest was in La Méjanelle back in 1986, when he admits that he did not know much!

They make two Pic St Loup. The first is Bonne Pioche, a blend of 65 per cent Syrah, 15 per cent Grenache and 20 per cent Mourvèdre, aged in 27- and 37-hectolitre *foudres* for 12 months, with black fruit spice and elegant concentration. Then there is Les Clous, which is more experimental, from Syrah and Grenache, made from hand-picked grapes crushed by foot, with no pumping, fermented in small vats and put into *foudres* for a two-year *élevage*. A pump is not even used at bottling. It was an intriguing difference. The flavours of the first wine were more conventional; the second was fragrant and concentrated, with stony mineral fruit. Pierre discerns three different zones in the Pic St Loup, which you can identify by the colour of the soil, *brune, blonde* and *rousse*. He has Syrah on all three and it behaves quite differently, producing tiny grapes from the *blonde* and much bigger, open bunches from the *rousse*. For him the great originality of Pic St Loup comes from its climate – it is much cooler, and that should be emphasized; Pic St Loup is not about power or ripe fruit.

We also enjoyed the white wine, Cascaille Blanc, made from seven different varieties, namely Grenache Blanc, Roussanne, Vermentino, Clairette, Viognier, Marsanne and Muscat à Petits Grains. They are all fermented together, with the juice of each grape added as it is picked. The oak is well integrated and there are mineral flavours, with structure and length all beautifully balanced.

Nothing ever stands still for Pierre; he is inherently experimental and is looking forward to discovering Montpeyroux. His vineyards are opposite Cocalières, on a single south-facing slope, in two plots. They are 50 kilometres away from Assas, so it will be complicated to bring the grapes to the cellar: 'We are intrepid!' he counters. Pierre enthused about the incredible diversity of wine, his own curiosity and the pleasure of encountering the new. 'Thirty years ago, wine was a *un produit alimentaire*, just a food product; these days it is a meeting, an encounter.' His open-mindedness and enthusiasm are infectious, and I like the way that all the wines are labelled Vin d'Artisan.

Château de Lancyre
Valflaunès 34270
www.chateaudelancyre.com

Régis Valentin is a cheerful, stocky *vigneron*, with a friendly smile, who has long-established roots in Lancyre. His father and two uncles were born in the hamlet and when the wine estate came up for sale in 1969, they bought it. The first bottling was in 1985. Régis started working on the property after studying oenology at Montpellier. His first vinification was in 1988. He is now president of the syndicat du Pic St Loup and the estate has grown gradually, now consisting of 78 hectares, in three main blocks, with an extensive range of wines. White AOP Languedoc includes La Rouvière, from 80 per cent Roussanne with 10 per cent each of Marsanne and Viognier, with some salty notes and a hint of peach. Régis observed that some estates are working towards an appellation with more southern varieties, while others favour IGP with Chardonnay and Sauvignon. The area should be suitable for white wine, with a good diurnal exchange and more rain than other parts of the Languedoc. At Lancyre they have a lot of Roussanne. La Grande Cuvée comes from older vines of Marsanne and Roussanne that were grafted onto Carignan, and is aged in *demi-muids*, with a rounded textured palate. Pic St Loup Rosé comes from Syrah, Grenache and Cinsaut, with some herbal notes and a fresh finish. For reds, we began with Coste d'Aleyrac, so called because the vines are near the Romanesque chapel, and a blend of Syrah, Grenache Noir and Carignan, kept in vat, to make for some cheerful spiciness.

Régis observed that he is moving towards shorter *cuvaisons*, and that the picking date is critical. In his view, 'You have to have *vins joyeux*; and Syrah is the *cépage emblématique* of the appellation.' Clos des Combes comes from Syrah, planted in 1975, and Grenache Noir, also from the 1970s, in one single plot, with spice and freshness. A Cuvée Vieilles

Vignes is more structured and the Grand Cuvée from 75 per cent Syrah with Grenache and Mourvèdre, aged in 400-litre barrels, is rich and sturdy with ageing potential. Madame was the final *cuvée*, virtually pure Syrah, it has 18 months' *élevage* in cement, with some satisfying fruit

Régis talked about the Pic St Loup, considering that until about 2005 people were working on the discovery of the different grape varieties in order to understand everything better. Initially there was too much extraction, whereas nowadays people go for less structure but know how to retain it – less is better. Drinkability is a key consideration; wines that are digestible, with fresh fruit and spice, black olives and *garrigue* flavours. Pic St Loup should be fresh and harmonious. The wines are more elegant and the growers more professional, especially with their work in the vineyards. He noted with pride how people now think of the wine rather than the mountain in connection with Pic St Loup. There has been a lot of investment in the area, with estates changing hands and the arrival of outsiders, making for some interesting developments. He believes that 'We need to work together and go in the same direction.'

19

GRÉS DE MONTPELLIER, WITH ST GEORGES D'ORQUES, LA MÉJANELLE, ST DRÉZÉRY AND ST CHRISTOL

The Grés de Montpellier covers a broad swathe of vineyards, below the hills and above the sea, forming a large amphitheatre, all around Montpellier. However, it does not have the same focused homogeneity as some other appellations of the Languedoc. It stretches from the banks of the Hérault, with Château St Martin de la Garrigue the most westerly estate, around to the vineyards of Sommières, with Château Grès St Paul outside Lunel the most easterly property. It touches Pézenas at Montagnac and Pic St Loup at Guzargues, and also incorporates several smaller areas, namely St Georges d'Orques, La Méjanelle, St Drézéry and St Christol.

Grés de Montpellier was recognized as an *appellation régionale* of the Coteaux du Languedoc in 2004, for red wine only, and hopes to achieve a full appellation. Any white or rosé is IGP or AOP Languedoc. As the name implies, *grès*, or sandstone, is the dominant soil and common unifying feature of the area. There are slight climatic variations, with the vineyards to the east being slightly warmer than those in the west, with a more marked maritime influence than for Pézenas. Rainfall is lower than in the Terrasses du Larzac and the altitude of the vineyards ranges from sea level up to 150 metres. Currently it includes 48 estates, in 46 different *communes*.

Producers

Domaine Roquemale
Villeveyrac 34560
www.roquemale.com

Valérie Ibanez is a welcoming hostess in her tasting *caveau* in the centre of the village of Villeveyrac. She and her husband, Dominique, set up their estate in 2001. They are both children of growers, who were members of the cooperative at nearby Poussan. Valérie laughingly observed that they are considered foreigners in Villeveyrac, even though Poussan is the next-door village. Dominique worked in the electricity business and Valérie sold wine for Skalli on the export market, but they really wanted to work together, so they found vines outside the village of Villeveyrac in an isolated valley. The name Roquemale, the *lieu-dit* of their vineyards, means *mauvaises roches*, in other words poor stony soil, perfect for vines. Altogether they have 12 hectares, which are cultivated organically. The old viaduct that was used for transporting bauxite runs in front their vineyard. They found a *maison de vigneron* in the heart of the village, with a substantial cellar, in time for the 2006 harvest.

The quality of the grapes is fundamental to their work. They have a lot of Alicante Bouschet, as well as Cinsaut, Syrah and Grenache, and some white varieties, such as Marsanne, Roussanne, Grenache Blanc and Gris, Vermentino and Viognier, for their white wine, Rocs Blancs. They are all in the same plot, and are picked and vinified together to make an original white, a balance of freshness and weight. They are also considering Piquepoul and Clairette, as they are not so happy with the Roussanne and Marsanne. Méli Mélo, Pays de l'Hérault, is an original blend of 80 per cent Alicante Bouschet, with some Syrah and Cinsaut. However, most of their red wines are Grés de Montpellier. Les Grés is mainly Syrah, the most traditional *cuvée* of the estate; Lema is predominantly Grenache Noir; and Mâle comes from one plot of particularly good, ripe Syrah, vinified by carbonic maceration. My tasting finished with what Valérie termed *un vieux* Mâle, from the 2010 vintage, with quite obvious oak and some intriguing leathery fruit.

Clos de l'Amandaie

Aumelas 34230
www.closdelamandaie.com

Clos de l'Amandaie is situated in Aumelas, which is not so much a village but a collection of small hamlets, in a lost corner of the Languedoc north of Montpellier. Philippe Peytavy explained that it is one of the coolest parts of the Grés de Montpellier. His grandfather made wine, but his father preferred to join the cooperative at Le Pouget. Philippe worked for a *négociant* in Gignac, but really wanted to do something with the family vineyards, and made his first vintage in 2002. He began by renting a cellar but now has his own modern one, built in time for the 2010 vintage, and his father's 8 hectares have been increased to 17 and planted with the usual Languedoc quintet of varieties. However, he uses the Mourvèdre for his IGP since it does not ripen well because the valley is too cool. He also has some Petit Manseng, planted in 2003, that goes into a Vin de France, as well as Grenache Blanc, Roussanne and Vermentino, and he is wondering about other varieties, such as Clairette and Carignan Blanc. All are grown on clay and limestone, with vineyards at an altitude of 150 metres. The wild boars are a problem. Philippe has tried electric fences, not to mention scarecrows and loud music, but with little success. *Lutte raisonnée* is the viticultural policy.

A range of Pays d'Oc called Chat Pitre, a play on words, forms his entry level. More interesting is the Clos de l'Amandaie range. The white is a blend of Grenache Blanc and Roussanne, with some *élevage* on lees to make a nicely textured white wine. In contrast Huis Clos is aged in barrel. The red Clos de l'Amandaie comes from roughly one-third each of Syrah, Grenache Noir and Carignan with 15 per cent Cinsaut, all kept in vat, except for the Syrah, for 12 months. It has ripe, peppery fruit, black olives and tapenade. Huis Clos is a blend of Syrah and Grenache, all aged in wood, after blending, for 12 months, with more depth on the palate. Philippe takes a fairly measured approach to his wine making: 'You just have to accompany it.' Our tasting finished with the Petit Manseng, named Les Ménades, after the maenads who were followers of Dionysus. The grapes are left to dry on the vines, picked between the middle of November and the middle of December, and the whole bunches are pressed and the juice put into an acacia barrel. It is a slow process; the 2015 harvest was still fermenting in September 2016. From 30 ares, the average yield is about 7 hectolitres. Philippe ruefully observed that the partridges eat even more grapes than the wild boars, but he usually manages to make some each year. The 2014 vintage was rich and intense, honeyed with balancing acidity. I was left with an impression of a quietly thoughtful winemaker who is not afraid to experiment.

Château St Martin de la Garrigue

Montagnac 34530

www.stmartingarrigue.com

Any discussion of Grés de Montpellier would be incomplete without mention of St Martin de la Garrigue but the property also produces prize-worthy Picpoul de Pinet, so it is to be found in that chapter, on page 205.

Domaine de Saumarez

Murviel-lès-Montpellier 34570

www.domainedesaumarez.com

Liz and Robin Williamson in Murviel-lès-Montpellier could make St Georges d'Orques but prefer to stay with Grés de Montpellier. The cooperative dominates the production of St Georges, accounting for 70 per cent of the *cru*, which does not facilitate things for the smaller producers. They also feel that St Georges is just too close to Montpellier, with the vineyards fighting against the urban sprawl, and that nothing really distinguishes St Georges from the surrounding appellations. 'Past performance is no guarantee of future success,' Robin observed dispassionately. He is one of several Plumpton graduates who were attracted to the Languedoc for the opportunities it offers. 'Land is cheaper and it is a dynamic region, with a new generation of outsiders, and fewer restrictions than in other parts of France. And you get ripe grapes every year.' Although Liz comes from New Zealand, her family originated in Guernsey, where *saumarez* means 'the salt of the sea'.

Robin and Liz produce an eclectic range of wines that would be difficult to fit into any other region of France. Rosé Pétillant Brut, *méthode traditionnelle*, is a blend of Grenache Noir, Syrah and Cabernet Sauvignon, with some crisp fruit. Their AOP Languedoc Blanc S'Blanc comes from Grenache Blanc, Marsanne and a drop of Roussanne and is partially fermented in oak, to give rounded fruit and a textured palate. As for reds, they have grafted Sangiovese, simply because they like it, and also Petit Verdot and Malbec, and are considering Tempranillo. I liked the Petit Verdot Vin de France, with some cassis fruit and sturdy tannins. Their Grés de Montpellier Trinitas comes from one-third each of Grenache Noir, Syrah and Mourvèdre, aged in old wood for 15 months, to make a rounded, spicy wine, with a touch of vanilla. They prefer not to use the syndicat bottle, thinking it rather old-fashioned with its embossed neck, even if it provides some visual recognition. Their AOP Languedoc, S'Rouge, from Syrah and Grenache, is eminently drinkable, which is just what they want.

ST GEORGES D'ORQUES

St Georges d'Orques was a *terroir* of the Coteaux du Languedoc, with a long history. There is record of a purchase of St Georges d'Orques by the Earl of Bristol in 1715. Thomas Jefferson appreciated the wines when he was ambassador of the newly independent United States in Paris and encourage their importation across the Atlantic. In the early nineteenth century, English interned in Montpellier during the Napoleonic Wars acquired a taste for the wine. As for the name, there are about a hundred *communes* in France that include St Georges in their name, whereas *orque* may be a term for what the French call a *jarre*, or an *orci* in Italian. Another suggestion is a mythical dragon. As for the wine, it comes from five villages, of which Murviel-lès-Montpellier, along with St Georges d'Orques, are the most important, with a nucleus of wine growers, together with Pignan, Lavérune and Juvignac on the outskirts of Montpellier. It is relatively close to the sea, and as for soil, the village of St Georges has *villefranchien* galets while Murviel is mainly clay and limestone. There are also *chailles*, small pebbles.

Producers

Domaine Belles Pierres
Murviel-lès-Montpellier 34570
www.domaine-bellespierres.com
Damien Coste has been considered one of the pioneers of white wine in the Languedoc since his very first vintage in 1992. He planted Petit Manseng in 1990, well before it was allowed in the Languedoc, and made his first Clauzes de Jo in 1994. Quizzed as to why he opted for white, which accounts for 40 per cent of his production, he replied quite

simply that he likes making it and likes drinking it, and wanted to do something that others were not doing. Originality was his inspiration. He was convinced, and remains convinced, that the Languedoc can produce very good white wines. In addition, he is a fervent exponent of St Georges d'Orques, talking about its associations with the American president Thomas Jefferson and pointing out that his wines have been chosen by the Elysée Palace and served to the last three presidents of France, thereby continuing the tradition. For Damien, St Georges d'Orques is about its history, its *terroir* and its typicity. There is a slight maritime influence in the climate and his *terroir* is clay and limestone, with large stones and quartz and some iron influence. Damien would like St Georges d'Orques to include white as well as red and rosé when it eventually becomes an *appellation communale*.

Les Clauzes de Jo Blanc is mainly Roussanne, with Viognier, Grenache Blanc and Vermentino, fermented and then given 12 months' ageing in wood, and blended just before bottling. The wine is nicely textured with a hint of honey, with *clauzes*, the Occitan for little walls, making a *clos* or walled vineyard. Damien observed that he was quite free with his winemaking; he aims for healthy grapes and lets nature take its course: 'The wine finds its natural balance, and the malolactic fermentation happens if it wants to.' Chant des Ames Blanc is a blend of equal parts of Viognier and Roussanne, from a slightly warmer vineyard with 18 months' ageing in wood, making for a rich, peachy wine. Inéptie is a blend of 50 per cent each of Gros and Petit Manseng, having been made since 1996 and leaving 15 grams per litre residual sugar, with attractive honeyed notes on the palate. It is a Vin de France and Damien calls it Vin de Belle Table.

Damien's Languedoc Rosé is a blend of Cinsaut and Mourvèdre and is unusual in being vinified and aged in wood until its bottling in March. Again, in the spirit of doing something different, Damien does not follow the crowd and the wine has good structure and body, very much making it a food rosé. Les Clauzes de Jo Rouge is a St Georges d'Orques. The blend is Syrah, Grenache and Mourvèdre, with 12 months' ageing in wood, with some firm but rounded fruit. Chant des Ames Rouge, from Syrah and Mourvèdre with 18 months' barrel ageing, is tight-knit and elegant, portraying the typicity of St Georges with its subtle tannins. For Damien, you should be able to drink St Georges as a young wine, or keep it for several years. His latest red wine, first made in 2015, is Magma Rouge, a pure Mourvèdre, 'à l'état pure', as Damien put it, with some elegant concentration. Finally, there was a delicious late harvest Vin de France, called Monica el Encuentro, after his wife, who sadly died a few years ago. She came from Colombia and it is now members of her family, Pedro and Johann, who help Damien run the estate. The current blend is Syrah with a little Grenache and Muscat à Petits Grains Noirs and the flavour is rich and sweet, with 60 grams per litre of residual sugar. Another late harvest is Passidore, a blend of Petit and Gros Manseng, which was rich and intense with good acidity on the finish, reminding me of a Jurançon Moelleux.

Domaine de la Marfée
Murviel-lès-Montpellier 34570
www.la-marfee.com

I first met Thierry Hazard for an earlier book, when he was using the ground floor of his house in the suburbs of Montpellier as a barrel cellar. Things have moved on and he now has a modern cellar, built for the 2008 vintage, outside the village of Murviel-lès-Montpellier. The very first vintage of Domaine de la Marfée was 1997 and the initial 5 hectares have grown to 9, with Chardonnay, Roussanne and some young vines of Vermentino, as well as Mourvèdre, which enjoys the maritime influence of his vineyards, and Syrah, a little Grenache Noir and Carignan, but no Cinsaut. The name la Marfée goes back to his childhood and his roots in the Ardennes; there was a bois de la Marfée near Sedan where his grandfather lived, which, as a child, captured his imagination, and seemed rather mysterious, and the name has stayed with him.

Thierry immediately strikes you as a thoughtful and questioning winemaker. His cellar includes ten eggs, as well as *barriques* for his red wine, and *demi-muids* for his whites. He observes the differences. The eggs are less oxygenating and more impermeable and the wine moves in the egg. You cannot actually see it, but it has the effect of making for more polished tannins than with *barriques*.

Thierry makes a range of serious red wines. Les Gamines, a blend of 50 per cent Mourvèdre, 40 per cent Syrah and 10 per cent Grenache with two years' ageing in old wood, has some firm, peppery fruit and well-integrated oak. He prefers to blend after *élevage*. Della Francesca is almost pure Mourvèdre, with two years' ageing, including 25–35 per cent in eggs. Altogether he has about 20 different plots and vinifies each plot separately. With Della Francesca he aims for elegance, but also enhances the natural power of the Mourvèdre. When I asked him if his winemaking had changed over the years, he replied that he had become lazier! What he meant was that he was less interventionist, preferring to let the wine take its course. Les Vignes qu'on Abat is almost pure Carignan, from 60-year-old vines, which spends two years in barrel, and combines structure, acidity, tannin and elegance on the palate. Les Champs Murmurés, St Georges d'Orques, comes from equal proportions of 40-year-old Mourvèdre and Syrah, with two years in wood, making an excellent combination of elegance and power. That is what Thierry looks for and that is what he has achieved.

Thierry made his first white wine in 2002. Frissons d'Embelles is a blend of 30 per cent Chardonnay to 70 per cent Roussanne, planted because those are two grape varieties that he likes, with Meursault a particular favourite. I found plenty of nuance, with white blossom, fennel and a saline note, well integrated oak and ageing potential. The 2008 did not taste significantly older than the 2013. As for projects for the future, Thierry admitted to planting 30 ares of Counoise five years earlier, but the young vines were affected by the drought and he has yet to make any wine from them.

Thierry's vineyards could be Grés de Montpelier, St Georges d'Orques, or plain Languedoc. He feels that St Georges d'Orques does have a clear sense of identity, but is rather disparaging about Grés de Montpellier, observing that there are no real stars, nor is it very homogenous. I think Thierry does qualify as a star, but he would be much too modest to agree.

Domaine Henry
St Georges d'Orques 34680
www.domainehenry.fr

Laurence and François Henry of Domaine Henry are in fact the only wine producers in the village of St Georges, apart from the local cooperative. François established the reputation of Château St Martin de la Garrigue in the 1980s and when that family property was sold, there was an opportunity to come to St Georges, where his first vintage was 1993. He has 11 hectares in 22 plots, with a variety of soils, *villefranchien*, limestone and flint, all cultivated organically around the village of St Georges.

Tasting with Laurence and François is rewarding for the diversity of opinions as well as the original range of wines. They are fun and enthusiastic, and not afraid to express an opinion. Their white wine is Pays des Collines de la Moure, a blend of 70 per cent Chardonnay with all three colours of Terret, *complanté* in the same vineyard from the 1950s, as well as Clairette and Muscat. It is very fresh and pure. François is very interested in *complantation*, the mixed planting of different varieties and the variations in ripening times; the excesses of one variety can mask the defects of another. He picks when the balance is right for all the varieties to be fermented together.

Vin Vermeil is light red in colour. The grapes are given a 24-hour pre-fermentation maceration so that fruit is extracted, but not tannin, and the resulting wine is ripe with soft tannins and some acidity. Paradines Grés de Montpellier is 40 per cent Grenache Noir, 30 per cent Syrah and 10 per cent each of Mourvèdre, Carignan and Cinsaut aged in vat. François rarely uses barrels any more, maybe if the wine is particularly powerful, but this has lovely ripe fruit and supple tannins. Next came St Georges d'Orques from Grenache Noir and equal parts Syrah and Mourvèdre with some 50-year-old vine Cinsaut. It was elegant with supple fruit but with more structure than the Grés de Montpellier. François's most original wine is Le Mailhol, a Vin de France because it includes a host of grape varieties that do not feature in any appellation, namely Oeillade Noir and Gris, Aspiran both Noir and Gris, and likewise Terret, as well as Ribeyrenc, Morastel and Calitor. The flavour is delicate and spicy with quite a firm dry finish and an older vintage demonstrated how well it aged, with perfumed fruit. St Georges Villa Franchien comes from Grenache Noir, from vines planted in 1920, blended with another plot from 1947. It is redolent of ripe cherry fruit and utterly delicious. Les Chailles comes from equal parts of Mourvèdre, Grenache Noir and Cinsaut, but there was none left to taste. Although he is fascinated by the other grape varieties, François is adamant that St Georges d'Orques is the emblematic wine of the estate. All his labels carry a depiction of St Georges, without the dragon, that comes from an iron that was once used to brand barrels.

François talked about the path toward the appellation. They do not want to restrict the percentages of grape varieties, but allow some flexibility. Although the cooperative works well, all its bottled wine is labelled St Georges d'Orques, which places a commercial brake on prices.

It should be more aware of the hierarchy of the regional appellation, Languedoc; the sub-regional appellation, Grés de Montpellier, and then the *appellation communale*, St Georges d'Orques, at the top of the pyramid, with wines priced accordingly.

Château de l'Engarran

Lavérune 34880
www.chateau-engarran.com

The château de l'Engarran was built in the eighteenth century and has been in the hands of the same family for five generations, since 1924. The gardens *à la française* were designed by a pupil of Le Nôtre, with elegant paths and statues at strategic points. The façade of the château bears a frieze depicting the three ages of woman, a young girl, a mother who looks to her future and an old woman surveying her past. Diane Losfelt, who has been the winemaker at L'Engarran since 1983, after training at Montpellier, is bright, vivacious and very competent. Tasting with her is fun and informative.

The rosé St Georges d'Orques is from Grenache Noir and Cinsaut, with some ripe fruit and good vinosity. Diane observed that rosé from the Languedoc is becoming a much more serious proposition, with the development of what she called *rosé de terroirs*, with discernible differences depending on their origins. Diane is particularly enthusiastic about Sauvignon for her white wine, with two cuvées, both Pays d'Oc. La Lionne Blanc is fresh and pithy, while Adélys includes some barrel ageing and is richer and more textured with a satisfying stoniness on the palate.

As for red wines, the Pays d'Oc includes 78 per cent Cabernet Franc as well as some Grenache Noir and Merlot, with soft tannins and rounded fruit. An AOP Languedoc, Sainte Cécile has fresh peppery fruit. Next come two Grés de Montpellier. Tradition is a blend of 53 per cent Syrah with some Grenache and Mourvèdre, of which one-third has been in wood for 12 months, with some rounded spicy fruit. Grenat Majeur is three-quarters Grenache Noir with some Syrah and Cinsaut, making an interesting contrast. Their flagship wine is Quetton St Georges, St Georges d'Orques, from 80 per cent Syrah with some Grenache. Half the blend has been aged in barrel for 12 months, followed by a further year in vat, and the wine is serious and structured with ageing potential. A recent addition to the range, but only in the best years, is Le Parc from one small plot of Syrah. The wine is aged in barrels, half new and half one fill, and it is rich and concentrated with ripe fruit and a fresh finish. In some years Diane makes a late-harvest Grenache Noir, Caprice de l'Engarran.

Diane Losfelt, Chateau de l'Engarran

Domaine de la Prose
Pignan 34570
www.domaine-de-la-prose.fr

Bertrand de Mortillet has been making the wine at Domaine de la Prose since 1995, after his parents bought a run-down property in 1990. It is an attractive spot, approached by a track lined with holm oaks and olive trees, that climbs gently to about 100 metres in altitude. Bertrand has 14 hectares that were converted to organic viticulture in 2004 and is now working biodynamically. He is a thoughtful, reflective winemaker and his range has evolved gently over the years. Cadières Blanc is a refreshing Vermentino with some sappy herbal fruit that is kept in vat. Embruns, from oak-aged Roussanne, with Grenache Blanc and Vermentino from vat, has well-integrated oak, with some rounded fruit and body. Prose Rosé is quite serious for a rosé – *un petit Bandol*, Bertrand suggested, with good fruit and a firm balance. Cadières St Georges comes from Grenache and a little Syrah, with some rounded fruit and a firm finish. Embruns Rouge, a Grés de Montpellier from 70 per cent Syrah with 20 per cent Cinsaut and 10 per cent Grenache Noir, spends two years in vat and is rounded with good fruit and depth. The Grande Cuvée St Georges d'Orques comes from equal parts of Mourvèdre and Syrah with a balance of 20 per cent Grenache Noir. It is firm and structured, with ageing potential. In addition, Bertrand makes the wine of his neighbour, Philippe Sala, at Domaine de la Rime.

LA MÉJANELLE

Méjanelle was one of the original *terroirs* of the Coteaux du Languedoc, a small area to the south-east of the city of Montpellier, close to the airport, within the *communes* of Mauguio, St Aunès and Montpellier itself. These days, sadly, it seems set to disappear. Château de Flaugergues is the principal property in the area, but they no longer use the name as 'it is so badly known and no longer means anything'. Pierre Clavel, the other exponent of Méjanelle, ceased renting his vineyards at Mas Calage in 2016.

Producers

Château de Flaugergues
Montpellier 34000
www.flaugergues.com

The château de Flaugergues was built at the end of the seventeenth century. Today it is open to visitors; the facade is Italianate and the interior contains a magnificent staircase, hung with Brussels tapestries depicting the life of Moses. There is a wonderful old kitchen with an enormous fireplace and copper pans. The elegant gardens leading to the vineyards are planted with an enormous variety of different trees. This is one of the few wine estates in the Languedoc with its own restaurant and there is a welcoming tasting *caveau* and shop. Pierre de Colbert is a descendant of Louis XIV's minister Jean-Baptiste de Colbert who did so much for the economy of France in the seventeenth century.

Flaugergues is fighting a rearguard action against urbanization, with new buildings threatening the vineyards, even causing an alleyway of 160-year-old maple trees to be cut down. Pierre admitted that in 2000 they had 40 hectares in production but these days it is just 25, with the others 'en repos', resting. The soil is the distinctive *galets roulées* and there is quite a strong marine influence with sea breezes. However, Pierre is also looking to the future, for he built a new cellar in time for the 2016 harvest. A pneumatic press has replaced the Vaslin press from 1985 and Pierre admitted that they needed to relearn their winemaking with the new cellar.

They make Pays d'Oc, AOP Languedoc and Grés de Montpellier, and, unusually for France, most are bottled with a screwcap. A Pays d'Oc Muscat had good varietal character, while the AOP Languedoc Blanc, a blend of Grenache Blanc, Roussanne and Vermentino, was lightly herbal. There are two qualities of Viognier, one peachier than the other. A fresh rosé followed and then a selection of reds, first some varietal Pays d'Oc Syrah, Merlot and Marselan and their AOP Languedoc, a blend of Grenache, Mourvèdre and Syrah with some peppery black fruit. La Sommelière is an unoaked blend of 65 per cent Syrah, 30 per cent Grenache and 5 per cent Mourvèdre, with black fruit, while Cuvée Colbert is the same blend, but aged in oak for 12 months. It is richer and more structured. Maybe Pierre will develop a more expensive La Méjanelle cuvée, but for the moment he prefers to concentrate on Grés de Montpellier. He would also like to be able to sell his wine more expensively, at €30 rather than €20, observing ruefully that a prophet is not appreciated in his own land. The future of La Méjanelle certainly seems in the balance, but I am optimistic that Pierre will continue to protect his patrimony from urban development. It is a lovely spot away from the madding crowd. Do go and visit.

ST DRÉZÉRY

St Drézéry and St Christol are another two of the original *terroirs* of the Coteaux du Languedoc; there was a third, Vérargues, but that wine has disappeared without trace, with no one producing it anymore. St Drézéry and St Christol are also aspiring for appellation status. Theoretically they are both part of Grés de Montpellier, with St Drézéry accepting the relevant conditions, but the forty-seventh commune of Grés de Montpellier, St Christol, has said *non*. It all revolves around the more detailed delimitation carried out for the new appellations. Originally whole villages were classified, now the INAO conducts a detailed vineyard selection, inevitably resulting in the removal of less satisfactory plots from the appellation. St Christol does not want this to happen and for the moment it is holding up the recognition of Grés de Montpellier as an appellation. Meanwhile St Drézéry is hoping to become an *appellation communale* by 2020. It is quite different from St Christol as the *terroir* depends upon *galets roulées*, and the climate is hotter than most of the Grés de Montpellier, with less maritime influence. For the moment St Drézéry includes only vineyards in that village, but they are hoping to extend the area to include adjoining vineyards in Sussargues and Castries, which would have the beneficial effect of increasing the number of producers. For the moment, they lack sufficient clout.

Producers

Château Puech-Haut

St Drézéry 34160
www.puech-haut.fr

Château Puech-Haut dominates the viticultural landscape of both villages. You approach the property along a driveway lined with olive trees and lavender bushes, and at the end there is a stylish visitor area where anyone is welcome to taste. From the visitor centre, you look down on the barrel cellar, including a large collection of *barriques* painted by various artists, some more well-known than others. The first *barrique* was painted by Hervé de Rosa, who received 150 bottles of wine in return.

Alain Asselin is director of oenotourism and an articulate ambassador for the estate. He explained that it was created by Gérard Bru in 1985, when he planted 25 hectares of vines, half red and half white. The first wines were made in the mid-1990s. Gradually the estate has been extended to include 40 hectares in the Pic St Loup, for which 1999 was the first vintage, and more recently Gérard Bru bought the St Christol estate of Château les Hospitaliers. When I met him in the late 1990s, he was very proud of the fact that he was a self-made man, happily describing himself as a bulldozer, which sounds better in French than English!

At St Drézéry, the vineyards are planted with Syrah, Grenache and Mourvèdre, on undulating hillsides, with vines of various ages and differing yields, and therefore different expressions of flavour. Altogether there are 90 different plots, with one vat per plot, to enable a very detailed *sélection parcellaire*. The *bordelais* oenologist, Michel Rolland, used to consult here, but these days it is Philippe Cambié. They have some concrete fermentation tanks, made in Italy, in a special shape designed to keep the *chapeau* of grape skins submerged during fermentation, so that you obtain better extraction. The bottom is square, with a tapered top, with Alain describing them as *Le Rolls de la cave*.

The range comprises two rosés, La Closerie du Pic, a blend of Cinsaut, Syrah and Grenache, with raspberry fruit on the palate, and Tête de Belier, which is an almost pure Mourvèdre and is more rounded and riper, with good structure. The name of this *cuvée* originates from a Roman sculpture of a ram or *belier* that was found in the vineyard, which they have reproduced to sit at the foot of several barrels. Next came their red wines, a Prestige Rouge, St Drézéry, from equal parts Syrah and Grenache, with solid black fruit on the nose and palate, and oak, vanilla and tapenade. The wine spends six months in barrel, none new, but slightly toasted. Tête de Belier is two-thirds Syrah, with some Grenache, Mourvèdre and Carignan. The aim is *un grand vin du* Languedoc, given 18 months' ageing with two-thirds of the *cuvée* in new oak. The flavours are intense, with ripe vanilla, tapenade and supple tannins, and a sweet, long finish. Clos du Pic, Pic St Loup, comes from Syrah and Mourvèdre given 24 months' *élevage* in barrels, two-thirds of which are new. It was sweet, dense and sturdy, and possibly a little atypical.

The final red wine was le 40ème, St Drézéry, made only in the best vintages. It is a natural wine, with no added sulphur. The grapes, from one plot of Syrah and one plot of 65-year-old Grenache, are crushed by foot, with a carbonic maceration, and a 24-month *élevage*. The flavours recall ripe chocolate, vanilla and soft tannins, with a sweet finish. The tasting concluded with two white wines. Prestige, from 80 per cent Marsanne and 20 per cent Roussanne, vinified in vat, had a rounded, peachy palate, with some acidity. Tête de Belier comes from 20 per cent Viognier with 80 per cent Grenache Blanc and a little

Roussanne, vinified in wood, with *bâtonnage* for eight months, making for a rich, leesy, oaky palate. Asked about the typicity of the domaine, Alain replied '*chaleureux,* aromatic, with a touch of elegance'. As for the typicity of St Drézéry, 'there isn't any. St Drézéry has lots of *galets roulées*, but essentially it is a question of the style of the individual *vignerons.*'

Mas d'Arcaÿ

St Drézéry 34160
www.arcay.fr

Jean Lacaustre is an eighth-generation grower, proudly asserting that all four of his great-grandfathers were *vignerons,* with one involved with the syndicat that created the VDQS of St Drézéry in 1951. The family's 42-hectare holding of vines is gradually being extracted from the village cooperative, with a first bottling in 2010. They have built a spacious cellar, well equipped with stainless steel tapered vats as well as concrete ones. For Jean, the typicity of St Drézéry comes from the *galets roulées* that retain the heat so well to give really ripe grapes. St Drézéry is only ever red, with a minimum of two grape varieties and Syrah usually the dominant variety.

Jean's white wine, Cheveux d'Ange, after a white flower that you find in the vineyards, is a blend of one-third Roussanne to two-thirds Marsanne, fermented and aged in oak for six months. It is ripe and textured with good balancing acidity. An AOP Languedoc Rosé, Le Nom de la Rose, is a blend of pressed Grenache and Cinsaut, with a fresh lift on the finish. A Grés de Montpellier 1779, from Carignan, Grenache Noir and Mourvèdre, is given 12 months in vat, with a rounded palate, while a St Drézéry Valentibus, from 50 per cent Syrah with 20 per cent Grenache and 30 per cent Mourvèdre, is aged in *barriques* and *demi-muids*, with rich, peppery fruit, with more tannin and depth. Jean asserted that St Drézéry is quite different from Grés de Montpelier. For him the appellation is a combination of men and the natural environment, the *galets* and the climate. He is focused and deserves to do well.

ST CHRISTOL

Producers

Frères Guinand

St Christol 34400
www.domaineguinand.com

Fabien Guinand's father is one of three brothers running a large property based in a sixteenth-century *bastide* just outside the village of St Christol, who are now approaching retirement. The family has been there for 200 years, and after a period in the cooperative, began making wine again in 1993. They have 60 hectares, of which 40 are St Christol and the rest Pays d'Oc for Chardonnay, Merlot and so on. For Fabien, St Christol is a land of *galets roulées* on gentle hillsides and the wine must be vinified in the village. They have a modern cellar, adjoining the *bastide*, allowing for plenty of *sélection parcellaire*, with numerous small vats, and their tasting *caveau* is in the old *bergerie*, sheepfold, adjoining the barrel room. Their entry-level wine is a simple AOP Languedoc. There are two St Christol, Les Frênes, with Syrah and 40 per cent Carignan, and Grande Cuvée, with Syrah and 40 per cent Grenache, with an *élevage* in new oak for 12 months. The oak gives some body, and Fabien likes the effect of carbonic maceration: 'It gives some good things and, if you hand-pick, you can retain the stalks.'

He explained that St Christol consists of a minimum of two grape varieties and a maximum yield of 42 hectolitres per hectare. Altogether there are six growers in the village, as well as a cooperative, who do not want to be part of Grés de Montpellier for fear that they will lose their identity. St Christol consists of about 400 hectares, of which about 100 are not planted, and if they were incorporated into Grés de Montpellier they would lose a significant amount of the overall area. 'It is a question of visibility.' Fabien also asserted that St Christol is better known than St Drézéry, with a more august history, and that St Drézéry has no reputation and is dominated by Château Puech-Haut. 'Grés de Montpellier will help St Drézéry, whereas St Christol does not need the help of the Grès de Montpellier.' Grès de Montpellier came later and there is no market for Grés de Montpellier in St Christol. Indeed, he does not make a Grès de Montpellier. For the moment, this not unusual *histoire de clochers* is blocking the progress of the recognition of the various appellations.

Domaine Catherine Bernard

Restinclières 34160

cb.castelnau@wanadoo.fr

I met Catherine Bernard just as she was finishing her thirteenth harvest, which she described as '*une bombe*'! She took to wine as a second career, having worked as an economics journalist for a number of years, and first came to Montpellier as a correspondent for *La Libération*. Obviously, this meant that she was covering wine and her interest was sparked. She dreamed of being a farmer; it could have been cows or wheat, but realistically in the Languedoc it had to be wine. She loves turning solid grapes into liquid, and something sweet into something dry. She has worked at Domaine Arlot in Burgundy, with Dominique Hauvette in Provence, and Elisabetta Foradori in Trentino and now has 4.6 hectares of vines that could be classified as St Drézéry, although she prefers Pays de l'Hérault. She built her own cellar outside the village of St Christol for the 2015 vintage, describing it as *bioclimatique*; it is partly underground, and all the water is recuperated.

Her vineyards are planted with Grenache Noir, Mourvèdre, Marselan, Cinsaut and Terret, but she admits that if she were starting afresh today, she would concentrate on Carignan and Cinsaut for red wine, and Carignan Blanc and Terret for white. As it is, she makes a rosé from Mourvèdre and Carignan, of which a very small proportion is given some *élevage* in wood, to add some extra structure. The first red wine is a pure Carignan, Vin de France, made with minimal sulphur, and there is Carbonnelle, a blend of Grenache, Mourvèdre, Marselan and Cinsaut from a vineyard where the land was once used for charcoal burning. The flavours are rich and characterful, rather like Catherine herself, who is fun and energetic.

20

SOMMIÈRES, LANGLADE AND PAYS DES CÉVENNES

Recognized in 2011, Sommières is the most recent denomination of the Languedoc appellation. Previously the wines were simply part of the large Coteaux du Languedoc, and subsequent AOP Languedoc, and, before that, part of Vin de Pays du Gard or d'Oc.

As you might expect, the vineyards are centred on the attractive town of Sommières. It sits below an imposing château, with an arcaded central square and a Roman bridge over the Vidourle. The wine area includes 18 *communes*, adjoining the Pic St Loup at Brouzet-lès-Quissac and also the Grés de Montpellier, with nearby villages of St Christol and St Drézéry. The new appellation of the Duché d'Uzès lies to the north, between Anduze and Uzès.

The criteria for Sommières are climatic, with vineyards protected by the first hills of the pre-Cévennes. It can be windy, with the influence of the Mistral coming down the Rhône valley, but it is not as wet nor as cool as Pic St Loup, and not as hot as Grés de Montpellier, which also has more of a maritime influence. The *vent marin* is rare in Sommières. The departmental boundary also plays a part in the delimitation, with Sommières in the Gard, while Grés de Montpellier is in the Hérault. Most of the wine growers of Sommières also make Pays de Cévennes, particularly as Sommières is only red.

The soil includes limestone, both hard and soft, marl and red clay and some flint, and the grape varieties are the usual red quintet, in particular, Syrah and Grenache Noir, which must account for a minimum of 50 per cent of the blend. Sommières can only ever be red and requires 15 months of ageing before sale. Ideally, the whole area would be farmed organically; in practice, over half of the estates are organic, but not all. Otherwise it is a region of polyculture; olive trees are important, for nearby Nimes has an appellation for its olive oil, and there are apricot orchards and fields of wheat as well as vineyards. The estates tend to be small family concerns, with less outside investment than in the Pic St Loup or Grés de Montpellier.

Producers

Domaine de Coursac
Carnas 30260
www.domainedecoursac.com

Domaine de Coursac is in the village of Carnas on the western edge of the appellation, and was created by David Codomié, who has previously worked in the transport business. In 2000, he took the opportunity to buy just 1 hectare of vines; more followed, which were vinified at the cooperative, but by 2007 he needed to make a choice and opted to turn full-time *vigneron*. The estate now comprises 25 hectares, with a new cellar built in 2013, and his son Morgan is set to follow in his father's footsteps. David is one of the enthusiasts of the area; he has an enquiring mind and is clearly enjoying what he describes as 'the big adventure'. Nor is he afraid to voice his opinions. 'I am in a hurry. You have to be energetic, but humility is also necessary with wine.' He is also ambitious, and wants his wines to be well known. For me they stood out in a tasting of several Sommières estates.

The cellar is well equipped with tronconic cement vats and some fat eggs – David called them tulips – with closed tops, which are good for micro-oxygenation, giving a better exchange between the juice and the skins. The juice moves, as it does in an egg, with the lees in suspension. Asked about the typicity of Carnas, he observed that it was cooler than Aspères, a nearby village closer to Sommières, as it is surrounded by hills. The soil is very calcareous, and they have about 500 millimetres of rainfall a year. Carnas means *pays aux pierres*, or land of stones, in Occitan. David has employed a Chilean winemaker, Catherine Muller; he wanted a feminine palate, 'structure with *une belle finesse*'.

His Pays de Cévennes Blanc is a blend of Sauvignon, Chardonnay and Viognier, picked and fermented together, with some pithy fruit and peachy notes. The Viognier provides the link between the Sauvignon and the Chardonnay. A red Pays de Cévennes from Pinot Noir had some fresh raspberry fruit with a rustic note. Les Garriguettes is Roussanne, Grenache Blanc and Viognier, fermented in 600-litre wood, in a cold room maintained at 5C°, with four months in barrel and then in a tulip, and it is characterful with well-integrated oak. Red Garriguettes, Pays de Cévennes, is a blend of Grenache, Cinsaut and Syrah, with some nicely peppery fruit. La Patience is Sommières, with a first vintage in 2015, with Grenache and Syrah, accounting for 90 per cent of the blend, with a drop of Carignan and Mourvèdre. Eighteen months in 600-litre wood makes for some rounded spice. A late-harvest Vin de France from Muscat à Petits Grains was lightly honeyed with some orange notes – a *sympathique* finale to our tasting.

Mas des Cabres
Aspères 30250
www.masdescabres.com

Florent Boutin is president of the Sommières syndicat. He is quietly competent with an engaging smile and you immediately sense his commitment to his appellation. His family has been in the village of Aspères since 1724. His father sold wine *en vrac* but, valuing his independence, was never a cooperative member. Florent bottled his first wine in 2003. He farms 13 hectares. Cabres is a reference to goats, implying some very stony, infertile land, where goats would graze happily. Florent makes Pays de Cévennes as well as Sommières, explaining that you are allowed the same grape varieties for Pays des Cévennes as for Pays d'Oc, but with a slightly lower yield of 80 rather than 90 hectolitres per hectare.

Florent's white wine is a blend of Vermentino, Viognier and Roussanne, with some ripe fruit. His rosé comes from Grenache Noir, Cinsaut and a splash of Muscat Hamburg, with some grapey fruit. Red Cuvée Equinoxe includes 55 per cent Merlot and 35 per cent Cinsaut with some more Muscat Hamburg, with some spicy fruit, making for easy drinking. His two Sommières, Draille and Terres d'Aspères, are immediately more serious, with longer macerations. La Draille, a reference to the summer transhumance of sheep, is a blend of Grenache Noir, Mourvèdre and Syrah, aged partly in barrel, with firm fruit, integrated oak and ageing potential. Terres d'Aspères is mainly Syrah with some Grenache Noir, with some firm black fruit and tapenade, again with ageing potential. Florent is optimistic for the future appellation of Sommières. 'It will take time to achieve, possibly eight or ten years. It is not so easy to stand out as an IGP whereas Sommières is known as an old market town.'

LANGLADE

The village of Langlade is situated between Nimes and Sommières, in an area called la Vaunage, which forms a natural amphitheatre and lies within the area of Sommières, although nobody in the village of Langlade mentions Sommières on their labels. Langlade first enjoyed a reputation for its wine in the seventeenth century. The leader of the Camisard revolt, Jean Cavalier, is said to have overindulged on the wine of Langlade, with the disastrous consequence that he lost the battle of Nage to the troops of Louis XIV. It is in the nineteenth century that the wines received the most praise. In 1868 there were 625 inhabitants and 600 hectares of vineyards, with viticulture almost the sole agricultural activity, and the wines fetching higher prices than those of neighbouring villages. Phylloxera struck a severe blow to the viticulture of the village, from which it never really recovered. Although it became a VDQS in 1945, earlier than most other VDQS of the Languedoc, it was not incorporated into Coteaux du Languedoc as a separate *terroir* in 1985. In the 1980s its reputation was maintained virtually single-handedly by Henri Arnal, of Domaine Arnal, an energetic man who had come to wine after selling a business manufacturing steel girders. Sadly, his sons did not have their father's talent and the estate has now disappeared from view. There are now about 60 hectares of vines in Langlade, with five estates.

Producers

Roc d'Anglade
Langlade 30980
contact@rocdanglade.fr
The mantle of the reputation of Langlade has now been taken on by Rémy Pedreno of Roc d'Anglade. He is very proud of the area, describing it as a 'mini Priorat', referring to the Spanish denomination outside the city of Tarragona, which also has a natural amphitheatre. Appar-

ently, there was never a cooperative here, nor a distillery, and at one time the wines sold for the same price as Châteauneuf-du-Pape. Unusually for someone who is now so enthusiastic and sensitive a winemaker, Rémy did not touch a drop of wine for the first 22 years of his life, even though his parents were regular consumers. His first job was in IT, with a project for the Maison des Vins in Tavel and it was a bottle of Vacqueyras les Amouriers that sparked what he called his first '*grande émotion*'.

Rémy made his very first wine in 1996 from some Carignan, just enough for one barrel. The following year he rented 30 ares of Syrah and produced four barrels, in his parents' garage. In 1999, he went into partnership with René Rostaing from Côte Rôtie who was looking for vines with which to improve his *vin de table*, which he makes in addition to his appellation wines. The solution was 4 hectares in the village of Langlade, and the two worked together, with René giving Rémy carte blanche for four vintages. In 2001, Rémy constructed a simple cellar adjoining his house just outside the village. Meanwhile he had started buying vineyards of his own, and in 2002 made his first wine from his own vines. He now has 10 hectares, of which half are Carignan, a quarter Mourvèdre and the rest Syrah, Grenache and Cinsaut. For his white wine, he has mainly Chenin Blanc with some Chardonnay, Grenache Gris and Blanc, and also Carignan Blanc.

Rémy combines modesty with confidence, and displays commitment and dedication. He has studied, 'so that I know what *not* to do'. He never analyses his grapes, only tastes them, and states very firmly that he makes wine according to his own taste. He only makes one red wine from his vines, taking time to get the right blend each year. His vines are on a mosaic of different *terroirs*, with sand, clay, alluvial soil and some vines facing north. 'The main thing is enjoyment'; he is not looking for concentration in his wines, but sheer drinking pleasure. Wine is after all made to be drunk and enjoyed.

His vineyards are organic, and he is working on biodynamics, following the moon, but not necessarily using all the preparations. Everything is hand-picked; he ferments mainly whole bunches, using natural yeast and keeps the sulphur levels as low as possible. The wines are aged mainly in *foudres* from the Austrian cooper Stockinger. 'The wines of the Languedoc are too rich for *barriques*; those are better for less ripe wines, with less concentration.' Rémy does not like too much extraction. He enthused about Carignan, calling it the Pinot Noir of the Languedoc, 'a fabulous variety'. His Carignan vines are quite old: between 30 and 60 years.

However, Rémy's real ambition is to concentrate on the original *terroir* of Langlade, 6 hectares on slopes just outside the village, which he considers to be the best land of all, and which will generate what he calls the renaissance of Langlade. He bought the land in 2008 and first planted rootstocks, allowing them to become established, field grafting with a massal selection. The vineyards are only now producing grapes, nearly ten years later.

Tasting with Rémy is a leisurely experience. We began with his rosé, Pays du Gard, a blend mainly of Mourvèdre, with some Carignan, Grenache Noir and Cinsaut, which had firm, dry fruit. Then we went on to reds, also Pays du Gard, as Remy's oldest Carignan is not classified within the appellation. There are no rules in the final blend; he describes how each variety evolves, and may begin blending in the fermentation vat, with the final blend after about 12 months. The style is elegant and harmonious, with tension and youthful fruit. Older vintages follow, a rich leathery 2009, with supple flavours, while the 2008, with a later harvest date, was fresher, with cedary notes. '*Ça pinotte*', observed Rémy. The 2004 was a ripe vintage, with some smoky flavours, notes of the *garrigue* and a long finish. The 2015 white vinified in *demi-muids* and *foudres*, with six months in stainless steel vats, is fresh and honeyed, with lovely texture and depth, from Chardonnay, Chenin, Carignan Blanc and Grenache. Our tasting finished with the 2006 white, a pure Chenin, with honeyed fruit and firm acidity, quite belying its decade of bottle age.

PAYS DE CÉVENNES

Pays de Cévennes covers a large area of the department of the Gard, from Sommières as far as St Hippolyte and Alès in the north. It includes the vineyards of Sommières and the appellation of Duché d'Uzès, recognized in 2012 and now considered part of the Rhône valley even though the parallel IGP comes within the Languedoc. As will be seen, Pays de Cévennes covers a multitude of different grape varieties and an eclectic range of wine styles. Asked about the typicity of their wines, the wine producers will offer freshness, diversity, authenticity and character. There is a feeling that everything is possible.

Producers

Mas d'Espanet

St Mamert-du-Gard 30730
www.masdespanet.com

Agnès and Denis Arman have been at Mas d'Espanet for 34 years; the property was originally bought by Denis's parents in 1980. They have 20 hectares of vines with 60 hectares of land altogether, on clay and limestone, in the middle of the *garrigue* outside St Mamert-du-Gard, divided equally between red and white, including some old vines of Carignan, Grenache Noir and Cinsaut from the 1960s. They have planted Pinot Noir and white varieties: Grenache Blanc and Gris, Sauvignon Blanc, Viognier, Piquepoul, Chenin Blanc, Vermentino, Roussanne and Petit Manseng, and also a little Riesling, which has been less successful. White wine, with higher yields, account for 70 per cent of their production, which is half Pays de Cévennes and half AOP Languedoc. As well as wine, they grow wheat and have a flock of sheep that perform a useful function in the vineyards, eating weeds and providing manure.

With such a diversity of grape varieties, they make some original blends. Freesia Blanc is mainly Viognier with some Sauvignon, Chasan and Chenin, aged in oak. Eolienne Blanc, which they described as '*le rock star du domain* that really got us known', is 80 per cent Grenache Blanc, with 10 per cent Piquepoul and 10 per cent Viognier, and some satisfying texture. Camille, named after their daughter, is a blend of equal parts Grenache Blanc and Piquepoul. The young wine was firm and oaky with good acidity but a 10-year-old wine had evolved beautifully to develop lovely nuances of flavour.

They have gradually shifted from *barriques* to *demi-muids* to restrain the oak, observing that it is important to follow the wine as it ages in barrel. Denis is self-taught; he has developed his own gentle way of pressing the juice, which makes for finer lees, and although he has an oenologist, 'I am the one who decides. We do not always agree.' He considers that he works *à la bourguignonne* for red wine, destalking, with a couple of short *remontages* and fairly short macerations of about ten days. 'You have to be lazy and let the wine make itself.'

Freesia Rouge is a refreshing Cinsaut and Le Pin Ôt has fresh raspberry fruit, with some ageing in *demi-muids*. Eolienne Rouge is a Languedoc AOP, a blend of Grenache Noir and Carignan, with 12 months in *foudres*. Denis explained that St Mamert is the last *commune* of the Languedoc and touches the Duché d'Uzès. The request to be AOP Languedoc was made in 1998 and finally granted in 2012, and maybe they will eventually become part of Sommières.

Meanwhile their son Guillaume is making the wine at Clos Vacquerolles, an estate within the *commune* of Nimes. You sense that Agnès and Denis are quietly energetic and nothing stands still; currently they are experimenting with amphorae for Camille.

Domaine le Sollier
Monoblet 30170
www.domainelesollier.fr

Domaine le Sollier is in the hills outside the village of Monoblet, in the Parc National des Cévennes. We met Thomas Olivier, who is young and keen. He explained how the family had made wine until 1970, when they had joined the cooperative at St Hippolyte. His brother studied oenology, so when he qualified in 2006, they began retrieving the family vines from the cooperative, and Thomas joined his brother in 2010 after doing business studies.

It was the first day of the harvest, with Viognier arriving at the cellar, and we walked into a vineyard to taste some Cinsaut that was still not quite ripe. The vines are all close by and surrounded by woods, with their nearest neighbours six kilometres away. The soil is clay and red sandstone. The cellar is simple and well equipped, with Thomas pointing out that they are content with their fibreglass vats, preferring to spend money on their vineyards.

As well as making Pays de Cévennes, they overlap with the Duché d'Uzès. Altogether they make two white, one pink and five red wines, with different blends and grape varieties, some more unusual than others. Les Alisiers, a blend of Viognier with 10 per cent Chardonnay and 20 per cent Vermentino has some peachy Viognier fruit. Les Acacias comes from equal parts of Viognier and Roussanne, partly fermented in oak, with rich, peachy fruit and texture. L'Ombre des Jumelles, named after the two hills that dominate the nearby landscape, is a rosé from a blend of pressed Cinsaut and Syrah, with fresh raspberry fruit. A pure

Merlot, made with natural yeast and no sulphur, with eight months in vat, was nicely rounded with fresh fruit. Terre Ronde is a blend of Syrah with 20 per cent each of Grenache and Cinsaut, with some fresh fruit and supple tannins.

Les Linthes, Duché d'Uzès, from 80 per cent Syrah with some Grenache, with 12 months in old wood, was quite firm and peppery. Les Quatre Chemins, from 70 per cent Cinsaut with some Syrah, first spends 12 months in new oak and then 12 months in old wood, with some elegant fruit from the Cinsaut. Finally, there was Mon Oncle, from 80 per cent Alicante tempered with some Grenache Noir. They were going to pull up the Alicante, but realized that it had potential, and named the wine in memory of the uncle who bought the estate. It was solid and spicy with some well-integrated oak. They would like to expand the estate to 15 hectares and plant some more Grenache, both Noir and Blanc, and perhaps also varieties with such aroma, such as Chenin or Gros Manseng. There is exciting potential to fulfil.

Mas de Seren
Anduze 30140
www.mas-seren.fr

Emmanuelle Schoch bought her vines, between Monoblet and Frayssac, from Daniel Faure, who produced some exemplary wine at Domaine Puechamp for a number of years. As I remembered from visiting Daniel, the vineyards are in the middle of nowhere, whereas Emmanuelle's compact cellar is under her house on the outskirts of Anduze.

We sat outside in the September sunshine and Emmanuelle related how she had come to wine. Although her name is Swiss-German, she was brought up in Lyons and worked as an event organizer. Like all good *lyonnais*, she loves wine, and when she arrived in Montpellier she found herself meeting wine producers, and those encounters sparked her enthusiasm. So she studied in Montpellier and then worked for various growers and cooperatives in both vineyard and cellar, and with the oenologist Jean Natoli. In 2009 she made the decision to buy some vines with her partner, Loïc Perols. He restores old cars, but has been a great support.

Emmanuelle opted for the Cévennes, saying she loves the sun, the freshness, the mountains, the old soils, the mixture of the Mediterranean and the more continental climate. She called it *un joli bijou*. Her vines are very difficult to work because they are isolated and on stony slopes, requiring a lot of manual work. There is Syrah, Cinsaut and Grenache for reds and Roussanne, Grenache Blanc, Vermentino and Viognier for whites, with vines aged between 20 and 60 years in one plot, but with a variety of soils: limestone, red sandstone, blue marl and layered schist. Altogether Emmanuelle does as many as 15 different vinifications in her very simple cellar under the house. She has lots of vats, but no barrels; 'Oak is not my thing,' she says. She concentrates on freshness and fruit in the grapes, and supple tannins. Twice a year she uses a horse to earth up the vines at the end of the season and then to *débutter* in the spring, and maybe to weed in June or July. She keeps the grass between the rows, but her neighbours' sheep oblige by keeping it well cropped. Daniel had already converted the vines to organic viticulture.

Etincelle is her entry-level wine. The white is a blend of 70 per cent Vermentino with some Viognier; the rosé is mainly Cinsaut with some Syrah; and the red a blend of Syrah and Cinsaut. She is particularly keen on the Cinsaut: '*J'adore ça.* It is a magic grape and I pamper them.' It gives freshness, spice and fruit. Etamin, another star, is a blend of 80 per cent Roussanne with 20 per cent Grenache Blanc, with good texture and a honeyed finish. Emmanuelle talked about the importance of producing accessible wines. Working so hard to improve its reputation, the Languedoc has concentrated on serious wine, completely forgetting the pleasure of simple, undemanding wines in the style of Beaujolais. Lilith is another star; I learnt that she was the first companion of Adam before Eve and the first independent woman, but she was repudiated and became a demon and is remembered in a star. The blend is equal parts of Cinsaut and Grenache, with Cinsaut giving freshness and Grenache Noir opulence. They complement each other, with perfumed fruit. Mintaka, from 75 per cent Syrah with some Grenache, and the only wine without Cinsaut, has firm, peppery fruit, with what Emmanuelle called the 'exuberant quality' of Syrah.

Over lunch we talked about the traditions of area, which is very Protestant, with a large Protestant church in Anduze. The history of the Cévennes is dominated by the revolt of the Camisards, who were Protestant, and there is the isolation of a hillier region set slightly apart from the mainstream of the Languedoc and defending its independence.

Domaine des Arnasseaux

Cardet 30350

www.domaine-arnasseaux.com

The unusual thing about Domaine des Arnasseaux is their plantings of Riesling and Gewürztraminer, varieties usually associated with Alsace. They wanted to plant white varieties but not the ones that everyone else has, like Viognier and Roussanne, and so they opted for the two Alsace varieties, which does indeed help with sales.

Domaine des Arnasseaux has been an independent cellar since the end of the nineteenth century. Guilhem Peladan explained that initially they did not concentrate on wine, but then his grandfather began producing large quantities, particularly of Aramon. His father sold his wine in bulk, but was never tempted by the cooperative, and replanted his vineyards with varieties like Merlot, Cabernet and Syrah. Guilhem took over in 2004, after finishing his studies in Montpellier, and did his first bottling the following year, of two reds and one rosé. Altogether they have 25 hectares, in about 35 different plots, all around the hamlet of Arnasseaux. Guilhem commented that in 2017 he had produced 1,600 hectolitres from 25 hectares, compared with his father's crop of 3,000 hectolitres or more in 1977 from the same number of hectares, but with completely different grape varieties. All the vineyards are Pays de Cévennes and climatically they are indeed very aware of the effect of the Cévennes. When the warm air from the sea meets the cool air from the hills, it rains, and the area is generally cooler and wetter than the rest of the Languedoc.

Guilhem makes an eclectic range of wines. The single varietal Riesling and Gewürztraminer show convincing varietal characteristics; Duo de Blancs is a blend of Sauvignon and Chardonnay. It was Guilhem who planted the white varieties; his father did not want them. However, their main wine, accounting for half of their production, is Perle de Gris, coming mainly from Grenache Noir with a little Cinsaut, with a very pale colour. The traditional rosé of the Languedoc is much darker; *gris* as a colour does not exist officially, only *gris de gris*, from *gris* varieties, notably in the IGP Sable de Camargue. Guilhem has invested in a pneumatic press and the necessary chilling equipment for white and rosé.

As for red wines, there is a Pinot Noir, a Merlot, and Heritage, which is a blend of Syrah, Marselan and Grenache, with some fresh red fruit. Réserve is the same wine, in contact with oak staves for eight months,

giving the palate a little vanilla and structure. Guilhem currently practises *lutte raisonnée* and is gradually moving towards organic viticulture. He would also like to produce some sparkling wine, maybe from
Gewürztraminer. As we left, we admired his great grandfather's indestructible concrete vats. This is an estate that has successfully effected a
generation change to evolve in its own quiet way. As Guilhem observed,
'Our generation is in the process of writing the history of quality in the
Languedoc.'

21

MUSCATS: FRONTIGNAN, MIREVAL AND LUNEL

It cannot be denied that the various Muscat appellations, namely Frontignan, Mireval and Lunel, are fighting a rearguard action, faced with a market that says it prefers dry to sweet. Consequently, the traditional *vins doux naturel*, the sweet Muscats, have declined dramatically in popularity. The wines are delicious but underappreciated, so the handful of producers who remain are diversifying their offer, making dry and sparkling wine, late-harvest wines and even red wines.

MUSCAT DE FRONTIGNAN

Frontignan has a long history. It was appreciated by Pliny the Younger, who called it *viae apianae*, the paths of bees. 'Frontiniac' was drunk in England in the seventeenth and eighteenth centuries, with the political philosopher John Locke singing its praises in 1676. Voltaire ordered wine from Frontignan, writing to his supplier in 1774: 'Keep me alive by sending me a small quarter of the best wine of Frontignan.' Perhaps its most famous consumer was Thomas Jefferson, who visited Frontignan in 1789 when he was the American ambassador in Paris. His correspondence with a Dr Lambert, who was mayor of Muscat and a producer of the wine, has been preserved. In 1790, he asked for ten dozen bottles to be sent 'to our President, General George Washington, and five dozen for me, both white and red, but more of the latter'. Evidently Frontignan produced red Muscat as well at that time. Indeed, Victor Rendu, writing a century or so later in *Ampélographie*

Française, also refers to red Muscat, comparing it to Vin de Constance, the Constantia of South Africa. Muscat de Frontignan was one of the earliest appellations of the Languedoc, recognized in 1936.

Like all the Muscats of the Hérault, Muscat de Frontignan comes only from Muscat à Petits Grains. Confusingly, Muscat de Frontignan may also be a synonym for that grape variety elsewhere in France, while other names for it have been used, such as Muscat Frontignan in California and even white Frontignan in Australia. It grows mainly on the white, chalky soil known as Calcaire de Frontignan, *calcaire lacustre* (lacustrine limestone), where the sea withdrew, leaving very fine alluvial soil that does not compact, something peculiar to this small area. Apparently, the chalk acts like a sponge, soaking up the water during the wetter months and then gradually releasing it so that the vines never suffer from stress. There is also some harder limestone, mixed with clay and stony deposits from the nearby hills of La Gardiole. Most of the vineyards are on the eastern side of the étang de Thau, which, combined with the proximity to the sea, ensures a suitably warm microclimate.

Producers

Château de la Peyrade

Frontignan 34110
www.chateaulapeyrade.com

The Pastourel family bought Château de la Peyrade in 1977. Bruno Pastourel, son of original owner Yves, produces an exemplary range of wines, which has allowed for some experimentation and diversification. I tasted the range with Bruno in his welcoming tasting *caveau*, next to a busy roundabout on the outskirts of Sète. He remembered how sweet wines used to be expensive 40 years ago. They have made Muscat Sec since 1990: 'You cannot live on sweet wine alone,' notes Bruno.

Cuvée des Lilas, Muscat Sec, IGP Collines de la Moure, is hand-picked and enjoys a cool fermentation to retain the freshness. It is firm and pithy, benchmark dry Muscat. L'EntreDeux is a Muscat *moelleux*, Pays d'Oc, with about 34 grams per litre residual sugar. The fermentation is stopped by chilling and filtering, so that it is honeyed and deliciously grapey. Next came the traditional Muscat de Frontignan, *muté* at 110 grams per litre and 15% abv. The Cuvée Prestige benefits from a *sélection parcellaire* of older vines, 50 to 60 years old. Only the first juice is used and there is an *élevage* in vat, making for a lemony, honeyed wine. Sol

Invictus is even more strictly selected, the best juice of specific plots it is delicately elegant. Barriques Oubliées is based on traditional Muscat de Frontignan, but spends four years in barrel, so that it becomes dark in colour, with concentrated flavours of orange marmalade. Vendanges d'Automne, Vin de France, comes from overripe grapes, picked a month later, without any *mutage*. The fermentation stops with chilling and filtering and the wine is honeyed and unctuous, with enough acidity to retain the freshness. Finally, YP, in memory of Yves Pastourel who died in 2016, is a Vendange Tardive aged in acacia barrels for two years. It was smooth and unctuous, and could almost be mistaken for Sauternes.

Bruno observed that people are eating much less sugar, and are much more conscious of sugar intake; he thinks that they are at the lowest ebb, *dans le creux de la vague*, and fervently hopes that things will improve. However, he has reduced his vineyard area, not renewing rental agreements. He lost a flourishing export market when the euro rose in value and now concentrates on the home market, running a successful shop where you can buy other local products as well as Muscat from Frontignan in all its forms.

Other producers, such as Château de Stony and Mas de Madame, while continuing to produce Muscat, are also turning to red wine, a poignant illustration of the fall from grace of Muscat.

MUSCAT DE MIREVAL

The vineyards for Muscat de Mireval cover two villages, Mireval and neighbouring Vic-la-Gardiole, on stony limestone soil. The differences between the Mireval and Frontignan appellations are minimal, though Mireval did not acquire appellation status until 1959, thanks to the *histoire de clochers* that prevented its association with Frontignan, and it continues to maintain its independence.

Producers

Domaine de la Rencontre
Vic-la-Gardiole 34110
www.domainedelarencontre.com
Domaine de la Rencontre is a new estate. If I were starting a new venture in the Languedoc, I am not sure that one based on Muscat would be my

first choice, but that is what Julie and Pierre Viudes have done, making their first wine in 2010. Their enthusiasm is infectious and I am full of admiration for their energy and determination.

Neither of them had any immediate links with wine. They met in Mexico, and that is one reason for the name of their estate. It also recalls an 1854 work by Gustave Courbet called La Rencontre, which apparently was painted close to their vineyards, with a view of the Mont St Clair in the background. There is a Route Courbet, which covers seven paintings in seven villages and La Rencontre is set between Vic-la-Gardiole and Mireval. Julie worked for a Swiss company in London where she had colleagues who were keen wine enthusiasts. Pierre had worked in *prêt à porter* and has also been an actor, which is a useful skill at wine fairs, where he has learnt to play to his audience very effectively. Looking for a change, he went to Mexico and met Julie, who was also travelling there.

Julie Lorimer Viudes and Pierre Viudes, Domaine de la Rencontre

Pierre has links with Sète and his grandfather was a *régisseur* on an estate outside Béziers so in a way he has come back to his roots. His parents had a friend with vineyards in Frontignan, so he went to work there, for a member of the cooperative who really knew how to convey his love of vines. The next step was to sign up for a part-time course at the Lycée Agricole, on viticulture and oenology. When the moment was right to buy their own vines, one plot of 7.5 hectares in the *garrigue* overlooking the sea. Pierre happened to go into the cooperative in the village, where the secretary said: 'My husband wants to sell his vines; he is pruning at the moment; let's go and see.' And that is how it happened. At the time, they did not even own a bucket or a pair of secateurs! Then in 2010 they bought a house, with an adjacent building for a cellar. The 7.5 hectare plot was committed to the cooperative until 2014, so in 2009 they rented 5 hectares and made their own first wine in 2010, just 6,000 bottles. Their range has gently evolved and now includes seven different variations of Muscat. Their new cellar, with a state-of-the-art press that is having a very positive impact on quality, was ready for the 2014 vintage.

Our tasting began with Muscat, Rencontre, a dry Pays de l'Hérault. They use just the free-run juice, with no malolactic fermentation and just a little *élevage* on the lees, and the young vintage was fresh and grapey, with the bitter note on the finish that is characteristic of good Muscat. Then Pierre opened their very first wine, the 2010. I would never have expected a Muscat to last as long as seven years, and not only to last but also to remain fresh and vibrant, with the slight petrol note that you may associate with mature Riesling. Next came Philosophe, first made in 2011, a blend of the dry Muscat and some late-harvest wine from the previous vintage that had been aged in barrel. You may add up to 15 per cent of an earlier vintage to a blend. The wine has some elegant honey, with spice and notes of citrus fruit. Poète comes from raisined grapes. This entails detailed work in the vineyards, with leaf plucking on the side of the rising sun, to encourage the grapes to dry and concentrate the sugar, while retaining acidity. There is an *élevage* in vat, which retains the freshness. The fermentation stops naturally at 65 grams per litre residual sugar, leaving some elegant honey and balancing acidity. There is only half the amount of sugar as for the *vin doux*.

Hédonisme, their Muscat de Mireval, is made from vines aged between 55 and 80 years old. The sugar level is a minimum of 110 grams per litre, but there is talk of reducing it to 100 grams or even 90 grams, which would make for a different equilibrium. Acidity is essential to balance the honey. Éclat, a second Muscat de Mireval, comes from younger vines and is fresh and concentrated. The two vineyards are on neighbouring plots and the wines are made in exactly the same way, with a difference of only two days in the picking time. They think the difference in flavour can only come from the older vines, with their deep roots tapping underground water. The final sweet wine is Sagesse, from grapes that are *passerillés* and may even have *pourriture noble*, noble rot. Julie talked about the difficulty of explaining to the pickers the difference between grey and noble rot. The best way is to make them taste the difference. The wine is given some barrel ageing and the flavours are concentrated and honeyed, with the unctuous notes of elegant Sauternes, and a long lingering finish. Our tasting concluded with Bulles Libres, a sparkling wine, for which they make the still wine. The juice is sent to a *prestateur* in the Var, who bottles it and keeps it on the lees for at least two years, the longer the better because that reduces the residual sugar. At 10 grams per litre it is *brut*, but at 12 grams per litre, *demi sec*. The wine is deliciously grapey. Julie lamented that importers tend to say the market is for dry wines; but when you give consumers your wine to taste at a fair, they really enjoy the lightly sweet wines. Asked about the future, they admitted that they would like some vineyards for red wine, but in the *arrière pays*, not on the coast.

The other important producer of Muscat de Mireval is the Jeanjean estate of Mas Neuf. The village cooperative, which accounts for about 70 per cent of the appellation, is also working well, under the guidance of a new president. It is called La Cave de Rabelais because Rabelais praised Muscat de Mireval in his *Pantagruel*, which was published in 1532.

MUSCAT DE LUNEL

Muscat was produced around Lunel as early as the sixteenth century. Felix Platter, a student from Basle, wrote in 1552: 'On leaving Nimes, the road crossed a plain planted with olive trees as far as Lunel, where I drank my first Muscat wine.' Jean-Jacques Rousseau wrote of enjoying the Muscat de Lunel at the Auberge du Pont du Vidourle towards 1750 and Laurence Sterne in 1760 described Muscat de Lunel as the best Muscat wine of the whole of France. Thomas Jefferson came to Lunel at the end of the 1780s, and mentioned the impossibility of obtaining older wine, for the demand was such that the harvest was sold the first year. Some years later, Pauline Borghese sent Muscat de Lunel to her brother, Napoleon Bonaparte, when he was in exile on the island of St Helena.

The appellation of Muscat de Lunel dates from 1943 and covers four *communes*, Lunel, Lunel-Viel, Saturargues and Vérargues. The vineyards are all relatively low-lying, at 50 metres, and just a little higher than the coastal plan. The soil is a mixture of limestone and red clay, originating from the alpine deposits of glaciers from the Rhône. The sea breezes bring humidity. The production is dominated by the cooperative of Lunel, which was founded in 1956, accounting for about 80 per cent of the appellation, with five or six independent producers, and no more than 100 hectares in production.

Producer

Domaine le Clos de Bellevue
Lunel 34400
www.domaine-le-clos-de-bellevue.com

Nicolas Charrière bought this estate in 2010, after an earlier career running a cooperative in the Ardèche. It is an attractive property, and easy to visit because it is very close to the motorway exit for Lunel. The property is situated on a small hill, with views towards the sea and La Grande Motte, and towards the Pic St Loup and St Christol in the other direction. The highest point of the appellation is just 50 metres. For red wines, his vineyards are within the confines of St Christol, but of his 20 hectares, 16 are planted with Muscat, making him the largest producer of Muscat de Lunel.

Nicolas admitted that he knew very little about Muscat when he arrived there, only the theory from his studies. Muscat Tradition, Lacoste – the name has been retained in memory of the previous owner who developed the estate – comes from younger vines and is delicately honeyed and grapey. Clos de Bellevue, Vieilles Vignes, comes from vines that are 60 years old or more, old bush vines, just outside the cellar. The *mutage* is *sur jus*, rather than on the grape skins, and the yield is lower than for the Tradition, 15–20 hectolitres per hectare as opposed to 30. The grapes are picked about ten days later, with an identical vinification but the wine has more concentration and depth than the Tradition, as you might expect. Vendanges d'Octobre, Cuvée Passerillée, Vin de France, comes from grapes picked a month later. The fermentation stops naturally, and the wine spends 12 months in barrel, making for some rich honey balanced with a streak of tannin. The range is completed by a Pétillant that is fun and frothy and also a Cartagène.

Happily for the appellation of Muscat de Lunel Nicolas has a very positive approach; he has replanted Muscat and really believes in it. The market for Muscat Sec is growing and he is optimistic for the future. It would indeed be sad if these delicious wines were to disappear, as they enhance the rich diversity of the Languedoc.

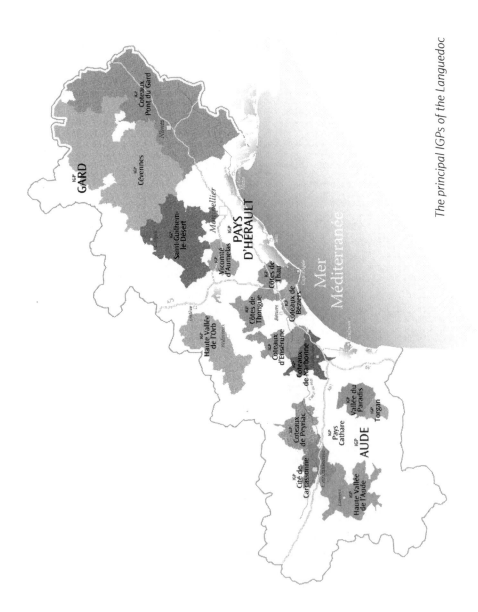

The principal IGPs of the Languedoc

22

IGPS: PAYS D'OC, CÔTES DE THONGUE, HAUTE VALLÉE DE L'ORB AND OTHERS

The *vins de pays*, or Indications Géographiques Protégées (IGP) as they are now rather clumsily called, are an important part of the viticultural landscape of the Languedoc. In volume terms, they are more important than the appellations, but not in terms of prestige, with rare exceptions. However, several wine growers have established a fine a reputation with an IGP as well as with an appellation. They have the distinct advantage that the regulations are much more flexible and allow for grape varieties not permitted within an appellation.

The IGPs are generally demarcated by administrative and political geography rather than by geology and *terroir*. A rare exception to this is Sable de Camargue, where the sand of the Camargue and the coastal sandbars are the determining factor. Otherwise there are IGPs that cover a department, such as Pays de l'Hérault or Pays de l'Aude, and others that cover a zone within a department, such as Côtes de Thongue or Vallée du Paradis. Largest of all are the regional IGPs, of which Pays d'Oc is the one that covers the whole of Languedoc-Roussillon, with the four departments of the Pyrénées-Orientales, Hérault, Aude and Gard, parts of which are outside the scope of this book. The regional name allows for blending between smaller IGPs and many producers prefer to use it, with its significant marketing clout, in preference to a small, unknown name with little identity. Others, on the other hand, feel overwhelmed by the anonymity of the all-encompassing Pays d'Oc and opt for the smaller area, which they can promote on a personal level.

There is no part of the Languedoc without an IGP, even if it lacks an appellation. Usually the two cohabit, allowing the wine growers to make two wines; depending on their approach, the IGP can be very much better or very much worse than the appellation, or just completely different because it uses grape varieties that are not allowed in the appellation. Some of the more obscure IGPs have disappeared, to be swallowed up by a larger zone, or the departmental IGP.

The IGPs allow for an imaginative flexibility as to which grape varieties may or may not be planted, and have firmly established the presence of varietal wines on the French market, an aspect of marketing that is generally ignored by the appellations. Pays d'Oc was recognized in 1987, initially to provide a marketing tool for the plethora of varietal wines produced in the south of France, enabling them to confront the challenge of the New World. It is now a very established part of Languedoc viticulture, but has progressed since the early beginnings. In 1987, 24 grape varieties, 9 red and 15 white, were included; by 2017, that list had grown to 58, with Albariño the latest addition. The more popular are of course the obvious, Cabernet Sauvignon, Merlot, Chardonnay, Sauvignon Blanc and Viognier. *Bis cépages* were introduced in 1996 to allow for two varieties on the label. Some of the more unexpected grape varieties that I encountered for this book include not only Albariño but also Touriga Nacional, Nebbiolo, Primitivo and Sangiovese. Plantings are often initially on an experimental basis, and then established usage comes into play so that the newcomers are accepted. Once decried varieties, such as Carignan Blanc, Aramon and Alicante Bouschet, are also now permitted. Some of the departmental IGPs are even more flexible than the Pays d'Oc, which for instance only recognized Carignan Noir as a single variety – it had long been acceptable in a blend – in 2016. For Jacques Gravegeal, the president of the Pays d'Oc, the focus is indisputably on the grape variety and after 30 years the Pays d'Oc accounts for half the production of Languedoc-Roussillon

PAYS D'OC AND PAYS DE L'HÉRAULT

Producers

Mas de Daumas Gassac

Aniane 34150
www.daumas-gassac.com

The most famous example of an IGP is Mas de Daumas Gassac, a humble Pays de l'Hérault produced in the hills outside the village of Aniane. The story has often been told how Aimé Guibert, and his wife Véronique, bought a holiday house in the Gassac valley. Wine was far from their thoughts, but the leading geologist from Bordeaux University at the time, Henri Enjalbert, came to visit and told Aimé that he had unique soil, a red glacial powder with the potential to make great wine. Aimé took up the challenge and set Mas de Daumas Gassac firmly on the wine map of the Languedoc, daring in the early days of the 1980s to charge what seemed a totally exorbitant price, which of course these days has long since been superseded. For better or for worse, Aimé energetically and successfully opposed Robert Mondavi's ambitions to produce wine in the Languedoc, from land that he had cleared in the hills above Gassac valley. The story features in Jonathan Nossiter's film *Mondovino*, released in 2004, about the impact of the globalization of wine.

These days Mas de Daumas Gassac is run by Aimé's children. I spent a friendly morning with Samuel, the eldest son, who is both winemaker and export manager. We walked through the vineyards in the spring sunshine. They have 50 hectares altogether, in 67 different plots, surrounded by woods on the valley hillsides, with an eclectic selection of grapes, essentially Cabernet Sauvignon and 15 other red varieties. Their oldest vines, one-third of a hectare of Cabernet Sauvignon planted in 1972, make their top *cuvée*, a homage to Emmanuel Peynaud, the *bordelais* professor of oenology who helped so much with the winemaking in the early days. For their white wine Chardonnay, Chenin Blanc, Viognier and Petit Manseng are most important, with a further 15 varieties, planted in the 1980s. Everything is as ecological as possible, with a flock of 50 sheep to keep the weeds at bay. The grapes are all hand-picked, with Samuel observing that as much as 90 per cent of the Languedoc is now machine picked, which is all too understandable, given the bureaucratic constraints of employing friends and family to help in the vineyards. The microclimate is relatively cool, with humidity from the river, which slows down the ripening process.

The cellar was originally a watermill, with grain grown on the land until the 1960s. It is naturally cool and well-equipped with stainless steel vats for the white wine and barrels for *élevage* of the red. The white wine sees no oak; there is some cool pre-fermentation skin contact and the flavours are ripe and peachy with some body. I have always found the white Daumas Gassac to be a tad too sweet for my taste, and Samuel admitted that it does have some residual sugar, on average about 7.5 grams per litre. Rose Frizant comes from almost unripe Cabernet Sauvignon, picked at the end of August, with the wine bottled under pressure, to retain some bubbles, with fresh raspberry fruit. However, the reputation of Mas de Daumas Gassac really stands on its red. Samuel explained how the style has changed; the wine was much more robust in the early days, but a *grand cru* should have finesse. It depends on the generations; the older generation wanted tannins they could chew on, but then there was a shift to more elegance, helped, he thought, by the age of the vines. Aimé's last vintage, the 2015, tasted from vat, had elegant, ripe, cedary fruit. It was tightly knit and finely balanced, with a long finish and ageing potential after 15 months' *élevage*. Cuvée Emile Peynaud is only made in the years when there is a significant difference in the quality of the two wines. A decision is taken after 12 months and the wine given a further eight months of *élevage*, to produce about 1,500 to 2,000 bottles. There is also a luscious dessert wine, Vin de Laurence, made from Sercial and Muscat à Petits Grains.

They also run the Moulin de Gassac label, for a range of varietals mainly from leased vineyards, and some of their own, using the facilities of the cooperative at nearby Villeveyrac. The range includes a cheerful white Moulin de Gassac from Sauvignon Blanc, Clairette, Grenache Blanc and a drop of Terret. The red comes from Syrah, Grenache, Mourvèdre and Carignan, with some easy spice and supple tannins. Samuel is particularly pleased with the Pinot Noir Pays d'Oc, describing it as a challenge, and a big learning curve, as it is so different from Cabernet Sauvignon.

Domaine la Grange des Pères

Aniane 34150
Tel: +33 (0)4 67 57 70 55

There is no doubt that others have been inspired by the success of Mas de Daumas Gassac and the village of Aniane includes several estates making serious wine with an international reputation. The closest neighbour is Domaine de Capion, which has recently been sold to Russians, after a somewhat chequered history. Driving back down the hill, you pass Terrasse d'Elise and Mas des Armes, to reach La Grange des Pères, where Laurent Vaillé has created an extraordinary reputation for both red and white wine in a relatively short space of time. I last visited him in 2007 and greatly enjoyed his wines, but these days he is completely reclusive and virtually impossible to visit.

Domaine Terrasse d'Elise
Aniane 34150
terrassedelise@gmail.com

Fortunately, Xavier Braujou at Terrasse d'Elise is much more welcoming. He made his very first wine in 1998, at St Jean-de-Fos, where his family have had vineyards for several generations. A great-grandfather was a cooper in Aniane, making barrels for storing olives and capers, rather than wine, though he did repair wine barrels, and his maternal great-grandmother was one of the very first women *négociants* before the First World War. Both his grandfathers were cooperative members, growing Carignan, Aramon and Cinsaut. Xavier began with just 40 ares of Syrah, from which he made a few barrels but has gradually expanded his vineyard holdings to 14 hectares. Family problems prompted him to leave St Jean-de-Fos so he now has an efficient cellar outside Aniane, where most of his vineyards are too.

Xavier Braujou, Domaine Terrasse d'Elise

You sense immediately that Xavier is thoughtful and very committed. He talked about his winemaking, how he vinifies each grape variety and each plot separately. All his wines are Pays de l'Hérault, apart from one Terrasses du Larzac. He has a variety of soils, *calcaire* (limestone), *argilo-calcaire* (calcareous clay) and *galets roulées*. Elegance and balance are his aim, and that is what he has achieved. Siclène is a blend of 40 per cent Marsanne and Roussanne with some Chardonnay; Xavier considers Marsanne and Roussanne the best varieties for the area, and Chardonnay adds volume in the mouth. I found the flavours fresh and firm, with herbal notes, good acidity and an elegant finish.

There is a pair of Cinsaut; Pradel, from six *terroirs* and three plots, given one year's ageing in barrels, is fresh and ripe, while Les Hauts de Carol's with two years' ageing, from four different *terroirs*, variations of limestone in two plots, is more substantial, but with the fresh cherry fruit of the Pinot of the south. Xavier uses old barrels, observing that you need to know their source. L'Enclos comes from Mourvèdre, given 12 months in wood; Pigeonnier is a pure Carignan, with some fresh red fruit; XB is pure Syrah, kept in vat; and Elise, Terrasses du Larzac, is a blend of two-thirds Syrah to one-third Mourvèdre, given two years in wood. Elise was his father's aunt, and by all accounts she was considered a saint for her kindness. She had some land at a *lieu-dit* called Terrasse, hence the name of Xavier's estate. The 2010 combined the freshness and finesse of the Terrasses du Larzac, with some dry cherry spice and firm tannins.

Domaine La Voute du Verdus

St Guilhem-le-Désert 34150
www.lavouteduverdus.com

Mélanie Estival was brought up in St Guilhem-le-Désert and met her husband Pierre while studying oenology in Montpellier. They both work for other estates but also make wine from some of the vineyards belonging to Mélanie's parents, which they have extracted from the Montpeyroux cooperative, beginning with 2 hectares in 2011. La Voute des Verdus is one of two estates in the enchanting village of St Guilhem-le-Désert. We met under the centuries-old plane tree in the Place de la Liberté and they led us down a side street away from the madding crowd to their small cellar, built by a great-grandfather in 1850, at the bottom of the hill. The stream, the Verdus, runs right by it. They explained that although their vineyards are potentially Terrasses du Larzac, St Guilhem-le-Désert was not included in the appellation because the handful of growers in the village were members of the Aniane cooperative and short-sightedly did not appreciate the significance of the classification. Since then the Aniane cooperative has closed and Mélanie and her husband have elected to make their wine in the village as an IGP St Guilhem-le-Désert.

Mélanie Estival, La Voute du Verdus

They have a tiny vaulted shop, run by Mélanie's parents, in the rue Descente du Portal, and that is where we tasted. Their white wine is a blend of 70 per cent Colombard with Grenache Blanc; they chose Colombard for its acidity, and the result is a simple, fresh, fruity white wine. The rosé, from 80 per cent Cinsaut with some Syrah, has some delicate raspberry fruit. They also make two reds. The first, from 40 per cent each Syrah and Grenache, with 10 per cent each Carignan and Mourvèdre, has some rounded spicy fruit, with notes of the thyme of the *garrigue*; and Le Grand Saut, mainly from Carignan and Mourvèdre, with some *élevage*, is sturdier and more concentrated. Their oldest vines are 50-year-old Carignan and they have also planted more Carignan, considering it so well suited to the climate. It has tough branches and skins, enjoying the heat and resisting the drought. I was left with the impression of a young couple who really enjoy what they do, and are quietly committed to their village. I also learnt that an inhabitant of St Guilhem is called a Sauta Roc, a reference to goats jumping from rock to rock. In winter, just 250 people live in the village, but during the summer the population explodes with tourists during the day.

Laurent Miquel

Cessenon-sur-Orb 34460
www.laurent-miquel.com

Laurent Miquel has family estates at Cazal Viehl, within the appellation of St Chinian, where he also produces very successful IGPs based particularly on Chardonnay and Viognier. In 2009 he bought a property, les Auzines, in the hills outside Lagrasse in the Corbières, where above all he makes Albariño. By concentrating on white wine, which accounts for 50 per cent of his production, he is certainly not typical of the Languedoc. The first plantings of Viognier at Cazal Viehl were in 1992, with a first harvest in 1995, and Viognier now accounts for 40 hectares of a 150-hectare property.

Laurent is energetic, focused and very committed, with an enquiring mind. His Irish wife, Neasa, is a highly competent and engaging right-hand, efficiently running the estates when Laurent is travelling abroad. For his *vins de cépage*, Laurent favours Pays d'Oc. First, we tasted a pair of Albariño, with delicate, peachy fruit and convincing varietal character. So-las was the lighter of the pair. Laurent mentioned that when they bought Auzines, the elderly *régisseur*, who had been there for years, confided that given the choice he would have planted white varieties, so building on his experience with Viognier, Laurent opted for Albariño and now has 25 hectares in production, as well as some Viognier and Chardonnay. He said his aim is to create a new style of wine in the Languedoc. Apart from Laurent, Vignobles Foncalieu have 4 hectares of Albariño and Domaine de Cendrillon in the Corbières includes a tiny amount in their white wine. The vine cuttings came from both Spain and Portugal and Laurent sees a fresher version of the denomination of Rías Baixas in Galicia as his benchmark.

Solas Viognier is unoaked, with lightly peachy, rounded, elegant fruit. Nord Sud Viognier – named after the aspect of the vineyards, with the vines planted north–south so the grapes are protected from the midday sun, but exposed in the morning and evening – with 30 per cent oak ageing, was richer with a tannic streak. Verité Viognier, from the best plots, with a selection of the best juice, and fermentation and then ageing for 12 months in oak, is more powerful with rich, peachy fruit and texture. The three made a fascinating comparison. Solas Pinot Noir comes from vineyards north of Béziers and has some fresh, raspberry fruit, with a firm finish.

Neasa and Laurent Miquel

Appellations followed. Pas de Géant, AOP Languedoc, comes from young vines at Cazal Viehl, and that is just what the Languedoc has done, 'taken a giant's step'. The wine is supple and peppery. Faugères, Kinsale, named in recognition of Neasa's Irish roots, is a blend of Syrah and Grenache, with spice and freshness. Nord Sud Syrah has good peppery fruit, with varietal character. Next came a trio of St Chinian. Cazal Viel Vieilles Vignes comes mainly from Syrah planted in the 1970s and is aged partly in *foudres*, with some appealing spice. Bardou, a *lieu-dit*, is Syrah with just 5 per cent Grenache, with firm structure and spice after ageing for 14 months. Finally, Larmes des Fées is fermented in small *foudres*, with the malolactic fermentation and *élevage* in new oak, so that the wine is ripe and opulent with rich fruit, good structure and ageing potential.

Mas de la Chevalière

Béziers 34500

www.larochewines.com

Mas de la Chevalière is the *languedocien* outpost of the Chablis producer Domaine Laroche. Michel Laroche, who is no longer part of Domaine Laroche since its sale to Advini, bought Mas de la Chevalière in 1995, with a small eighteenth century château and sufficient land for the construction of a streamlined cellar. The purchase of vineyard land followed, so that they now farm 150 hectares, of which they own 40.

Their vineyards of Chardonnay are in an isolated spot in the hills, at the *lieu-dit* of Peyroli near Lunas, at an altitude of some 400–500 metres. We took a winding dirt track out of La Bousquet d'Orb, through the *garrigue* to emerge into a large vineyard. There is a week's difference in ripening between the top and the bottom of the steep slope, which faces north-west. The soil is stony limestone and perfect for Chardonnay. Wild boars are a problem, and electric wires protect the vines. Their other significant vineyard is in St Chinian, at Roqua Blanca, on land that once belonged to the nearby abbey of Fontcaude. It forms an amphitheatre of vines, with quite different terrain, and is much warmer and more Mediterranean. These vineyards were planted in 1999, 'in the spirit of Burgundy' as winemaker Géraud Blanc put it, with a denser planting than was the norm for the Languedoc at the time.

Back at the elegant château, I tasted a range of their wines. A Chardonnay Pays d'Oc was lightly buttery, kept on its lees in barrel. For this they own other vineyards and also have a partnership in Limoux, and another elsewhere in the Hérault. Peyroli is much more serious, made from the best grapes, pressed whole bunches, and kept in 500- and 600-litre barrels. Part of the wine does a malolactic fermentation, which is unusual in the Languedoc, and makes a nicely buttery palate, with some nutty notes, with texture and length, and balanced acidity.

A Viognier Pays d'Oc, coming from three partners with vineyards near Minervois, is lightly peachy. A fresh Pinot Noir, from Limoux, with red fruit and acidity, is given four or five days' cold maceration and then fermented, to reach about 27°C at the end of the fermentation. The final wine was Roqua Blanca, from 70 per cent Syrah and 30 per cent Grenache, of which a third is aged in 500-litre barrels, with some youthful, peppery fruit and ageing potential. A comparison of two vintages was intriguing, with the cooler 2012 more northern, and 2013 more southern and riper in character.

Domaines Paul Mas

Montagnac 34530
www.paulmas.com

Jean-Claude Mas started his business in 2000, with an inheritance of 35 hectares near Conas. He is a fourth generation *viticulteur*, but a first generation *vigneron*, with far-reaching ambitions. After a varied career, including working for Bernard Magrez and Domaines Virginie, with the help of his Japanese importer he bought Domaine Astruc in Limoux. He has steadily expanded his vineyard holdings – at the last count, he had 12 estates totalling 650 hectares, from the Gard to Limoux, with his most recent purchase being Château Lauriga in Roussillon. He would not consider buying a vineyard that was further than 15 minutes from the motorway.

The harvest usually takes about 13 weeks, from late August until the middle of October. Jean-Claude aspires to being fully organic by 2023, gradually increasing by 5–10 per cent each year. The main thing is to stop the use of chemicals for the treatment of mildew and oidium, and not to use herbicides or insecticides, but favour pheromones that create sexual confusion instead. He talked of the importance of biodiversity in the vineyards to revive the soil and also of the need to reduce the use of sulphur in the cellar. Accordingly, he makes a couple of wines without any sulphur at all. A further 1,300 or so hectares are farmed under contract with 80 partners, of which 10 partners are responsible for 60 per cent, with a *négociant* activity for purchased grapes, rather than wine.

It is an enormous enterprise, which has grown steadily, with numerous successful brands and labels. Jean-Claude would describe the style as Old World wines with a New World attitude; daring to be different. He emphasizes the modern technology, the rural roots, the *terroir* and the family business. The Mas style is affordable, full-bodied wine, with fruit and soft tannins,. He is best known for his label The Arrogant Frog, with its witty back label casting the frog as an endangered species. His aim is to control the entire production process from vine to bottle, so 70 per cent of his wine is made in his own cellars, with a further 20 per cent made in cellars where he is not the owner but is none the less in control, and the final 10 per cent bought *en vrac*. IGPs constitute 80 per cent of his port-folio. He exports to over 30 different countries and is a keen marketer, with a broad vision of the Languedoc, identifying areas where there is a good *rapport qualité–prix*. There is the traditional side of the Languedoc with appellations, while the IGPs represent the modern side. It is possible to do both and to be good at both; it is a meeting of cultures.

Jean-Claude Mas, Domaine Paul Mas

Jean-Claude is also very aware of the importance of wine tourism and has opened a restaurant, Côté Mas, near Montagnac. You eat well there, with a range of Domaines Mas wines on offer, but Jean-Claude is quite dispassionate: he does not make money from the restaurant but it is a vital showcase for his wines, with a tempting shop on the ground floor. Tasting with Jean-Claude is always a lively and demanding experience, with wines from all over the Languedoc. Each estate has its own personality.

Domaine Ste Rose

Servian 34290

www.sainterose.com

Ruth and Charles Simpson are an English couple who came to wine as a second career, buying Domaine Ste Rose to make their first wine in 2002. They had looked as far afield as Central Otago and Western Australia, but realized that they wanted to be closer to home and found Domaine Ste Rose, with an elegant nineteenth-century château, outside the village of Servian, with 40 hectares of vines. They replanted 20 hectares right away, pulling up Cinsaut and Aramon, and now have 43 hectares with 14 different grape varieties. They produce an extensive range of IGPs, mainly for the export market. Charles laughingly points out that they have made a new wine with each vintage. The most recent addition is their sparkling wine, and 2017 saw their first crop of Pinot Noir for still wine.

Having successfully established Ste Rose, they have taken on the new challenge of making sparkling wine in Kent, outside Canterbury. This prompted Charles to observe that in France wine is easy to make, but difficult to sell, whereas in England it is difficult to make and easy to sell. Having embarked on English sparkling wine, they felt they should make some sparkling wine in France as well, so they now produce a pure Chardonnay, Blanc de Blancs, Vin de France, given 30 months on the lees, and also a rosé from Pinot Noir, given 18 months on the lees, as well as an original sparkling Shiraz, with fresh fruit and a tannic streak. A *prestateur* in Marseilles fine tunes the sparkling wines for them.

Both Charles, especially with his previous experience in the corporate world of Glaxo, and Ruth have a developed sense of the market and work hard to produce wines that conform to those demands. They would describe their wines as Old World, using New World methods. Highlights among their still wines, which are all Pays d'Oc for simplicity's sake, include a punchy Sauvignon, Montagne et Mer, and Le Marin Blanc, a blend of Roussanne and Marsanne, with a hint of Viognier. There is a barrel-aged Roussanne with more depth. Coquille d'Oc is a blend of Syrah, Grenache Noir and Mourvèdre, while La Garrigue has more Grenache Noir than Syrah, with some spicy fruit. Les Derniers Cépages refers to the last two varieties to be harvested, Petit Verdot and Mourvèdre, which is rich and structured. Syrah le Pinnacle is co-fermented in barrel with 5 per cent Viognier, to give firm, youthful spice, and a Vin de France Roussanne comes from two rows of Roussanne, that were late harvested and almost forgotten when the grapes would not fit in the press. I left with a taste of lemony honey and fresh fruit.

CÔTES DE THONGUE

Some IGPs stand out more than others, usually those without a parallel appellation, such as the Côtes de Thongue, which covers villages on lower-lying land south of the appellations of Faugères and St Chinian. The Thongue is a tiny stream that flows into the Hérault near Pézenas. At the end of summer, it is barely a stream, but after heavy rain, it has the potential for serious flooding. Twenty-three villages make up the area, which is about 30 kilometres in length, forming a triangle between Faugères, Béziers and Pézenas, stretching from St Thibéry and Nézigan l'Eveque in the south to Neffiès and Vailhan in the north. There are now about 65 wine producers, with the 7 cooperatives playing a less important role than in some areas, accounting for between a quarter and a third of an average production of about 50–60,000 hectolitres. A few years ago, the Côtes de Thongue aspired to an appellation but that aim seems to have evaporated, meaning the area is less dynamic than it once was. However, as Guy Bascou from Domaine Condamine l'Evêque pointed out, the great advantage to being an IGP rather than an appellation is that 'we can do what we like, and we would lose that with the appellation', not to mention that the yield for the appellation would be 50 hectolitres per hectare as opposed to 80 for an IGP. There are some wine growers who focus on quality and work well, but opt for Pays d'Oc, or promote their own name, rather than Côtes de Thongue. Nonetheless the Côtes de Thongue does retain a certain identity, with the two largest producers committed to their area.

Producers

Domaine la Croix Belle

Puissalicon 34480
www.croix-belle.com

Here I must declare an interest, as Jacques and Françoise Boyer have become good friends since I wrote my book on the wines of the south of France and I often taste and drink their wines. Their tasting *caveau* is open most days during the summer months, and makes an ideal destination for friends in need of wine, with Françoise often there to give you a friendly welcome. Behind the *caveau* you can admire the enormous *foudres* that were once the tradition of the Languedoc. The village of Puissalicon now has a lively tapas bar and wine shop, Le Picomandil, which provides a second reason to go there.

Francoise Boyer, Domaine la Croix Belle

Jacques Boyer is an energetic man with a firm sense of purpose and a strong commitment to his region. He took over the family property in 1977 and bottled his first wine in 1984, not without fierce arguments with his father who could not see that quality, rather than quantity, would pay. The original focus of the region, as for most of the Languedoc, had been very much centred on the latter. Jacques now runs 142 hectares, all within a close radius of Puissalicon, which is an attractive *circulade* village. In the early days he replanted, changing the composition of his vineyards dramatically, replacing Aramon, Alicante Bouschet, Ugni Blanc and Carignan with Syrah, Mourvèdre, Chardonnay, Sauvignon Blanc and so on, and at the same time improving the viticultural practices, with denser plantings. The cellars have gradually been modernized and Jacques is very aware of new technological developments; one time I visited at harvest time and found him trialling a new mechanical sorting machine.

The range of wines, all Côtes de Thongue, is very logical. The entry level is Caringole, in three colours, but more interest comes from the next level, Les Champs. Champs des Lys is a blend of Grenache Blanc, Chardonnay and Sauvignon Blanc; Champs des Grillons rosé comes from Grenache Noir, Syrah and Cabernet; and there are two reds, Champs du Coq, from Syrah and Grenache Noir, and Champs des Calades, a contrasting blend with Cabernet and Syrah, aged in oak. There are also some single varietal wines, notably Muscat and Syrah, as well as Merlot and Chardonnay. Cascaillou, one of my favourites, is predominantly Grenache Noir, with some lovely rich fruit, and No 7 in all three colours is the flagship of the estate. The first vintage of the red was 1996, a blend of the Mediterranean and Bordeaux, with seven different grape varieties – apologies for the list but it demonstrates the diversity of the Côtes de Thongue – namely, Syrah, Mourvèdre, Cabernet Sauvignon, Grenache Noir, Merlot, Carignan and Cinsaut, aged in oak and demanding some bottle age. No 7 Blanc, first made in 1997, consists of Chardonnay, Viognier, Grenache Blanc, Sauvignon Blanc, Grenache Gris, Muscat à Petits Grains and Carignan Blanc. No 7 Rosé followed in 2012 and comes from almost the same varieties as No. 7 Rouge, but includes Petit Verdot rather than Cinsaut. The final *bonne bouche* is Soulenque, a late-harvest dessert wine made from a blend of Muscat, Viognier and Sauvignon Blanc, with delicious honeyed fruit. The name recalls the celebratory meal at the end of the harvest.

Domaine de l'Arjolle

Pouzolles 34480
www.arjolle.com

Domaine de l'Arjolle is a family estate, based in the village of Pouzolles, with large cellars and a smart tasting *caveau*. Altogether they have 110 hectares of vines in Pouzolles and the surrounding villages, including Margon, which is dominated by its imposing château, built by the architect Violet-le-Duc, who is best known for his restoration work on the city of Carcassonne. On earlier visits to Arjolle I have met Louis-Marie Teisserenc, who was an early pioneer of the Côtes de Thongue, planting an eclectic mixture of grape varieties, beginning with Sauvignon Blanc in 1981, and subsequently including Zinfandel and Carmenère. These days Louis-Marie has retired and it is the next generation that runs the estate, dividing their responsibilities, and including one outsider, Geoffroy de la Besnardière, who I met on my last visit. They make an extensive range of wines, all Côtes de Thongue, with just two exceptions, Zinfandel and Carmenère, which are Vin de France. The name Arjolle means a small clay amphora in Occitan and the elegant outline of half an amphora features on all their labels and barrels.

Louis-Marie and François Teisserenc, Domaine de L'Arjolle

Geoffroy treated us to an extensive tasting, but by no means included all the different wines they produce. The Equilibre range implies wines that are easy to drink; then there is Equinoxe with more depth; Paradoxe, with a red and a white; and Etonnant that includes both the Zinfandel and the Carmenère, as well as an original Chardonnay, Dernière Cueillette. We compared Equlibre and Equinoxe Chardonnays; the first was lightly buttery with only a tiny amount of *élevage*, while Equinoxe comes from riper grapes and is aged in barrel from October to May, with some *bâtonnage* so that the oak is well integrated. A blend of Sauvignon and Viognier Equilibre had some fresh, pithy fruit, while the Viognier was more apparent in the Equinoxe, with more oak ageing. Geoffroy observed that they are obsessed with freshness and acidity in the grapes; they must not be picked too early, but certainly not too late. Paradoxe, also from Viognier and Sauvignon, is a selection of the best barrels, with more weight and oak.

With such a diversity of grapes, the harvest takes two months, beginning with Sauvignon in the middle of August to the last Cabernet Sauvignon around mid-October. Syrah Equilibre is fresh and peppery; Equinoxe Merlot Cabernet had some appealing cassis fruit, resembling a ripe claret. The Carmenère vines came from Bordeaux and two-thirds of the wine is aged in barrel for 12 months, giving tannin and dry spice. Zinfandel is very rich and generous, with black fruit, and rounded tannins. Arlequin, currently a blend of Cabernet Franc, Syrah, Grenache Noir and Cabernet Sauvignon, but shortly changing to just Cabernet Franc and Syrah, is rounded and elegant with black fruit and ageing potential. The first vintage of Arlequin was 2012 and it illustrates how the estate is moving with the times, recognizing Cabernet Franc in the Languedoc as being more successful than Cabernet Sauvignon, but tempered with the more southern flavours of Syrah. They are wondering what to plant next – maybe Pinotage?

Domaine Condamine l'Evêque
Nézignan l'Evêque 34120
g.bascou@wanadoo.fr

Guy Bascou and his son Guilhem at Domaine Condamine l'Evêque in Nézignan l'Evêque fit into several areas and appellations, for they make Picpoul de Pinet, Côtes de Thongue and AOP Languedoc. It is Guilhem who is now in charge of the winemaking. He studied oenology at Montpellier and then spent six months with Roederer in California, followed by some time at Robertson in South Africa, returning to the family estate in 1997. Guy himself is *un fils de vigneron* from the village of Pomerols, with his grandfather founding the cooperative of Pomerols (see p. 203). Guy's Picpoul de Pinet is produced under the auspices of that cooperative.

At Condamine l'Evêque they have always grown an enormous variety of different grapes, Viognier, Sauvignon Blanc, Muscat à Petits Grains, Piquepoul and Petit Manseng, and for red, Syrah, Mourvèdre, Merlot, Cabernet Sauvignon, Petit Verdot, Cinsaut, and Marselan, which is a Grenache Noir–Cabernet Sauvignon cross. Altogether the estate totals 65 hectares. Condamine means 'master's field' and all the wines are named after former bishops of Agde, who had a palace in Nézignan l'Evêque. They preferred to live inland, because of the danger of malaria on the coast.

A tasting chez Bascou includes various Côtes de Thongue, such as Sophrose, a pithy Sauvignon; Fronime, a grapey Muscat à Petits Grains; a peachy Viognier; Georges, a Mourvèdre; and Vermiste, a Syrah with some peppery notes. Château la Condamine l'Evêque, AOP Languedoc, is a selection of the best plots of Syrah and Mourvèdre, from vines that are 40 years old, giving good fruit and body with ripe spice. A lovely finale was Folie Douce, which comes from Petit Manseng harvested in December and kept in *demi-muids*, with no sulphur, so that it ferments very slowly for two or three years, stopping naturally when the yeasts are exhausted. The colour of this dessert wine was golden amber, and it had intriguing notes of orange, dried figs, walnuts and orange marmalade with some refreshing acidity.

Lou Belvestit
Magalas 34480
www.loubelvestit.com

This estate is a relative newcomer to the Côtes de Thongue. Emilie Alauze and her sister took over family vineyards, bottling their first wine in 2011. They have built a new cellar, with cheerful, purple concrete vats, which they used for the first time in 2016. Emilie laughingly recalled that she had assumed that the choice of colour for your vats was either grey or red, so she was thrilled to discover that other options were possible and the colourful vats certainly provide a welcome splash of colour. Altogether they have 19 hectares, mainly outside Magalas, including some Carignan planted in 1947, as well as Aramon, Grenache Noir, Cinsaut and Syrah. The Cabernet Sauvignon and Merlot go to the *négoce* and they have just planted some white varieties, Grenache Blanc, Carignan Blanc and Roussanne. The Côtes de Thongue is put in bottle and the rest of their production is sold as Pays d'Oc *en vrac*.

The wines are given names that relate to members of the family, so Carignan Maem is for her sister Marie, as well as Emilie. It displayed some convincing red fruit on both nose and palate, with a *sympathique* touch of rusticity on the finish. Emilie explained that she had tried carbonic maceration but was not convinced by it; however, she likes Carignan for its particular character, which you do not find anywhere else. L'Embe, for her mother Béatrice, is a blend of Syrah and Carignan, with youthful fruit. Roem, for her father Roland, is a pure Syrah, and most original of all is a Vin de France, a pure Aramon, with ripe fruit, hints of the *garrigue*, and a rustic finish. It was a surprising example of a much-despised grape variety that is possibly beginning to establish a new reputation. As Emilie observed, the image of Aramon is one of overproduction, it was the grape variety of her grandparents, but other grape varieties can overproduce too. It can oxidize easily and is not suitable for barrel ageing, but vinified in vat, it makes for enjoyable, easy drinking.

Emilie is optimistic. Asked about the typicity or originality of the Côtes de Thongue, she talked of its diversity, the variety of different styles of wine, and pointed out that above all it is *une histoire d'hommes*, a story of the people who developed the region. There is more liberty than with an appellation, with a more relaxed *cahier des charges*. 'You can play with the blends and bring out the best of each vintage.'

HAUTE VALLÉE DE L'ORB

There are two areas of the Languedoc where Pinot Noir grows particularly successfully. The first is Limoux, where it is often used for sparkling wine, but also produces exemplary still wine as Haute Vallée de l'Aude. The second area is the Haute Vallée de l'Orb, where there is no parallel appellation. That covers the area between Bédarieux in the south, with the most northern vines at Joncels above Lunas.

Producers

Domaine de Bon Augure
Joncels 34650
www.domainedebonaugure.fr

The Faugères producer Abbaye Sylva Plana has a vineyard of Chardonnay at Joncels, at Domaine de Bon Augure, not too far from the Chardonnay vineyards of Mas de la Chevalière. They make the wine in the '*esprit de* Chablis', with the harvest as much as two months later than in Alignan where they have Chardonnay for Côtes de Thongue. They consider it a great area for white wine, with an altitude of 400 metres, and half of the wine is fermented and aged in barrel, giving acidity and minerality. There are two further wines from white varieties: a Chardonnay, with just 10 per cent Petit Manseng, which spends 12 months in barrel, and an orange wine, from Grenache Gris, Sauvignon and Chardonnay. Their first vintage of Pinot Noir, Les Petits Apôtres, was 2017.

Domaine de Clovallon

Bédarieux 34600
domaine@clovallon.fr

I first visited this estate, just outside Bédarieux, back at the end of the 1990s when Catherine Roque was making an original range of wines that included grape varieties not usually found in the Languedoc, as well as exemplary Pinot Noir, notably Les Pomarèdes. These days Catherine concentrates on Faugères at Mas d'Alezon (see p. 160) while her daughter, Alix, runs Clovallon, with her first official solo vintage in 2014. Alix studied in Montpellier and has worked around the world, in Chile, Tasmania, for Louis Latour and notably for Marie-Thérèse Chappaz, an inspirational biodynamic wine grower in the Vaud in Switzerland. Alix is very aware that she has taken on a 30-year heritage since her mother made her first wine at Clovallon, but things will continue to evolve. She probably has a more natural approach than her mother, so some *cuvées* will remain and she will develop new ones, from 10 hectares of vines, with as many grape varieties.

Her first new *cuvée* is Les Indigènes, which comes from an extraordinary secret garden, a walled 1-hectare vineyard, approached by the narrowest of roads, in the hills above Bédarieux. The original vineyard was planted in the 1850s, ungrafted as the soil is quite sandy; inevitably some vines have been replaced but others survive, and Alix made her first wine from it in 2016. There is Oeillade, Servant, Aramon, Terret, Bourboulenc, Clairette, Jacquez, Carignan, Cinsaut, Alicante and Muscat, all mixed up together. The vines were farmed conventionally, and now that Alix is cultivating them biodynamically, life is returning to the soil. The flavours are intriguing with perfumed fruit and supple tannins.

Aurièges, a blend of Viognier, Roussanne, Petit Manseng, Petite Arvine, Clairette and Riesling, is given a long maceration until the following August to make an orange wine with structure. I tasted the 2016, from vat, in early September 2017; the grapes had been pressed on 2 August and the wine had some firm tannins with grip. As for the 2015, the Riesling had spent ten months in vat and the other varieties in barrel, and as well as tannin there was some peachy fruit, with sweetness on the finish. There are usually two *cuvées* of Pinot Noir, but in September 2017 Alix was licking her wounds; her vineyards had been devastated by frost, so that she had lost as much as 90 per cent of her crop. It was the first time that had happened for 50 years. Normally she would have made two Pinot Noirs, one simpler and the other, Les Pomarèdes, from a single vineyard with more depth and flavour. In 2016, she also tried her hand at a Pinot Noir *en blanc*, which smelt and tasted not unlike champagne, but without the bubbles. It was original and intriguing.

Alix is very enthusiastic about her patch of the Languedoc. It is a zone of hills, where everything is possible. That is the advantage of the Haute Vallée; she would much rather be here than in a more rigid appellation, although she does not actually use the label Haute Vallée de l'Orb.

Les Coteaux de Capimont

Hérépian 34600
www.coteaux-capimont.com

The cooperative at Hérépian is probably the most enthusiastic protagonist of the Haute Vallée de l'Orb, with an attractive range of wines under the brand name Vallée des Arômes. The cooperative was founded in 1939, and now covers about 280 hectares around St Gervais, Olargues and Bédarieux. The wines are mainly single varietals, refreshing examples of Chardonnay, Sauvignon and Muscat, amongst others, that benefit from the cool nights and cooler conditions of the valley, enhancing the natural aromas of the grape.

Le Temps des Cerises

Le Mas Blanc, La Tour-sur-Orb 34260
Tel: +33 (0)6 87 77 56 37

Axel Prüfer has a cellar in a small hamlet between Bédarieux and La Tour-sur-Orb. He came to winemaking, and indeed natural winemaking, by a circuitous route, arriving in France in 1998, from East Germany, in order to avoid military service. He had no money and spoke no French but got a job as picker in the Pic St Loup, where the neighbouring estate of Mas Foulaquier triggered his interest in *vin nature*. Then he travelled, visiting other natural wine growers, including some of the original pioneers like Marcel Lapierre in Beaujolais. His girlfriend came into a small inheritance and they bought their cellar, which was in a state of ruin, needing urgent repairs to the roof, and rented some vines. Axel made his first wine in this cellar in 2004. We sat there and chatted, sipping a glass of Avanti Populo, with Axel apologizing that he was not able to offer a tasting of his 2016s because they were not yet '*en place*'. Avanti Populo is pure Carignan, and the name a revolutionary slogan. He does not add any carbon dioxide to the vat because that can make the tannins hard, and he does not use any sulphur. The grapes are hand-picked and chilled so that the fermentation starts gently and takes its natural course, without any temperature control, in an open top tronconic vat. The flavours were fresh and juicy.

Axel now owns 7 hectares on the *causses* above Bédarieux, including Chardonnay, Cinsaut and Grenache. He makes what he calls a *gamme horizontale*, avoiding blends, and preferring *les parcellaires*, which show a definite sense of place. La Peur du Rouge is Chardonnay; Cuvée Brutal is based on Cinsaut; Un Pas de Côté comes from Grenache Noir on limestone; and Les Lendemains qui Chantent is a second Grenache, which ripens last and usually gets eaten by the wild boars. He also makes a Pét-Nat, which is fermented dry before late-harvest juice is added and the wine bottled. Maybe he might try a red Pét-Nat.

Talking to Axel about *vin nature*, he insists upon transparency: 'You say what you do and you do want you say, and it must also be a *vin de terroir*.' Some people do not care about *terroir*, but he does, passionately. Nor does he have an oenologist. Would he be a wine producer if he had not discovered natural wine? He is not sure. He is a passionate purist, with an engaging sense of humour.

VIN DE FRANCE

Producers

Domaine de la Fontude
Brenas 34650
www.lafontude.fr

François Aubry works from his cellar at Mas du Blanc just outside the little village of Brenas. This is one of the wetter areas of the Languedoc, with as much as 1,200 millimetres of annual rainfall. However, François is also able to irrigate with water from the lac de Salagou, which is sometimes essential because the soil is very free draining, with small water reserves. Technically his vineyards are not in the Haute Vallée de l'Orb, but would be part of the Coteaux du Salagou. However, he does not have the red soil that is really typical of those vineyards and, as it happens, he prefers to use the Vin de France label for all his wines. As well as 5 hectares of vines, planted with Terret Blanc, Cinsaut, Grenache, Carignan and a little Aramon, he has a flock of 25 sheep.

His first vintage was 2003. He studied ecology at Montpellier, with agriculture and winemaking coming later. Essentially, he is self-taught, favouring biodynamics, with natural compost from his flock, and minimum intervention in the cellar. He does not have an oenologist and laughingly observed that it is his bank manager who advises him to add sulphur, as then he can sell his wine quicker! We chatted and tasted wines from vat in his simple cellar. Jour de Fête, Terret Bourret, kept in vat, is firm and stony with good acidity, despite undergoing a malolactic fermentation. Carnaval rosé is a refreshing blend of Grenache and Cinsaut; Pierre de Lune is a pure Grenache Noir, grown on basalt, with ripe cherry fruit and spicy minerality; Entremonde comes from Carignan, with a little Grenache, Aramon and Cinsaut, fermented together, with some structure and fruit; and finally Fontitude is a pure Cinsaut, with fresh vibrant fruit. You sense that François is a thoughtful winemaker, with a strong sense of independence, and very much his own man.

Domaine Ribiera
Aspiran 34800
www.ribiera.com

Régis and Christine Pichon are also natural winemakers, with a firm sense of purpose and commitment. He comes from Brittany, from the most westerly point of Finistère, and I spotted the Breton flag flying at the entrance to their property. He has already had a career in Paris as a sommelier and wine merchant, and studied at the *école viticole* in Mâcon. Quite simply, sunshine brought him to the Languedoc. They drove 10,000 kilometres all over the south to find '*un bel endroit*', arriving here in 2005 when it was still relatively easy to find vineyards for sale. These days there is more pressure on the vineyards, as the children of the cooperative members are tending to take over their parents' vineyards, either staying in the cooperative, or creating new estates. The name

Ribiera comes from the Occitan for river, and the Hérault runs nearby.

Régis makes an intriguing range of wines, and you sense that he loves to experiment. Nothing stands still so his wines follow the spirit of the year. He admits to a low boredom threshold, 'but vines are long-term and impose their own rhythm', which he accepts. He works biodynamically, but also makes decisions according to the actual conditions in the vineyards. Good Friday is apparently the absolute worst day to do anything in the biodynamic calendar. Sometimes Régis makes two versions of a wine, with and without sulphur to see the difference and he is not interested in new wood. His cellar is mainly full of fibreglass vats. In the vineyard, he favours the grape varieties that can cope with drought, namely Cinsaut and Clairette.

Causse Toujours is a blend of Grenache and Cinsaut, with vibrant red fruit, and balancing acidity and tannin. Régis noted that he now does less *pigeage* than in earlier years; indeed he has almost given up *pigeage* and just does a couple of *remontages*. He does not press his grapes, preferring just to use the free-run juice. Cinsaut has very thin skins and liberates the juice easily. Tintorella, meaning balance in Occitan, comes from Cinsaut with a little Grenache Noir, kept in vat, with firm spicy, black cherries. Amassa, meaning *assemblé* or blended in Occitan, is Cinsaut and Grenache, blended in April and bottled in July with a waning moon. The Grenache fills out the Cinsaut. La Vista comes from 40-year-old Cinsaut with perfumed cherry fruit. Our tasting finished with a Cartagène, from Grenache, which was ripe and opulent. Then we went to look at the remains of the Roman villa outside the village of Aspiran, where you can still see the vestiges of the *dolia* or vats.

Domaine Gregory White

Aspiran 34800
Tel: +33 (0)6 63 22 57 85

Despite his name, Gregory is French. Although his father is English, he was born in Paris and has spent all his life in France. Wine represents a complete career change for him, as he was originally a sports journalist based in Paris, but his wife comes from the Médoc and he admits to a road to Damascus moment in some vineyards there. He then went on to study oenology in Beaune. He bought two plots of old vines, totalling 5 hectares in the village of Aspiran. Although they are classified Pézenas for the red wine and Languedoc for white, Gregory prefers to make

Vin de France because the administrative hassle is so much less. He has replanted the old vineyards with Grenache Noir, Syrah, Cinsaut, Carignan and for white wine Terret and Grenache Blanc.

Gregory's first vintage was 2013, made in shared rented cellar space in the village of Aspiran and he makes his wines as naturally as possible, using natural yeast and as little sulphur as possible, preferably none at bottling, but 'it is not a dogma'. He produces the best grapes possible, picking them all by hand, and favours fairly short macerations and daily *remontages*. So far, he has not tried any *élevage* in oak; he favours fruit. His labels are witty. White is Blanc, from two parts Terret to one part Grenache Blanc, is firm, stony and structured. Terret does not have a lot of aroma, but it does have acidity, and Grenache Blanc gives drinkability.

White is Rosé is a pure Cinsaut, *saignée* after a few hours, with a perfumed nose. Jamais Pas Soif, from Grenache Noir, Cinsaut and Carignan, with a classic vinification of destemmed grapes, has some spicy red fruit, with a slightly rustic note from the Carignan. White is Rouge is based on Syrah and the oldest Carignan with a little Grenache and Cinsaut, and is more structured and peppery. In 2014 Gregory had made two versions of this wine, with and without sulphur, and found that the sulphur closed up the wine. When I suggested that I often found natural wines lost their regional characteristics, he explained that the cool carbonic maceration favoured by many producers diminishes any regional differences, making Carignan taste like Gamay.

Domaine de la Colombette

Béziers 34500
www.lacolombette.fr

Domaine de la Colombette is a large estate outside Béziers. Altogether the Pugibet family has three estates, amounting to 250 hectares, run by François and, increasingly, his son Vincent, who began working with his father in 1997. Domaine de la Colombette first came to notice for producing some particularly successful Chardonnay in the 1990s, and then they developed a range of wines, Plume, with lower alcohol levels, for which the excess alcohol is removed by a process of osmosis. Their aim for these wines, one of each colour, is drinkability. As Vincent notes, alcohol is essential for wine, but it is also a drug, and it is a question of the appropriate dose. A little can be very beneficial, and can invigorate us, but too much and the flavours of a wine can be masked, and we become less perceptive. White Plume, based on Chardonnay, is light and refreshing; the rosé comes from Grenache Noir, with some delicate fruit; and Red Plume, a blend of Grenache Noir and Syrah, is supple and easy. They may not be great wines but they perform a useful role and account for half their total production.

The Pugibets' current research is concentrated on developing vines with an inbuilt resistance to disease, notably to oidium. They are horrified by the amount of pesticide used by the French wine industry, with the average grower treating their vines 14 times per year; in Champagne that figure rises to as much 23 times. Happily, in the Languedoc, with the drying winds, usually only about 7 treatments are necessary. However, the apple industry is overall the worst offender, with as many as 20 treatments. The Pugibets were already farming organically but organic viticulture allows for the use of copper and sulphur, and copper is a heavy metal that stays in the soil. Since it does not disappear it is simply not ecological. Consequently, they have been working on producing grape varieties that will resist oidium, crossing existing local varieties with *Vitis amurensis*, which has some resistance to rot. I tasted a white wine that is a crossing of Sauvignon and Muscat with *Vitis amurensis*, with delicate herbal notes and a touch of citrus. It is a Vin de France. Creux du Nid, both red and white, also come from experimental vines, with some convincing flavours. When François Pugibet compared the use of pesticides to the use of asbestos, his message really struck home.

Domaine Coutelou
Puimisson 34480
www.coutelou.fr

Jean-François (Jeff) Coutelou has 13 hectares of vines, as well as 400 olive trees. His father planted his oldest vines back in 1966 and the estate has been organic since 1987. He was one of the pioneers of organic viticulture in the Hérault, when there were just seven organic wine growers in the department, with a total of just 40 hectares, registered with Nature et Progrès. These days Jeff is an ardent exponent of biodiversity. The soil in his vineyards is very mixed, with several different grape varieties: Syrah, Grenache, Carignan, Mourvèdre and Cinsaut for reds, and for whites Sauvignon Blanc, Muscat and a little Viognier, as well as some more recently planted Grenache Gris, Macabeo, Clairette Musqué and Carignan Blanc, plus just 120 plants of Castet, a rare red variety that you also find at Château Simone in Palette. Jeff is continuing his interest in old vine varieties with plantings of Terret Blanc and Noir, Morastel, Piquepoul, Ribeyrenc Noir and Gris and Aramon Noir and Gris.

Back at the cellar in the village, that number of grape varieties raises the question: how many wines does he make? The answer is that it depends on the year. In 2015, he made eighteen; and in 2016, just four. The wine named after his address in Puimisson, 7 rue de la Pompe, is a constant, a blend of Syrah, with a little Grenache. Jeff follows the precepts of the Association des Vins Natures and does not add any sulphur. If the grapes are healthy, the sulphur comes naturally. I have also enjoyed the Vin des Amis, with fresh fruit, reminiscent of liqueur cherries. Flambadou is a pure Carignan, and Mourvèdre just that.

I thought our tasting had finished, when Jeff said, 'but you haven't seen the other cellar'. Little did we know that he is a master of soleras for dessert wine, making the most deliciously matured Grenache, but without any *mutage*, or addition of alcohol. The cellar itself is a treasure trove of old wine artefacts, with walls covered with old vineyard equipment. Jeff showed us an old box that was used for sending a small sample of wine in the post; you put the stamp directly onto the box. As for the wines, which Jeff calls, *pépites*, or nuggets, we tasted from a series of barrels, lovely mature wines that had spent three years or more in old wood, making for a flavour of walnuts with hints of orange, not unlike a Tuscan Vin Santo; another reminded me of an oloroso sherry. Some were sweeter; some were drier, with length and depth, layers of flavour and great complexity. Words began to fail me and for some reason my tasting notes became increasingly less coherent. It was a wonderful example of the unexpected; you never quite know what you will encounter in a Languedoc cellar.

23

VINTAGES SINCE 2000

The Mediterranean climate is generally temperate so that vintage variations are much less extreme than in northern France, but there are differences none the less, with varying amounts of sunshine and, more significantly, varying amounts of rain, affecting the water stress, *stress hydrique*, of the vines. In an ideal world, the water reserves are replenished during the winter, spring is mild and the summer warm and sunny, with a couple of storms, usually around the two public holidays of the summer, 14 July and 15 August, to refresh the vines. September should be dry and sunny for the harvest, with the weather beginning to break around the equinox. But each year brings its own variations on the theme. The wine growers can expect enough sunshine to ripen their grapes; the key quality question these days, especially with the growing awareness of global warming, is drought and rain. The amount of rainfall may not have changed significantly; what has changed is when it rains. The harvest date is generally earlier than even ten years ago. The CIVL's vintage report of 2000 talks of the harvest starting on 15 September; in 2017, most of the Languedoc had finished picking by that date. Generally, however, the growers of the Languedoc are less concerned by specific differences than in Bordeaux and Burgundy, especially as the concept of wines for ageing is relatively recent in the Languedoc. Obviously, there are quite considerable local variations in the climate between the cooler regions of Limoux and Malepère and the Haute Vallée de l'Orb and parts of the Terrasses du Larzac compared with the warmer areas of Pézenas and the Grés de Montpellier.

2017

Without exaggeration, this is one of the most difficult vintages the Languedoc has ever experienced. Frost was the first problem in late April, with the vegetation well advanced after an early spring. Some areas were affected more than others, with the cooler parts such Malepère, Limoux, Cabardès and the Haute Vallée de l'Orb particularly badly hit, but there were patches of damage elsewhere. There was no serious rain from the middle of May until after the harvest, so the combination of frost and drought had an impact on the quantity, resulting in an average 20–30 per cent reduction in crop, and sometimes more. However, the quality was very good, with very healthy grapes, and despite the summer drought, the wines have retained their freshness and fruit. The comment was made that with a little rain at the right moment, the quality could have been great rather than merely very good. These are wines that will offer enjoyable drinking in years to come.

2016

A mild winter and an early bud break, followed by a dry summer, one of the driest since 1943 and 1944, resulted inevitably in a small crop. However, the quality was good, with beautifully balanced wines, that have elegance and freshness. The one real disaster of the year was the hail storm that hit the Pic St Loup on 17 August, devastating half the vineyards of the appellation.

2015

A regular year that started with winter rain, followed by some spring rain, so the vines did not suffer from drought. In most areas there was enough sunshine, neither too much nor too little, combined with cool nights. There was a little hail in the Terrasses du Larzac at the end of August, and some in La Clape in the middle of June. Limoux harvested early, in mid-August, as did Cabardès. Overall the quality is very good, the result of beautifully balanced, ripe grapes.

2014

This was quite a challenging year. The first six months of the year were drier than usual, with a warm spring, and a May that was more like July in temperature, resulting in an earlier bud break. There was some hail in La Clape and in the Minervois. The summer itself was relatively cool, with the first couple of weeks of September warm and sunny, but then came the rain, which caused problems for those with later-ripening varieties and those who favour a late harvest. However, on the whole the wines are balanced, with freshness and fruit, and developing well.

2013

The Languedoc fared very much better than the rest of France, with 320 days of sunshine. The spring was cool and the summer was late, with a late harvest, as much as three weeks later than usual, and the latest for 30 years. The Muscats were not picked until the end of August, a whole month later than in 2017. However, the grapes were very healthy, and the wines have benefited from the cool summer night-time temperatures to give wines with balance and elegance.

2012

Winter was dry, with a very cold February. The spring was cool, and rain allowed replenishment of the water reserves. July was cool and August hot; September was overcast, but there was no rain. Corbières considers 2012 a cooler, more complicated year. However, the grapes were generally healthy, making elegantly fruity wines with good acidity, but less concentration than in some years.

2011

September made the vintage, with ideal harvest conditions. A dry January and February were followed by heavy rains in March, and then a warm April with an early bud break. May was also hot, which meant an early flowering. The summer was mixed, hot and cold, and there were some storms in August. Minervois considers it an ideal year, with sufficient but not too much water. The wines are balanced, with fresh fruit and acidity.

2010

Winter rains ensured good water reserves, so there was no water stress. The spring was cool and the warm weather arrived at the end of June. August was hot, but with cool nights, making for a later harvest than usual and a lower than average crop. Corbières claimed textbook weather. Overall the wines have great balance and are drinking well. Comparisons have been made with other great Languedoc vintages – 2001, 2005 and 2007.

2009

A normal winter, followed by a wet April and a warm May, so that the vegetation was ahead of its cycle. The summer was late, with June and July enjoying cool nights, and then August brought a heatwave. The grapes were healthy, the harvest early, and yields were between 10 and 40 per cent below average.

2008

A small but healthy crop. The winter was mild, with little rain. Bud break was early, with a wet spring, followed by some rain in June. July and August were mainly dry with some localized hail. Faugères had a dramatic hailstorm the week before the harvest was due to start, on 4 September. This was one of the coolest vintages of the past ten years, and the harvest generally started ten days later than in 2007.

2007

A mild, dry winter was followed by a warm, wet spring and an early bud break. The summer was dry, but cooler than usual, until mid-August, when the temperatures rose. The fine weather continued throughout the harvest, and the crop was small, but good, in contrast with many other parts of France. Enthusiasm for the vintage was widespread, with fresh, balanced wines

2006

There was good rain, and even some snow in January, so the water reserves were replenished. A cool spring followed, with good weather at flowering. Overall a hotter year than either 2007 or 2005, with a very warm July, leading to talk of a heatwave, and then a storm on 15 August. Muscats were picked as early as the middle of August. Some hail in Limoux. Comparison were made with 2003, but with the difference of better water reserves. Le Grand Vin Blanc from Château d'Anglès in La Clape was drinking beautifully when it was ten years old, illustrating the unexpected ageing potential of the white wines of the Languedoc.

2005

A wet winter made for good water reserves. Spring was late and the summer warm, with rainfall at the appropriate moment. Some heavy rain just before the harvest caused some problems but the ensuing Indian summer produced ripe fruit and beautifully balanced wines. The best wines have lasted well.

2004

The climatic conditions were described as capricious. A wet autumn in 2003 made for good water reserves. The weather was good at flowering and there were storms in late August and early September; the grapes ripened slowly and conditions were cooler, especially in comparison to 2003, making for ripe grapes with good acidity levels. A 2004 Limoux Chenin Blanc from Château Rives Blanques evidently benefited from the good levels of acidity and was drinking beautifully when it was 11 years old. Cantilène from Domaine Ste Eulalie in the Minervois was another star at a similar age.

2003

The year of the heatwave. However, there was no drought because there had been heavy rainfall during winter. The spring was fairly dry and the summer very hot and dry, with temperatures reaching 40°C. A little rain in mid-August refreshed the vines. Inevitably the harvest was early, with very ripe grapes, and the later-ripening varieties like Carignan and Mourvèdre performed well. With lower acidity levels, the wines will have lasted less well than some.

2002

Generally a wet year, described by some as *une année terrible*. Rain at the end of August and in September complicated the harvest, with floods in the eastern half of the Languedoc, while the western part of the region fared much better. The wines are generally quite light and delicate, but none the worse for that, with more weight and concentration in Minervois and Corbières.

2001

A dry year with a warm spring and a dry summer with a couple of good storms. The dry summer made for ripe fruit, with good sugar levels and concentration. Cool nights and drying north winds also helped the ripening process and contributed to the quality, making wines with good ageing potential. A pair of Faugères were drinking beautifully when they were 15 years old, and also a St Chinian from Domaine Borie-la-Vitarèle.

2000

The floods of November 1999 had affected about 400 hectares of vines, mainly in the Corbières, but with no lasting damage. Vines are remarkably resilient. July was relatively cool, and followed by a hot August and early September, so that the grapes ripened well with an excellent *état sanitaire*. Some of the wines are quite long-lived, notably a 2000 Mas d'Alezon enjoyed in September 2017, and a Fitou, Jean Sirven from Domaine Bertrand Bergé, was delicious in November 2016. The difficulty is in finding these older vintages, since they are not generally available on the market.

GLOSSARY

Some French winemaking terms are so much more precise and less clumsy than the equivalent English term, and the same goes for wine descriptions too. If you are talking to French winemakers inevitably some French words creep into the notes and the subsequent text.

Aligot. Delicious creamy mashed potato, liberally laced with garlic and cream.

Are. Historical unit of measurement, equivalent to 100 square metres.

Arrachage. Pulling up of vines; in the past growers were paid a subsidy to do so, with *primes d'arrachage*.

Assemblage. Blend.

Barrique. Barrel of 225 litres.

Bastide. Country house.

Bâtisse. A large building, edifice.

Bâtonnage. Lees stirring.

Bonbonne. A demijohn or large glass jar used to store wine outside to turn it into *rancio*.

Bordelais. Adjective of Bordeaux, often used in the context of barrels.

Buvabilité. Literally, drinkability.

Cahier des charges. The document that lays down the regulations of the appellation and what the wine producer may or may not do.

Capitelle. Little dry-stone building that looks like an igloo.

Carbonic maceration. A method of fermentation whereby whole bunches are put into a vat filled with carbon dioxide and left to ferment. Contrary to a usual fermentation, the pressed juice is better than the free-run juice.

Cépage. Grape variety.

Cépage améliorateur. Describes grape varieties like Syrah, Grenache Noir and Mourvèdre, which were seen to improve the once despised Carignan and Aramon.

Champenois. Adjective, from Champagne.

Chapeau flottant. A cover for a vat, for which the height can be adjusted.

Circulade. A traditional village of the Languedoc, built in a circle around a central point for reasons of defence.

CIVL. Comité des vins du Languedoc, which runs the appellations of the region.

Commune. The unit into which French departments are divided; it can be big or small.

Compagne (f)/Compagnon (m). Emotional, but not necessarily business, partner.

Complanté. Grape varieties planted together in a vineyard, making for a field blend.

Cru. Literally, a growth, and part of the French wine hierarchy.

Cuvaison. Time in vat with grape skins in contact with the juice.

Cuvée. Almost a synonym for a wine; a wine grower will produce several different *cuvées* or wines.

Cuverie. Tanks in a cellar.

Débutter. Unearthing of the vines.

Défricher. To clear scrubland or *garrigue*.

Délimitation parcellaire. The precise delimitation of vineyard plots within an appellation.

Demi-muids. Usually about a 500- to 600-litre barrel.

Dosage. For sparkling wine, the addition of some sugar, with some wine, after disgorgement to determine the final degree of sweetness.

Élevage. Literally, 'the rearing'; the educating or ageing of wine, usually in barrel.

En echalas. A vine planted with just one supporting post and without any wires.

Enjambeur. A tractor that is high enough to straddle a row of vines; used in high-density vineyards.

En vrac. Wine in bulk.

Esca. Vine trunk disease.

Fermage. Term for renting a vineyard.

Finesse. Tasting term that implies elegance.

Foudres. Large barrels, anything from 5 to 500 hectolitres.

Fraîcheur. Freshness, but even more so, with a certain refreshing quality.

Fût de chêne. Oak barrel, usually small.

Galets roulées. Large, round pebbles, most typical of the vineyards of Châteauneuf-du-Pape but also found quite extensively in the Languedoc.

Garrigue. Mediterranean scrubland, with the typical vegetation of laurel, thyme, juniper, cistus and so on.

Gobelet. Bush vines.

Gourmand. Literally greedy, but when describing a wine, implies rich, warm and appealing flavours.

Grappillon. Small, unripe grape bunch.

Grand cru. Literally, a 'great growth', above *premier cru* in the pecking order.

Gras. Literally, 'fat'; a wine with some weight.

Gris. A term used to describe a grape variety that has a pale pink skin when ripe, such as Grenache Gris as opposed to Noir or Blanc.

Histoires de clochers. Literally a 'story of bell towers'; in other words, parish politics.

IGP. Indication Géographique Protégée, the term which has replaced *vin de pays*.

INAO. Institute National des Appellations d'Origine, the government body that controls all the details of an appellation.

INRA. Institut National de la Recherche Agronomique, the French national institute for research in the agricultural sciences.

Intercep. Piece of vineyard equipment that enables you to weed mechanically between the vines within the row.

Jarre. Amphora.

Lattes/sur lattes. For sparkling wine, describing the resting time on the lees of the second fermentation. *Lattes* are the boards that support the bottles.

Lieu-dit. Small plot of land on a map; literally, 'place named'.

Liquoreux. Very sweet; richer than moelleux.

Lutte raisonnée. Sustainable viticulture; you think before you spray, rather than spraying irrespective of climatic conditions.

Maison de maître. A substantial village house of serious proportions.

Marcottage. The traditional way of propagating a vine. A vine shoot, still attached to the vine, is pushed into the ground, so that it grows roots. It may then be cut from the parent vine.

Matière. Literally, 'matter'; implies a wine with some substance.

Mazet. Small building in the vineyards.

Méthode traditionnelle. Champagne method for sparkling wine.

Moelleux. Lightly sweet.

Monocépage. Single grape variety in a wine.

Mutage. The stopping of the alcoholic fermentation by the addition of grape spirit, for the production of *vin doux naturel*. When the wine is *muté sur grains*, the alcohol is added before the juice has been run off the skins; when *muté sur jus*, the alcohol is added just to the juice.

Négociants. Merchants who buy grapes, juice and wine in varying stages of preparation and then make their own blends.

Occitan. The *langue d'oc* – the original language of the Languedoc, also spoken in other Mediterranean areas and today enjoying something of a revival.

Passerillé. Raisined grapes, dried on the vine in the autumn sunshine.

Pétillant. Lightly sparkling.

Pigeage. Pushing down.

Pinotter. When a mature wine takes on the characteristics of Pinot Noir; particularly used in Beaujolais for the mature crus, and seen as a compliment.

Premier cru. A first growth, usually below *grand cru* in the hierarchy.

Prestateur. Literally someone who provides a service; in the case of producers of Blanquette and Crémant de Limoux, they riddle and disgorge the bottles.

Primes d'arrachage. Subsidies for pulling up vineyards.

Prise de mousse. For sparkling wine, the process of the second fermentation.

Quai de réception. Arrival point for the grapes.

Rancio. Wine aged in barrel, so that it oxidizes gently and deliciously; usually fortified and making a delicious dessert wine. An old tradition.

Rapport qualité–prix. The ratio of a wine's quality to its price.

Régisseur. Estate manager, and usually also its winemaker.

Remontage. Pumping over.

SAFER. Société d'Amenagement Foncier d'Etablissement Rural, the organization responsible for the development of rural France, with a say on who buys which vineyards.

Saignée. Term used for making rosé; literally, means 'bleeding' the vat and running off juice.

Sélection massale (massal selection). Choosing vine cuttings from a vineyard rather than buying clones from the nursery.

Sélection parcellaire. Site or plot selection.

Stage. Work experience, or a short apprenticeship.

Stagiaire. A trainee student doing work experience.

Syndicat. Union, as in the growers' union that runs the appellation.

Taille. For sparkling wine, a pressing of juice.

Tailler. To prune the vine.

Terroir. A French term impossible to translate directly into English. It includes soil, but also aspect and altitude, and encompasses the overall environment of the vine.

Tonnelier. Cooper.

Tronconique vat. Tronconic vat – a large, tapered vat that may be in wood, stainless steel or concrete and which is used for fermentation or *élevage*.

VDQS. *Vin Delimité de Qualité Supérieure*, the category beneath *appellation contrôlée* and now virtually defunct.

Véraison. The moment when the grapes begin to change colour, particularly noticeable with black grapes.

Vers de la grappe. Larvae from two insects, cochylis and eudemis, that can do considerable damage to vines.

Vigneron. Wine grower; they make their own wine as well as growing grapes.

Vinification intégrale. A recently developed technique entailing the fermentation of red grapes in a small oak barrel, from which the top is removed so that it is possible to put the grapes in the barrel.

Viticulteur. Grower of grapes; does not make wine.

METRIC MEASURES AND U.S. EQUIVALENTS

$1°C = (1 \times 5/9) + 32 = 33.8°F$

1 centimetre (cm) = 0.39 inches

1 gram (g) = 0.03 ounces

1 hectare = 2.47 acres
   (an 'are' is 100 square metres; a hectare is 100 ares)
1 kilometre (km) = 0.621 miles
1 litre = 1.75 pints (a hectolitre is 100 litres, roughly 26.5 US gallons)
1 metre (m) = 3.28 feet
1 millimetre (mm) = 0.04 inches

BIBLIOGRAPHY

Berry, Charles, *In Search of Wine*, London: Constable & Co, 1935, republished by Sidgwick & Jackson, 1987

Bertrand, Gérard, *Wine, Moon and Stars*, New York: Abrams, 2015

Boissieu, Jean, et al. *Les vins du Rhône et de la Méditerranée*, Laussane: Editions Montalba, 1978

Bousquet, Jean-Claude, *Terroirs viticoles: Paysages et géologie en Languedoc*, Prades-le-Lez: Editions Ecologistes de l'Euzière, 2011

Clavel, Jean, *Le 21ème siècle des vins du Languedoc*, St Georges d'Orques: Editions Causse, 1999

Deyrieux, André, *A la rencontre des cépages modestes et oubliés*, Paris: Dunod, 2016

Dion, Roger, *Histoire de la vigne et du vin en France des origines au XIXème siècle*, Paris: Flammarion, 1959

Jaroniak, Florence, and Nagel, Sharon, *Un terroir des hommes: Le Pic Saint Loup*, Mauguio: Pure Impression, 2014

Gasparotto, Laure, and Jullien, Olivier, *La mécanique des vins*, Paris: Grasset, 2016

George, Rosemary, *French Country Wines*, London: Faber & Faber, 1990

George, Rosemary, *The Wines of the South of France, From Banyuls to Bellet*, London: Faber & Faber, 2001

George, Rosemary, *The wines of Faugères*, Oxford: Infinite Ideas, 2016

Gorley, Peter, *The Wines and Winemakers of Languedoc-Roussillon*, eBook, Hamilton John Publishing, 2015

Guyot, Jules, *Etudes des vignobles de France*, Paris, 1868

Healy, Maurice, *Stay Me with Flagons*, London: Michael Joseph, 1949

Jeanjean, Maurice, *Vigne et Vin en Languedoc-Roussillon, l'Histoire de la*

Famille Jeanjean, Toulouse: Editions Privat, 2007

Jefford, Andrew, *The New France*, London: Mitchell Beazley, 2002

Jullien, André, *Topographie des tous les vignobles connus*, Paris, 1866

Karlsson, Britt, and Karlsson, Per, *Biodynamic, Organic and Natural Winemaking*, Edinburgh: Floris Books, 2014

Lachiver, Marcel, *Vins, vignes et vignerons: Histoire du vignoble français*, Lille: Fayard, 1988

Legeron, Isabelle, *Natural Wine*, London: Cico Books, 2014

MacKenzie, Alastair, *Daumas Gassac: The Birth of a Grand Cru*, London: Segrave-Foulkes, 1995

Moon, Patrick, *Virgile's Vineyard, A Year in the Languedoc Wine Country*, Leicester: Matador, 2014

Pomerol, Charles, (ed.) *Terroirs et vins de France*, Paris: Total-Edition-Presse, 1984

Rendu, Victor, *Ampélographie française*, Paris, 1857

Robinson, Jancis, Harding, Julia, and Vouillamoz, José, *Wine Grapes*, London: Penguin, 2012

Sagnes, Jean, Pech, Monique, and Pech, Rémy, *1907 en Languedoc et Roussillon*, Montpellier: Espace Editions, 1997

Smith, Michel, *Corbières*, Paris: Editions Jacques Legrand, 1996

Strang, Paul, *Languedoc-Roussillon: The Wines and Winemakers*, London: Jeanne and Paul Strang Partnership, 2017

Waldin, Monty, *Biodynamic wine*, Oxford: Infinite Ideas, 2016

Wilson, James, *Terroir*, London: Mitchell Beazley, 1998

Woon, Basil, *The Big Little Wines of France*, London: Wine and Spirit Publications, 1972

ACKNOWLEDGEMENTS

Books about wine are above all about people, so my thanks must go first to all the wine producers who feature in these pages. About 250 *vignerons* contributed to the book, but sadly constraints of space determined that there was not room for all of them to feature in these pages. But quite simply, without them there would be no book. I thank them wholeheartedly for spending time with me, answering my questions, opening bottles and sharing their challenges and successes, and thereby making this book possible.

Next come the representatives of the various regional organizations who all helped in various ways, facilitating my research. They organized trips, arranged visits and tastings and answered questions tirelessly.

Firstly, at the Comité des Vins du Languedoc, Jérôme Villaret, Christine Behey-Molines, Jean-Philippe Granier, Bernard Augé, Fanny Lopez, Estelle Nijhof, Thibault de Gregori and Philippe Cabrit.

Next come the representatives of the various wine syndicats, who made my life so much easier, not just arranging cellar visits but even driving me around, thereby saving on 'getting lost' time! Stéphanie Ramé from Cabardès; Marlène Tisseire, director of the Cru Limoux; Catherine Verneuil, director of the Syndicat Général AOC Corbières; Virginie Gouxette-Blasco, of the Syndicat Corbières Cru-Boutenac and also for Minervois La Livinière; Marie-Pierre Puech from the syndicat AOC La Clape; Marie Vidal-Vigneron from the Syndicat AOC Minervois; Nelly Belot, director of the Syndicat Cru Saint-Chinian; Flore Olivieri from the Syndicat AOP Faugères; Sophie Landreau from the Syndicat des Vignerons du Pic Saint Loup; Eléanor Anger, the *sympathique* stagiaire with Danny Peregrine at the Fédération des Vins IGP du Gard. We were

351

delighted to discover that we shared a birthday; she was born on my fortieth birthday and the day that my first writings on the Languedoc were published in French Country Wines! Sarah Hargreaves from In the Mood to Discover, who, with Jean-Pierre Fontanel, organized a rewarding visit to Fitou, and also to Minervois La Livinière, and finally Jean-Luc Bonnin from Agence JLB.

Friends supported and advised and shared wine visits. It is always good to have a sounding board after a visit, so thank you Alex McCormick, Lynne Snowden and Lits Philippou.

A very big thank you to Gary MacDonald for his wonderful photographs; my prose needed lightening with some effective images that capture the diverse personalities of the various wine growers.

At Infinite Ideas I would like to thank Richard Burton for commissioning this book, and thereby enabling me to spend more time than usual in my favourite part of France, and his colleague Rebecca Clare for her efficient editing of my text. Every author needs a second pair of eyes.

Last, but certainly not least, my husband Christopher Galleymore, who has lived patiently with a gestating book, provided support and encouragement. He was often my chauffeur in France, and back in London braved the supermarket so that I could 'just finish a chapter'. Fortunately, he loves the wines of the Languedoc as much as I do.

INDEX

Numbers in **bold** refer to the main chapter areas. Winemaking terms are not indexed but can be found in the Glossary.